The Older Liszt

Franz Liszt at the piano. Photograph by Franz Hanfstaengl, Munich 1869.

The Older Liszt
Music, World and Spirit

Peter G. Coleman

The Lutterworth Press

The Lutterworth Press

P.O. Box 60
Cambridge
CB1 2NT
United Kingdom

www.lutterworth.com
publishing@lutterworth.com

Hardback ISBN: 978 0 7188 9715 4
Paperback ISBN: 978 0 7188 9713 0
PDF ISBN: 978 0 7188 9714 7
ePub ISBN: 978 0 7188 9712 3

British Library Cataloguing in Publication Data
A record is available from the British Library

First published by The Lutterworth Press, 2023

Copyright © Peter G. Coleman, 2023

All rights reserved. No part of this edition may be reproduced, stored electronically or in any retrieval system, or transmitted in any form or by any means, electronic, mechanical, photocopying, recording, or otherwise, without prior written permission from the Publisher (permissions@lutterworth.com).

*To fellow members of the Liszt Society
past, present and future*

Table of Contents

List of Illustrations ix

Preface xiii

1. Understanding Liszt through His Correspondence — 1
2. Psychological and Spiritual Crises in Liszt's Earlier Life — 8
3. Liszt and His Correspondents in His Fiftieth Year (1860-61) — 33
4. Returning to His Religious Vocation (1861-65) — 77
5. Disappointment and Conflict (1865-71) — 113
6. Pursuing Divergent Goals (1871-76) — 143
7. Bearing a Heavy Burden (1876-80) — 177
8. Through Triumph and Disaster (1881-86) — 211
9. Seeing Liszt Whole: Music, World and Spirit — 253

Editions of Liszt's Correspondence Consulted 293
Other References Cited 294
Index 297

List of Illustrations

Unless otherwise stated, all images are held in the collection of Ernst Burger, Munich.

1	Franz Liszt at the piano	ii
2	'A matinée at Liszt's'	3
3	Beethoven's 'kiss of consecration'	11
4	Félicité de Lamennais	15
5	Countess Marie d'Agoult *Musée Carnavalet, Paris*	16
6	Carl Alexander, Grand Duke of Weimar *Klassik Stiftung Weimar, Herzogin Anna Amalia Bibliothek, KGr/00921*	25
7	Princess Carolyne de Sayn-Wittgenstein and her daughter Marie *Klassik Stiftung Weimar, Museen, BV Graphik Nr. 2320*	27
8	Princess Marie de Sayn-Wittgenstein *University of Notre Dame, Indiana, Snite Museum of Arts, L.1980.059.013*	29
9	Liszt photographed in 1858	32
10	Princess Carolyne in 1860	37
11	Anna Liszt, née Anna Maria Lager *Liszt Museum, Budapest*	49
12	Blandine, Daniel and Cosima Liszt *From the collection of Edme Jeanson, Paris*	50
13	Baron Antal Augusz *From the former collection of Robert Bory, Coppet*	58

14	San Carlo al Corso, Rome	79
15	Oratorio della Madonna del Rosario	94
16	Abbé Liszt after ordination	106
17	Abbé Liszt with Pope Pius IX	110
18	Liszt conducting the first performance of his *Legende von der Heiligen Elisabeth*	112
19	Marie d'Agoult photographed c. 1866	116
20	The Forum Romanum and the Monastery of Santa Francesca Romana	123
21	Liszt photographed in 1867	125
22	Princess Marie de Hohenlohe *Klassik Stiftung Weimar, Museen, BV Graphik 1960 Nr. 2317*	134
23	Princess Carolyne painted in 1873 *Klassik Stiftung Weimar, Museen, BV Graphik 1960 Nr. 2323*	135
24	Europe in 1870 and the principal destinations of Liszt's 'Vie Trifurquée'	145
25	Piano concert by Liszt in Budapest, 18 March 1872 *Gesellschaft der Musikfreunde, Vienna*	146
26	Olga von Meyendorff *Originally published in Robert Bory,* La Vie de Franz Liszt par l'Image *(Paris: Éditions des Horizons de France, 1936)*	151
27	Richard and Cosima Wagner *Nationalarchiv der Richard-Wagner-Stiftung/ Richard-Wagner-Gedenkstätte, Bayreuth*	155
28	Title page of *Aux Cyprès de la Villa d'Este* *From the former collection of Robbert Bory, Coppet*	176
29	Contents of Liszt's *Années de Pèlerinage, Troisième Année* *From the former collection of Robbert Bory, Coppet*	176
30	Garden of the Villa d'Este *Nationalarchiv der Richard-Wagner-Stiftung/ Richard-Wagner-Gedenkstätte, Bayreuth*	176
31	Liszt photographed in 1876	178

List of Illustrations xi

32	Hans von Bülow Published in Adrian Williams (ed.), Franz Liszt: Selected Letters *(Oxford: Clarendon Press, 1998)*	180
33	Franz Liszt and Count Géza Zichy	202
34	Pastel portrait of Liszt by Franz von Lenbach, 1884 *Nationalarchiv der Richard-Wagner-Stiftung/ Richard-Wagner-Gedenkstätte, Bayreuth*	210
35	'Poor composer' Liszt photographed in 1881 *Gemeentemuseum, The Hague*	212
36	Agnes Street-Klindworth Originally published in Robert Bory, La Vie de Franz Liszt par l'Image	219
37	Liszt photographed in 1884	232
38	Liszt's last letter to Princess Marie de Hohenlohe *Harvard University, Houghton Library, AM 16 (2), album III/80*	252
39	The 100th anniversary of Liszt's birth in 1911 *Collection of Eleonore Recher, Munich*	259
40	Liszt and Lina Schmalhausen	263
41	Liszt listening to Mass, 1885 *Musée de l'Opéra Paris*	268
42	Liszt and Alexander Siloti	289

Preface

I have known and loved Liszt's music since I was very young. My grandmother taught me as a boy to play on the piano an adapted version of the lively theme from his Hungarian Rhapsody No. 2. Although Liszt was not my first musical love – that was Chopin – by the time of my late teenage years he had become particularly special to me. By then I had attempted to play many of his pieces, most well beyond my limited expertise, but, more importantly, I had joined the Liszt Society and even become acquainted with some of his later works. Throughout my life his music has accompanied me and been a solace in some of my most difficult moments. Comments I notice online about recordings of Liszt's piano music capture similar feelings of wonder and gratitude: 'Is it possible to live without Liszt?'; 'Without Liszt the world would be a mistake'; 'Only Liszt could have possibly conceived of this music'.

Early in my career as a gerontologist I began appreciating the value of studying individual lives in detail and of understanding the particular pathway taken by a person in its own right rather than as an example of a general rule or pattern. I have written much about how growing older involves adapting to the losses, physical and social, that usually accompany ageing. Most research of this kind involves detailed interviewing of particular living persons over time as they respond to the challenges they face. However, it is also possible to learn from the complete lives of people in the past where sufficient evidence survives on their experience of ageing, for example, in diaries, interviews and other records. Although Liszt did not keep a personal diary, he was a prolific correspondent and kept up a regular exchange with the important people in his life. Fortunately, most of these letters survive. However, relatively little survives of letters sent to him apart from those of Carolyne zu Sayn-Wittgenstein, his partner, principal supporter and friend from mid-life onwards. For others' perceptions of Liszt, such as those of his first partner Marie d'Agoult and their second daughter Cosima, we have to rely on their surviving personal diaries and other writings.

Many biographies of Liszt have been written starting in his own lifetime, some highly critical of Liszt, others much more sympathetic, but none as far as I know which employ psychological theory to provide deeper understanding of the course his life took. Although I am confident that it would be possible to compose a psychobiography of Liszt's life, no one has yet attempted this. Liszt's personality and behaviour have been both praised and maligned but only rarely examined in depth. This book does not claim to be a psychobiography of Liszt – for that a much more detailed examination of Liszt's early years and the influences acting upon him throughout his life would be necessary – but it does attempt to understand the latter part of his life in psychological terms. Most importantly, it focusses on Liszt's spiritual development. Throughout the successes and failures of his life Liszt remained deeply religious, but it was in his later years that his spiritual life was most evident in his music, his writings and his actions. For purposes both of psychological and spiritual analysis this study draws principally on what Liszt tells his correspondents about himself and life in general.

This book has been a long time in preparation. I have been reading about Liszt for many years and I conceived the idea of writing about his difficult later years when I was still middle-aged. Now I have reached the age at which Liszt died and like him have been looking back at my own life. I thank those who have encouraged me to complete this task and commented on draft material, particularly my wife Maria Calcagno and our son Leonardo, but including also Frank Capocci, Nicholas Dakin, Francis Davis, Audrey Ellison, Leslie Howard, Craig Lawson, Jamie Moran, Alexei Nesteruk, Timothy Tims, Jim Vincent and Ros Williams. I thank also Samuel Fitzgerald at The Lutterworth Press for his encouragement and prompt assistance in answering my queries, and those at the University of Southampton who have helped me produce illustrations for this book, especially Paul Reynolds and Lynn Campbell. Alan Walker, Liszt's principal biographer, has been exceptionally kind throughout my journey by answering my many queries and reinforcing my interest in Liszt's religious life and compositions. I owe especial thanks to Patrick Rabbitt, my psychology tutor at Oxford University in the 1960s, who read a first draft of the whole manuscript and provided valuable critical comment. I am also very grateful to my music teacher of thirty years, Carol Bishop, who has listened to my stories about Liszt, and also read all the material I produced, and strengthened my belief that such a book as this could also be valuable for those who enjoy playing and listening to Liszt's music, especially the diverse and extraordinary music of his later life. Certainly, getting to know Liszt better has led me to appreciate his music even more. I hope my readers will have the same experience.

Southampton, October 2022

1

Understanding Liszt through His Correspondence

The life of the Hungarian musician Franz (Ferenc) Liszt (1811-86) was exciting and eventful. He was a most creative musician and a pianist of supreme talent and artistry. His character and behaviour fascinated others. He appears from most accounts to have been an extremely charming and captivating person. The period of European history he lived through included revolutions, the rise of nationalism, both German and Italian unification and the beginnings of the collapse of multi-ethnic empires. Liszt himself was acquainted with and admired some of the key political characters of the time, such as Napoleon III and Pope Pius IX, and his friends and relatives included major players in the dramas of the time.

He also knew well virtually all the other important European musicians of his lifetime and was friends at one stage or another with other musical geniuses such as Berlioz, Chopin, Saint-Saëns, Schumann and Wagner. He encountered much personal disappointment as well as success in his life. The renown he achieved as a pianist was unprecedented and his reputed talent in this regard remains almost incredible. Nevertheless, for a still underappreciated composer, Liszt suffered greatly from the negative judgements of music critics of his time. He also had to face up to many disappointments in his personal life. He loved many women but never married. His amorous affairs were seen as scandalous and he came to be ashamed of some of his past actions but not of his capacity for love. His three children from his relationship with a countess early in life brought him joy but also sorrow. Two died prematurely and the third treated Liszt at the end of his life in a way that he could not have expected.

Liszt did not write an autobiography and he expressed some disapproval of the one biography written of him in his lifetime, not because it presented him in a negative light – it was largely sympathetic – but because he felt it should have concentrated only on the kind of music he was trying to promote. He wrote to others that he did not feel his personal life deserved such scrutiny. Yet, on the other hand, he enjoyed being fêted as a celebrity and he clearly liked writing about himself and his experiences of people and places as well as his musical successes and failure. His life can seem to have been full of contradictions. His correspondence is varied and full of life and incident as well as of personal commentary. It is for the most part both very interesting and pleasurable to read.

His biographers, of course, have drawn on his correspondence but, in my opinion, have not always given it the detailed consideration it deserves, particularly in regard to his spiritual life. In this book I have aimed to reveal what we can know about his personality from a close reading of his personal correspondence over the last twenty-five years of his life. This period of his life also has the advantage that there is a sufficient variety of consistent correspondents to allow the reader to draw contrasts as well as similarities in the views of himself that Liszt presented to different people. I have also included material written about him by his contemporaries and his many subsequent biographers. However, I give priority to Liszt's own words about himself. This might seem a little naïve but I think that it is the fairest approach to understanding any person; one starts from his or her self-understanding. I also include my own interpretations and suggestions, based on my own experience and expertise as a gerontologist. My particular interest is in using concepts and theory drawn from the psychology of ageing and adult development as a key to understanding Liszt's thinking and feelings in his later years.

A consideration of the major psychological and spiritual issues in Liszt's earlier years follows in Chapter 2, but there is one feature of his life from his youth onwards which is worth stressing at the outset: his various attempts at quite major self-transformation which continued until his death. In middle age he aimed to change his primary identity from pianist to composer and incurred difficulties with others' acceptance of this change for the rest of his life. He also often returned, not only in his imagination but also in his actions and musical compositions, to his early felt vocation to adopt a religious life. At the same time, he

'A matinée at Liszt's'. Lithograph by Josef Kriehuber 1846. Liszt is at the piano, Hector Berlioz and Carl Czerny in front of him, the violinist Heinrich Ernst to his right and Kriehuber himself to his left.

was greatly taken by many of the attractions of the nineteenth-century European world he grew up in, its new forms of literature and art, rapidly changing political events as well as the pleasures of aristocratic society, to all of which his intelligence, talent and charm gave him ready access. However, above all, Liszt maintained his engagement with the world of music in which direction his father had set him at an early age. His constant involvement in his musical life, initially as one of the world's first travelling concert pianists, and subsequently as the leading advocate of new forms of Western music, left him less time and psychic energy for the fulfilment of other important roles such as parental ones. Eventually there had to be a reckoning of the choices he had made and the directions both followed and those not taken. Liszt's correspondence illustrates how reviewing his life became ever more salient to him as he grew older.

There have been many accounts written of Liszt's life, the most detailed being Alan Walker's highly regarded, three-volume biography of Liszt, a massive work involving investigation of surviving records of his various activities from his earliest years onwards, including his concert performances as well as his many musical innovations. Walker pursued this mammoth task with the utmost conscientiousness over many years.[1] Nevertheless, it is also instructive to contrast his usually carefully measured conclusions with those of other recent biographers who have made more provocative suggestions about Liszt's life and character. This applies in particular to the most recent account by Oliver Hilmes which, on the basis of new material identified by the author, throws new light particularly on Liszt's personal life while he was living in Weimar in the 1850s.[2]

Most closely resembling a psychological and spiritual analysis, although it does not explicitly refer to psychological concepts and theory, is the account of Liszt's final decade by the musicologist Dolores Pesce.[3] She draws on analysis of his correspondence with two of the most important women in his life in these years, his long-term partner Carolyne zu Sayn-Wittgenstein as well as his newly acquired friend, Olga von Meyendorff. Pesce contrasts the different ways in which he presented to these two women his thoughts and feelings on his past and present life. Her work examines closely Liszt's musical compositions of his last decade, paying particular attention to the religious music which dominated his output in this period. This contrasts with the approach of other biographers who have concentrated on the more experimental compositions which shocked contemporaries but have impressed later generations.

In this book I am attempting a broader examination of Liszt's later life beginning in his fiftieth year in 1860-61 and continuing until his death in 1886. It shares a focus on Liszt's spiritual life with Pesce's work as well as with Paul Merrick's earlier work on religion in Liszt's music.[4] The music Liszt produced in the latter part of his life can then be appreciated in the context both of his earlier ambitions to take music forward into the future but also his more recent ideas for reforming church music. The age of 50 as a starting point has been chosen not because it is a 'significant' marker of ageing, but because many biographers including

---

1. A. Walker, *Franz Liszt: The Virtuoso Years, 1811-1847* (London: Faber & Faber, 1983); A. Walker, *Franz Liszt: The Weimar Years, 1848-1861* (London: Faber & Faber, 1989); and A. Walker, *Franz Liszt: The Final Years, 1861-1886* (London: Faber & Faber, 1997). The three editions are hereafter cited by their subtitles, *The Virtuoso Years*, *The Weimar Years* and *The Final Years*.
2. O. Hilmes, *Franz Liszt: Musician, Celebrity, Superstar* (New Haven, CT: Yale University Press, 2016).
3. D. Pesce, *Liszt's Final Decade* (Rochester, NY: University of Rochester Press, 2014).
4. P. Merrick, *Revolution and Religion in the Music of Liszt* (Cambridge: Cambridge University Press, 1987; reissued 2008).

Walker have recognised it to be the beginning of Liszt's 'third' period. This was the year in which he resigned his musical position in Weimar and moved to Rome with the intention of marrying his long-term partner Carolyne on his fiftieth birthday and beginning a new way of life with a renewed focus on religious forms of musical composition. This division also formed the basis for the first publication of his selected letters by La Mara whose second volume is entitled *From Rome to the End*.[5]

Before beginning the presentation of the analysis of Liszt's correspondence some consideration needs to be given both to the ideas underpinning it and the nature of the material itself. Chapter 2 sets the scene by considering key psychological and spiritual issues in Liszt's earlier life which might have repercussions for his later years. This involves paying attention to the major crises and turning points in his earlier life as reported by his biographers. Although Liszt's younger achievements as a pianist and composer for the piano were outstandingly successful, they were accompanied by personal turmoil whose consequences were to trouble him for the rest of his life.

In Chapter 3 I begin the analysis of Liszt's self-presentation in his correspondence by giving a survey of his letter writing in his fiftieth year as he prepared for the dramatic step of moving to Rome from Weimar. I also draw a little on material from his previous years in Weimar to illustrate his likely major concerns and preoccupations at this time. Liszt had endured many disappointments in his middle years, damaging both to his reputation as a musician and as a person of moral standing, and these problems were to continue as he grew older. The chapter provides an overview of his relationships and surviving correspondence with each of the important people in his life at this point.

Both in this chapter and throughout the book I present Liszt largely in his own words based on a thorough analysis of his correspondence. I have read all that I have found available in published form, some 2,000 letters written by Liszt from 1860 to 1886, as well as a selection of his letters written earlier. The principal sources available are the edited letters published by La Mara and translated into English by Constance Bache in the two decades after Liszt's death.[6] Complete volumes of his

---

5. La Mara [Lipsius, Ida Marie] (ed.), *Letters of Franz Liszt*, trans. Constance Bache; *Volume 1: From Paris to Rome: Years of Travel as a Virtuoso*; *Volume 2: From Rome to the End* (New York: Charles Scribner's Sons, 1894).
6. La Mara (ed.), *Letters of Franz Liszt*, trans. Constance Bache; *Volume 1: From Paris to Rome: Years of Travel as a Virtuoso*; *Volume 2: From Rome to the End* (New York: Charles Scribner's Sons, 1894).

unedited correspondence to particular people began to appear in the second half of the twentieth century: Liszt's writings to Carolyne's daughter Marie;[7] to his own daughter Cosima and her daughter Daniela;[8] to his later-life friend Olga von Meyendorff;[9] and to a close friend from his Weimar period Agnes Street-Klindworth.[10]

Particularly valuable is the one-volume, 1,000-page selection of his total correspondence translated into English by Adrian Williams.[11] For the latter part of his life this includes a large number of his letters to Carolyne. This has also been the major source for my knowledge of Liszt's correspondence during the earlier part of his life. Unfortunately, there has still been no successful attempt to provide a complete edition of all his correspondence. A full list of the volumes of his correspondence which I have consulted is provided at the end of the book. Although Liszt's mother tongue was German, his early years in Paris led him to favour French as his principal mode of correspondence. In this book I have presented his letters in English translation, for the most part already provided by previous editors. During his later years, Liszt often included words and phrases from other languages, particularly Italian and Latin, to special effect. I have left these expressions in their original language, following the model set by Williams.

Analysis of Liszt's correspondence from his arrival in Rome in 1861 until his death in 1886 has been divided into the next five chapters. They follow his achievements, his disappointments, joys and sorrows over the remaining years of a relatively long life for someone living in the nineteenth century. He faced many unexpected challenges and a number of tragic losses, but he never lost his faith in humanity and his hope for a better world. I have given particular attention to his ways of coping with stress and to his inner life which sustained him through some dark periods. As he aged, he strove with greater impetus to follow the Christian teaching of the Cross, especially as exemplified by his favourite saint, St Francis of Assisi.

---

7. H.E. Hugo (ed.), *The Letters of Franz Liszt to Marie zu Sayn-Wittgenstein* (Cambridge, MA: Harvard University Press, 1953).
8. K. Hamburger (ed.), *Franz Liszt: Lettres à Cosima et à Daniela* (Sprimont, Belgium: Mardaga, 1996).
9. W.R. Tyler (ed.), *The Letters of Franz Liszt to Olga von Meyendorff, 1871-1886* (Washington, DC: Dumbarton Oaks, 1979).
10. P. Pocknell (ed.), *Franz Liszt and Agnes Street-Klindworth: A Correspondence, 1854-1886* (Hillsdale, NY: Pendragon Press, 2000).
11. A. Williams (ed.), *Franz Liszt: Selected Letters* (Oxford: Clarendon Press, 1998).

Throughout these chapters I have sought to understand Liszt through his own account of his daily life rather than being led by his biographers. At the same time, I engage with their views on Liszt's motives and intentions at key decision points in his later life, beginning with his and Carolyne's refusal to marry despite Carolyne's long battle to obtain an annulment of her first marriage and even after her previous husband died. The concluding chapter brings together what I consider to be the key elements in any description of Liszt's life, his musical achievements, his relationships with women and his Christian faith. I am frank about what I see as the weaknesses as well as the strengths of his character. I focus on his self-examination as he looked back in old age on his creative but troubled life. I consider his views on the future of music and on religious faith as it confronted the increasing challenges posed by new forms of secular thinking. I believe that Liszt still has much to communicate to us today, not only in his music and writings on music, but also in his advice on dealing with life's problems.

2

Psychological and Spiritual Crises in Liszt's Earlier Life

One might expect later-life development to have its roots in strengths of character and forms of adaptation that have been built up in earlier life. Few lives run smoothly but earlier problems surmounted can be the source of resilience in dealing with new challenges. By contrast early sorrows and trauma that remain unhealed can lead to chronic unease and distress. An examination of what Liszt's biographers have said about the difficulties he faced in his earlier years and how he coped with them helps to focus on areas for investigation of his correspondence in his later years.

There are three distinct periods of Liszt's earlier life where his biographers have recognised that he faced major challenges. The first is his unusual childhood as a musical prodigy living in cosmopolitan Paris separated in culture from his Hungarian origin. The second and perhaps the most obvious is the sudden and increasingly stormy relationship he began at the age of 22 years with an already married older Parisian countess. This produced three children but also much heartache as the couple came to quarrel bitterly. The third is the disappointing response to his innovative musical initiatives that Liszt received after he gave up his life as a travelling pianist and took on a post as music director at the grand ducal court of Weimar in Germany.

Psychological Issues in Liszt's Early Life

Liszt grew to adulthood in the period of high Romanticism and his music is often cited as a key example of what Romanticism means, including the removal of restraints to self-expression along with rebellion against the old order of deference and submission to authority. Like Byron, Liszt is often classed as the romantic artist *par excellence*, and there is no doubt that he lived up to that image in many of the ways in which he presented himself to the outside world. The self-absorption shown in his correspondence, one of its many striking qualities, is characteristic of high Romanticism.

Even so, some biographers have drawn some surprisingly specific conclusions about his inner life. One example is Bryce Morrison's *Franz Liszt*, published in the series, *Illustrated Lives of the Great Composers*.[1] This is a much praised, short introductory book by a well-regarded expert on piano music but it also includes some rather strong inferences about Liszt's personality and motives throughout his life. As early as the Preface, after referring to the contrasting responses that Liszt's music has produced in listeners, Morrison proposes what appears as a major psycho-biographical statement:

> [A]t the risk of seeming unfashionably psychological, I would like to suggest that while Liszt undoubtedly created out of a contradictory mixture of religious zeal and vainglorious mastery, he also wrote out of a profound sense of inner uncertainty and disharmony. The facts of his life point inevitably to such a state which can, however, be seen in a positive rather than a negative light.[2]

In this book I shall give particular attention to the relationship, at times conflicting, between, on the one hand, Liszt's evidently strong spiritual beliefs and his expressed wish at times for a life of withdrawal and meditation, and, on the other, his equally clear attachment to continuing to live in a world in which he enjoyed being the centre of attention. However, what are the facts of Liszt's life that might lead one to infer 'inner uncertainty and disharmony'?

We understand better now how parenting is a crucial factor in human development and Liszt was more fortunate than most in this regard. His relationship with both his mother Anna and his father Adam appears to have been very close and there is no evidence to contradict the view that he had a very happy early childhood. He was an only child and that already made him the centre of both parents' attention, but he also became the special focus of Adam's own personal ambitions, both spiritual and musical. The most significant claims of psychological

---

1. B. Morrison, *Franz Liszt* (London: Omnibus Press, 2014).
2. Ibid., p. 11.

disturbance in his early life which have been made by biographers relate to the time his father was presenting him as a *wunderkind* pianist in Paris in the 1820s and in the period after Adam's sudden death in 1827.

Adam had himself felt a Christian vocation when young and spent a time as a novice in a Franciscan monastery. Later he had hoped for a successful musical career and played the cello under the direction of the great court musician Joseph Haydn when he worked on the Esterházy estate in Eisenstadt.[3] It was therefore natural that from an early age Adam both recognised and encouraged his son's musical talent and early love for the piano. He was ambitious enough to enrol Franz for studies with the famous piano teacher Carl Czerny in Vienna, the nearest large city to their home in Raiding, in 1822 at the age of ten. Liszt remembered Czerny as a good teacher and took steps to honour him later in his own life. Two years later and more ambitiously still, Adam sought entrance for his son to the Paris Conservatoire. As Hilmes points out, Czerny was critical of this step and concerned that Liszt's father was turning his son into a business, 'Adam Liszt & Son'.[4] Certainly, it removed Franz from his previous environment, confronting him with a new language and culture. Nevertheless, his undoubted ability, aided by his charming appearance, soon came to delight audiences and it was not long before he was even invited to play in London where he twice performed in the presence of King George IV.

Within a short time he had become well known as a child 'prodigy'. One journalist in Paris was convinced from the performance he saw that little Franz had to be the reincarnation of Mozart:

> I am convinced that the soul and spirit of Mozart have passed into the body of the young Liszt, and never has an identity revealed itself by plainer signs. The same country, the same wonderful talent in childhood, and in the same art. ... His little arms can scarcely stretch to both ends of the keyboard, his little feet scarcely reach the pedals, and yet this child is beyond compare; he is the first pianist in Europe. ... The features of our little prodigy express spirit and cheerfulness. He comes before his audience with exceeding gracefulness, and the pleasure, the admiration which he awakens in his

---

3. Now in Burgenland, Austria, but throughout Liszt's lifetime in the Hungarian part of the Austrian Empire.
4. Hilmes, *Franz Liszt: Musician, Celebrity, Superstar*, p. 14.

hearers as soon as his fingers glide along the keys, seem to him an amusement which diverts him extremely.[5]

The last of these statements already suggests the external attitude of the expressive and responsive public performer that Liszt was to adopt later. But there is no evidence that his success gave the boy an inflated sense of himself at this stage of his life.

We have now become much more aware of the dangers of becoming a 'child prodigy' to subsequent mental health. However, is there any evidence in Liszt's case? It is true, as Walker notes, that we have no indication that Liszt in Paris at the age of fifteen had any real friends of his own age. His only companion seems to have been his father, as his mother remained with her sister in Graz. 'Small wonder', Walker writes, 'that this brilliant boy became withdrawn and introspective.'[6] Nonetheless, the only major source for this commonly expressed view is an unpublished diary[7] which the fifteen-year-old Liszt wrote in Paris. It contains quotations from St Paul and St Augustine as well as Liszt's

Beethoven's 'kiss of consecration' of the young Liszt. An imaginary depiction in a lithograph published in 1873 to celebrate the 50th year jubilee of Liszt's 'Vienna debut'. (Liszt's own record of the original event indicates that it did not take place in a public concert.)

---

5. From *Le Drapeau Blanc*, cited in Walker, *The Virtuoso Years*, p. 99.
6. Ibid., p. 116.
7. Held in the National Archives of the Richard Wagner Museum in Bayreuth: info@wagnermuseum.de.

own thoughts at the time. Walker gives three examples which stress the importance of 'not wasting time', of 'pleasing God above all' and that 'most things can be achieved with effort'.[8]

Liszt's later testimony indicates that by this age he already knew very well the famous early-fifteenth-century Catholic book of spirituality, the *Imitation of Christ* by Thomas à Kempis. What this demonstrates is that young Franz was a highly religious child, not necessarily different from many other well educated, religious young people throughout Catholic Europe at that time. From my own experience of a Jesuit education in the 1950s and early 1960s such intensity of religious engagement with the *Imitation of Christ* would not even then have been unusual. What is striking about Liszt's religiosity is its consistency over time. He remained a devoted Catholic until the end of his life.

Much of previous biographers' discussion of Liszt's 'religious crisis' as a youth comes from his own words as an older man both in his conversations with his first biographer Lina Ramann and his correspondence with close women friends. As later chapters deal with this material in detail it is sufficient to mention here that it shows that he and his father while in Paris talked much about having a religious vocation. One can imagine their discussions alone in their rooms of an evening after a busy day practising and performing. Adam as a young man had been in a religious seminary and so he could speak from his own experience. In the end he seems to have persuaded his son that music should be his vocation and that this was not only compatible with but conducive to serving and loving God. It is also important to note that in this period the young Franz had already begun composing music, variations on popular opera melodies by Mozart and Rossini and even writing an opera for which his father organised a performance. His father encouraged him greatly, writing with pride to Czerny in Vienna about how much his son enjoyed composing and expressing the hope that this would in time become his main profession rather than performance.[9]

The real tragedy of Liszt's early life is that his father died so suddenly while Franz was still only fifteen years old. Adam was taken ill with typhoid fever on the first day of a short holiday they were taking in Boulogne in August 1827, a trip to the seaside which they had enjoyed before in order to rest from their hectic life in Paris. Realising he was

---

8. Walker, *The Virtuoso Years*, p. 117.
9. Cited in ibid., p. 121.

very ill, his father asked his son to write to ask his mother to come.[10] Unfortunately, Adam died before Anna could arrive. Thus, Liszt lost his principal guide and overnight found himself in charge, not only of deciding his own musical future but of supporting both himself and his mother. He and his mother found accommodation in Montmartre and Franz began to earn money as a piano teacher.

Fortunately, it was relatively easy for Liszt to find pupils as his name was already well known in Paris. Nevertheless, it was an arduous life that involved travelling across the city to give lessons from early morning to late in the evening. He had no time for composition. It is significant that Liszt preferred to teach rather than continue performing. He gave an interesting explanation for this decision, written in an essay some ten years later:

> When death had robbed me of my father ... and I began to foresee what art *might* be and what the artist *must* be, I felt overwhelmed by all the impossibilities which surrounded me and barred the way which my thoughts indicated as the best. Besides, finding no sympathetic word from anyone harmonizing with me in mind ... there came over me a bitter disgust against art, such as it appeared to me: vilified and degraded to the level of a more or less profitable handicap, branded as a source of amusement for distinguished society.[11]

He did, however, give two public concerts, following the second of which Liszt was heavily criticised for reducing music making to conjuring tricks and 'brilliant frivolities'. Walker attributes this to the emotional upheaval resulting from the sudden end of 'his first love affair' with one of his pupils, Caroline, daughter of Pierre de Saint-Cricq, a minister in Charles X's government. When he realised what was happening, Saint-Cricq, not wanting his daughter to marry someone of a lower station, ended the relationship, much to both his daughter's and Liszt's distress.[12] The whole episode is supposed to have awoken Liszt to the fact that his position in Parisian society was not what he had imagined. Despite this,

---

10. His endearing letter to her survives: 'Best of Women, Mother! At the very moment I write to you, I am anxious about my father's health ...'. Cited in ibid. p. 123.
11. Cited in ibid. p. 130.
12. Ibid., pp. 131-33.

in time his mother's care and attention is said to have helped him to recover from what Walker described as a 'nervous breakdown'.

Lina Ramann gave the first account of this story in her life of Liszt and it has been repeated in most subsequent biographies. There is a danger, however, in taking oft-repeated stories at face value without further critical examination. Gert Nieveld has pursued the matter in considerable detail and published an account of his investigations for the Liszt Society.[13] His conclusions are that biographers have exaggerated the importance of the young Liszt's love for his even younger pupil, and this is supported by his subsequent meetings with her and his comments to others about their relationship.

What does remain clear is that Liszt became depressed for many months after his father's death and that it was only the need to earn money to support himself and his mother that kept him going. It could be that it was in this state that he met and found a sympathetic ear in the young Caroline. Liszt was in search of deeper understanding of life and we know that he was beginning to read widely, especially French literature, including philosophical and religious books, and also the new Romantic literature that was emerging on the tail of Chateaubriand's *René*. He was searching for his way forward. It was in this period that he later told Princess Carolyne that he 'implored' his mother to allow him to enter a seminary for the priesthood. However, Anna, like his father a few years previously, was successful in persuading the young Franz to continue on his musical path.

Nevertheless, Liszt's spiritual searching did not cease. He attended meetings of the Saint-Simonist movement in Paris, an early form of Christian socialism, along with other musical and literary figures closely involved in Paris's developing critical culture such as Hector Berlioz and George Sand. More importantly, in 1834 at the age of 22 he met his first major spiritual mentor, the Abbé Félicité Robert de Lamennais, a charismatic liberal Catholic thinker to whom all of France at the time was paying particular attention. Liszt had been reading his writing, particularly his recent powerful critique of papal authority which argued for a return to a purer Christianity, *Paroles d'un croyant*. He wrote to Lamennais praising the book and its importance to him personally, and Lamennais replied, inviting the young man to his retreat in Brittany. Liszt stayed there for many weeks over the summer and afterwards Lamennais wrote to his friend Montalembert, another liberal Catholic,

---

13. G. Nieveld, 'Caroline de Saint-Cricq: Siren with a Heart of Ice', *The Liszt Society Journal*, Bicentenary Edition, Vol. 31 (2011), pp. 28-70.

telling him how much he liked Liszt, calling him 'a young man full of soul'.[14]

Lamennais was clearly an honourable person, also intelligent and brave, who campaigned against social injustice and suffered imprisonment and other penalties from Church and State for his actions right up until his death in 1854. That he was so impressed by Liszt's qualities as a young man is high testimony and cannot easily be dismissed by those critical of Liszt's character. He also tried to intervene to help Liszt in the romantic problems he soon encountered and remained in contact with him for many years afterwards. Alan Walker has argued that Liszt 'discovered himself as a composer' that summer he spent in Brittany with Lamennais.[15] He began composing what would become his *Harmonies poétiques et religieuses* and other works influenced by his spiritual mentor's writings and actions. Lamennais had defended the silk-weavers of Lyon, some of whom died in street-fighting while protesting against their desperate living conditions. Liszt wrote an early composition on this subject entitled simply 'Lyon' which showed that he was already developing ideas on the role of artist in society.

Félicité de Lamennais (1782-1854). Lithograph by Delpech based on a drawing by Belliard c. 1835.

Liszt's Relationship with Countess Marie d'Agoult

Biographers' repeated interest in the story of his early love for one of his pupils is understandable, given their frequent focus on Liszt's relationships with women throughout his life and, particularly, with the already married Countess Marie d'Agoult who bore Liszt three children. Unfortunately for Liszt, his reputation as a 'womaniser' became established early in his lifetime. Marie d'Agoult's later descriptions of Liszt in her writings after the break-up of their relationship have also been most damaging to him.

However, as Walker insists, there is no evidence that Liszt was a sexual predator at any stage of his life. Nor indeed does he seem to have been sexually reckless. He never encountered venereal disease as some

---

14. Cited in Williams, *Franz Liszt*, p. 973.
15. Walker, *The Virtuoso Years*, p. 157.

contemporary musicians, artists and writers did. The only three children he appears to have fathered were conceived in the context of a loving relationship. That neither this nor his subsequent relationship with Carolyne zu Sayn-Wittgenstein matured into a full and lasting one might also be thought to arise from some 'inner disharmony' or other personality defect. This also would be an incorrect inference. The breakdown of his relationship with Marie was due in large part to incompatibility of personality and ambition. His subsequent major relationship with Carolyne lasted for the rest of his life and the fact that it did not lead to marriage was largely due to circumstances beyond Liszt's control.

Nevertheless, the question remains whether Liszt could and should have acted differently with the first real love of his life. Liszt was introduced to Marie d'Agoult early in 1833 by another of his young pupils, who happened to be her niece, at an artistic gathering in one of the salons of Paris. Marie describes in her memoirs how she was overwhelmed by the manner and conversation of this young man who was seven years younger than her. She was a lover of music and enjoyed writing, was very beautiful but also came from a family with a history of mental illness and was herself of a depressive nature. Most crucially, she was dissatisfied in her marriage with an older man whom she admired but did not love.

Liszt and d'Agoult soon fell in love and the relationship developed quickly as they sought ways of meeting together secretly. According to Walker, Liszt's time away with Lamennais in Brittany the following year was to give the pair of them time and space to reflect on their situation.[16]

Countess Marie d'Agoult (1805-1876). Oil painting by Henri Lehmann 1843.

However, on Liszt's return to Paris, he was confronted by Marie, in great distress after the death of her six-year-old child following an acute illness. Initially reluctant to see Liszt, she eventually succumbed and came to see him at his apartment early in 1835, and the fire was lit.

It is interesting that Liszt wrote about his situation to Lamennais, the only person besides his mother in whom he confided his intention to run away with Marie. Lammenais responded immediately, coming back to Paris and going directly to Marie to try – unsuccessfully – to dissuade her from taking such a drastic step. Marie and

---

16. Ibid., p. 201.

Psychological and Spiritual Crises in Liszt's Earlier Life

Liszt arranged to travel separately to Switzerland where they met up in Geneva. As Marie's brother later commented, it had been too late to stop a fire that was already ablaze:

> I even believe that he [Liszt] is not altogether to blame: he says that he asked Abbé Lamennais to help him. It is true that he did so only after having pretty well set the house on fire, but I feel that we should make allowances for his being only twenty-two years old; only the future can prove what there really is in this man and what consideration he may merit.[17]

On the 18 December 1835 their first child Blandine was born in Geneva and then given to a local wet-nurse. When a few months later the couple went travelling, the baby was entrusted to a local Protestant pastor and his family, until they could provide a home of their own. This was common practice at the time throughout Europe.

For another three years their love flourished and Marie did indeed provide Liszt with support for many of his early and very beautiful compositions as they led a bohemian life around Europe. His wonderfully innovative piano compositions, representing his impressions of what he experienced in their travels together, first in Switzerland and later in Italy, were eventually published in two volumes given the titles *Années de pèlerinage*. This was a reference to Goethe's 1821 novel, *Wilhelm Meisters Wanderjahre, oder die Entsagenden* ('Wilhelm Meister's Years of Travel, or the Renunciants'), in its first French translation, itself a harbinger of the romantic movement in its notion of the importance of self-realisation. Liszt prefaced most of the pieces with lines from recent writers.

We know from Marie's diaries and memoirs that she was close to him while he was composing many of these pieces. Thus, for one of his early Swiss pieces, *Le lac de Wallenstadt*,[18] Marie had a very clear recollection: 'Franz wrote for me there a melancholy harmony, imitative of the sigh of the waves and the cadence of oars, which I have never been able to hear without weeping.'[19]

---

17. Cited in ibid., p. 225.
18. For which Liszt chose a caption from Byron's 'Childe Harold's Pilgrimage', Canto III, Stanza 68: 'Thy contrasted lake / With the wild world I dwell in is a thing / Which warns me, with its stillness, to forsake / Earth's troubled waters for a purer spring'.
19. Cited in Walker, *The Virtuoso Years*, p. 211.

Sposalizio ('Wedding Ceremony') from the Italian set was inspired by a painting by Raphael,[20] a copy of which Liszt placed on his published manuscript. He must have seen this in the Brera Gallery in Milan during his many visits there in the later 1830s. Albert Brussee[21] has also argued that its themes reflect both the sound of bells of the area around Bellagio on Lake Como where they were staying in 1837 and even the very church litany which they heard (and can still be heard) on the first Sunday of October in the nearby village of Visgnola. Marie comments on this litany in her diary entry for Sunday, 1 October 1837 when she and Liszt visited the church in Visgnola for the Feast of the Madonna. This was shortly before the birth of their second child Cosima in Como itself. She too was given into care.

It was also in Italy, specifically in Venice, that it is possible to trace the beginnings of the lovers drifting apart. So far, they had shared projects but now they began to clash. Liszt at one important level of his being was very committed to action in the world. Marie, on the other hand, wanted to continue their life of exploration and withdrawal from the world. Something of this dissatisfaction is already clear from Liszt's letters to Lamennais, with whom Liszt had kept in contact. For example, in May 1836, writing from a trip back to Paris and indicating his expectation of meeting him soon, Liszt revealed his need for spiritual advice:

> Dear and venerable Father, I shall expect you. Whatever sorrow there is in the depth of my soul, it will be sweet and consoling to me to see you again. You are so wonderfully good to me! and I should suffer so much by being so long away from you! – Au revoir then, once more – in eight days at latest it will be, will it not? I do nothing else than keep expecting you. Yours, with the deepest respect and most sincere devotion. (Paris, 28 May 1836)

A year later in Italy in December 1837 Liszt expressed how he was eagerly awaiting Abbé Lamennais' next work[22] and indicated his unease with his own present life:

---

20. *Lo Sposalizio* or *The Marriage of the Virgin* depicting the marriage of Mary and Joseph.
21. A. Brussee, 'Franz Liszt at Lake Como', *The Liszt Society Journal*, Vol. 41 (2016), pp. 39-62.
22. *Le Livre du Peuple*, which had just been published and was yet to reach Liszt.

> I am hoping and longing ardently for your next book, which I shall read with my whole heart and soul, as I have read all that you have written for four years. I shall owe you just so many more good and noble emotions. Will they remain for ever sterile? Will my life be for ever tainted with this idle uselessness which weighs upon me? Will the hour of devotion and of manly action never come? Am I condemned without respite to this trade of a Merry Andrew and to amuse in drawing-rooms?
>
> Whatever may be my poor and humble destiny, do not ever doubt my heart. Do not ever doubt the deep respect and unalterable devotion with which you have inspired me. (Como, 18 December 1837)

The expression 'Merry Andrew' is an unusual one nowadays but its use indicates how strongly Liszt felt about the restrictions of his current position and that he aspired to a more serious and less 'clownish' role for himself in society.

In March 1838, while the couple were in Venice (to which Liszt and Marie reacted very differently – he found the city fascinating and she tawdry), Liszt heard about the major floods of the Danube that had very badly affected Hungary and Pest, in particular. He insisted that he must go to Vienna to help to raise funds for the relief effort. His charity concerts there were a great success and included for the first time his very skilful transcriptions of Schubert's songs which caught public attention. Unfortunately, while he was away Marie became ill and, more importantly, very concerned about her health. It was some weeks before he returned to her and only after she had begged him to do so. Marie definitely did not want Liszt to enter public life as a performer, but to continue his recent focus on composing.

Still, they continued their travels in Italy visiting Lake Lugano, reading Dante and Petrarch together, and visiting the museums in Milan. By then Marie was pregnant again and both her physical and mental health had declined. They decided to move to Rome, where on 9 May 1839 their son Daniel was born and entrusted to a local woman. However, another more significant quarrel soon followed. Liszt heard that the initiative to raise a monument to Beethoven in Bonn, the place of the great composer's birth, was failing and spontaneously offered his own help which was eagerly accepted by the memorial committee. Inevitably, this meant a major programme of concerts on Liszt's part. Marie objected strongly. She felt that this development would not only leave her more isolated but be detrimental to Liszt's career as a composer. In this she may well have been right. Nevertheless, Liszt was determined to go ahead and began to organise concerts in Vienna. Marie could not accept this situation and so decided to return with her two daughters to Paris where she succeeded in resuming her previous life. She accepted Liszt's proposal to place their two girls with his mother, although somewhat reluctantly as she regarded Anna as coming from a lower class of society.[23] She had no choice, however, because under French law Liszt had custody of his children as their father.

This was only the beginning of eight years for Liszt of constant travelling around Europe and of the so-called phenomenon of 'Lisztomania' as people flocked to hear him play the piano in cities and towns large and small. In the process, besides enjoying an exciting lifestyle, he raised large sums of money for various good causes. Despite his earlier misgivings about being an 'entertainer', he must have felt that this was his way for the present of being active and useful in the world. He certainly succeeded in raising the profile of the pianist and his art, moving beyond the salons to provide music to a wider public. Not all his fellow musicians and pianists saw it this way; some in fact, like Schumann, were horrified. Nevertheless, through his skilful transcriptions of important music, especially opera compilations, he provided an education to the wider European public, from Limerick and Lisbon in the West to Moscow and Constantinople in the East, in a way that was unprecedented. He also did much to encourage pride in subjugated cultures by his readiness to promote their music through his improvisations on local melodies, not only in his native Hungary but also further east in Wallachia and Moldavia. He achieved a great deal in those years, his so-called *Glanzzeit* ('heyday').

Was Liszt selfish in pursuing his own worldly career path against Marie's wishes? The answer to this question has to be yes. However, the incompatibility between his and Marie's wishes had already become very clear. Her own diary entries while she was in Venice showed that there were times when she realised this: 'I feel myself an obstacle to his life. I'm no good to him. I cast sadness and discouragement over his days.'[24]

The private life that she had imagined with Liszt was too far removed from his need to have an impact on the world. Could they have reached a compromise? He and Marie still corresponded lovingly and met when they could. Perhaps she was hoping that his travelling would end sooner

---

23. Daniel joined his sisters when he reached two years.
24. Cited in Walker, *The Virtuoso Years*, p. 252.

than it did and he would come back and settle down with her in Paris. She came to spend time with him while he was on tour in London in 1840, but it was not a success and she did not join him at work again. They also spent some holidays together, twice on the island of Nonnenwerth in the River Rhine in 1841 and in 1843. It was on the second occasion that Marie seems to have come to the conclusion that they could not continue their life in this way and they needed to make a definite break.

Was Liszt unfaithful to her in these years? He certainly met many attractive women and news of them came back to Marie in Paris. Walker defends him strongly.[25] Hilmes is much less sure. Certainly, it would seem remarkable from our present-day perspective if Liszt never succumbed to the many temptations he would have come across. However, Liszt, though often acting as the enchanter in public, was capable of great caution in private. Interestingly, the issue of fidelity was a matter they even discussed in their correspondence, Marie once, perhaps wanting to make Liszt jealous, seeking his opinion on how he would view her if she had an affair with one of the many men she met in the salons of Paris. His reply was disarming:

> You know my way of looking at that kind of thing. You know that for me the facts, the deeds, are nothing. The feelings, the ideas, the shades of meaning, especially the shades of meaning, are everything. I want and I wish you always to have complete freedom, because I am convinced that you would always use it nobly, tactfully.[26]

The final straw for Marie seems to have been the embarrassing publicity in 1844 around Liszt's connection with the so-called 'Lola Montez', an enterprising entertainer born in Limerick who succeeded in gaining Liszt's attention in Dresden and then followed him around on his travels across Europe. When she also arrived in Paris to dance at the Opéra, it is understandable that Marie may have suspected that Liszt had something to do with her getting such a prestigious billing. Marie and Liszt dined together in Paris in April and Marie wrote a letter to him soon afterwards indicating she was parting from him. Liszt protested in vain and it was reported that in a subsequent quarrel she told him that 'she did not object to being his mistress but she objected to being *one* of his mistresses'.[27]

---

25. Ibid., p. 390ff.
26. Cited in ibid., p. 385.
27. Cited in ibid., p. 395.

Their letters to each other in this period were more sorrowful than angry. For example, Marie expressed herself gracefully in her letter of parting:

> Were it not my conviction, my dear Franz, that I am not and cannot be in your life anything but an affliction and a tiresome irritant, please believe that I should not take the decision that, with the utmost sorrow, I am taking. You have much strength, youth, and genius. Many things will yet spring up for you on the grave in which our love and our friendship are laid to rest. If you wish to spare me a little in this last crisis, which with a little pride and clear sight I should not have postponed so long, you will not respond with anger and irritation to the few requests I have to make.[28]

She even suggested to Liszt choosing Lamennais as one of a number of possible intermediaries in making a final settlement of their affairs, referring to him as he 'who loves you and has never considered me as anything but a calamity in your life'.

The end of Liszt and Marie's relationship need not have been so tragic and painful as it became. Most biographers agree that the lasting damage was the semi-autobiographical novel *Nélida*[29] that Marie began writing in 1843 and published in 1846. It tells of a beautiful heiress who sacrifices her marriage, reputation and aristocratic way of life for a relationship with a middle-class painter. Success goes to his head and he deserts her. However, eventually his life ends in failure, unable to carry out the great commission he has been awarded to paint a huge fresco in a major public building. He becomes ill and calls for Nélida, dying in her arms as she forgives him. The parallels are very specific to their own lives, even to the imaginary couple's flight to Geneva and the painter's last appointment to the court of a small duchy in Germany – Liszt had recently taken up an appointment in Weimar.

The novel had considerable success, was republished in Liszt's lifetime and is still readily available today, continuing to be advertised as a novel about the author's relationship with Liszt. Walker argues that it captured all Marie's pent-up feelings of rage and resentment that Liszt did not need her any longer:

---

28. Cited in Williams (ed.), *Franz Liszt: Selected Letters*, p. 210.
29. An anagram of the first part of the pen name Marie adopted – 'Daniel Stern'.

> In Marie's quest for her 'great man' it was clearly implied that she, and she alone, would be his guiding light, his inspiration. Liszt soon made it plain that she was to be nothing of the sort. Whatever the reasons that made him love her, she was dispensable as far as his art was concerned.[30]

People at the time, including Liszt's mother, thought *Nélida* to be an attack upon him but he would not agree. In fact, he never acknowledged that the artist character was a depiction of himself. When Marie asked him in writing whether he was offended by the novel, he denied it and wished her further success, although he indicated some irritation at being repeatedly asked this question by so many people. In my view, some doubt must remain about whether Marie consciously intended her novel to be an attack on Liszt rather than being a product of her creative and thus partly unconscious imagination.

It is interesting that even at this late stage of their relationship Lamennais remained involved. Marie sent him a draft manuscript of *Nélida* for criticism. He refused to comment and suggested a proper critic who in fact advised against publication. In 1845 Liszt wrote a long letter to Lamennais justifying the actions which he had taken, and was planning, in regard to his children. He was arranging for them to be educated in Paris but wanted them to be regarded as Hungarian not French. He was intending to ask the Emperor in Vienna for 'complete legitimization' under Austro-Hungarian law. Presumably, Lamennais had been contacted by Marie about Liszt's intentions in this regard. Besides indicating his continuing huge respect for Lamennais, the letter also expresses his regret at their recent lack of communication and his acknowledgement of his 'youthful follies': 'If, as I have some ground for hoping, the outcome is favourable, my children will then be in the best possible position, and I shall have made good my youthful follies as honourably as the situation allowed.' (Grenoble, 18 May 1845)

Once she realised the situation, Marie expressed extreme anger to Liszt over the arrangements he had made to exclude from her parenting responsibilities:

> You are capable of the worst cowardice of threatening *from a distance*, and *on grounds of legality*, a mother who claims the fruit of her womb! ...

---

30. Walker, *The Virtuoso Years*, p. 388.

> From now on, sir, your daughters no longer have a mother; that is what you wanted. Their fate lies in your hands; no amount of heroic devotion will ever be strong enough to fight against your madness and your wild egotism. ...
>
> One day, perhaps, your daughters will ask you: where is our mother? You will reply: it did not suit me for you to have one. (Paris, 3 June 1845)[31]

For a further two years Liszt corresponded with Marie, sending her rather polite letters about his activities and travels, and continuing to express his bewilderment at her rejection of him:

> A singular correspondence, ours! But since we no longer have anything but words for one another, why not say them? They will not close our wounds, it is true, but they will not reopen them either. To what are we condemned? Do we know? We used both of us to be noble natures, and you have cursed me, and I have banished myself from your heart because you misunderstood mine. Is it a test we are undergoing – or an affliction of fate? The future will tell us. ... (Valenciennes, 23 January 1846)

He also made sure she knew of his successes while congratulating her on her own writings. She asked him about his 'intimate life' to which he replied that it would require having an 'intimate relationship'. On that occasion he was writing in February 1847 from Woronińce in Poland[32] where he told Marie he had just met 'a most extraordinary woman, a truly extraordinary and outstanding woman'. She was his future partner Princess Carolyne zu Sayn-Wittgenstein. Marie replied sarcastically.

The tussle with Marie over their children haunted Liszt over the following years and he was as a result often reluctant to visit Paris, preferring to correspond regularly with his mother and his children. When three years later, in 1850, Blandine innocently wrote to him about how, in their grandmother's absence, she and Cosima had decided to call on their mother, that it had been a great joy for them all and that they were making plans for further meetings, Liszt responded furiously. He wrote angrily back to Blandine, accusing his daughters

---

31. Ibid. p. 406-7.
32. Present-day Voronivtsi in Ukraine.

of deceiving and being cruel to their grandmother. He then took the drastic step of removing them from his own mother, to Anna's distress, and placing them with an experienced French governess who had helped to educate Princess Carolyne in Poland. She and her sister were to keep a very close surveillance on the two girls from now on. How one might ask could Liszt have been so insensitive to his children's emotional needs? By today's standards of course such behaviour appears completely unacceptable. However, it also shows how deep the division had become by then between Liszt and his former lover. If this rift were not to be healed both were likely to carry a heavy burden for the rest of their lives.

Liszt's Years as Court Musician in Weimar

By his mid-30s Liszt had become dissatisfied with his life as a concert pianist and wanted to return to composing. As already noted, even from a young age Liszt had never been properly content with the life of an entertainer, brilliant pianist though he was. He wanted to be a composer and had already produced outstanding work. Many have noted the influence on the young Liszt of seeing Paganini's violin performances and the huge following he achieved. Certainly, Liszt did succeed in emulating him with the piano. However, while honouring Paganini's achievements, he also came to distance himself from the life that the Italian virtuoso led. As he reflected, he doubted more and more its value. He also needed more stability of position in order to develop his compositional talents.

Fortunately, he was noticed by Carl Alexander, the son of the Grand Duke of Weimar, who unlike his father had a strong interest in music and was eager to promote Weimar as a centre of culture as it had been in Goethe and Schiller's time. In 1842 he persuaded his father to give Liszt the honorary title of *Kapellmeister Extraordinaire* at the court of Weimar. In this he was supported by his mother, the Grand Duchess Maria Pavlovna, sister of the Russian Tsar Nicholas I, who was herself an accomplished musician. Over the years the friendship between Liszt and Carl

Carl Alexander
(1818-1901), Grand Duke
of Weimar (1853-1901).
Lithograph 1856.

Alexander grew and Liszt could be candid with him about both his present situation and his ambitions:

> The moment is coming (*Nel mezzo del cammin di nostra vita*[33] – 35 years!) for me to break out of my chrysalis of virtuosity and to allow my thoughts to take free flight. ... Were it not for the wretched money matters which so often keep me in a stranglehold, and also the various more or less alluring whims of my youth, I could be 4 or 5 years more advanced. Such as I am, thank God, I have not lost too much, and honour, too, is saved. (Aboard the *Galatea*, between Pozsony [now Bratislava] and Pest, 6 October 1846)

Liszt's aim was now in fact an even more ambitious one, to transform music, both by his own compositions and by promoting the work of like-minded composers.

It was in the following year on his last international concert tour that he met a Polish woman who had responded generously to the charity appeal he had attached to a concert he gave in Kiev [Kyiv]. When Liszt went to look for her, the two of them found themselves in harmony both of mind and soul, and she invited him to come and visit her on the large estate which she had inherited from her father. She was living there with her young daughter Marie but was estranged from her husband. Her maiden name was Carolyne Iwanowska and her husband was Prince Nicholas zu Sayn-Wittgenstein of a noble family of German origin whose father had been a field marshal in the Russian Imperial Army during the Napoleonic wars. What seems to have impressed Liszt so much about Carolyne was her exceptional intelligence and the range of knowledge which she had acquired under her father's guidance, but he would also have appreciated her idealism and strong Catholicism. She was also an extremely determined and decisive person. There is no doubt that she fell madly in love with Liszt in a very short period of time and together with him devised a plan to leave her home and join him, with her daughter, in his new venture in Weimar. She believed that her previous marriage could be annulled on the grounds that her father had compelled her to marry against her will.

In April 1848 Carolyne organised her and her daughter's escape from the Russian Empire unnoticed, no easy matter, and in all of her subsequent

---

33. 'In the middle of the journey of our life' – the first line of Dante's *Divine Comedy*.

action she demonstrated a very strong sense of purpose. She became Liszt's staunch supporter in the musical ventures he tried to achieve in Weimar. She urged him to compose and to put his many musical ideas into practice. Indeed, he was very productive in these years creating innovative music in various genres, for orchestra, choir, solo voice (*Lieder*) as well as piano. Carolyne came to think that she was crucial to Liszt's success in these years. Maybe she was right because, as his letters to Lamennais showed, Liszt had tended to suffer from feelings of inertia and thus perhaps needed Carolyne's chivvying. Much later she told a friend how she achieved this:

Princess Carolyne de Sayn-Wittgenstein and her daughter Marie. Lithograph 1844.

> I have always worked in the same room as him, otherwise he would never have composed any of the works that date from his Weimar period. He wasn't lacking in genius, he just lacked the ability to sit still for any length of time, a virtue no less important than hard work and perseverance.[34]

Liszt himself also wrote and published a lot about music in his time in Weimar. His energy and creativity continued to impress Carl Alexander: 'Liszt grows up in an undisputable importance. He grows up like a spiral because he always shows new facets – extraordinary person. I would not be surprised to see him withdraw entirely from music in order to take up literature only.'[35]

Liszt and Carolyne's residence in Weimar, the Altenburg, granted for their use by the royal family, became a musical centre where the pair hosted other notable musicians such as Berlioz and Wagner, as well as Liszt's piano pupils who came from all over Europe. These included major future musicians, including Hans von Bülow and Carl Tausig. Liszt and Carolyne also hosted literary figures from outside the world of music, including the soon-to-be-famous novelist Mary Ann Evans

---

34. Cited in Hilmes, *Franz Liszt: Musician, Celebrity, Superstar*, p. 126.
35. Extract from Carl Alexander's diary for the year 1851, cited by Nicolas Dufutel, 'Liszt and Wagner', Foreword to *The Collected Writings of Franz Liszt: Dramaturgical Leaves, II (Richard Wagner)*, ed. Janita R. Hall-Swadley (Lanham, MD: Rowman and Littlefield, 2016), xv-xxxviii.

whom we know better by her pseudonym of 'George Eliot' and who left a vivid picture in her own letters of hearing Liszt play the piano.[36] It was at the Altenburg that Liszt composed the great orchestral works of his middle period, the 'Faust' and 'Dante' Symphonies and his various symphonic tone poems, as well as his ground-breaking Sonata in B minor for piano. Politically, the first years Liszt and Carolyne spent in Weimar were marked by revolution against elitist rule across Europe beginning in Paris and Vienna and leading to the long but unsuccessful struggle for Hungarian independence from Hapsburg rule. Liszt followed these events closely and his Hungarian rhapsodies based on folk music reflected his growing identification with the land of his birth.

Liszt was developing what came to be called the 'New German School' and is now commonly referred to as 'Programme Music', in which music reflects and is sometimes intertwined with themes from literature including novels as well as poetry. As well as writing such music himself, he encouraged the performance in Weimar of other like-minded composers, including Berlioz and Wagner. He had to put great effort into these ventures because the orchestral resources at his disposal in Weimar were limited and, therefore, he had to find the money to import musicians from elsewhere in Germany. He also took great risks, for example, putting on Wagner's operas *Tannhäuser* and *Lohengrin* in the years immediately after the revolutions of 1848 when Wagner himself was a wanted man on the run after he supported a failed revolution in Dresden.

In fact, it was Wagner who early on noticed that Liszt was not getting the support he deserved in Weimar and that too many court official and people in the town were sabotaging his efforts. He saw how frustrating this situation was for Liszt and that he was suffering greatly under his generally peaceful façade.[37] Although the programme music that Liszt promoted in Weimar had initially been seen positively, within a few years criticism of his work began to increase. Conservative musicians, including Brahms and Joachim to both of whom Liszt had previously offered encouragement and hospitality, grouped together to oppose the new trend of seeking extra-musical associations for composition in favour of the abstract paradigms music had traditionally come to rely on. Powerful and articulate opponents, most noticeably the influential, Vienna-based, music critic Eduard Hanslick harshly condemned Liszt's attempt to fuse the arts in the symphonic 'poems' he was creating. Major

---

36. Walker, *The Weimar Years*, p. 248.
37. Hilmes, *Franz Liszt: Musician, Celebrity, Superstar*, p. 121.

compositions for the piano, including his Concerto in E flat and Sonata in B minor, were also heavily criticised. By 1857 audiences were actively intervening in performances of his and other new composers' works in order to discredit them, eventually even in Weimar itself. Particularly painful to Liszt was the repeated suggestion that he should give up promoting this so called 'New Music' and go back to his life as a piano virtuoso.

Liszt's time in Weimar was also not an easy one for personal as well as musical reasons. They had both expected that Carolyne would fairly promptly obtain an annulment of her marriage from the Roman Catholic Church and that therefore they would become free to marry. Agreement seemed to have been reached in Rome in 1852 but objections were immediately raised by the Roman Catholic authorities in Russia. As the Grand Duchess of Weimar was the Tsar's sister, Liszt and Carolyne's domestic situation became embarrassing. Soon Carolyne was not only excluded from court functions but also generally shunned by Weimar society, which was strongly influenced by the pastor of the city and head preacher to the Protestant court. The situation deteriorated further after Prince Nicholas' visit to Weimar the same year. He demanded that Carolyne and her daughter return to Russia and, when she refused, he asked the Grand Duchess Maria Pavlovna to take charge of Marie in place of her mother. Eventually, he wrote to the Tsar asking him to summon Carolyne back to the Russian empire.

When she also refused the Tsar's request, she was exiled, her assets in Russia confiscated and placed into trust for Princess Marie until she married or reached the age of 21.

Carolyne bore all these burdens well. Her loving support for Liszt never wavered, but the strain was evident on both her and Liszt. As Walker suggests,[38] some of Liszt's most moving, personal piano music of this period, such as his *Consolations* of 1849-50, reflects the painful circumstances Liszt and Carolyne had to endure in Weimar in these years. It was a situation that could not last long. Carolyne was now increasingly dependent financially both on Liszt as well as on her own daughter Marie, who still had access to her father's wealth and

Princess Marie de Sayn-Wittgenstein (1837-1920). Oil painting by Ary Scheffer 1855.

---

38. Walker, *The Weimar Years*, p. 145.

was his principal heir. Fortunately, Marie was consistently supportive of her mother and had an excellent relationship with Liszt. He had in many ways a closer relationship with Marie than with his own daughters as he had lived with her and nurtured her from the age of eleven. By then, however, Marie was approaching 20 and the question of her marriage was occupying Prince Nicholas, Carolyne and Liszt.

As his years as Kapellmeister passed, Liszt saw both his professional and personal life beset by obstacles. His music continued to be opposed by powerful critics and even in Weimar itself he received inadequate support. What direction should he now take? On the positive side, he still had the support of Carl Alexander who had now succeeded his father as Grand Duke. Liszt had for some time been thinking of resigning his position but on each occasion that he raised the issue had been persuaded by Carl Alexander to stay. However, from the end of 1858 a number of critical events succeeded one another over the following twelve months. On 15 December there was huge embarrassment at the performance of an opera, *The Barber of Baghdad*, composed by his colleague Peter Cornelius, which Liszt himself was conducting. A significant part of the audience hissed, seemingly supported by the new theatre director. Liszt could take no more and he finally wrote two months later to Grand Duke Carl Alexander asking to be released from his contract.

At the same time Carolyne and Liszt's marriage hopes had been raised by a mysterious visitor named Okraszewski, a lawyer from Carolyne's lands in Ukraine, who indicated that annulment of her former marriage might finally be approved by the Roman Catholic hierarchy in Russia. (In the meantime, Prince Nicholas had obtained a Protestant divorce and remarried.) However, it was highly suspicious that Okraszewski said he required a huge payment to complete this task. Nevertheless, Carolyne was eager to proceed and, although she herself had no available money, her daughter Marie, who was by now 22 years old and thus financially independent, agreed to make the payment on her behalf.

Meanwhile, Prince Konstantin, a member of the branch of the ancient and noble Hohenlohe family living in Vienna, had proposed marriage to Marie and gained Prince Nicholas' approval. Carolyne had refused previous marriage proposals for her daughter and also had reservations about this one, but Liszt who knew the Hohenlohe family well persuaded her to agree and the marriage eventually took place in the Catholic church in Weimar in October of 1859. It must have been a very sad day for Carolyne, losing not only a daughter but the one person who had been both her constant companion and close supporter over so many years.

Finally, in December Liszt suffered a most grievous and unexpected blow with the death of his youngest child Daniel at the young age of 20. In recent years they had grown much closer to each other. Daniel had done exceptionally well at the Lycée Bonaparte in Paris, winning the national *prix d'honneur*. After being awarded his baccalaureate at the end of 1856, he had spent almost four months with Liszt in Weimar. There they decided that the best course for Daniel was to study law in Vienna where he could turn for any help to Liszt's cousin Eduard Liszt. Daniel could meet with his father when Liszt came to give concerts in Vienna. However, by 1859 Daniel, who had never had a strong physique, was already ill with consumption. He arrived for a late summer holiday in Berlin with his sister Cosima and her husband, Liszt's former pupil Hans von Bülow, but weakened quickly over the following months. Fortunately, Liszt arrived in time to be with Daniel in his last days and could grieve together with his daughter. He responded with a musical composition, a setting of a poem by Lamennais, *Les morts*, a work he asked also to be played at his own funeral.

In March 1860 came the good news that an annulment of Carolyne's marriage to Prince Nicholas had been granted by the Roman Catholic hierarchy in Russia, but this was followed by the refusal of their local German bishop to recognise it. Carolyne realised that she would have to go herself to Rome to plead her case before the Pope himself. She left Weimar in May and after a few months in Rome realised that there were clerics in high places in the Vatican who opposed her. Fortunately, there were also supporters. In September she succeeded in having an audience with Pope Pius IX. He was kind to her, giving her his assurance that he would call a meeting of cardinals to decide and two weeks later he gave his assent to the annulment of the marriage. Carolyne had every right to feel exultant but, again, she was to be blocked by the local bishop in Germany who objected, citing evidence of perjury, as a result of bribery, on the part of the Catholic authorities in Russia as well as new evidence from cousins of Carolyne who had attended her wedding. They were prepared to testify that Carolyne had entered her marriage willingly.

The situation became even more painful for her with the growing realisation that her new son-in-law Prince Konstantin was opposed to the annulment of Carolyne's original marriage, no doubt because it would declass the status of his new wife. This became evident when he refused to allow Marie to make the payment to Okraszewski on her mother's behalf. It was only with considerable difficulty that she and Liszt managed to pay this large sum by withdrawing a previous investment they had made in Vienna with the help of Liszt's cousin Eduard.

On 8 January 1861 the College of Cardinals reaffirmed its earlier decision. In fact, as Walker notes,[39] it was the original decision of 1852 that was upheld by Pope Pius IX, thus avoiding all the complications arising from the recent accusations of bribery and corruption within the Church itself. Carolyne was triumphant. She and Liszt could have married within days but, for various reasons, they waited before finally making arrangements to marry in Rome itself on 22 October, Liszt's fiftieth birthday.

Franz Liszt. Photograph by Franz Hanfstaengl 1858.

---

39. Ibid., p. 528, footnote.

3

Liszt and His Correspondents in His Fiftieth Year (1860-61)

In the later nineteenth century as today, musicians, as well as artists, writers, politicians and businessmen, were often reaching their peak achievements in their fiftieth year. Liszt, by contrast, was facing a second crisis point in his creative life. By resigning his position in Weimar, he had already signalled that he was making a change but his subsequent decision to move to Rome would have greatly surprised the contemporary musical world. He was moving away from its German-speaking centre to a land more famous for opera than for orchestral or piano music. Admittedly, he had produced many new operas in his twelve years as court musician in Weimar and also composed some superb transcriptions of opera highlights for piano. However, what precisely did Liszt have in mind for his future musical career?

In the intervening time between the Pope's original agreement to Carolyne's remarriage in September 1860 and his own arrival in Rome in October 1861, Liszt concentrated on piano composition, including further opera transcriptions. He also travelled to Paris in May, where he stayed a whole month, to see his mother who was by now disabled and living with her granddaughter Blandine and Blandine's new husband. While in Paris, he was invited to dine at the Tuileries with Emperor Napoleon III and Empress Eugénie. Then in August he helped to host a large music festival in Weimar which featured his former pupils, colleagues and friends including Richard Wagner. The main item was his 'Faust' Symphony, which his son-in-law Hans von Bülow conducted. He then closed the Altenburg and made ready to join Carolyne in Rome.

Liszt's correspondence in his fiftieth year provides insight into his attitude as he prepared to leave Weimar for Rome and provides the starting point for this psychological and spiritual analysis of his later years. I shall approach this subject by considering the various people with whom he was corresponding in 1860 and before his journey to Rome in the autumn of 1861. We are particularly fortunate in Liszt's case to have his letters to so many different people. Our sense of self is to a large degree constituted by our various and different relationships, whether harmonious or not. William James was one of the first psychologists in modern times to make the point that we can have as many 'social selves' as persons to whom we relate. As Liszt was living apart from Carolyne, he wrote to her regularly in this period and his letters to her indicate not only the state of their relationship but also his thinking about their future together. He also wrote to various family members, other close friends and colleagues in the world of music. Most but not all of these letters were included in La Mara's published collections (1893-1918). They have subsequently been republished in their original form without her editing and exclusions.

Before turning to his major correspondents in his last year in Weimar, there is another most important document that Liszt wrote at the beginning of this period which reveals a great deal about his state of mind at the time. This is his will. It is a substantial document, more than six pages as reproduced as an appendix in Alan Walker's second volume of his Liszt biography.[1] It seems likely that Liszt had been pondering this over a considerable period of time, perhaps since Carolyne's departure for Rome. Besides affirming his strong commitment to Catholic belief, it is notable for the devotion and gratitude he expresses towards her, whom he also named as the will's executrix, and also for the strong complaints he expresses about how they had been frustrated so far in their wish to be allowed to become husband and wife. The following passages from the beginning of the document are cited unaltered and without omissions:

> I am writing this on September 14, the day on which the Church celebrates the Festival of the Holy Cross. The name of this festival is also that of the glowing and mysterious feeling that has pierced my entire life, as with a sacred wound. ...
>
> Yes, 'Jesus Christ crucified', 'the foolishness and the exaltation of the Cross', this was ever my true vocation. ...

---

1. Ibid., pp. 557-63.

I have felt it in my innermost heart ever since I was seventeen years old, when I implored with tears and supplication that I might be permitted to enter the Paris seminary, and when I hoped that it would be granted to me to live the life of the saints and perhaps to die the death of the martyrs. This has not happened, alas! Yet, in spite of the numerous transgressions and errors which I have committed, and for which I feel sincere repentance and contrition, the divine light of the Cross has never been entirely withdrawn from me. At times, indeed, it has overflowed my entire soul with its glory. I give thanks to God for this, and I shall die with my soul fixed to the Cross, our redemption, our highest bliss; and in acknowledgement of my belief, I wish before my death to receive the holy sacraments of the Catholic, Apostolic, and Roman Church, and thereby to obtain the forgiveness and remission of all my sins. Amen.

My best thoughts and actions over the past twelve years I owe to her whom I have so dearly wished to call by the sweet name of wife, a wish that human malignity and the most deplorable chicanery have so far obstinately prevented –

To Jeanne-Elisabeth-Carolyne, née Iwanowska.

I cannot write her name without an ineffable thrill. All my joys are from her, and all my sufferings go to her to be appeased. Not only has she become associated and completely identified with my existence, my work, my worries, my career, helping me with her advice, sustaining me with her encouragement, reviving me with her enthusiasm and with her unimaginable prodigality of attentions, anticipations, wise and gentle words, ingenious and persistent efforts; more than that, she has often renounced herself, abdicating whatever there is of a legitimate imperative in her nature, the better to bear my own burden, which she has made her wealth and her only luxury!

I kneel before her in thought in order to bless her and render thanks to her as my guardian angel and my intercessor with God; she who is my glory and my honour, my forgiveness and my rehabilitation, the sister and the bride of my soul! What words can I use to tell of the wonders of her devotion, the courage of her sacrifices, the greatness, the heroism and the infinite tenderness of her love? I should have liked to possess an immense genius to sing in sublime harmonies of that sublime soul. Alas! I have but scarcely succeeded in stammering a few scattered notes borne away by the wind. If, however, there were to survive something of my musical toil (to which I have applied myself with an overriding passion for the last ten years), let it be the pages in which Carolyne had the greatest share because of the inspiration of her heart! I beg her to forgive me for the inadequacy of my artistic legacy, as well as the still more distressing insufficiency of my good intentions intermingled with so many shortcomings and disparities. She knows that the most poignant grief of my life is to feel myself unworthy of her and not to have been able to elevate myself to that holy and pure region which is the abode of her spirit and her virtue. If I continue to remain on this earth for some time, I vow to strive to become better, to diminish my failings, make amends, to acquire more moral stability, and to neglect nothing in order to leave behind a reputation of some good example.

Lord have pity on me; have mercy on me, and may Thy grace and blessing be upon her in time and in eternity! (Weimar, 14 September 1860)

This document has been given relatively little emphasis by many of Liszt's biographers, some of whom seem to have doubted its sincerity. However, even if one takes account of the passionate and romantic language of the nineteenth century, it still reads as a remarkably strong statement of a man's attachment towards a woman. For a Christian believer the strong association made between devotion to Christ and devotion to a fellow human being might even be thought inappropriate, as also the depiction of Carolyne as Liszt's 'guardian angel'. Nevertheless, if one refuses to accept the cynical comments of Liszt's critics who have continued to see him as a 'showman' and never to be taken seriously even long after his performing days were over, this preamble to his will provides strong evidence of the strength of his commitment to Carolyne. Moreover, it indicates the debt he felt to her, not only for her support and partnership in all his activities, but also the moral example she provided to him, including in the exercise of his Christian faith. At this turning point in his life Liszt clearly admired Carolyne as a person of the highest quality. He loved her but there was also something more that explains his commitment to her and makes understandable the use of the words 'guardian angel'.

Princess Carolyne

The only letters that Liszt received and seems to have subsequently kept are those from Carolyne. Her correspondence to him, which is even larger than his to her, is preserved in the Liszt archives in Weimar.[2] Both sets of correspondence were donated by Carolyne's daughter Marie after her mother's death. That Liszt preserved Carolyne's letters but not those of many other of his closest friends indicates the special importance she had for him from the beginning of their relationship. Therefore, the obvious starting point of any analysis of Liszt's correspondence in his later years is from a reading of his communication with Carolyne.

Princess Carolyne in the clothes she wore for her audience with Pope Pius IX in the Sistine Chapel. Photograph by Fratelli d'Alessandri, Rome 1860.

As already noted, Carolyne was a well informed and particularly determined person whom Liszt acknowledged to have superior education and intelligence to himself. She was particularly knowledgeable about religious matters and sustained Liszt in his Catholic faith throughout their relationship. However, she also understood and appreciated music well and was a strong advocate for Liszt's compositions. She also encouraged other composers. Berlioz dedicated his opera *Les Troyens* to her because of the encouragement she gave him during its creation at a moment of depression and self-doubt. Wagner was also greatly impressed by her lively manner and how she became involved with everyone around her.[3]

An edited version of Liszt's letters to Carolyne in the original French was published by La Mara in 1900 and they also provide a major part of Adrian Williams' compilation of Liszt's correspondence translated into English. Alan Walker has consulted the originals in Weimar, as has Dolores Pesce for her study of Liszt's last ten years, but no critical edition as yet exists of Carolyne's some two thousand letters to Liszt. There appears to be a major problem with the legibility of her handwriting to

---

2. archiv@hfm-weimar.de.
3. Ibid., p. 234 and p. 410.

which both Walker[4] and Pesce[5] refer. Nevertheless, Carolyne's writings deserve a fuller study not only because she was the central figure in Liszt's later life but also because she was a prominent female intellectual of her time who was prepared to question the organisation of the Roman Catholic Church.

Carolyne and Liszt exchanged many letters with one another while Carolyne was living alone in Rome from May 1860 to October 1861. Through these letters one can experience the ups and downs in Carolyne's search for an annulment of her marriage to Prince Nicholas and corresponding fluctuations in Liszt's emotions. As stressed in the previous chapter, Liszt was conscious of how much Carolyne had suffered in Weimar for his sake. Now he needed to respond to her sufferings in Rome:

> The end of your latest letter, 'I am treated so harshly by everything and everyone', breaks my heart! Yet there is no question of weakening just now. Let us remain steadfast, strengthening ourselves through God! We must, by our faith and our love. I shall write to you more often, since you ask me to – although I don't know how to speak to you as I should like. While you were listening to the Psalm 'Caeli enarrant'[6] at Santa Maria Maggiore, I was working at mine for male-voice chorus. I finished it yesterday, and it seems to me that it hasn't turned out too badly. ... I shall produce the 'Caeli enarrant' for you ... I hope – and I fancy that you will like the verse 'Et ipse tamquam sponsus procedens'.[7] (Weimar, 22 August 1860)

In Carolyne's letter to Liszt a week later she named Monsignor Gustave Hohenlohe, her son-in-law's uncle, as one of the principal clerics who were opposing her. Having befriended her when she arrived in Rome, he had subsequently presented her to the Pope as a 'ridiculous old woman who, by wishing to re-marry at her age, was exposing her daughter to the charge of illegitimacy'.[8] Liszt wrote back a supportive letter. It was at this point that Liszt decided to write his will. At this stage

---

4. Ibid., p. 35.
5. Pesce, *Liszt's Final Decade*, pp.6-7.
6. 'The heavens declare (the glory of God)' – the first line of Psalm 18(19).
7. 'And coming forth as a bridegroom' – Psalm 18:6.
8. Walker, *The Weimar Years*, p. 522.

he was still expecting Carolyne to return to Weimar with or without the annulment: 'When you return I shall show it to you – and you will tell me what I should add or change. In the meantime, I am leaving it in one of the drawers of your desk, in our blue room.' (Weimar, 17 September 1860)

Carolyne and Liszt's concern was transformed into joy when, following her audience with Pope Pius IX, the Council of Cardinals on 22 September pronounced in favour of the annulment of Carolyne's marriage as proposed by the Russian Catholic authorities. The joy was short-lived, however, as the judgement was not accepted by the Catholic authorities in the German diocese of Fulda (which included Weimar). At the same time, more evidence was brought forward suggesting that Carolyne had voluntarily entered marriage with Prince Nicholas rather than being forced into it by her father. It was at this stage that Liszt himself took further action; he travelled to Vienna in October where he met with his cousin Eduard to arrange payment to Carolyne's Ukrainian lawyer and also with the Papal Nuncio to Vienna, as well as Gustav Hohenlohe who was visiting his family. Liszt by now fully accepted that the Wittgensteins and Hohenlohes were working together to obstruct the annulment as is indicated by his correspondence with Agnes Street-Klindworth.[9] He would have realised how considerable were the forces of opposition arrayed against them by these two noble families, made more powerful by their lack of transparency.

At this point in the winter Liszt appears to have succumbed to depression:

> I am smitten with remorse at sending this letter so late. Various small external circumstances made me fall into this fault of omission, which this morning fills me with bitter sorrow. On awaking I was overcome by a fit of unspeakable sadness. ... May I see you again soon, and resume my true, my only life – beside you, at your feet. (Weimar, 3 February 1861)

A month later Liszt wrote to Carolyne in elation at hearing the news that the Pope had confirmed the annulment of her marriage to Prince Nicholas. In fact, it had been his Catholic parish priest who informed him. He told Carolyne that he would wait in Weimar for further instructions from her and that it might be possible for him to be in

---

9. Letter from Liszt to Agnes of 8 November 1860.

Rome by Holy Week. Nevertheless, his subsequent letters to Carolyne indicate continuation of his depressed mood. He told her of his difficulty in concentrating on his musical obligations, his wish to work as before next to her, his looking for her as he came back to the house in the evenings, and his need to listen to her counsels (having recently received a warning article from her about the dangers of drinking absinthe).

The celebration of Easter on 31 March came and went without Liszt and Carolyne meeting, let alone marrying. Liszt wrote to Carolyne on that day telling her that Carl Alexander was pressing him to know why they were delaying their marriage, particularly given the threatening situation in Rome itself. Italian unity had been proclaimed in the same month and nearly all papal territory was under the control of the new Italian government. Only Rome itself remained under papal control, protected by a French garrison installed by Napoleon III. However, Liszt had explained to the Grand Duke that he needed to join Carolyne in Rome and that she, who had suffered persistently from bouts of poor health in Weimar, had discovered that Rome's climate suited her. Therefore he was now preparing to go to Rome himself:

> I come back to Rome where you have to remain – and say in confidence that the prospect of pitching my tent there, for the few years of life that perhaps still remain to me, in this time of 'profound degradation and arrant perfidy', attracts me singularly. The time to make a definite plan has not yet come; and I remark solely that my opinion will be fully in harmony with yours, if you decide to settle in Rome. In any event, I shall not continue my mode of life, such as it has been these last ten years or so. I absolutely must have more peace, solitude, self-communion, and independence. My expenses must also be more restricted and better regulated, my work more continuous, lets in fits and starts – it must hollow out its bed like a broad river. God grant that I give you a little satisfaction! (Weimar, 31 March 1861)

This letter shows that Liszt was determined to change his way of life. For some time, he had been complaining about his current lifestyle, his need both to limit the extravagance of the spending that accompanied it and to concentrate more on his musical composition. He was also now prepared to live in Rome if that was what Carolyne also wanted. The situation that threatened papal Rome, to which Carl Alexander referred, seems to have been a positive rather than negative factor. Both he and

Carolyne, who must now have felt extremely grateful to Pope Pius IX for his support of her case, were prepared strongly to identify with the papacy in its hour of need.

However, in the following months Liszt's doubts about whether they would be allowed to marry returned. He wrote to Carolyne about the explanation he had recently given the Grand Duchess.

> The obstacles which have got in the way of our marriage may continue indefinitely. I am no longer taking it into my head to count on a solution favourable to us. On the contrary, I am expecting only bad luck, so that I can as well as possible protect us from its blows. Such as we are made, both of us, we fundamentally need only one another. Several people could undoubtedly, and in good conscience, have done us good turns. But since, instead of that, we have done only a good many bad turns, it really is necessary to look facts in the face and, without surrendering anything of our right, readily to accept the fate which has been prepared for us. (Weimar, 29 June 1861)

Later, in this same letter to Carolyne, he addressed her directly on this point: 'All my decisions are based on a negative eventuality, one which so far as our marriage is concerned I regard as probable.'

These are startling statements given the fact that the Pope had already pronounced on two occasions in favour of the annulment of Carolyne's marriage to Prince Nicholas. Does it suggest that Liszt knew so much about the opposition, whose strength he had personally witnessed in Vienna, that he believed it was still capable of overturning the decision already made in Rome? If so, why did he and Carolyne not try to arrange a secret marriage outside of the orbit of these powers? Did not any Catholic priest now have the authority to marry them? Carl Alexander immediately suggested the same but Liszt, as he told Carolyne in the same letter, rejected his proposals:

> When Monseigneur asked me repeatedly if he couldn't do me some service, either by letter or by taking some direct step – I replied explicitly, 'No, and again no!'... The proposal for us to get married clandestinely at one of Monseigneur's country seats – Zella, in the Oberland I believe, where there is a Catholic priest – was brought up again. Since Monseigneur said, 'This is not unfeasible', I cut him short by retorting, 'Unfeasible thrice over!'

If simply getting married was their aim, surely Liszt and Carolyne should have accepted such a proposal. However, clearly, they wanted something more than this, namely, to marry in full view of the highest church authorities. Whatever the reason, their decision to wait for a suitable occasion appears to have been one they took together.

In the following weeks, Liszt kept Carolyne informed about his preparations for the music festival in Weimar. He was looking forward to a new start away from Weimar: 'Oh! How I long to be quit of all this, and to breathe another air! Last night I again woke up saying an Ave Maria and thinking of Our Lady of Loreto!' (Weimar, 19 July 1861)

He described his emotions on closing their rooms at the Altenburg in the company of his cousin Eduard who had carried out an inventory of the couple's possessions:

> Just as I telegraphed to you, I left this house – where for 12 years you so ardently practised the Good and sought the Beautiful – at 2 o'clock in the afternoon, in full sunlight, arm and arm with Eduard, who, I believe, has faithfully carried out all your instructions. He left for Vienna at 4 o'clock. When I went through the rooms in the morning I could not restrain my tears. But after making a final stop at your prie-dieu – where you used to kneel with me before I went on a journey – a comfortable feeling of release came over me. (Weimar, 12 August 1861)

After leaving Weimar, Liszt stayed for some weeks in Löwenberg in Silesia as the guest of Constantine, Prince of Hohenzollern-Hechingen, a music enthusiast, before moving to Berlin to see Cosima and Hans and their new child. It was there that he received news of the arrangements for their marriage that Carolyne had made:

> Blessed be your dear letter of 28 September which settles everything. ... How to respond to the sentiment which made you choose the 22nd of October, and to the words that this sentiment inspires in you? However long I still have to live will not suffice, in my opinion! I am also happy about the coincidence of your parish church being under the invocation of your patron, St Charles. After him it is certainly Antonelli[10] who is our great patron in Rome. (Berlin, 4 October 1861)

---

10. Cardinal Giacomo Antonelli, secretary of state at the Vatican who was one of Carolyne's main supporters during 1860 and 1861.

Ten days later, as he prepared to embark for Italy, he wrote the final letter of this longest period of absence they had experienced since their first meeting:

> These are the last lines I am writing to you. My long exile is about to end. In 5 days I shall again find in you my country, hearth and altar! May the clemency and mercy of God, who 'raiseth up the poor out of the dust, and lifteth the needy out of the dunghill',[11] be blessed without end! May I give you days of peace and tranquillity, as we approach the evening of our lives! (Marseilles, 14 October 1861)

What do Liszt's letters to Carolyne reveal about his relationship with her at this point of transition? He expresses a strong sense of dependence on her and appears determined to please her by settling in Rome. This may all seem normal for lovers. However, Liszt and Carolyne had been together already for thirteen years. While it is hard to doubt the genuineness of his strong sense of loyalty to Carolyne, the sense of dependence he expresses appears excessive, perhaps rather unhealthy. What does seem sure is that at this crucial point in his life Liszt wanted their destiny, uncertain though it was, to be decided on her terms rather than his. Liszt's invocations of God's mercy would no doubt have impressed Carolyne and there is no reason to think they were also not real prayers of his own. Liszt after all was heading into the unknown.

Princess Marie zu Hohenlohe-Schillingsfürst, Carolyne's Daughter

Liszt had welcomed Carolyne's daughter Marie at the age of eleven into his life in 1848 together with her mother. He acted as a stepfather to her from the beginning and they had developed a very close and trusting relationship by the time of her marriage in 1859 into Viennese nobility. She had been the focus of Carolyne's and Liszt's shared personal concerns in the years leading up to her marriage. Marie's appreciation of Liszt is evidenced by the many actions Marie took to honour his memory after his death. On his travels he wrote to her regularly and independently of her mother. As part of the renewed interest in Liszt in the second part of the twentieth century, his letters to Marie, which were in the possession of Harvard University, were some of the first to be

---

11. Psalm 112/113:7.

published separately in English translation.[12] They appeal by their great charm and the evident mutual understanding that developed between Liszt and his intended stepdaughter. They also show Liszt in a different character from his other letters. With Marie he appears to have tried to keep up the light and playful mood he adopted to her as the child he first met. However, it seems to me that Liszt's biographers have tended to pay much less attention to his letters to Marie than they deserve. They reveal another side to Liszt's personality and one that is very attractive. An edition of the correspondence in the original French has been published only relatively recently.[13]

Unfortunately, Marie's marriage into the noble Hohenlohe family led to immediate friction between mother and daughter as Carolyne believed, with good reason, that the family were conspiring to prevent her marriage to Liszt and thought that Marie did not offer sufficient resistance to her husband's actions. Liszt continued – at least initially – to write to her regularly after she moved in 1859 to Vienna as the wife of Prince Konstantin. However, there is a large unexplained gap of almost nine years in the correspondence between 4 June 1860 and 31 March 1869.[14] What are the possible explanations? It seems too much of a coincidence for it not to be related to the obstacles Marie's husband Prince Konstantin was putting in the way of Liszt's marriage to Carolyne from the summer of 1860 onwards. As Hugo emphasises, the two parts of the correspondence, up to 1860 and from 1869 onwards, do have a different character. Liszt addresses her much more respectfully in the later correspondence. Nevertheless, their close confidence in each other is still very evident. It also seems difficult to believe that Liszt ceased writing to Marie altogether in this long period of nine years. However, the puzzle of what happened to any missing correspondence has not yet been solved.

Liszt's letters to Marie in the first half of 1860 provide her with detailed accounts both of his musical and other activities, and those of friends and colleagues such as Wagner and Cornelius, whom she knew, as well as general pleasantries about events in the German-speaking world. For her birthday on 18 February, he told her of presents he was arranging to send her:

---

12. Hugo (ed.), *The Letters of Franz Liszt to Marie zu Sayn-Wittgenstein*.
13. P. Pocknell, M. Haine and N. Dufetel (eds), *Lettres de Franz Liszt à la Princesse Marie de Hohenlohe-Schillingsfürst née de Sayn-Wittgenstein* (Paris: Vrin, 2010).
14. Hugo (ed.), *The Letters of Franz Liszt to Marie zu Sayn-Wittgenstein*, p.137.

It's a simple offering that I give you for this 18th of February – merely my impoverished heart, bereft of all that makes for glory and fame in this world. I had arranged a little gift, however, to act as my interpreter on this date: Chopin's Songs, with your name inscribed. The binding, alas, wasn't ready in time, and it's so far from here to Vienna! Still let me be with you on this day and all others, with all my heart and soul, - to pray for you, and to remain in the years to come even as in the years past, your very deeply grateful servant F. Liszt.

P.S. Since a painting ought never to be lacking on the 18th February, there will be a Tony Johannot to place itself at your feet. (Weimar, 11 February 1860)

For her part Marie sent Liszt a laurel wreath on the feast of his patron saint, St Francis of Paola (2 April). In thanking her, he told her how her mother and he were anxious to have news of her Ukrainian lawyer's mission to Russia where he was seeking approval for the annulment:

You can well imagine that for the past three weeks, all we've done is to wait for Okra's [Okrazewski's] arrival – Minette[15] can neither eat nor drink nor sleep – As for me, I continue to hope and hope and hope; the way the pine and the yew retain their leaves despite the ravages of the weather. (Weimar, 7 April 1860)

This seems to suggest that at this stage Liszt was not aware of Marie's husband's negative attitude to Carolyne obtaining an annulment.

However, the content of a letter Liszt sent the following month, after Carolyne had left for Rome, may indicate the beginnings of real tension between mother and daughter. Had Carolyne expressed such disapproval of Marie's distancing herself that Liszt thought he needed to deny that he shared this view? Whatever the background to this letter might have been, Liszt's approval of how Marie had grown into her new status is beautifully expressed:

From your letter to Minette, which has just reached me and which I am immediately sending on to Rome, I notice that a postscript was lacking in the one I sent you yesterday. Allow me to correct this omission, and to tell you in all truth, that I *approve* of you completely and even *admire* you for the

---

15. Liszt and Marie's pet name for Carolyne.

> perfectly simple and at the same time dignified way of life you are following, in the milieu where you are called upon to live and take root. For my opinion, it would be impossible to give further proof than you have shown of tack, charm, nobility of sentiment, and calm superiority of spirit.
>
> I suppose one might have expected it of you; still, it is with the charm of certain qualities, to which is added the perfume of noble virtue, as with the flowering of spring. One knows that it will come – yet at its approach, we feel a sort of thrill that is akin to surprise. (Weimar, 28 May 1860)

On the 4 June Liszt wrote the last letter that survives from this period of his correspondence with Marie. In it he tells Marie of the completion for publication of his 'cycle of 12 symphonic tone poems' and his plans for further composition. This letter indicates the closeness Liszt felt towards Marie, not only as his hoped-for stepdaughter but as someone he could still confide in. She understood his spiritual and musical ambitions and had witnessed his struggles in her years growing to adulthood in Weimar:

> Apart from the feeling that dominates my whole life and for whose honour I would gladly give all ten of my fingers – one after the other – and all of my worldly possessions, I have no other passion save that for my task. The contradictions, nay even the injustice occasioned by my work, far from thwarting me, arouse me still further; and they confirm me completely in the attitude I have had since my youth: that is, in the field of Music I have something to say; and no one else can say it for me. – Certainly this a small enough thing. I take no great pride in it; but come what may, I shall fulfil my task by God's good grace, to Whom I pray with genuinely resigned humility for what good or bad fortune I may encounter.

His last words to Marie were for her mother: 'I hope that Minette will enjoy her stay in Rome, and that God will grant her a few years of peace and quiet after so many trials and tribulations. Let us pray that it may be so!' (Weimar, 4 June 1860)

Can more be said about why there are no surviving letters to Marie for the following nine years? From reading Carolyne's correspondence, Walker identified that she was 'distraught' at the lack of letters from her daughter in 1860 and 'was convinced that her mail to Marie was being intercepted'.[16] Had the new obstacles that arose in her search for an annulment led Carolyne in the summer of 1860 to discourage Liszt from writing further to her daughter? It is also striking that Liszt does not appear to have sought to meet with Marie when he visited Vienna in October 1860 to seek his cousin Eduard's help in paying Okrazewski's fee and visiting the papal legate who was actively opposing Carolyne's annulment. If relations had remained normal, surely he would have wanted to see her in Vienna?

In the final volume of Walker's biography of Liszt, he cites a passage of a letter from Marie to Liszt which he found in the Weimar archives. It postdates Liszt's last surviving letter to Marie from 1860. Walker places it in a footnote but it seems to me to have huge importance in indicating not only Marie's state of mind at this time but also the great value she placed on Liszt's balanced opinion on what was at stake:

> In desperation, Marie had turned to Liszt, and in the summer of 1860, when the annulment case was still in turmoil, she had written to her 'dear, great and impartial judge' for help. Carolyne, she told Liszt, expected her daughter to obey her without hesitation, 'even if she ordered me to throw my fortune into the Danube. ... I suffer cruelly, for the rapid torrent of circumstances makes me more and more incapable of being good for anything. It is as much as I can do to maintain my peace of mind, confidence, and serenity. ... Burn this letter, dear Great One, and do not reply to it. The negotiations are secret.' (Vienna, 16 July 1860)[17]

Liszt's relationship with the young woman who could have been his stepdaughter was to remain a positive feature of the remaining years of his life, one based on mutual respect and admiration. In this way he was properly rewarded for the care he had shown Marie since taking a father's share of responsibility for her upbringing. His correspondence with her shows Liszt in an unequivocally positive light, sharing news eagerly, sympathising in times of trouble and loss, and always encouraging.

---

16. Walker, *The Weimar Years*, p. 522, footnote.
17. Walker, *The Final Years*, p. 31, footnote.

Liszt's Family: His Mother Anna and Daughters Blandine and Cosima

The one constant person in Liszt's life up to the age of 50 had been his mother. Not only had she been the strongest support to him in childhood but she had shouldered huge responsibilities for him throughout his adulthood. Born in Krems in lower Austria, she had worked for a time as a chambermaid in Vienna before crossing into Hungary to marry Adam Liszt. In coming to join the young Franz after her husband died, she gave up her previous ties, culture and language in order to provide a secure home background for the young man as he began his life as a travelling piano teacher in Paris. She counselled him through his time of emotional turmoil following his father's death, including his repeated wish to enter a religious life, and was one of his few confidants before he took flight with Countess Marie d'Agoult. Most remarkably, after this relationship broke down, she took it upon herself to raise his three children with the financial support he provided her and encouraged regular correspondence between Liszt and his children.

Many of Liszt's letters to his mother are included in Adrian Williams' compilation of Liszt's selected letters in translation.[18] Although always loyal to her son, Anna was also ready to criticise him, most evidently when he took his two daughters away from her in 1850 to place them under a governess and then five years later away from Paris itself without any prior warning, both actions intended to keep them away from the influence of their mother Marie d'Agoult. When she finally learned what her son was planning, she wrote to her son to express her dismay and condemned the insensitivity of his actions to his own children.[19] By then, after a fall down steps while visiting her son in Weimar in 1852, Anna had become somewhat disabled and so could not have continued looking after Blandine and Cosima. Nevertheless, their departure from Paris was a cruel blow to her. Fortunately for her Blandine returned soon to Paris.

Anna incurred a series of further accidents over the following years which finally left her virtually immobile. After she fractured a femur in 1860, she was taken to live with Blandine who was now married. Liszt was very grateful for the attention Blandine showed to his mother in her declining years. There was never any lessening of the close bond between Liszt and his mother. She remained the caring mother, as shown by the

---
18. Williams (ed.), *Franz Liszt: Selected Letters*.
19. Walker, *The Weimar Years*, pp. 450-51.

following excerpt from one of his letters in which he thanks her – somewhat belatedly – for a rug she had sent him:

> For several months it has been rendering me excellent service and delighting my eye with its beautiful green colour – the colour both of hope and of the Holy Ghost. Although silent and mute it tells me many nice things about you. It lies in my study under my desk, and while I write to you warms my feet, which for years have had a silly habit of freezing. That probably comes from the fact that in many things I am rather a hothead. (Weimar, 18 September 1860)

Anna Liszt, née Anna Maria Lager, Franz Liszt's mother (1788-1866).

Liszt spent time during his long stay in Paris in the spring of 1861 at Blandine's apartment, sitting often at his mother's bedside. No doubt they would have spoken much about Daniel, the son and grandson they had both recently lost, the youngest of Liszt's children and the one Anna had mothered the longest.

Blandine's son Daniel produced an edition of his mother's and grandfather's letters to one another.[20] However, relatively less of Cosima's correspondence with her father survives and, although a number of Liszt's letters to Blandine can be found in Adrian Williams' compilation, none of his letters to Cosima can be found there. For these we need to turn to Klára Hamburger's collection of all Liszt's surviving letters to Cosima in the original French.[21] It appears that Cosima was very selective in what she kept of her relationship with her father. Despite the many mentions of Cosima, whom Liszt liked to called 'Cosette' in his letters to Carolyne and others in 1860-61, there is only one surviving letter from Liszt to Cosima in this period, written on 28 May 1860 to ask why his daughter had not written to him recently – she was in the early stages of pregnancy – and tell her of Carolyne's travel to Rome.

Although Liszt saw little of his children as they were growing up, not visiting at all for a period of nine years 1844-53, he did take a great

---

20. D. Ollivier (ed.), *Correspondance de Liszt et de sa fille Madame Émile Ollivier, 1842-1862* (Paris: Grasset, 1936).
21. Hamburger (ed.), *Lettres à Cosima et à Daniela*.

interest in their education. However, only gradually in their later teens did Liszt's children get to know their father as a physical presence rather than a famous personage. Nevertheless, as described in the previous chapter, he was prepared to take great pains to remove them from their mother's influence once the girls began seeking and wishing to meet her on a regular basis. Cosima in particular seems to have become resentful to her father. In later life she wrote to her own daughter that 'my whole youth was a staying at home!'[22]

Blandine, Daniel and Cosima Liszt. From a water colour by Amélie de Lacépède 1843.

Both Cosima and Blandine married in 1857. Cosima married Liszt's most talented protégé Hans von Bülow, in whose mother's house she and Blandine had lodged in Berlin, after Liszt moved them from Paris to further their education but also to minimise contact with their mother. Hans was already developing a promising career as an orchestral conductor, as well as a pianist, and had become a strong advocate for Wagner's music as well as Liszt's. By falling in love with her father's favoured pupil, she might seem to have drawn closer to her father but her choice of husband would prove a mistake. Hans was highly neurotic and might now also be classified as bipolar. Following Cosima's marriage, Blandine returned to Paris and married a rising French politician Émile Ollivier to whom she had been introduced by Marie d'Agoult at one of her regular salons.

After their marriages, Liszt saw more of his daughters, travelling both to Berlin and Paris to be with them and their husbands and seeking to improve their relationship with Carolyne as well. On 12 October 1860 Cosima gave birth to a daughter whom she named Daniela, but she became very ill afterwards. She resisted complaining to her husband and it was left to Blandine, who was very close to her sister and thus understood her very well, to point out to her father that neither Hans nor his mother were ideal carers for his daughter. Liszt responded to Blandine's concern and persuaded Cosima to enter a sanatorium in the Bavarian Alps for some months in 1861, during which time her health recovered. He also took the opportunity to write to Hans urging him not to be a victim of his negative moods.

---

22. Cited by Walker, *The Weimar Years*, p. 438.

Liszt and Blandine kept in close contact throughout this period and Liszt's letters reveal a close and trusting relationship between himself and his eldest child:

> In the meantime let me thank you, dearest Blandine, for offering to accompany Cosima to the south; I hope such a trip will not be necessary and that the Reichenhall cure will be enough. Besides, Hans would not agree to his wife being away for several months unless he was with her ... but I am none the less moved by the affection you show your sister. Do, however, take care not to write and tell her too insistently to look after her health, for that is a topic which angers her very easily, as you know. (Weimar, 25 March 1861)

Blandine's husband Émile had also developed a good relationship with his father-in-law, as he wrote in his diary after Liszt's visit to Paris in May 1861: 'I have come to feel a most warm and genuine affection for him, and how transported, moved and filled with wonder I have been by his truly supernatural playing, it is impossible to describe.'[23]

There were thus grounds for thinking that Liszt would be able to continue building better relationships with his daughters even after he left for Rome. However, there remained the huge problem for both Blandine and Cosima of the disharmony between their parents. Émile sought to improve this situation and took care to cultivate close ties with Marie d'Agoult as well as with Liszt.

The Countess Marie d'Agoult, Mother of Liszt's Children

Countess Marie d'Agoult had been by far the major correspondent of Liszt in the years 1833-44.[24] Thereafter, their correspondence dwindled but they remained closely linked by their children. Unfortunately, their relationship deteriorated after Liszt sought to prevent contact with their mother and even removed Blandine and Cosima from Paris to Berlin without consulting Marie. Worse still, they communicated their disagreements openly with their daughters. As Walker has made clear, the battle over their children shows neither Marie nor Liszt in a good light.[25]

---

23. Cited by Williams (ed.), *Franz Liszt: Selected Letters*, p. 528.
24. See Williams (ed.), *Franz Liszt: Selected Letters*.
25. Walker, *The Weimar Years*, pp. 452-55.

It is therefore remarkable that Marie, when she heard that Liszt was coming to Paris in 1861, invited him to a luncheon party and then asked him to come back again for a more intimate meal together a few days later. He accepted both invitations. Marie has left a detailed account of her words and feelings recorded both in Émile Ollivier's journals and her own *Mémoires*. She was clearly moved by seeing Liszt again, writing the following after the first meeting:

> He has aged a lot, but he has remained handsome. His face has become tanned, his eyes no longer have their sparkle, but his manner is young. His beautiful hair falls in long straight tresses on both sides of his noble, saddened face.
>
> Ever since his appearance, I have been preoccupied with him. On the first night I had difficulty in sleeping.[26]

After the second meeting she was more critical and described him in terms one might expect from the writer of *Nélida*: 'He gives the impression of a man who is content to be rich, to lead an elegant life, to be *à la mode* in Paris and to be well connected. But sad, profoundly sad at bottom. And he has certainly not reached his goal.'[27] Liszt saw her for a third time on the day he left Paris. Marie was again overwhelmed: 'While saying goodbye, I spontaneously got to my feet and hugged him, deeply moved. ... Inexpressible charm! It is still him and him alone who makes me feel the divine mystery of life. With him gone, I sense the emptiness around me and weep.'[28]

Liszt gives his own account of seeing Marie again in two long letters to Carolyne, seemingly written on the same day, when he was back in Weimar. It is very different from Marie's description:

> I promised to tell you about my visit to the Hôtel Montaigne. Alas! The memories which led me there are extremely sad, and the one which has been added to them is not of a kind to make them more serene. Nélida did not see me again to tell me of anything that could have interested us – but only because many people were speaking to her of me, of my little successes and even of my *bons mots*. My daughters' names

---

26. Cited by Walker, *The Weimar Years*, pp. 542-43.
27. Cited by Hilmes, *Franz Liszt: Musician, Celebrity, Superstar*, p. 183.
28. Cited both by Walker, *The Weimar Years*, p. 543, and by Hilmes, *Franz Liszt: Musician, Celebrity, Superstar*, p. 183.

were pronounced only casually, at the end of my last visit, the day I left Paris. She then asked me why I had prevented Cosima from following her real vocation – that of an artistic career!! According to Nélida, that was what was most suitable! On this point, as on so many others, I am unable to share her opinion. This radical disagreement in our temperaments showed itself right at the start of our first interview, when we chatted about very general things only, such as the principle of nationalities, Hungary and Poland, the politics of the Tuileries and of Cavour, etc. (Weimar, 29 June 1861)

At the second meal, which Liszt described as 'excellent and served to perfection', he was again conscious of the differences in their opinions:

Nélida maintained, of course, that in France there was no longer either good taste or good form – that there was no longer either talk or conversation – that all interest in matters of the intellect had disappeared – that plenty of building work was going on, but that it certainly didn't amount to architecture, etc., etc. You can imagine how all this nonsense was to my taste. And so I did not fail to cast a good many stones into the fine flower-beds of her blossoming rhetoric – by maintaining, stoutly, that our own age was at least as good as any other, that there was always a prodigious amount of intelligence in France, and that the Seven Wonders of the ancient world put together did not equal the reconstruction of Paris being carried out by the Emperor Napoleon.

It was Liszt who took the initiative to visit Marie again but this time on his own before he left Paris. On this occasion at least they could speak of more personal matters, Marie's success in her latest novels and Liszt's musical ambitions. They brought up their previous mutual friend, Marie's fellow novelist Aurore Dupin, who wrote under the pseudonym of George Sand and with whom Marie had not recovered her previous friendship:

'What about you,' she went on, 'have you remained a good friend of hers?' – 'Your estrangement rather cooled my relations with her – for although *au fond* I regarded you as being in the wrong, I stood up for you none the less.' – 'I believed the contrary.' – 'Groundlessly, as of old.'

Liszt went on to refer to the English novelist Mary Anne Evans ('George Eliot'), who also used a male pseudonym. She had visited him in Weimar together with her partner George Henry Lewes, who was researching material for a biography of Goethe:

> In connection with Goethe and his biographer, Lewes, I mentioned Miss Evans, George Eliot. It seems that she has written two novels – whose titles I forget – which are very highly spoken of, so much so that several well-known critics in England regard Miss Evans as Mme Sand's only rival. This was a sore point for Nélida. Fortunately her superiority as a historian and publicist remains intact.

What do these letters suggest about Liszt's attitude to his former lover. He was impressed by their very different attitudes to contemporary literature and politics, including French policy towards Italian unification and the actions being taken by Cavour, the prime minister of the Kingdom of Piedmont-Sardinia and first prime minister of a united Italy, to promote it. However, more importantly, he clearly felt that they were or had become incompatible characters, referring to 'radical disagreement in our temperaments'. He also seemed to enjoy scoring points against Marie when showing his acquaintance with and knowledge of the work of a 'rival' contemporary female novelist. Most striking is his repeated reference to Marie as 'Nélida', the name of the principal character in her earlier quasi-autobiographical novel. Clearly this still greatly rankled with him. Most sad of all is the evidence that they could not talk in harmony about their three children.

Nevertheless, there were some hopeful signs of a coming together of views in Liszt's account of their last meeting. He had turned the conversation to himself and boldly even used the name 'Guermann', his artist self in *Nélida*, to refer to himself. Liszt's account of what he said to Marie d'Agoult is very important also for what it reveals about his own self-conception in his fiftieth year:

> After we had chatted about various literary and political matters, I gave the conversation a more personal turn. Wagner, the Music of the Future, the part I was taking in the present-day musical movement, etc., had been touched upon several times in my very first visit; I returned to these topics in more detail – and showed her very plainly that to continue along my path I needed neither friends nor party

nor newspapers. 'Guermann's walls are already painted', I told her, 'and he will paint others too – without bothering in the least about rubbish spoken or printed by others'. She was struck by my voluntary isolation, and perhaps, too, by the strange significance of my artistic life. Not that she has ever much noticed it, but at that moment it seemed to flash upon her. Hearing me talk of myself like that, of my egoism and my ambition, of the part I play for the public and of the one which remains reserved for the artist, of the total identification of my endeavours of former days with my ideas of today, of the permanence of this self that she had found so 'hateful' – she felt some kind of emotion, and her whole face filled with tears. I kissed her on the forehead, for the first time for many long years, and said, 'Look, Marie, let me speak to you in the language of the peasants. May God bless you! Don't wish me ill!' – She could make no response at that moment – but her tears flowed still more abundantly. Ollivier had told me that when he was in Italy with her, he had several times seen her weeping bitterly in various places which reminded her more particularly of our youth. I told her that I had been touched by this remembrance. All but stammeringly, she said, 'I shall always remain faithful to *Italy* – and to *Hungary*!' Thereupon I quietly left her. On my way downstairs I thought of my poor Daniel! His name had not once been mentioned during the 3 or 4 hours I had spent talking with his mother!!!

Was a lasting reconciliation possible between Liszt and Marie? It is not part of the purpose of this book to come to an evaluation of Marie d'Agoult's character. Nevertheless, it would seem to me that Alan Walker is less sympathetic to her than he might be. The hero of his biography is understandably Liszt himself and he defends him successfully against many false accusations. However, Marie was also a person with talents and ambitions which she succeeded in realising to a large extent. Both the breakdown of her relationship with Liszt and the way it affected their children were tragedies and at this point in the story there could still be hope that some at least of these issues could be resolved to the benefit of both. A major problem admittedly was the hostility Marie had developed towards Carolyne, despite never having met her, but was Liszt interested in seeking a reconciliation? Unfortunately, his view of Marie as 'Nélida' seemed to be fixed in stone.

Eduard Liszt, His Cousin

Although Liszt had left behind his extended family in Hungary and Austria when he was still a young boy, he did have a number of cousins with whom he was to recover relationships later in life. However, there was one cousin who had already become an important person in Liszt's life. This was Eduard Liszt, a half-brother of Liszt's father. Liszt preferred to call him cousin rather than uncle as Eduard was in fact five years younger than him. He lived in Vienna and was a well-respected lawyer. By 1861 he had become assistant imperial prosecutor to the Habsburgs. His trusted status had led both Liszt and Carolyne to rely on him for both legal and financial advice and to entrust their savings to him. Liszt had also asked Eduard to take on the role of guide and protector to his son Daniel when he came to study in Vienna in 1857.

Liszt's letters to Eduard show that he was 'one of the very small number of persons whom it gives me pleasure to tell of my thoughts and feelings'.[29] After Daniel's death in December 1859, he expressed his deepest thanks for the support Eduard had given him both at that time and throughout his years in Weimar:

> By the loving friendship which you have shown me, especially during the last decade in which so many trials have been laid on me, our close relationship in heart and character has been for ever firmly sealed, dearest Eduard. You are, and will ever be to me, a support and a courage-giving comforter in the battles and straits of my life. God grant me grace to go through them without wavering, as a faithful servant of the truth in Christ! (Weimar, 28 December 1859)

Eduard was very interested in the new musical developments Liszt was instigating and Liszt kept him informed both about his latest compositions and the work of other composers such as Wagner. Eduard also befriended Liszt's colleague, the composer Peter Cornelius, after he moved from Weimar to Vienna in 1859 following the fiasco of the reception of his opera, *The Barber of Baghdad*. Clearly, Liszt felt a close affinity with Eduard as he reaffirmed in his letter the following year:

> You remain perpetually in the home of my heart, not at all in countless company, but all the more in picked company.

---

29. Letter to Eduard from Liszt in Gotha, 29 March 1854.

When I think I have done anything pretty good I think of you and rejoice that what I have done will be a pleasure to you – and in the hours when sadness and sorrow take hold of me you are again my comfort and strength by your loving insight into my innermost wishes and yearnings. (Weimar, 9 July 1860)

He also wrote in September 1860 to console Eduard at his disappointment in failing to obtain the promotion he was expecting in Vienna.

In July 1861 Eduard was Liszt's house guest in Weimar when he held his last music festival there before his departure. Eduard had also been invited to make an inventory of the contents of the Altenburg before it was closed. Carolyne had advised Liszt to do this carefully as the building now contained many valuable and precious mementoes of Liszt's achievements and of the precious furnishings Carolyne had bought over the years. Alan Walker's reading of Carolyne's letters to Eduard at this time demonstrates her trust in him as her financial advisor at this difficult turning point in their life, especially following the loss of her inherited assets in Russia.[30]

Liszt's Closest Friends in Music

Liszt had numerous friends and acquaintances as the long lists of names in the various volumes of his assorted correspondence indicate.[31] Most of his closest friends came from the world of music, but only to a select few of these did he reveal his inner self, his underlying goals in life. I have picked out the persons who seem to me to have been his most intimate correspondents in music, life and spirit as he approached the age of 50 years. I have placed them in order of length of acquaintance.

Baron Antal Augusz

When Liszt came back to Hungary to give concerts in 1839-40, he acquired new friends in his native land. His patriotic stance was greatly appreciated. After his performance at the National Theatre in Pest, he was awarded with a ceremonial sword by a group of noblemen. Liszt's

---

30. Walker, *The Weimar Years*, pp. 550-51.
31. See, for example, La Mara (ed.), *Letters of Franz Liszt*; Williams (ed.), *Franz Liszt: Selected Letters*.

rousing impromptu response in French (he had never learned to speak Hungarian) – which, as Walker notes,[32] may have appeared as a call to insurrection – was translated by Baron Antal Augusz, one of the group, and read back in Hungarian to the audience. Augusz subsequently became one of Liszt's closest friends and a regular correspondent. When Liszt returned to give a series of concerts in Hungary in 1846, he stayed at Augusz's house in Szekszárd and celebrated his birthday there on 22 October. The local people gathered outside to wish Liszt well and he had the piano brought towards the open windows so that he could play the arrangement he had made of the *Rákóczy March*, which had become the unofficial Hungarian anthem. Two years later came the unsuccessful Hungarian struggle for freedom from Hapsburg rule; lasting a year and a half, it was followed by brutal suppression. Liszt followed these painful events from afar. He had learned from his previous experiences in Paris to be wary of violent revolution, as Augusz was as well. Liszt's response was his piano elegy, *Funérailles*, a profound meditation on human ideals and suffering in situations of conflict.

Liszt's friendship with Augusz grew such that he could confide in him his disappointments in the reception of his orchestral compositions in the 1850s. Criticisms were largely negative and harsh comparisons drawn with the symphonies of Haydn, Mozart and Beethoven. Liszt and Augusz had in common that they could draw on similar spiritual resources. While on a visit to Pest in April 1858, Liszt, Augusz and another Hungarian nobleman were admitted together to the order of St Francis as 'confraters'. After mass in the church which Liszt had known in his childhood, they ate with the monks. They were toasted by the father superior, who then conducted the ceremony of admission. Liszt gave a detailed account of these events in correspondence. He was, as he wrote to Carolyne, 'in very good and reliable company'.[33]

Baron Antal Augusz (1807-1878). Lithograph by Strixner, c. 1855.

His subsequent letter of January 1860 to Augusz after the death of Daniel is a particularly interesting document as it expresses some of Liszt's most important values. It begins by confirming the bonds between Liszt and his Hungarian friend and

---

32. Walker, *The Virtuoso Years*, p. 326,
33. Liszt's letter to Carolyne from Vienna 13 April 1858.

then provides much insight into the closeness Liszt felt towards his son which is not available in his letters to others. He confided in Augusz how Daniel had also expressed a vocation to the priesthood, which as Walker notes,[34] reflected Liszt's own feelings at a similar age, as well as feeling of obligation to live up to his inherited Hungarian identity:

> I have spoken little to you about my son. He had a dreamy, gentle, deep nature. His soul's yearnings elevated him above the earth, as it were, and he had inherited from me a powerful propensity towards that region of ideas and aspirations which brings us ever closer to the divine mercy. And so the thought of entering the priesthood had been taking firmer and firmer root in his mind. My sole desire was that before carrying out this holy resolve he should undertake solid and serious studies, in order to fit himself for the task of giving good service to the cause of religion. You know how much he applied himself to responding fully to my expectations of him, and to what he rightly considered an obligation imposed by his name. After he had carried off the *prix d'honneur* at the *Concours Général* in Paris, he was preparing to sit his law examination in Vienna, and would, I doubt not, have acquitted himself with honour. On the eve of his death he spoke to me about it again and strove to explain to me the chapter from the *Code* dealing with the different kinds of obligations. A little earlier he had taken pleasure in reciting to me by heart a few lines of Hungarian, to prove to that he was keeping the promise he had given me to acquire a good knowledge of this language even before the completion of his legal studies! (Weimar, 14 January 1860)

Liszt, as noted in the previous chapter, had been determined from their childhood that his children should be registered as Hungarian by birth.

In the same letter Liszt expressed his worries to Augusz about the continuing turmoil in their native land:

> Patriotism is a great and admirable sentiment, to be sure; but when in its exaltation it reaches the point of disregarding necessary limits, and takes for counsel solely the inspirations of hotheads, it too will end by 'sowing the wind to reap the

---

34. Walker, *The Weimar Years*, p. 472, footnote.

whirlwind'. It is not for me to get involved in judging these events, for I don't feel called to take an active part in them. Nevertheless, I firmly hope not to fail in my task, and shall apply myself ceaselessly to bringing honour to *my country* (as I told HM the Emperor) by my work and by my character as an artist.

Liszt continued, condemning the tendency of some Hungarians to honour their own culture to the exclusion of all others, including neglecting the contribution of gypsies to Hungarian culture. Liszt had recently incurred harsh criticism for writing about their important influence on Hungarian music:

[E]ven if not precisely in the way understood by certain patriots, for whom the Rákóczy March is more or less what the Koran was for Omar and who would gladly burn – as did the latter the Library of Alexandria – the whole of Germanic music with this fine argument; 'Either it can be found in the Rákóczy or it is worthless'. ... The fuss made about my volume on the gypsies has made me feel much more truly Hungarian than my antagonists, the Magyaromanes, for loyalty is one of the distinctive features of our national character. Now is it loyal, I ask, to steal from those we have *patronized*? Haven't Bihary, Lavotta, Csermák, Boka and a score of other gypsies left us a mass of compositions signed with their names and which have taken root in the very heart of our memories? And so why not render unto the gypsies the things that are the gypsies, while retaining for the Hungarians their own rights and possessions? – and have I done anything other than this?

Grand Duke Carl Alexander

Carl Alexander had taken an interest in Liszt from the pianist's first concert performance in Weimar in 1841. His Russian mother, the Grand Duchess Maria Pavlovna was a talented musician who played the piano very well, sang and also composed. She it was, rather than her husband, who supported her son in his ambition to bring Liszt to Weimar in order to help renew the artistic and spiritual heritage of the city. Over the years Carl Alexander had become Liszt's friend as well as his patron. At the same time, he had disappointed Liszt even after he succeeded his father as Grand Duke in 1853. The resources he made available to his court musician were never sufficient to realise Liszt's ambitions despite his entreaties. If he had really wanted to make Weimar a centre of musical excellence, why did he not commit the necessary funds for a major orchestra, even perhaps dared to employ Liszt's friend Wagner in addition as Liszt urged him? However, Carl Alexander, although sharing Liszt's ideals, was shy and retiring and remained, understandably in the German context of the time, cautious about opposing his financially prudent ministers. Similarly disappointing was his inability to defend Carolyne from insults at court.

Carl Alexander's failure in these respects did not detract from his genuine appreciation of Liszt's talent and his liking of him as a man. Moreover, there was no deterioration in their relationship in 1859 when Liszt finally resigned from his position as court Kapellmeister in anger, following the disrespectful behaviour of the theatre director and the audience at an opera while Liszt was conducting. Liszt made clear his displeasure in his subsequent correspondence with the Grand Duke, referring not only to the treatment of his musical work, but also to the ill will displayed to Carolyne and even mentioning the unjust treatment of her daughter Marie, who had been taken away from her mother for some years and placed in the ducal palace at the insistence of her father Prince Nicholas.

Still, Carl Alexander tried to persuade his court musician to stay in Weimar. Two months later Liszt wrote back an exceptionally long letter, explaining his position in great detail and giving his patron a last chance to give Liszt the position he had always desired. It demonstrates by its tone and frankness Liszt's confidence in his secure friendship with his patron:

> The Weimar theatre has had significance only under Goethe, and Goethe never needed to appear in it in public. If you desire my services in the musical category, exempt me from the *letter* which kills and thus leave free place to the *spirit* I represent, a spirit of initiative and encouragement in the domain of art.

As Liszt no doubt realised, it was not possible for the Grand Duke to grant his request and he ended his letter accordingly:

> Rather than retain me here in the only way in which I can remain, people will persuade you that you cannot be *good* to me. I am entirely prepared for it, and if, despite that, I talk

to you of the manner in which I could serve you, it is only so as not to respond by a bitter silence to the friendship your words express and for which I am never less than grateful, something I shall remain whatever the circumstances – as too, Your Royal Highness's very faithful servant. (Weimar, 6 February 1860)

Despite his inability to grant Liszt's request, both Carl Alexander and his wife took a remarkably close interest in the negotiations for the annulment of Carolyne's marriage and the arrangements for a subsequent marriage to Liszt. When the situation took a downturn in the summer of 1860, Liszt appealed for his help in dramatic language:

Save me, sire – you can do it! Wherever the obstacle might be, you are in a position to remove it. My gratitude is of such little use that I forbear to mention it at this moment. But the feeling of having done a good and noble thing will bear a reward worthy of you, and God who rules our conscience will bless you.

Do not abandon me, then. You know that in this union with the princess lies all the honour and all the happiness to which I aspire and hope in this world. (Weimar, 19 August 1860)

Carl Alexander responded by writing both to Cardinal Antonelli, the secretary of state at the Vatican, and the Russian ambassador in Rome. Moreover, as Liszt's letters to Carolyne show, the Grand Duke persisted in trying to find solutions for Liszt and Carolyne, even going as far as to suggest that he find a Catholic priest who would marry them on one of his estates outside Weimar. Liszt, by contrast, remained pessimistic about the final outcome, implying that he possessed a deeper knowledge of the situation.

Liszt's final letters to Carl Alexander at the end of his time in Germany show him returning to the previous, often jovial, content of their correspondence, satisfying his patron's curiosity about recent historical personages whom he had learned about in his travels and sharing new pieces of information. One of his last letters refers to Goethe's apprehensive attitude to Beethoven's influence on music, as revealed in the recently published letters of Felix Mendelssohn Bartholdy (perhaps Liszt was thinking that the same applied to himself less than 30 years later): 'This is the limit of what people were able to listen to in 1832 – five years after Beethoven's death.' (Löwenberg, 7 September 1861)

Richard Wagner and Hector Berlioz

By 1860 Richard Wagner already owed a great deal to Liszt's help. Although Liszt had scarcely taken note of him when they first met in Paris in 1840, he had become greatly impressed by his work after attending his opera *Rienzi* in Dresden in 1844 and Wagner's subsequent music dramas convinced him of his genius. Once established in Weimar, Liszt put on a performance of *Tannhäuser* in February 1849 especially for the benefit of Grand Duchess Maria Pavlovna who had also become interested in hearing Wagner's new work. Then, only a few months later, Wagner arrived in Weimar as a fugitive begging for Liszt's help. He had joined in the revolutionary fervour that followed the popular risings across Europe in 1848 and been forced to flee Dresden. Liszt not only bravely offered him sanctuary in his home but skilfully organised Wagner's escape from German lands to Paris with false papers.

Subsequently, Liszt went on to promote his friend's work by all means possible, powerful testimony not only to his sense of loyalty but also to his faith in the value of Wagner's work. As Walker points out, 'for five years Liszt was the only conductor in Germany who would have anything to do with Wagner's compositions; the others were either fearful of the political consequences or disdainful of the music'.[35] Throughout this time Liszt helped sustain his friend's morale by his championship of his music, both performing it and also writing about it in depth. In Walker's opinion, he put the promotion of Wagner's work before his own musical development. He kept up a regular encouraging correspondence, met Wagner when he could outside Germany, and also responded generously to Wagner's constant appeals for money. Wagner acknowledged the practical help as well as the inspiration that he received from Liszt. In grateful response he dedicated his next major composition *Lohengrin* to Liszt, who gave its first performance in Weimar in 1850. On a number of later occasions Wagner admitted how much Liszt had influenced him in his understanding of harmony. Indeed, it is clear that both composers learned from one another in the 1850s and their relationship has been described as one of the greatest friendships in music.

However, Wagner had major defects of character which over time came to irritate Liszt. When, at the end of 1858, Wagner wrote rudely to him from Venice demanding he send him money as soon as possible rather than his own compositions, Liszt made it clear that this was unacceptable behaviour. The following year he wrote candidly to

---

35. Ibid., p. 118.

his son-in-law Hans von Bülow, who was by then Wagner's principal conductor, offering both his opinion of Wagner and his advice on dealing with him, in particular, advising him to be cautious in following his instructions in detail. He also wrote to von Bülow that he particularly disapproved of the pretentious way Wagner acted requiring people to treat him as if he was a 'great Sovereign'.[36]

Nevertheless, Liszt continued to express the same affection towards the person who for so long had been his greatest ally in moving music forward. In 1860 he wrote how eager he was to learn more of Wagner's recent projects including *Tristan und Isolde*, the great cycle of music dramas of *Der Ring des Nibelungen*, on which he was already working, as well as a new version of *Tannhäuser*:

> Your letter, dearest, unique one, means more to me than the most beautiful, blossoming May day. May you, too, rejoice in the heartfelt joy it has given me!
>
> How gladly would I telegraph *myself* to Paris! Where could things go so well for me as with you – in the magic circle of *Rheingold, Walküre, Siegfried, Tristan und Isolde*, all of which I yearn for! I mustn't think of this for the time being, however; but I shall certainly come, and as soon as I can. ...
>
> And so there will soon be a *Tannhäuser* with ballet and a *contest of translators* as well as of *singers*! It will be quite a tough piece of work for you, and I advise as many walks and cooling baths as possible. During the rehearsals Fips [Wagner's spaniel] should give you a lecture on philosophic patience. ... Meanwhile, I remain, with all my heart. Your own. F. Liszt (Weimar, 31 May 1860)

In the same letter he confided in Wagner the good news he had recently received from Carolyne, that the intrigues around them had been overcome and that he expected that they would be free to marry soon.

However, a year later in May 1861 when Liszt did succeed in coming to Paris, the mood between them had changed. Walker provides a detailed account of the underlying tensions.[37] Wagner was resentful towards Liszt for not coming earlier to the performances of his new *Tannhäuser*. These

---

36. Dufetel, 'Liszt and Wagner', Foreword to *The Collected Writings of Franz Liszt: Dramaturgical Leaves, II (Richard Wagner)*, xviii-xix.
37. Ibid., pp. 543-47.

had not been successful and he thought – quite unreasonably – that Liszt's presence would have made a difference. Moreover, Wagner was annoyed that after the first performances of *Tristan* a music critic, Richard Pohl, had questioned his originality, attributing the origins of this new harmonic world to Liszt. This was not something he thought that should be made public in this way and he was convinced without any good reason that Carolyne had had something to do with this. By now, Liszt had been distressed to learn from his son-in-law Hans that Wagner considered Liszt was unduly dominated by Carolyne, was opposed to their marriage and was dismayed that Liszt should leave Germany for Italy.

There were other more fundamental differences in world view between Liszt and Wagner. However much they might have admired each other's musical compositions, they were at variance in how they conceived the context and meaning of the music they created. Liszt had retained his strongly spiritual view of the creation of music which he interpreted within his strong Catholic religiosity. Wagner was not a believer in anything as definite as Christianity and particularly disliked Catholicism. The two men were moving in very different directions. Carolyne could see this clearly but Liszt tried to apprehend the Christian sources and meanings in the stories and legends that fascinated Wagner. Nevertheless, they were both involved in the fledgeling Allgemeine Deutsche Musikverein (the German Music Association) which was founded in Weimar in August 1861 to further the 'New German School' of music. The association's first president was Franz Brendel until his death in 1868. Its founder members included Liszt, Richard Wagner, Hans von Bülow and Franz Brendel.

Liszt's loyalty to Wagner had resulted in a loosening of his ties to Hector Berlioz, with whom he had been friends for much longer. They had first met when Liszt was only nineteen years old and Berlioz 27 years, after Liszt had been entranced by the first performance of the older man's *Symphonie fantastique*. Liszt's highly successful career in transcribing orchestral music to keyboard began two years later when he performed a skilful piano version of this work. Liszt even acted as an official witness to Berlioz's marriage with Harriet Smithson in 1833. The two musicians shared similar enthusiasms for the new spirit that had emerged in Paris after the July Revolution of 1830 and, particularly, for the movement known as 'Saint-Simonism', which combined early forms of socialism and ideas of Christian brotherly love against traditional autocracy and theocratic rule. They were both enthusiasts for literature and art as well as music and they honoured the memory of the recently deceased Beethoven. They particularly appreciated the great composer's later works, such as his piano sonatas and string quartets, at a time when these works were still considered strange and disturbing.

After Liszt established himself in Weimar in the later 1840s and began promoting 'new music', he gave Berlioz pride of place, organizing week-long Berlioz festivals which the composer attended. Carolyne also responded warmly to Berlioz and they developed a correspondence of their own. Unfortunately, however, Berlioz did not share Liszt's huge enthusiasm for Wagner's compositions and this began to undermine their friendship as Liszt devoted more and more attention to promoting the German composer's work.

Berlioz like Liszt had suffered greatly both from the lack of appreciation given to his work and the persistence of troubled family relationships, which in his case were dogging him still as a result of a second marriage. In his long visit to Paris in May 1861 Liszt met Berlioz along with other musicians including Bizet, Gounod, Rossini and Wagner. He commented to Carolyne again on Berlioz's unhappy psychological state:

> Our poor friend Berlioz is thoroughly dejected and filled with bitterness. His domestic life weighs on him like a nightmare, and outside he encounters only vexations and disappointments! I dined at his place with d'Ortigue, plus Mme Berlioz and her mother. It was dismal, sad, desolate! Berlioz's voice has become feebler. He generally speaks very quietly – and his whole being seems to incline towards the grave! I don't know how he has managed to isolate himself here in this way. In fact, he has neither friends nor supporters – neither the great sun of the public, nor the gentle shade of people close to him. (Paris, 16 May 1861)

He noted that Berlioz had lost any hope of having *Les Troyens* performed at the Opéra in Paris now that he had fallen out with its director in regard to changes the latter had requested to the libretto. Moreover, Liszt disapproved of his critical articles on Wagner which he considered had harmed not only Wagner but also himself.

Agnes Street-Klindworth

During his Weimar years Liszt acquired many musical friends among the many pupils and immediate colleagues of and interested visitors to the 'School of Weimar'. However, there is one pupil in particular who became a very close confidant of Liszt. This is the mysterious Agnes Street-Klindworth. Her cousin Karl Klindworth was already studying with Liszt, so it was natural that Liszt also accepted Agnes when she came in 1853 to Weimar, where she stayed for two years. She presented as a young woman estranged from her husband. Nevertheless, Agnes does not seem to have come to Liszt primarily for piano lessons. She was also a spy, working for her father Georg Klindworth, one of the master spies operating in the maelstrom of European affairs in this period of rising nationalism. His original paymaster was Prince Clement Metternich, the long-serving chancellor of the Austrian Empire, but Klindworth also worked for the Russian Tsar, as well as at times for the French and British governments. His main target for enquiry seems to have been Prussia and the momentum of the German states towards unity, but he also worked on issues relating to the movement towards Italian unity and the future of the Papal States. The Duchy of Weimar was a useful place to position his daughter as a spy to observe interstate German politics, and Liszt was also known to have friends in both the French and Russian legations there.

Agnes' role in Liszt's life remained unknown for many years after his death. The evidence of a romantic relationship between them (and even Agnes' name) was removed from the letters La Mara published in a separate volume with the title *Briefe an eine Freundin*. Furthermore, presumably because they revealed her role as a spy, Agnes refused to hand over many of her letters to La Mara, intending perhaps one day for them to be published by her sons. The publication by Pauline Pocknell of the complete correspondence in English translation, very carefully annotated together with the original French text, was a major event in Liszt biographical studies.[38]

From these letters it is clear the Liszt and Agnes were lovers for three years (1854-57), both while Agnes was living in Weimar but also after she left for other cities in Europe where Liszt arranged assignations with her. Pocknell's analysis shows that there were many striking elements to their relationship one of which was the use of cabalistic cyphers and codes.[39] This evidence shocked Liszt's admirers, showing him to be a man apparently in love with two women at the same time, while confirming for others his reputation as an incorrigible 'womaniser'. However, what is perhaps just as remarkable is that Liszt and Agnes

---

38. Pocknell (ed.), *Franz Liszt and Agnes Street-Klindworth: A Correspondence, 1854-1886*.
39. Ibid., pp. xliii-xlv.

succeeded in transforming their relationship into a genuine friendship. Agnes became someone in whom Liszt could confide both his musical and personal difficulties. The two also shared similar political interests, Liszt like the Klindworths opposing German unification. Carolyne seems never to have known about the true nature of their relationship. Liszt burned Agnes' letters to him and urged her to do the same.[40]

Liszt's letters to Agnes between 1860 and 1861 provide further detailed evidence on Liszt's state of mind in his fiftieth year as he finalised his move from Weimar to Rome. The 29 letters Liszt wrote to Agnes between May 1860, when Carolyne left for Rome, and October 1861, when Liszt left Weimar to join her, are only exceeded by the number he wrote to Carolyne herself (46 in Williams' incomplete selection). Do they provide evidence on Liszt's thinking and mood consistent or divergent from his other correspondence, especially that with Carolyne?

The themes and the relative frequency of Liszt's letters to Agnes over this period of time are distinct from those to Carolyne, other family and friends. There are references in common to the important people in his life, in particular, his concerns for Carolyne in Rome, the health of his mother and also that of his daughter Cosima, whom he clearly wished Agnes to come to know better. However, the most frequent themes in his letters to Agnes are his musical activities, particularly his support of Wagner, and his curiosity about European politics, which Agnes was in an exceptionally good position to satisfy. He also sought opportunities to meet Agnes in person. He suggested in his letter to her of 28 May that she find an opportunity to 'break her journey' in the vicinity of Weimar. When she sent him a photo of herself in June 1860, he referred as before to how deeply she affected him:

> The photograph is ravishing; in its colourless silence it conveys nonetheless a little of that intelligent and many-hued grace, whose appeal is so irresistible in the original! Thank you very much for having sent it to me – it will give me the best service *as a nurse* by prolonging the *illness* indefinitely. (Weimar, 14 June 1860)

As the subsequent letters indicate, they met in Weimar or close by in mid July 1860. A few months later, as he considered a visit to Paris in order to see his mother and to support Wagner, he planned to visit Agnes in Brussels where she was living at the time. His Paris visit, however, had

---

40. Ibid., p. 218.

to be deferred and it was not until June the following year that he finally saw Agnes again and met for the first time her second child. Liszt also succeeded in meeting Agnes a few weeks later in Weimar.

A frequent feature of Liszt's correspondence to Agnes in this period concerns his relationships with Wagner. The majority of the letters refer to him in one way or another, expressing Liszt's enthusiasm for his talent, Wagner's recent creation of *Tristan* and his concerns about the difficulties Wagner would face in obtaining a proper reception of this opera. Liszt also confided in her the difficulties he had in sustaining a constantly good relationship with Wagner. As Agnes had also become a friend to Wagner, Liszt encouraged her in the support she gave him:

> I am well acquainted with Wagner's bitter and despairing moods. Alas! there is hardly a way of curing them – but no one more than you could commiserate tenderly, so at least to charm away, even what it is impossible to *mend*. I thank you on my behalf for the affection you feel for Wagner, and ask you not to let yourself become disheartened by his deplorable rebuffs. He has a heavy mill-stone round his neck! (Weimar, 27 June 1860)

He thanked her again on further occasions early in 1861 for the help she was giving to Wagner and explained that he was also trying to assist him by seeking, unsuccessfully, to persuade Carl Alexander to invite him to conduct *Tristan* in Weimar.

However, there is one long and very interesting letter to Agnes, written in November 1860, in which Liszt reflects on his own musical ambitions. He agrees with Agnes that, although he has just been elected an honorary citizen of Weimar, he has been 'out of his element' there and reflects on the opposition he has met because of the type of music he was promoting. Nevertheless, he intends to continue to promote the 'new music':

> If, when I settled here in 1848, I had decided to attach myself to the *posthumous* party in music, to share in its hypocrisy, to flatter its prejudices, etc., nothing would have been easier for me through my earlier connections with the chief bigwigs of that crew. By so doing I would have certainly won myself more esteem and pleasanter relations in the outside world; the same newspapers which have assumed the responsibility of abusing me with a host of stupidities and insults would have

outdone each other in praising and celebrating me, without my having to go to much trouble about it. They would have gladly *whitewashed* a few of my youthful peccadillos in order to laud and boost in every way the *partisan* of good and sound traditions from Palestrina up to Mendelssohn.

But that was not to be my fate; my conviction was too sincere, my faith in the present and future of the art was both too fervent and too firm for me to be able to be content with the empty abjuratory formulae of our pseudo-classicists, who shriek until they are blue in the face that the art is being ruined, that the art is ruined. The mind's tides are not like those of the sea; they have not been ordered: 'Thus far shalt thou go, and no further'; on the contrary, 'the spirit bloweth where it listeth', and this century's art has its word to contribute, just as much as had that of earlier centuries – and it will do it inevitably.

All the same, I did not delude myself about the fact that my position was most difficult and my task an extremely thankless one, at least for many years to come. Since Wagner had so valiantly broken new ground and created such wonderful masterpieces, my first concern had to be to establish for these masterpieces firm roots in German soil, at a time when he himself was exiled from his homeland, and when all the great and small theatres in Germany were afraid to risk his name on a playbill. On my part, four or five years' *obstinacy*, if you want to call it that, sufficed to achieve this aim, despite the meagreness of the means at my disposal here. As a matter of fact, Vienna, Berlin, Munich, etc., have for five years done nothing more than copy what little Weimar (which they mocked at first) had dictated to them ten years ago. They would like to call a halt now, and to have some sort of impossible coupling, which would be like patching an old garment with new cloth, or putting new wine in old bottles … but it is a matter of different things entirely, to tell the truth, – and I am determined to make good the message that Wagner wrote for me under his portrait: '*Du weisst wie das werden wirt*.'[41] Therefore I shall have no respite as long as I live.

I do not know why I began to talk to you about things which you know at least as well as I do. (Weimar, 16 November 1860)

---

41. 'You know how it will become.'

This is a strong statement of Liszt's past, present and future position in music. Moreover, it makes clear one reason why he valued Agnes so much; he imagined that she already understood these things.

Another striking feature of these letters is Liszt and Agnes' exchange of views on European politics. To none of his other correspondents does he appear to show such persistent and lively interest in international affairs and he is constantly urging Agnes to send him more of her 'political columns'. His interests were wide ranging, from discussion of Hungarian politics, the Italian and, particularly, Papal situation, Napoleon III's policies in this regard, the likelihood of a pardon for Wagner within the German states, the coronation of Wilhelm I as King of Prussia in Königsberg and even the possibility of an *'entente cordiale'* between England and Russia'.[42] His views on Hungarian nationalism and his dislike of violent revolution are consistent with the views exchanged with his friend Baron Augusz. He expresses particular distaste for the words of *La Marseillaise*. At the same time, he is not averse to making jokes, even at Napoleon III's expense. His loyalty to the Pope is evident in the assurances he gives Agnes on the future of the papacy, despite the fact that the Pope's temporal rule by now had been reduced to Lazio, which included the city of Rome, and was guaranteed only by the presence of French troops.

Despite the evident secrecy around his meetings with Agnes and his concern to have their correspondence destroyed, Liszt indicated throughout these 1860-61 letters that his primary loyalty was to Carolyne. Indeed, as the time approached for him to leave Germany in order to marry her, he kept the promise that he had given to Carolyne not to tell anyone of his precise movements. In fact, he denied to Agnes the rumour already circulating in the newspapers that they would marry soon:

> The piece of news you mentioned to me is newspaper news. I shall tell you again that I refuse any longer to believe or disbelieve anything about this matter. When there is something definite I shall inform you. You know that for several months already there had no longer been any *religious* impediment to this news being confirmed by the deed – but for reasons of social convention and future expectations it might have to be postponed indefinitely. That is why I shall only mention it to you when there is good reason to do so. Without being at all inclined to make a mystery of it, since so

---

42. Letter of Liszt to Agnes of 16 September 1861.

to speak my whole life is played with my cards on the table, nevertheless in this case I must be more silent than I like, given the numerous threads entangled in it. (Löwenberg, 16 September 1861)

This was the last letter Liszt wrote to Agnes for two years.

Nevertheless, it is clear from a reading of Liszt's correspondence with Agnes that she was very dear to him, someone in whom he could confide both about his musical work and his personal concerns. In a number of these letters, he referred to her special qualities: 'you understand me and see into me so well'; 'you reply with such gentleness'; 'you are so very very generous'. Although most of Liszt's letters to Agnes in the period May 1860 to September 1861 are light and cheerful in content, there are a further two, rather long, letters which show him to be in evident distress. The first was sent after his return from Vienna in October 1860 when he wrote to Agnes not only detailing the 'unpleasant days' he had spent there in meetings concerning the annulment of Carolyne's marriage, but also the whole long saga of the obstacles that had been put in Carolyne's path and which still had not come to an end. Liszt tells Agnes that she is the only other person with whom he can share his feelings about this one issue which preoccupies him above all others. The second letter, of March 1861, follows two months of not writing to Agnes, and is even more striking as Liszt admits that he is seriously depressed:

> I am mortally sad – and cannot say anything, nor hear anything. Prayer alone consoles me at times, but alas! I am no longer able to pray with much continuity, however imperious my need to do so. May God grant me the boon of passing through this mental crisis and may the light of his mercy shine in my darkness. ... This morning Lassen [a friend and fellow composer in Weimar, and Liszt's successor as court Kapellmeister] came to see me. We spoke only of things which have become fairly foreign to me – yet I was overcome all of a sudden with such a feeling of desolation that I could not hold back a flood of tears. Forgive me for wearying you with such futile things. You have often been gentle and kind to me, and I am indulging myself by talking to you as though you were right here in front of me – which I assure you I hardly do with others. (Weimar, 21 March 1861)

That Liszt experienced difficulties in this period is also evident from his letters to Carolyne, telling her on 3 February that he had been 'overcome by a fit of unspeakable sadness', on 6 March that his 'mind was not on musical matters', on 14 March that 'without you', he 'had no desire to see anyone', on 20 March that he 'couldn't get used to living far from you' and on 31 March that he 'needed peace' in his life. These letters which Liszt wrote in this period to Carolyne and Agnes, laden with negative emotion, probably reflect the cumulative pain of living under constant stress in Weimar for so many years, but perhaps also the uncertainty he was facing.

Liszt in His Fiftieth Year

Liszt's correspondence with Carolyne and Agnes and also with Carl Alexander indicates that he was experiencing a major life crisis in his fiftieth year, even greater than the one which led him to give up his career as an international travelling pianist in his thirties. To most other people he preferred to present a positive picture of himself, and with Wagner it was Liszt himself who had to play the encouraging and supportive role. However, even Wagner heard from Agnes that all was not well with his friend and this surprised him:

> Of you I can never think except as someone who is surrounded by people, even at Weimar. Perhaps I have a good many erroneous notions in that respect; at least Madame Street gave me to understand as much when she described her visit to you. She said that you had been very sad, although in very good health. Well, I certainly cannot see why you should be particularly joyous; at the same time this news has struck me very much.[43]

Liszt's underlying sadness was also picked up by Marie d'Agoult in their meeting in Paris in May 1861, although as his 'discarded muse' she may well have been looking for signs of failure.

From his correspondence in this period Liszt gives the impression of someone who is no longer wholly in control of his life. This is very different from the younger Liszt who even in the midst of difficulties and challenges exuded self-confidence and understanding of the path he should take in life. As Wagner had perceived, Liszt had become dependent on Carolyne for the choice of where he should live and work, a power over his life he would never have granted Marie d'Agoult. It

---

43. Letter from Wagner in Paris to Liszt, 13 September 1860, cited in Pocknell (ed.), *Franz Liszt and Agnes Street-Klindworth*, p. 181.

is also at odds with the determination he had always shown in his musical career. He even asks Carolyne to 'cure him of his bad habits' as if he is himself helpless to change them. His attitude to Agnes, his love for whom he had repeatedly referred to as an 'incurable disease', also reflects passivity. Moreover, there is the startling appeal to his patron Carl Alexander beginning 'Save me, sire' which seems to strike a new tone of neediness in their relationship.

During Liszt's stay in Paris in May 1861, Émile Ollivier wrote an interesting comment on his father-in-law in his diary regarding his incessant coming and going (including travelling to visit Agnes in Brussels). Émile had been expecting Liszt to spend more time with his ailing mother whom he had seen little in recent years:

> During the early days he was with us often; little by little he was surrounded, lured away, and we ceased to enjoy the pleasure of his company. During the last week, he hardly appeared at his mother's and his last dinner, instead of being at her bedside was at Mme Obreskoff's. He has a weak character, spoiled by admiration, but upright, loyal, and charming.[44]

This was an insightful comment from an intelligent observer who was in a good position to judge Liszt's behaviour. Although Émile greatly admired Liszt for his excellent qualities, he also saw some of his faults, in particular, his strong need for approval.

Émile mentions Liszt's loyalty, one of his most admirable qualities. His concern for Carolyne had dominated his fiftieth year and he was willing to please her because of all that she had done for him. He had kept his promise to her not to divulge their wedding plans despite Agnes' curiosity. His loyalty to Wagner was even more exceptional, given Wagner's notorious egotism. This needs to be understood in reference to what Wagner meant to him. Liszt accepted that Wagner was the leading figure in the movement to create new music whereas his own position was secondary. He did not resent this at all, which exemplified another of Liszt's splendid qualities, his generosity of spirit.

His letters to his musical colleagues and friends such as Franz Brendel[45] also show Liszt as highly conscientious in his last year in Weimar.

---

44. Émile Ollivier's diary entry, 12 June 1861, cited in ibid., p. 206.
45. A musicologist, who in 1844 had taken over the editorship of the *Neue Zeitschrift für Musik* in Leipzig from its founder, Robert Schumann, and was an important supporter of the '*Neudeutsche Schule*'.

However, they hide the fact that in reality Liszt was becoming worn out by his musical efforts. They had become too onerous and unrewarding. His depressed mood had even led him to be pessimistic about how long he had to live – although his relatively good physical health suggested he should be prepared to live many more years. A self-deprecatory tone was a common theme in his correspondence with Carolyne, but at times appears exaggerated, for example, 'I succeed in very few things.'[46] The same tone can also be found in his letters to Agnes, signing himself, 'your very useless ...',[47] as a result of disappointing her over a delay in the delivery of a piano. Such remarks indicate that he was looking for a nurturing response from both women.

Yet, Liszt was also capable of responding sensitively to others' complaints of personal inadequacy. For example, Liszt wrote to Carolyne's daughter Marie early on in her marriage to console her as she adapted to her new role as a princess in Viennese society:

> You speak of your *uselessness*. In all truth, there are, I believe, those physicists who claim that we can see quite well enough without the sun, and that after a fashion this lovely star is merely *useless*. Your own state is similar.
> But let's talk about some other *useless* things. ...
> Excuse me for having related all these useless things to you; perhaps they'll distract you for a moment. (Weimar, 14 January 1860)

Was there not a danger that Liszt would come to feel useless himself in Rome? What was he to do there? Would he find the peace that he had been looking for? What about his long-nourished ambitions to change the character of music? There were hints in some of his letters to Carolyne in Rome in 1860 that he might be imagining the beginning of a new musical career in Rome itself, composing sacred music for the Roman Catholic Church:

> On Sunday I went to Leipzig to hear Allegri's *Miserere* and Lotti's magnificent *Crucifixus* at a concert given by the Riedel Society. ... Hearing these works has in a way brought me nearer to you in Rome and put me back, if I may put it thus, on to the 'ascending' slope of my fervent desire to compose

---

46. 26 October 1860.
47. 7 September 1860.

religious music. I must soon write the *Stabat mater dolorosa* and the *Stabat mater speciosa*, the text for which has been supplied to me by Émile. All this music is moaning, singing, and praying within my soul. For the moment I am entirely absorbed by the work[48] mentioned in my last letter. (Weimar, 11 July 1860)

On 24 July Liszt asked Carolyne whether she could obtain a memorandum on the reform of church music presented to the Vatican twenty years before. No doubt Carolyne would have been highly encouraging of any signs on Liszt's part of a desire to concentrate on composing religious music.

---

48. *Les morts.*

4

Returning to His Religious Vocation (1861-65)

A New Life in Rome

Liszt arrived in Rome on 20 October 1861 and the very same day went with Carolyne to an appointment she had already made for them at the Vatican. There they took oaths that they were both free to marry. In the evening of 21 October, they received communion in Carolyne's parish church of San Carlo al Corso, which had already been prepared for their marriage service the following morning. As Walker explains,[1] Carolyne, fearful of spies from Russia and elsewhere, had acted in the preceding weeks with particular care, concealing as far as she could Liszt's movements before his arrival in Rome, and then proceeding rapidly to finalise their marriage once he did arrive.

However, the powers opposed to her marriage had been at work in Rome. Archbishop Gustav von Hohenlohe had received a further delegation of Carolyne's cousins and relatives from her Polish family. They affirmed that they had seen Carolyne enter voluntarily into marriage with Prince Nicholas zu Sayn-Wittgenstein. Hohenlohe had then sought an audience for them with Cardinal Caterini, the prefect of the Holy Congregation of Cardinals, who had been the only member of the review committee to have voted against the annulment of Carolyne's marriage. He wrote to him that the motivation of his visitors was 'to forestall a great scandal'.[2]

---

1. Walker, *The Final Years*, pp. 26-30.
2. Letter in the Vatican Secret Archive consulted by Walker, *The Final Years*, p. 29.

At eleven o'clock, very late in the same evening of 21 October, Carolyne received a message from her parish priest telling her that Pope Pius IX had withdrawn his permission for the wedding to take place and that her case needed to be re-examined.

Carolyne could have continued fighting her case but she did not. Walker concludes that this 'devastating' last-minute intervention convinced Carolyne that the forces against her had become too great. They included not only the two noble families of the Hohenlohes and the Wittgensteins, but her own Polish family as well. Even if she were to marry Liszt, she would be fighting a never-ending battle over the legitimacy of her first marriage. She may have also come to accept that her own daughter's happiness had precedence over her own. Walker suggests that she underwent a definite change of personality as a result of the huge psychological trauma she had suffered. She withdrew into herself, into reading and studying alone in her apartment, and would not socialise as she had done before.[3]

What about Liszt? Up to this point his position had been more passive than active. He had followed the instructions Carolyne had given him. Nonetheless, as examination of his correspondence from earlier in the year has shown, the failure of their marriage plans would not have come as a surprise to him. He had understood, perhaps better than Carolyne herself, the power and influence that the noble families of the Austrian and Russian Empires could wield within the Vatican. At the time these events occurred, the popular press in Rome commented sardonically on this particular case and the power of money in decisions made by the Roman Catholic Church.[4] The Church's processing of requests for annulment of marriages was not perceived to be always fairly decided. Liszt knew that the Hohenlohe family connection had become the crucial element in the opposition within the Vatican to the annulment of Carolyne's marriage. Might Liszt by now have been regretting his support for the marriage of Marie to Prince Konstantin? It seems more likely that he too would have given priority to the happiness of the now Princess Marie zu Hohenlohe-Schillingsfürst. His enthusiastic letters written soon after her marriage indicated his concern for her and she in turn had put her trust in Liszt's 'wisdom', caught as she was between the interests of her husband and her mother.

This is one major incident in Liszt's later life where it is impossible to gauge Liszt's reaction. As Walker indicates, 'there is not a single letter,

---

3. See Walker, *The Final Years*, pp. 31-33.
4. Ibid., p. 29, footnote.

document or diary entry that would allow us to divine his true feelings'.⁵ Why should this be? Perhaps Liszt did not want to leave a record of his thoughts at this time and preferred that these events should pass in silence. Whatever the case may be, he now had to pursue a new path for himself and one that needed to be more independent of Carolyne. The thought of living together in Rome as they had done before in Weimar was inconceivable. They were loyal Catholics living close to the Vatican itself and the Church, although it had not formally pronounced on the validity of Carolyne's first marriage, was not eager to question it further. Carolyne herself seemed no longer willing to challenge its judgement. After her defeat, she had succeeded in achieving a measure of serenity, as she wrote to Liszt's cousin Eduard:

San Carlo al Corso, Rome. Photograph, c. 1920.

> But God is making resignation easier for me by the joy I have had, not only in seeing Liszt again, and seeing him in good and magnificent health, but still more, and above all, by finding in him again in every circumstance, however unforeseen, that same noble-mindedness, tact, and loftiness of view which make me admire, cherish, and esteem him more than ever.⁶

Sensibly, Liszt took time to adjust to his new life in Rome, becoming a tourist for a while. He rented rooms in the centre of Rome, bought a piano and acquired a manservant, Fortunato Salvagni, whose German wife was Carolyne's own housekeeper. His address was not too distant from Carolyne so he would have seen her probably almost every day, but we have no information of what passed between them in this time. Liszt did begin to send shorter notes to Carolyne as the months passed but not, of course, the long letters which he had written when they had been apart. He would comment, for example, on the events of the day which might alter his time of arrival:

> Good day dearest, very dearest, one! ... The excursion to the Vatican with Visconti and the Lovatelli is arranged for noon

---

5. Ibid., p. 33.
6. Cited by Williams (ed.), *Franz Liszt: Selected Letters*, p. 566.

today ... at 3 o'clock, in an archaeological outing, conducted by Mme Malatesta and illustrated by di Rossi, to the Christian Museum in the Lateran. I shall in any case be dropping in on you – not *'entre chien et loup'*[7] but between Vatican and Lateran! However, I strongly urge you not to expect me for lunch. The *Antinous*[8] might detain us for rather a long time – and between the wonders of pagan antiquity and those of Christianity I might not have enough leisure left to take refreshment! (Rome, February 1862)

He appears to have delayed writing to his family and friends, and seems to have first written extensively to Blandine, Carl Alexander and Franz Brendel towards the end of December, assuring them that all was well with him and that he was enjoying life in Rome and envisaging new compositions:

My life in Rome is more peaceful, more harmonious, and better ordered than in Germany. I am hoping, therefore, that it will be to the advantage of my work and that this will turn out well. ... Tenerani's and Overbeck's studio, the Quirinal, Santa Maria degli Angeli, and Santa Maria Maggiore are nearby, and I intend to go to them often, to take possession of them, for beautiful things belong to those who know how to feel and become imbued with them. On Sundays I go regularly to the Sistine Chapel to bathe and reinvigorate my spirit in the sonorous waves of Palestrina's *Jordan*; and every morning I am awakened by a concert from the bell-towers of the surrounding churches ... which charm me far more than all the concerts of the Paris Conservatoire could do. (Letter to Blandine, Rome, 25 December 1861)

To both Carl Alexander and Franz Brendel he expressed the hope that by Easter he would have finished a religious oratorio, *The Legend of St Elisabeth* [of Hungary], one on which he had been working since 1855, after seeing the recently painted frescoes commemorating stories from her life – including 'The Miracle of the Roses' – in Wartburg Castle close to Weimar. A princess from Hungary in the thirteenth century, she had lived her short life in the court of Thuringia and after her husband's early

---

7. At twilight.
8. An antique statue of Hadrian's favourite.

death devoted herself to charitable works in the spirit of St Francis. This work thus brought together Liszt's birth and upbringing in Hungary and the years he had spent in Germany.

He asked Blandine to keep him informed of his mother's progress in regaining some mobility indoors and also about the success of Émile's political speeches, which he had been reading about in the French newspapers. Liszt also wanted any news she might be able to tell him about Wagner's activities in Paris because, as he wrote to her in the same letter, his friend had by now made it plain to Liszt that he disapproved of his leaving for Rome: 'He replied so sourly to my last lines from Berlin that I don't quite know how to set about resuming correspondence with him.'

From Franz Brendel he was eager to know about musical matters in Germany and, in particular, to learn any news of his young musician friends there. The French, English and limited German papers to which he had access in Rome contained 'as good as nothing of what I care about in the domain of music'.[9] To Carl Alexander Liszt continued his previous habit of describing the important people he had recently met which the Grand Duke appreciated. He thanked him especially for putting him in contact with the Duke of Sermoneta, Michelangelo Caetani, whom he described as one of 'the most distinguished personalities that can be met with in the European aristocracy',[10] a scholar of Dante and, as Liszt had already found out, able to recite from memory every canto of the *Divina Commedia*. Liszt also described his visit to the Reverend Agostino Theiner, the distinguished scholar in charge of the Vatican Secret Archive, to whom he had been introduced by Carolyne. He worked and possessed a small printing press in the turret where Galileo had had his observatory in the seventeenth century.

Once Liszt's presence became known in Rome, he again attracted piano pupils, one of whom, Giovanni Sgambati, was to become famous and of great help later in promoting the performance of Liszt's own compositions. However, outside opera and church music, the musical life of Rome remained extremely limited, as Liszt lamented in a New Year letter to his friend Prince Constantine in Löwenberg. There was no concert hall as such so that even the expanding corpus of German and Austrian orchestral music was largely unknown. Music making of the quality Liszt desired could only be found in the homes of aristocrats

---

9. Letter from Liszt to Dr Franz Brendel of 20 December 1861.
10. Letter from Liszt to the Grand Duke Grand Alexander of 25 December 1861.

and the higher clergy and within some of the European embassies. Fortunately, Michelangelo Caetani was particularly welcoming to Liszt at the concerts he held in his own grand palace.

Throughout 1862 Liszt began to develop his musical life, keeping his earlier commitment to write two concert studies for piano, as well as an innovative piece inspired by thoughts of Allegri's *Miserere* and Mozart's *Ave Verum Corpus* while visiting the Sistine chapel. In his letter to Prince Constantine of 26 January but, more particularly, in his letter to the piano manufacturer Xavier Boisselot of 3 January, in which he thanked him for the 'delightful Boisselot upright piano which is the principal adornment of my sitting-room', he commented on the inspiration he received in Rome to compose religious music:

> As regards music in Rome, I am wholly enthralled by that of the Sistine Chapel, everything is grand, majestic, permanent, equally sublime in its general effect and in its radiance. Every Sunday I listen to that singing in the way that one must say one's breviary.
>
> Despite, or rather because of, this, I don't in any way share the opinion of those who claim that everything has been said in church music, that its vein is exhausted. On the contrary, I believe it should be excavated still further, and, at the risk of seeming presumptuous, I shall admit that this task tempts me singularly and that I shall endeavour to accomplish it by writing several works in the style and of the order of inspiration of my Gran Mass and of some Psalms which have been performed in Germany.
>
> For the moment I am wholly absorbed in *Saint Elisabeth*. (Rome, 3 January 1862)

During the year he wrote regularly to Blandine and his mother, and presumably also to Cosima, although no letters to her appear to have survived. He also corresponded many times with Brendel as well as with some other musical friends, but noticeably not with Agnes. In none of his correspondence, as far as we know, did he comment on the cancellation of the marriage ceremony or even on his relationship with Carolyne. He greatly welcomed the news of Blandine's pregnancy in April, agreeing to her request for him to be the child's godfather. In a later letter he described his prayers for her in considerable detail:

> That God will grant you the grace called for by your present condition, and pour out His blessings upon your motherhood,

Returning to His Religious Vocation (1861-65)

is what I ask ceaselessly. May the accomplishments of the duties it involves ever be accompanied for you by all the joys, delights, and satisfactions of a devout and clear conscience! May the doleful spectacle of the sorrows which follow forgetfulness or neglect of God's law serve to keep you well on your guard; believe me, there is no sophism in the world specious enough to atone for our faults. Let us therefore not flatter ourselves through the deceptive illusions of a wisdom of our own invention, as opposed to the true wisdom, the one which existed before us and will remain when we are gone, but strive simply to be good, upright, and sincere with ourselves and with others, without ever seeking happiness which does not go hand in hand with practice of the Good and the cult of the Beautiful, which alone lifts us up to that region where our souls breathe freely. (Rome, 9 June 1862)

Liszt clearly felt very close to Blandine in this period. He had already praised her in April for being 'very skilful and ingenious at charming people' after she persuaded the priest of the Paris Church of Saint-Eugène to have 'my Mass'[11] performed there because of its true 'Catholic feeling'. In his letter of 9 June, he said how much he enjoyed her letters:

Your latest letters, dear Blandine, are quite permeated with the sentiments that I love in you. And so to read your small handwriting, with its characters formed so firmly and prettily, gives me great joy and delight.

Have you already decided on your baby's names, for I assume you will bestow several patrons upon him? Tell me what they are.

He also told her of how 'radiant' Catholic Rome now was because of the presence of so many bishops, archbishops, patriarchs and cardinals who had come 'to attend the canonization of twenty-six Christians, almost unknown during their lifetimes, who were martyred in Japan in the seventeenth century'. For him, it demonstrated the power of the Roman Catholic Church despite the considerable loss of temporal power which it had suffered:

---

11. Presumably the early version of Liszt's *Szekszárd Mass for male voices* (*Missa quatuor vocum ad aequales*).

It is a majestic spectacle for the faith, an imposing affirmation for thought, this ecumenical assembly, more numerous and united in feeling than at the most memorable councils, forming an indestructible bundle to the principle of divine authority personified in the Pope ... and of whatever opinion one may be on this or that question of politics or philosophy, a prevailing fact that has to be recognized, under pain of blindness, is the immense vitality and unrivalled power of Catholicism.

I pray for you and embrace you from the depths of my heart. (Rome, 9 June 1862)

During this festive time in Rome there was a remarkable meeting for Liszt with a former pupil and friend from his early days in Paris whose life had been spiritually transformed. This event also brought back memories of Blandine's birth in 1835 since his friend had been present in Geneva at the time:

Grandmama has written me a wholly charming little letter in her most beautiful handwriting. Among other things she tells me about the Geneva portrait of me which belongs to that city's Conservatoire, and of your fondness for that picture. I can't tell you how moved I was to know this, and what inner happiness it gives me to talk with you, dearest child, in the chapel of my heart into which enter only those special thoughts which are an earnest of immortality! On the other hand, the memories which are connected with your birth in Geneva have been vividly illuminated recently by the presence of someone who had no reason to notice it, and to whom I did not even mention you very much. Guess who? The Revd. Father Hermann in person. (Rome, 8 July 1862)

Hermann Cohen, fondly known as 'Puzzi', had been one of Liszt's youngest and most devoted pupils during his early days of teaching in Paris and his subsequent tours in Europe. In 1841 an accusation of embezzling funds from concerts Liszt gave in Dresden had led to a parting of their ways, and Hermann's musical and personal life became disordered principally as a result of gambling. However, Liszt may well have had a lasting spiritual as well as musical influence on the young man, having introduced him to Abbé Lamennais and given him a Bible as a present. In his later twenties he underwent a religious conversion from Judaism to Christianity and eventually joined the strictly penitential Carmelite order. Although Liszt and Hermann subsequently renewed their friendship by correspondence, they had not succeeded in meeting until now.

Liszt and Hermann met regularly during the three weeks the latter was in Rome, walking and visiting various sites together. Liszt also went to hear Hermann preach at San Luigi, the French church in Rome, and told Blandine that he spoke eloquently, making a moving impression on his hearers. Liszt considered his friend to have 'grown in mind as well as heart' as a result of his conversion from Judaism to Roman Catholicism. Hermann told Liszt that Cardinal Wiseman, the first Archbishop of Westminster, whom he had met in Rome, had invited him to re-establish the Carmelite order in London and that Pope Pius had agreed his immediate transfer. As he would be travelling via Paris, Liszt asked Hermann to call in on his mother.

Altogether the summer of 1862 seems to have been a very happy time for Liszt. He had made new friends in Rome, as well as renewing friendships with old ones, and was happy there. 'Oh Rome! My country; city of the soul; the Niobe of Nations' were the words of Byron, which Liszt had written in a notebook earlier in the year,[12] one of the few occasions in his life when he actually kept a diary. He had completed his oratorio, *The Legend of St Elisabeth*. During the summer he wrote enthusiastically to Brendel not only about this work but also about Wagner's new work *Die Meistersinger von Nürnberg* that Cosima had described to him in detail. He received the excellent news that Blandine had given birth to a boy, that he was to be named Daniel after her brother and that mother and child were both doing very well. His sweet notes to Carolyne in this period also suggest great contentment: 'Good night, my good angel – you who are my peace, my tranquillity, and my light' on an evening when Rome was subject to a fierce thunderstorm; 'However pleasant this day may have been, it is no less a day lost for me – since I haven't seen you! – this was after Liszt had been on a full day's trip to the excavations at Ostia, the ancient port of Rome.[13]

Liszt's sense of gratitude for the blessings he had received in life is also reflected in an eloquent letter to his mother in which he remembered how much he owed to his parents. It shows how clearly he perceived that he had been remarkably fortunate to have had a father with such a clear

---

12. Walker, *The Final Years*, p. 46.
13. Undated notes from Liszt to Carolyne, probably of June/July 1862 cited by Williams, *Franz Liszt: Selected Letters*, p. 581.

intuition of his son's musical talent and the sense of self-sacrifice that had been necessary to develop that talent:

> Dearest Mother, If my letters give you even a hundredth part of the joy that yours cause me, that is enough to make me well content, for it would already be a good deal. Your handwriting, it seems to me, is becoming from year to year ever more beautiful; so much so, that I should like to take lessons in calligraphy from you. Something else which increases for me from year to year is the sweetness of the evidence of your love and devotion. I was moved to tears by your pious remembrance of my father, and thank you with all my heart for having on 28 August thought simultaneously of him and of me. My father's presentiment, that his son was to leave the track beaten by others of his social class and face the hazards of an uncommon destiny, quickly became a real conviction, I could almost say an *article of faith*, with him; that presentiment, I say, conceived in the circumstances of Raiding, the village, far removed from all civilization, whose social amenities were limited to games of tarot with a few country priests and colleagues in the service of Prince Esterházy, all of them inferior to him in intelligence and understanding nothing more of music than, perhaps, the strumming of his little prodigy of a son, aged eight or nine! How not to be struck by it? He did not hesitate for a moment, nor did he yield to all the rational arguments of rational people. He had to sacrifice his secure position, give up comfortable habits, leave his own country, ask his wife to share a doubtful future, meet the costs of our modest existence by giving Latin, geography, history, and music lessons; had, in a word, to quit the service of Prince Esterházy, leave Raiding and settle in Vienna, so that I could take lessons from our good, excellent Czerny and thereafter face the risks of a very problematical career. And all this with savings of no more than a few hundred francs! Certainly, dearest Mother, you are entirely right when you say that not one father in thousands would have been capable of such devotion, or of such persistence in that kind of *intuitive stubbornness* possessed only by persons of exceptional character. But since, as both a dutiful wife and a most devoted mother, you shared daily and

hourly everything that my father did and sacrificed for me, allow me to bring to you, with the most faithful respect and all the emotion of my gratitude, what is due to you. (Rome, 12 September 1862)

The Death of Blandine

Sadly, at the very time Liszt seems to have written this letter to his mother, a death had already occurred that would cut short this intense period of happiness for Liszt. His daughter Blandine died in Tropez on 11 September as a result of septicaemia following inflammation of her left breast and the probably unwise treatment she received from her doctor. It was just over two months since the birth of her son.[14] Liszt responded bravely and unselfishly, inviting her grief-stricken husband Émile Ollivier to stay with him in Rome, which greatly strengthened the bonds between them. During his time in Rome Émile also spoke for long periods with Carolyne alone in her own apartment. He wrote to her afterwards to thank her for her 'maternal welcome' and the support that she had given him in allowing him to voice his sorrow.

Liszt wrote to his mother two weeks after his previous letter to her. He had wanted to be the first to console her but she had already written to him. It was in fact her resignation and her faith which offered consolation to both Liszt and Émile:

> My first, my constant thought in this cruel calamity which has struck us, is you, dearest Mother: you, who played so great a part in this dear, gentle life which, alas, is no more – through the care, love, and devotion which you lavished daily, hourly, on her childhood; you whom she loved so devotedly and whom she felt happy, in her turn, to care for, soothe, cheer, and charm! What melancholy, what a void her disappearance has just caused us in this sad world! I weep and grieve more than I can say. But you, dearest Mother, truly show admirable resignation in such sorrow; and the letter you wrote to Ollivier, and which he has just shown me, gives me the sole consolation to which I am open at this moment: that of knowing that you are bearing your grief like a Christian. (Weimar, 27 September 1862)

---

14. A full account of this tragedy is given in Walker, *The Final Year*, pp. 47-53.

After he returned to Paris, Émile continued to have Anna Liszt cared for within his apartment in Paris, something for which Liszt would always remain grateful.

As he had done with the death of his son Daniel three years earlier, Liszt responded to the loss of his older daughter with composition of music, his piano *Variations on a Basso Continuo* from the first movement of Bach's cantata, *Weinen, Klagen, Sorgen, Zagen*. This is one of the most impressive pieces Liszt ever wrote for piano, a highly skilful treatment of a relatively simple theme, deeply moving in the ways its advanced chromatic harmony suggests the pain of grief, but advancing slowly towards its goal of acceptance. It is at the same time a very personal utterance and it is significant that, in his correspondence over the following months, Liszt, although he referred to other compositions he had completed, did not mention this work. Even today it is not as well-known as it should be.

However, the loss of his second child must have affected Liszt profoundly, and it needs to be borne in mind that he was still recovering from a long period of considerable anxiety and stress relating to uncertainty as to his musical future and to his marriage to Carolyne, as well as the death of his son only three years earlier. A depressive reaction was to be expected. As Walker relates,[15] people noted physical changes: his hair began to turn grey and the warts which marked his face in later life made their first appearance. Observations from others, including his new piano pupil Walter Bache, who saw Liszt on his birthday, confirm the sad appearance he presented to the world.[16] His letters also reveal the level of strain which he was bearing. In later October/early November he wrote a short note to Carolyne:

> I spent a bad night, and this morning I feel totally shattered – it's my nervous condition which takes hold of me for a day or two. I shall probably not resume my seat at your table today – unless I feel a little more presentable by about noon. At present I am doing nothing but yawn and stretch my arms! ... There is no illness at all in my condition – merely a great deal of *Abspannung*.[17]

---

15. Ibid., p. 54.
16. Ibid.
17. 'Weariness'. Undated note from Liszt to Carolyne cited by Williams, *Franz Liszt: Selected Letters*, p. 588-9.

In writing to thank Carl Alexander for his letter of condolence, he apologised for not having acknowledged the death of the Grand Duke's uncle: 'forgive me for having failed to do so at a time when so much grief was weighing upon me. There are certain states of the soul in which one hardly knows how one lives; someone else would seem to take this trouble for us!' (Rome, 1 November 1862)

Nevertheless, Liszt kept on working and was fortunate to be able to rely on musical composition as his mainstay in coping with his loss. In the same letter to Carl Alexander, he told him that he had completed *The Legend of St Elisabeth* and that he had also been inspired to compose *Évocation à la Chapelle Sixtine*, combining Allegri's *Miserere* and Mozart's *Ave verum corpus*, uniting the former's cry of mankind's distress with God's mercy, 'who shows us Love triumphant over Evil and Death':

> It is known that when he [Mozart] visited Rome he wrote down Allegri's *Miserere* during its performance in the Sistine Chapel, both to retain it better in his memory and, perhaps, to breach the prohibitive system, which, in the good old days, extended even to music manuscripts. How not to remember this fact, in that same enclosed space where it occurred? So I have often sought the place where Mozart must have been. I even imagined that I saw him, and that he looked on me with gentle condescension. Allegri was close by, and seemed almost to be committing an act of penitence for the celebrity that pilgrims, generally little given to musical impressions, have taken care to bestow exclusively upon his *Miserere*.
>
> Then, slowly, there appeared in the background, besides Michelangelo's *Last Judgement*, another shade, of unutterable greatness. I recognized him instantly and with joy, for while still an exile here upon earth He had consecrated my brow with a kiss. He too sang his *Miserere*, and until that time no sobs and lamentations of so profound and sublime an intensity had ever been heard. Strange encounter!

This third figure, of course, was Beethoven, who was said to have kissed the young Liszt on hearing the boy play in Vienna. Liszt went on to link his primary model as a composer with Allegri's *Miserere* in that Beethoven had also 'alighted on the same mode and on the same interval – a stubborn dominant' in various of his compositions which he enumerated for the Grand Duke. An egocentric and fanciful vision perhaps, but also a powerful illustration of to what extent music gave sustenance to Liszt's life and that it was interlinked with spiritual intuitions that he was not shy of sharing with those he trusted.

The origins of *Évocation à la Chapelle Sixtine* might have been thought enough for one letter but Liszt went on to describe to the Grand Duke his intention to compose a setting of the *Cantico di San Francesco*. He had already decided to conclude it with the verse St Francis had added when grieved by hearing of a major dispute between the bishop and the magistrates of Assisi. When they heard it sung, the conflicting partners embraced and asked for one another's forgiveness:

> *Laudato si', mi' Signore,*
> *Per quelli che perdonano per lo Tuo amore,*
> *E sostengo infirmitate e tribulazione!*
> *Beati quelli che sosteranno in pace,*
> *Che da Te, Altissimo, sirano incoronati!*[18]

It is at this point in his life that Liszt seems to have returned to the religious vocation of his early youth. In a letter to his mother in which he described in detail his work on *The Legend of St Elisabeth*, he raised the question as to why contemporary society had lost interest in the lives of the saints, and wrote of his own return to the spiritual yearnings of his youth:

> We are not saints, and at all times the saints have been exceptional beings, the elect. But why could we not – without raising ourselves to their heights, indeed simply contenting ourselves with the *practice of good* – at least seek in thought to become absorbed in the depths of their souls? If we so often tolerate what stands *below* the level of good, indeed if our tolerance is often subtly transformed into sympathy even, why do people so very much resist what rises *above* the good.
>
> You know, dearest Mother, how for several years on end during my youth I ceaselessly dreamt myself, so to speak, into the realm of the saints. Nothing seemed to me so self-evident as Heaven, nothing so true or so great a source of happiness as the goodness and mercy of God. Despite all the errors and

---

18. 'Praised be You, my Lord, / through those who give pardon for Your love, / and bear infirmity and tribulation. / Blessed are those who endure in peace / for by You, Most High, shall they be crowned.'

aberrations of my life, nothing and no one have been able to shake the belief in immortality and the salvation of the soul which came to me during my prayers in the churches of Raiding and Frauendorf, at the Mariahilf church in Vienna, and at Notre Dame de Lorette and St Vincent de Paul in Paris. All the storms notwithstanding, the good seed in me has germinated and is more deeply filled than ever before with all the truths of religion. When I now read the *Lives of the Saints* I feel as though after a long journey I am meeting old and venerable friends from whom I shall part no more. (Rome, 2 December 1862)

Liszt sent letters to a number of other friends and family towards the end of 1862, reiterating his wish to focus on composing religious music. He had been receiving various offers to engage in musical ventures. In a letter renewing his ties with his oldest Hungarian friend, Baron Augusz, he told him of the invitation from the Committee of the Pest-Buda Conservatoire to take up a position there. He had refused because of his fundamental need at that time to write music but said he would like to compose something more for Hungary, as he had done before with the *Missa Solemnis* for the inauguration of the basilica at Gran.[19] He also reminded Augusz of the help he had given him in providing material for his *St Elisabeth*. While continuing to offer advice to Brendel in regard to the next gathering of German musicians, he declined his invitation to become practically involved himself and stressed that having "as far as I could, solved the greater part of the *Symphonic* problem set me in Germany, I mean now to undertake the *Oratorio* problem".[20] He had a similar message for his friend Alexander Gottschalg, the court organist in Weimar.

Perhaps even more revealing of Liszt's inner thoughts in the autumn of 1862 than his letters to Carl Alexander and to his mother is the one he sent to his cousin Eduard Liszt in Vienna. In this letter he begins by explaining his previous silence and his efforts to come to spiritual peace over the course of the previous year:

Dearest Eduard, The feeling of our double relationship is to me always an elevating and comforting one. Truly you abide with me, as I do with you – *cum sanguine, corde et mente.*

---

19. Present day Esztergom.
20. Letter from Liszt to Dr. Franz Brendel on 8 November 1862.

> Accept my thanks for your kind lines, and excuse my not having written to you long ago. I might indeed have told you many a thing of more or less interest; but all seemed to me tiresome and insufficient in writing to you. I needed more than ever, and above all things, ample time to compose myself, to gather my thoughts, and to bestir myself. During the first years of my stay here I secured this. It is to be hoped that you would not be dissatisfied with the state of mind which my 50th year brought me; at all events I feel it to be in perfect harmony with the better, higher aspirations of my childhood, where heaven lies so near the soul of every one of us and illuminates it! I may also say that, owing to my possessing a more definite and clearer consciousness, a state of greater peacefulness has come over me. (Rome, St Elizabeth Day, 19 November 1862)

Liszt also explains how he thinks he has come to terms with the recent deaths of his children. He connects them with how he conceives the 'artistic task' that he has been set:

> Blandine has her place in my heart beside Daniel. Both abide with me bringing atonement and purification, mediators with the cry of '*Sursum corda*'[21] – When the day comes for Death to approach, he shall not find me unprepared or faint-hearted. Our faith hopes for and awaits the deliverance to which it leads us. Yet as long as we are upon earth we must attend to our daily task. And mine shall not lie unproductive. However trifling it may seem to others, to me it is indispensable. My soul's tears must, as it were, have lacrymatoria made for them; I must set fires alight for those of my dear ones that are alive, and keep my dear dead in spiritual and corporeal urns. This is the aim and object of the Art task to me.

He continues by describing to his cousin what he had achieved so far in Rome. He has completed *The Legend of St Elisabeth*, *Il Cantico del Sole*, the *Évocation à La Chapelle Sixtine* and settings of two Psalms. Now he is about to set himself 'the great task of an Oratorio on Christ' which he intends to complete within the next year. Despite discouragement from

---

21. 'Let us lift up our hearts.'

well-meaning people, he cannot do other than compose music, although he will not impose them on anyone simply offer them to any who may appreciate them. He describes the recent invitation he has received from the Conservatoire in Pest to take up a musical position in Hungary, that he will refuse it but may well in the future produce a religious composition, a '*Te Deum* or something of the kind', for their native land. Liszt thus made clear to Eduard also that musical composition and religious expression would be intertwined in his future activities.

In the course of his first year in Rome Liszt had already come a long way in marking out what was to be his new musical project but he was perhaps over confident in the demands that he was making of himself. The lack of letters in the early winter months of 1863 may suggest a depressed mood, as does his short note to Carolyne on 27 January in which he apologises for his behaviour the previous day. He explained that he had been in 'rather a distracted mood' for several days as a result of being 'unable to continue the work' he had begun. By the spring he was writing again, to his mother, showing concern for her physical and mental health and exchanging thoughts on the deaths of both Daniel and Blandine, and to his cousin Eduard, asking him to bind together some of his piano pieces for a friend who was now living in Vienna. However, it was in letters to his previous music colleagues in Germany, Brendel and Gottschalg, that Liszt provided an explanation for the feelings of malaise to which he had succumbed. He told Gottschalg in April that his *Christus* oratorio was progressing only slowly, owing to the many 'interruptions' he had had to endure during the winter, and 'thirsted' for time free of them.[22] He expanded on the 'interruptions' in his letter to Brendel:

> The last months brought so many interruptions in my work that I still feel quite vexed about it. Easter week I had determined should, at last, see me regularly at work again; but a variety of duties and engagements have prevented my accomplishing this. I must, therefore, to be true to myself and carry out my former intention, shut myself up entirely. To find myself in a net of social civilities is vexatious to me; my mental activity requires absolutely to be free, without which I cannot accomplish anything. (Rome, 8 May 1863)

---

22. Letter from Liszt to A.W.Gottschalg 14 April 1863.

Moving to a Monastery

By the summer Liszt had found a solution to his over-engagement in Roman social life. On 20 June he moved outside Rome to the Madonna del Rosario, an old monastery on Monte Mario, an hour's journey from Rome but with a magnificent view on the 'Eternal City'. He wrote to Brendel again on his good fortune: 'The view is indescribably grand. I mean now, at last, to try and lead a natural kind of life. I hope I may succeed in approaching more closely to my monastic-artistic ideal. – Meanwhile you may laugh at me about it.' (Rome, 18 June 1863)

It was his friend in the Vatican 'turret', the Reverend Agostino Theiner who had allowed him, together with his manservant, to occupy a large set of rooms in the almost uninhabited house attached to the monastery. One wonders how Carolyne herself would have interpreted his move to Monte Mario. However, the lack of letters between them in the following period would suggest that he continued to visit her on a regular basis. We also know from the letters of his new English pupil Walter Bache that Liszt regularly walked down to Rome to give piano lessons, as well as performances on the grand piano in the home of Monsignor Nardi. He reserved Monte Mario for his life of composition

Oratorio della Madonna del Rosario. Photograph c. 1970. Liszt occupied a number of rooms on the first floor (a white plaque can be seen beneath one of his windows).

and spiritual retreat, joining the monks in their services and sometimes accompanying them on the harmonium.

No doubt Carolyne would have been impressed to hear Liszt's news of the visit made to him three weeks later by Pope Pius in the company of Monsignor Hohenlohe, now the Pope's almoner, the very man in Rome who more than any other had worked to prevent his marriage to Carolyne. For Liszt, this was a huge honour, as he told both his mother and Brendel:

> This letter is so filled up with Royal Highnesses, Majesties, and illustrious personages, that it offers me a natural transition to tell you of an extraordinary, nay, incomparable honour I received last Saturday evening, the 11th of July. His Holiness Pope Pius IX visited the Church of the Madonna del Rosario, and hallowed my apartments with his presence. After having given His Holiness a small proof of my skill on the harmonium and on my work-a-day pianino, he addressed a few very significant words to me in the most gracious manner possible, admonishing me to strive after heavenly things in things earthly, and by means of my harmonies that reverberated and then passed away to prepare myself for those harmonies that would reverberate everlastingly. (Letter to Franz Brendel, Rome, 18 July 1863)

Pope Pius also received Liszt in a personal audience in the Vatican a week later and presented him with a cameo of the Madonna. As Walker notes,[23] there is also evidence that the Pope visited him a second time later in the year, on which occasion Liszt played for much longer, perhaps including some of his newly composed 'Legends', *St Francis of Assisi: Preaching to the Birds* and *St Francis of Paola: Walking on the Waves*.

What did this papal contact imply? Could it be that the Vatican authorities were actively seeking to draw Liszt to themselves perhaps as a court musician? Or was it more simply that the Pope was offering support to Liszt in his decision to live and work in Rome or even perhaps to show kindness to someone whose planned marriage in Rome the Church had been obliged to refuse. It is probably impossible to know but as Walker argues,[24] it seems unlikely that the Pope was considering giving Liszt a major musical responsibility in the Vatican. There was already a well-

---

23. Walker, *The Final Years*, p. 56, footnote 10.
24. Ibid., p. 56.

established director of the Sistine Choir, and, in any case, Liszt's style of music would have been thought too 'progressive' for the conservative leanings of most of the leading clergy in Rome. Probably the most likely explanation is that the Pope had learned of Liszt's strong religiosity from other clergy, including Hohenlohe, and was simply performing his pastoral duty in supporting Liszt's faith and his potential vocation to ordination as a cleric of the Church.

Liszt gave probably the most accurate short account of how he saw himself at this time in his first letter to Carl Gille since leaving Weimar. Gille had been his legal adviser and, by the time he left, had become a close friend:

> My stay in Rome is not an accidental one; it denotes, as it were, the third part (probably the close) of my life, which is often troubled, but ever industrious and striving upwards. Hence I require ample time to bring various long works and myself to a good ending. This requisite I find in my retirement here, which will probably become even more emphatic; and my present monastic abode provides me not only with the most glorious view over all Rome, the Campagna and the mountains, but also what I had longed for; quiet from without and peacefulness. (Monte Mario, Madonna del Rosario, 10 September 1863)

Since his move to Rome, Liszt and Agnes Street-Klindworth had not written to one another but their correspondence was renewed in the summer of 1863 when Agnes wrote to him. She had probably learned that Liszt's marriage to Carolyne had not taken place as expected. Liszt's reply indicates that she had learned Liszt's whereabouts from a newspaper article. In her letter she must have included a musical reference to their previous time together. Liszt acknowledged this and explained his recent spiritual developments but at the same time stressed that for him this did not exclude honouring his previous emotional attachments:

> Your *Music* is heard; it often echoes in my soul.
> No need to tell you that there has hardly been any great change in me, even less a lapse of memory. Only I am leading a simpler sort of life – and the Catholic piety of my childhood has become a regular and regulating feeling.
> For certain people piety consists of burning what they once adored. I am far from finding fault with them – but for my part I feel inclined and will try indeed to sanctify what I loved, I

will say that in this I am following the system used constantly in Rome with regard to the Christian monuments. Do not the magnificent pillars of Sainte Marie des Anges come from Diocletian's thermal baths, and has not the bronze from the Pantheon found a use as the baldachin of Saint Peter's altar? One could go on for ever listing similar transformations, for at every turn here, one is struck by the harmony in the divine plan between what was, what is, and what will be. (Monte Mario, Madonna del Rosario, 30 August 1863)

Liszt asked after her children and her father Georg Klindworth and encouraged Agnes as in the past to send him regularly news of European politics. Liszt's insistence on political news indicates that he was still very interested in European politics. Agnes responded generously and he in turn gave her news of Rome and of his musical work, including his ongoing major revision of his arrangements of Beethoven's symphonies for piano. It is of particular interest that Agnes is the first person to whom he appears to have written openly, if briefly and obliquely, about why he was in Rome and his present relationship with Carolyne: 'Since my *raison d'être* in Rome consists of one person, and since she mixes very little in society, my activities are centred on a few fixed points of affection, study and work.' (Monte Mario, Madonna del Rosario, 19 September 1863)

Liszt debated politics with Agnes in the three further surviving letters that he wrote to Agnes in the latter months of 1863. He referred to his contact with the Bonaparte family in Rome and defended strongly the current policies of Emperor Napoleon III. He was for Liszt 'the great man of a great age', whereas Agnes for her part was much less enthusiastic about the French ruler's abilities. Liszt also gave news of the Reverend Agostino Theiner who, by a happy coincidence, remembered Agnes as a child from the time he had visited her father in London.[25] He was sending her a rosary via Liszt and, since he would be coming to spend six weeks during the winter on Monte Mario where the pair of them would no doubt eat together, her 'political columns' would provide them with 'most delicious intellectual dessert'. Liszt reassured Agnes again that his feelings for her had not changed and that they would meet again soon:

> The apparition has not faded; I still see you and hear you in exactly the same way. In that regard my heart does not age;

---

25. Presumably on Vatican business.

despite the shadows which have gathered over it since then, the double *cypher* still retains all its luminous magic. I appeal against your '*presupposition*' so as not to contradict myself ... and we shall go into this topic more deeply when we see each other again – next year. (Rome, 6 December 1863)

In autumn 1863 Liszt was visited by another woman admirer, Charlotte von Oven, a famous German actress who had first met him in Berlin during his concert-playing days. She was one of the women whose encounters with Liszt had aroused Marie d'Agoult's jealousy. As Williams notes,[26] Charlotte's strong feelings for Liszt 'seem never to have waned'. In 1849 she wrote him a splendid compliment: 'Years have passed since I found and lost you, but I must admit that because of you I have been spoilt for all other men; for none, *not a single one*, can bear the least comparison. You are and remain *unique*.'[27] Now fourteen years later she wrote to Liszt after her visit to tell of the 'eternally unforgettable hours' spent with him. She also included a poem she had written inspired by a solitary pine which she had admired on Monte Mario.

Liszt responded in kind: 'When the winter frosts were threatening the *symbolic Pine*, you protected and adorned it, enveloping it in flowers of poetry and perfumes of memory. And so its sap will not grow cold, and its evergreen foliage will again be able to smile, dream, and gently murmur.'

He continued, providing a strong Christian association to the image of the solitary pine which they had shared together: a vision of the Cross which the Emperor Constantine was said to have received on Monte Mario before his victory in the battle of the Milvian Bridge in 312:

> The pine which overlooks the hills of Rome, like a hermit sunk in some mysterious meditation which holds him back on the very threshold of the Holy City, doesn't allow its thoughts to wander into vagueness. It stretches its branches towards the heights where the sign of the redemption of the world appeared in radiant triumph to Constantine; it is to that tree, noble beyond all others, whose leaves, fruits and buds bring forth every grace and every blessing, that it bears testimony; and it is the hymn of the *Crux fidelis* that it urges me to sing. As you know, the chapel commemorating the appearance of

---

26. Williams (ed.), *Franz Liszt: Selected Letters*, p. 967.
27. Quoted from a letter in the Weimar archives.

> the Cross to Constantine on Monte Mario stands very close to the symbolic pine and to my dwelling-place at the Madonna del Rosario. (Rome, 16 February 1864)

Religious sentiment and imagery had become dominant in Liszt's mind as his life gravitated more and more around the liturgies of the Church.

In March 1864 the Pope asked Liszt to play at a charity concert in Rome during Passion Week in a new building rising on the site of the old Praetorian Camp near the Baths of Diocletian. The concert began with the Sistine Choir singing a motet of Palestrina. Four sermons were then delivered, interspersed with four piano pieces of a religious character from Liszt, to which the audience responded enthusiastically. Liszt was awarded the 'Order of Pius IX, Third Class'. Most of Liszt's contacts in Rome were by now with clerics, including the chief astronomer, the Jesuit Father Angelo Secchi. He also began to spend a lot of time with Gustav Hohenlohe who took him in July to stay at the sixteenth-century Villa d'Este, north-east of Rome, with its famous fountains. Hohenlohe lived there as a tenant of the Duke of Modena with the right to keep possession of the villa for the rest of his life. He in turn gave Liszt an open invitation to stay at the villa whenever he wanted.[28] On this first occasion, Liszt wrote to Carolyne telling her of his need to compose music rather than perform it, but one still wonders what she would have thought of his staying in the house of the person who only four years earlier had organised the resistance to their marriage. Liszt also told Agnes that he and Hohenlohe had spoken about her father whom he also knew from Vatican political dealings.

Later in July he was invited to join the Pope, who now called Liszt 'his dear Palestrina', at his summer palace of Castel Gandolfo overlooking Lake Albano to the south of Rome. His concerts there were warmly applauded and, according to *Le Monde*, the Pope complimented him publicly saying that: 'Liszt recommended himself as much by his Christian belief as by the marvels of his musical genius.'[29] Liszt wrote another letter to Carolyne at the beginning of his stay in Castel Gandolfo, detailing his timetable there, which made further evident his growing friendship with Hohenlohe:

> I hope my stay at Castel Gandolfo will give you some satisfaction. The Holy Father is most graciously kind to me. ...

---

28. Williams (ed.), *Franz Liszt: Selected Letters*, p. 607, footnote 6.
29. Walker, *The Final Years*, p. 69, footnote 29.

I played him various pieces on an upright piano that Mgr. Hohenlohe had managed to find. ... For tomorrow, Monday, M. de Meyendorff [First Secretary at the Russian Embassy in Rome] has invited Mgr. Hohenlohe and me to dinner. ... Mgr. Hohenlohe is so affable and kind when insisting on keeping me longer, that I dare not refuse. ... [T]hanks to the most obliging good offices of Hohenlohe, my accommodation ... just ten paces away from His Holiness's Palazzo, is quite perfect. (Castel Gandolfo, 31 July 1864)

First Journey Back to Germany and France

In August 1864 Liszt made his first journey outside Italy, as he had intimated in his letter to Agnes the previous year, to attend the third German music festival in Karlsruhe. He had told Brendel in January that he was thinking of coming, but only on condition that his son-in-law Hans von Bülow was conducting, and he asked him not to mislead his friends into imagining that this temporary visit might lead to his returning to Germany: 'I am', he wrote, 'peacefully industrious in my seclusion here. Let me rest, let me dream.'[30] In his letters to Agnes in June, July and August he gave a detailed account of his travel plans. He would attend the music event at the 'insistence' of his friends who were endeavouring 'to consolidate and increase the little bit of *musical Good* I tried to do in Germany during the twelve years of my music-directorship in Weimar'. After the festival he would journey to Weimar and finally to Paris to see his mother. He also intended to visit Blandine's grave in Saint-Tropez. He hoped that Agnes would let him know while he was in Karlsruhe where they could meet. In the event, Agnes came to see Liszt in Karlsruhe.

Agnes' political news for Liszt concerned the rival ambitions of Prussia and Austria for German unity, as well as the Schleswig-Holstein crisis. Liszt praised Agnes' expertise: 'you handle the keyboard of political events with such virtuosity'. Liszt's main news for Agnes came directly from Cosima, who had recently written to her father about what she referred to as the 'miracle letter' that Wagner had received from King Ludwig of Bavaria. The King had invited the composer to live, compose and have his works performed at his expense as the King's guest in Munich. Liszt was very happy about this massive turnaround in Wagner's fortunes and enclosed for Agnes not only a copy of the

---

30. Letter from Liszt to Dr Franz Brendel on 22 January 1864.

King's letter to Wagner but also a timetable of Wagner's proposed performances of his works right up to 1872, in which Cosima's husband Hans would also be closely involved.

Throughout his journeys Liszt wrote long letters to Carolyne describing his various experiences on his travels but always offering reassurance of his continued devotion to her. He first wrote to her on arriving in Marseilles:

> When I leave you, my soul no longer follows my body. It remains entirely with you, for eternity! I did the little journey from Rome to Civitavecchia, and from there until here, always turned, or, to use the biblical word, 'converted' to you – praying for the day when, instead of looking behind, my eyes will seek you *in front*, on this same road. (Marseille, 12 August 1864)

At High Mass in Strasbourg on 15 August, the Assumption of the Virgin Mary, and thus her daughter Marie's name day, as well as the Emperor Napoleon's birthday, Liszt told Carolyne that he prayed for Marie, remembering 'all the beautiful drawings we used to take to her in the mornings of 15 August', and 'sang with all the power of my lungs: "Domine salvum fac Imperatorem nostrum Napoleonem"'.

Liszt was pleased with the performance of his works at the Karlsruhe festival but shocked to learn of the nervous condition of his son-in-law Hans von Bülow which prevented him from conducting. Cosima reassured her father that King Ludwig of Bavaria had offered Hans a fixed and generous salary as court musician. After the festival Liszt and Cosima travelled to Lake Starnberg in Bavaria to a villa which King Ludwig had made available to Wagner and his new musical company. He told Carolyne that he was dismayed to see Hans in 'so wretched a condition, both physically and morally, that these two days I have barely left him, and limited myself to sending you a telegram'. However, he was positive about Wagner, delighted with his success and optimistic again about their friendship:

> But let's come back to Wagner, whom I have entitled the Glorious One, *der Glorreiche*. At bottom, nothing can have changed between us. The great good fortune that has at last come his way will sweeten as much as possible certain asperities in his character. For the moment, I have to say that he is very much at his best, in all respects. Naturally we chatted at great length, for 5 hours on end. ... Wagner acquainted

me with his *Meistersinger*, and in return I showed him my *Beatitudes*, with which he seemed more than content! His *Meistersinger* is a masterpiece of *humour*, spirit, and lively grace. It is animated and beautiful, like Shakespeare! (Lake Starnberg, 31 August 1864)

What Liszt did not tell Carolyne, but Walker has deduced[31] from Wagner's 'Brown Book' diary,[32] is that Liszt must have reprimanded him for the attention he was paying to Cosima. No doubt Liszt had understood the underlying reason for Hans' distress, although he probably did not realise quite how far Wagner's relationship with Cosima had developed.

Very early on 5 September Liszt arrived back in Weimar after an absence of three years. He wrote to Carolyne later the same morning, telling her that he had placed his manservant Fortunato Salvagni (who had accompanied him on his journeys) in lodgings while he walked in the dark streets to the Altenburg: 'How many ghosts did I not meet! Schubert's *Doppelgänger* would be the nearest cousin to this spectral family!'" He wrote a week later to give news of people and events, but the memories he recalled were not happy ones:

> The sound of your weeping and of your prayers inside these rooms resounds within my soul! ... I was thinking to myself yesterday that there are towns which fulfil their functions in a manner that is the direct opposite of what orthopaedic institutions aim at. What is straight, they make crooked! (Weimar, 12 September 1864)

Liszt was somewhat at a loose end as the principal person he wished to see in Weimar, the Grand Duke Carl Alexander, was on business visit to Ostend. Therefore, he was pleased when Cosima arrived to visit her father again and they decided to go back to Berlin together. On the way they stayed with Liszt's friend Prince Constantine in Löwenberg from where he wrote to Carolyne that he was happier than in Weimar 'for I am convinced that people here sincerely wish me well' and that 'Cosette' would send her a more detailed report on their daily activities. He had

---

31. Ibid., p. 75, footnote 47.
32. Bergfeld, J. (ed.), translated by Bird, G., *The Diary of Richard Wagner, 1865-1882* (London: Gollancz, 1980).

Returning to His Religious Vocation (1861-65)

played piano versions of excerpts from pieces for his projected oratorio, *Christus*, as well as his two recent *Légendes* on Saint Francis of Assisi and Saint Francis of Paola. He thanked her for the support she had given him in Rome:

> Oh, when will the moment come when I shall belong to myself again – and can continue and complete our *Christus*! I swear to you that there is no other happiness for me than the one you have been giving me for nearly three years by your gentleness, your devotion, and your adorable concern for my true welfare, my sweet guardian angel! (Löwenberg, 16 September 1864)

He repeated a similar message on arriving in Berlin where he went with Cosima to visit Daniel's grave: 'You cannot imagine the extent to which journeys have become painful and disgusting to me! Arriving somewhere is just as unbearable as departing – and I feel that I can no longer stay anywhere other than at the Madonna del Rosario!' (Berlin, 21 September 1864)

Carolyne's husband Prince Nicholas had died in March 1864 and so the last remaining obstacle to her marriage with Liszt had been removed. Why did it not happen? This question must have been on many people's minds. When Liszt could at last meet with the Grand Duke, Carl Alexander raised the matter with him directly. Liszt reported their conversation to Carolyne:

> He reminded me that he had several times written to Antonelli [the Pope's secretary of state] in my favour, for which I thanked him very sincerely, and equally as much for his assurance that he would always do whatever he could to show his affection for me. By virtue of this affection and of the numerous proofs of it that he has given me, he did not hesitate to refer again to the simplicity of the solution that is now possible – being unable to conceive that people could have pursued a goal for 15 years, only to turn aside from it at the very moment when nothing any longer stood between them and its accomplishment. I remarked that I had not thus far spoken of this matter to anyone at all, and that I was not planning to break this silence in the future. (Wilhelmsthal, 29 September 1864)

No doubt Liszt's answer seemed unsatisfactory to the Grand Duke and it is still unsatisfactory to many commentators on Liszt today. Clearly, Carl Alexander was moved by the painful dilemma the couple faced as is evidenced by his diary entry for 29 September on his meeting with Liszt:

> It is impossible not to be affected by the fatalistic side of his destiny. The affection that he felt for the princess, her passion for him, the fetters that this created, his departure for Rome, his wedding that was thwarted at the last minute by the Pope just as he was on the point of celebrating it, two years of waiting then the death of the prince, the princess's husband ... this is one of the most curiously affecting psychological dramas that life could produce.[33]

Carl Alexander persisted with his quest for an answer, writing to Liszt six months later: 'Now that a year has passed since Prince Wittgenstein's death, there is no longer any human reason, nor earthly power which could oppose your union. If it is not accomplished, the reason lies in you, or in her.' (Weimar, 8 March 1865)[34]

Liszt responded with Pascal's dictum, 'the heart has its reasons which reason does not know', but would provide no further elucidation. Alan Walker's considered opinion is that the decision not to marry had already been decided mutually by Liszt and Carolyne.[35] Perhaps at their age they no longer considered it appropriate to marry, rather to remain close friends while they independently pursued their own interests, Liszt in music composition, Carolyne in writing. It does not seem possible to find out more of what they might have said to one another on the subject, at least at this stage of their lives. However, another possible reason was soon to make itself apparent.

After leaving Weimar Liszt again met up with Cosima at Eisenach, where they visited the historic Wartburg, and then they journeyed together to Paris to visit Anna Liszt who was confined to bed after a fall. They stayed in Ollivier's house, sleeping in Blandine's rooms while Émile was away, and went out to visit friends including Berlioz and

---

33. Cited by Hilmes, *Franz Liszt: Musicial, Celebrity, Superstar*, pp. 205-6.
34. Cited by Pocknell (ed.), *Franz Liszt and Agnes Street-Klindworth*, p. 234, footnote 5.
35. Walker, *The Final Years*, p. 32.

Rossini. They also met Marie d'Agoult whom neither had seen in the last three years. There is no account of this meeting from Liszt's viewpoint, but we do have one from Marie's diary:

> He said: I've always loved you. For three years I have loved you in a way that is a little less unworthy of you. I live alone etc. He says he is poor and that some of the deprivations that he suffers are hard to endure. Not even in Paris is he controversial. He works six hours. ... He speaks the language of Catholics. Seems to obey a strict morality and to continue to have a great deal to do with the aristocracy. He has aged during the last two years. Far less good-looking, but calmer and more affectionate. Great tenderness for Cosima.[36]

This seems to be a fair account of Liszt in 1864. Certainly, his finances had become more restricted. In his letter to Carolyne from Weimar he had complained about his need to spend more than he should do. Marie's comments are also consistent with the possibility of a reconciliation between her and Liszt after their years of conflict over their children's upbringing. From Paris Liszt and Cosima journeyed to Saint-Tropez where they again prayed together at a graveside. They stayed with Émile and his and Blandine's little child Daniel, before going their separate ways to Rome and to Germany.

Ordination at the Vatican

Liszt's letters to his various correspondents in the following months do not reveal anything of the important decision he was about to make. They speak of matters of health, of musical achievements and European politics. With Agnes, he repeated his conviction that the Church would adapt to the coming democratisation of European states, but not about his personal plans to enter the ordained clergy. No doubt he spoke about this matter with Carolyne when he was back in Rome but to everyone else his decision came as a surprise.

On 21 April 1865 Liszt left his accommodation on Monte Mario and went to stay for some days in the Lazarite monastery in Rome in order to prepare himself spiritually for ordination into the lowest rank of clergy. On 25 April he was tonsured by Archbishop Gustav Hohenlohe in a

---

36. Cited by Hilmes, *Franz Liszt: Musician, Celebrity, Superstar*, p. 206.

private chapel in the Vatican. In the evening he was given an audience with Pope Pius who gave Liszt his blessing *in extenso*. He then went to live in Hohenlohe's private apartments in the Vatican, on the same floor as the famous Raphael murals, and with another splendid view this time over St Peter's Square's itself. A fine piano was installed for Liszt's use. On 30 July he entered the four minor orders of the priesthood: acolyte, doorkeeper, exorcist and lector. He was now 'the Abbé Liszt'. He was not yet a priest, and so could not celebrate mass or hear confession, but he had started on the pathway towards the priesthood, and in the following months he studied Latin and theology with a view to taking the next step, ordination to the subdiaconate.

Abbé Liszt after ordination. Photograph taken in Pest by Canzi és Heller, August 1865.

He wrote to Carolyne in great detail during the three-/four-day retreat he undertook at the Lazarist Mission, after the ceremony and then when he had moved into rooms in the Vatican. Carolyne appears to have been totally at one with him in the decision he had taken:

> *Et ego semper tecum*! I feel very comfortable here, and these 3 or 4 days of transition are very soothing! No austerity is imposed upon me. Apart from extra spiritual reading, which I do very gladly, it is almost my life on Monte Mario. ... There are about 35 of us; I am seated at a separate table, alone. There is no talking, which suits me extremely well. (22 April 1864)
>
> My three days at the Mission have been very agreeable – I shall retain a profounder and more serene memory of them than of my alleged successes of former days! Man is really only what he is in the eyes of God! (Rome, 24 April 1865)
>
> Your lines of this morning have shone out over the whole of this happy day. Mgr. Hohenlohe will give you an account of it before you receive this. It gives me pleasure to go over it again with you. ... As you know, the tonsure must be in the form of a crown. ... It is so that on head of the cleric, and of the whole clergy, may be imprinted the image of the crown

of thorns of Our Lord Jesus Christ. It also denotes the 'royal dignity' of him who is admitted into the ranks of the clergy. The word 'cleric' comes from the Greek *kleros*, heritage, lot. ... May our dear good Lord heap upon you all His blessings! I enclose the *Manuel du chrétien*, in which I beg you to read for my sake Ps. 15 and 83. It is a very poor French translation – but your soul will sing them in their real language! I did not fail, this evening, to speak to the Holy Father of my gratitude and devotion to Hohenlohe, who once again has done everything for the best. (Rome, 25 April 1865)

No previous biographer of Liszt has commented, as far as I know, quite how remarkable this last statement is for Liszt to have addressed to Carolyne about the man who had prevented their marriage. Had she also come to appreciate past events differently?

Now Liszt had to explain to the world the step he had taken. Most of his family and friends were shocked. Émile Ollivier described it as 'a spiritual suicide'.[37] Wagner noted in his diary: 'To me this Catholic rubbish is repugnant to the very depths of my soul – Anyone who takes refuge in that must have a great deal to atone for.'[38] Carl Alexander wrote to Liszt: 'I read it with a feeling of deep personal anguish.'[39] Even Liszt's own mother cried:

> My dear child, people often talk of things at such great length that they finally happen, and so it is with your present change of status. There have been frequent reports in the newspapers here that you had chosen clerical status, but I have vigorously contradicted them whenever they were mentioned. And so your letter of April 27, which I received yesterday, upset me deeply, and I burst into tears. Forgive me, but I really was not prepared for such news from you.[40]

However, as Walker notes, Anna recovered and 'bowed to what she called the will of God. ... If the blessing of a feeble old mother can achieve aught with the Almighty, then I bless you a thousand times.' Why had Liszt not even told his mother of his plans once they had become definite?

---

37. Cited by Walker, *The Final Years*, p. 88.
38. Cited by Hilms, *Franz Liszt*, p. 198.
39. Ibid., p. 198.
40. Cited by Walker, *The Final Years*, p. 87.

Could he have been afraid that she would try to prevent him as she had done when he was young?

The 'world' in general could hardly believe what it had heard of Liszt's next step in life, and many writers on Liszt – although not Alan Walker – have belittled Liszt's step in becoming ordained. For some, it was yet another change in a life of ever shifting self-presentation. Even his most recent biographer Oliver Hilmes has not taken Liszt's ordination as seriously as Liszt evidently intended it. For example, he gives importance to the views expressed by Kurd von Schlözer in his *Römische Briefe*. Von Schlözer was a member of the Prussian embassy staff in Rome and a keen pianist, who enjoyed hearing Liszt play and had visited him on Monte Mario. He also enjoyed recounting gossip he heard in social groups, including the story which fancied Carolyne to have played 'the chief role' in what had occurred: 'Some maintain that fear that the unpredictable Franz might yet marry some young woman agitated her so much that she set the whole Vatican in motion to see that influential clerics gently propelled the good Franz into the clergy.'[41]

Hilmes also gives credence to alternative views that Liszt may have been aiming for a musical career in the Vatican or that his step towards the priesthood would protect him from any renewed pressure from Carolyne to marry her. More generously, he suggests that it 'represented a public sacrifice offered up to his former companion in life'.[42] By entering the clerical state, he was ensuring that marriage itself was out of the question for him, as he could not be both married and a cleric.

However, these perspectives fly in the face of the evidence from Liszt's own correspondence that his spiritual development had always been important to him and that it had become even more important to him after he moved to Rome. Once he and Carolyne had both lost the desire to marry each other, entering the religious state became a more natural step for him. His correspondence with friends who knew him much better than von Schlözer support this view. For example, on 1 May 1865 he wrote to Agnes to let her know what had happened to him. He did not expect her to be shocked: 'I think you will hardly be surprised at the realization of a decision already made some time ago, but about which I chose to inform, a few days in advance, only the three absolutely indispensable people.'[43] (Vatican, 1 May 1865)

---

41. From Kurd von Schlözer, *Römische Briefe* (1912), cited by Hilmes, *Franz Liszt: Musician, Celebrity, Superstar*, p. 198.
42. Hilmes, *Franz Liszt: Musician, Celebrity, Superstar*, p. 199.
43. Hohenlohe, the Pope and Carolyne.

He made clear to her that he would continue his musical work, completing his *Christus* oratorio, and in the summer would be going to Pest to conduct the first performance of his *Legend of St Elisabeth*. He hoped that it might be possible to meet her in or near Munich on the way back and asked her to send letters to his manservant at Carolyne's address.[44] He commented on his new dress and that her children must not be afraid of meeting him next in a cassock:

> I received widespread compliments that I wear it as though I had never worn any other garment. The fact is that I feel completely at ease in it and am as happy as I am capable of being.
> 'Deus charitas est, et qui manet in charitate, in Deo manet, et Deus in eo.'[45]

Later in the month he thanked Agnes for her reply – 'there is nothing sweeter and more tenderly loving than your letter' – and gave advice on a violin teacher in Brussels for her son Georges, then aged eleven, who was showing considerable talent.[46] He wrote with advice on not stopping his general education:

> In Georges' case, I simply urge you not to break off other studies too early, so that he learns thoroughly what is required to be an honour in every way to his mother, through his education and upbringing. It matters more than ever today that an artist be also an intelligent man and knows a certain amount of things beyond the exercise of his art. It is not enough to be a good strolling player, and one can no longer even manage to be that if one neglects to stock one's mind properly. (Vatican, 19 May 1865)

As Pocknell notes,[47] Liszt 'felt deeply his lack of formal education'. This was evident both in his letters to Carolyne and to Agnes.

Perhaps the fullest and at the same time most straightforward account which Liszt gave of his decision to enter religious orders was to his other

---

44. Fortunato Salvagni's wife was housekeeper to Carolyne.
45. 1 John 4:16, 'God is love, and he who abides in love abides in God, and God abides in him'.
46. Agnes took up Liszt's advice.
47. Pocknell (ed.), *Franz Liszt and Agnes Street-Klindworth*, p. 241, footnote 1.

Abbé Liszt with Pope Pius IX in the cloisters of the Church of
St John Lateran in Rome c. 1866. Wood engraving based on
a drawing by Paul Thumann.

patron Constantine, Prince of Hohenzollern-Hechingen. Although he had not played as major a role in his life as Grand Duke Carl Alexander, Prince Constantine was someone who greatly enjoyed hosting Liszt and promoting his music. As a Catholic he had a better understanding of Liszt's spirituality and had presented him with a valuable ivory crucifix:[48]

> Convinced that by this act I should be confirming to myself that I was on the right path, I accomplished it without effort, in total simplicity and uprightness of intention. Moreover, it accords with the antecedents of my youth, just as it does with the development undergone by my work of musical composition during these last four years – work which I intend to pursue with renewed vigour, since I consider it to be the least defective part of my nature.
>
> To speak familiarly, if 'the habit does not make the monk', neither does it prevent him being one; and in certain cases,

---

48. In his will of 1860 Liszt had asked Carolyne to give this crucifix to her daughter Marie.

when the monk is fully formed within, why not assume the outer garb as well?

But I am forgetting that I do not in the least intend to become a monk in the strict sense of the word. I lack the necessary vocation, and it is enough for me to belong to the hierarchy of the Church to the degree that the minor orders allow me. And so it is not the frock but the cassock that I have donned. (Vatican, 11 May 1865)

In this letter Liszt made perfectly clear what his intentions were. He wished to identify even more strongly with the Church in which he was educated. He would not become a priest but would work harder to combine his musical and spiritual vocations. This was not a new aim on Liszt's part. It was wholly consistent with what he imagined his life project to be when he was still very young.

Liszt conducting the first performance of his *Legende von der Heiligen Elisabeth* in the Redoutensaal in Pest on 15 August 1865. Wood engraving from the *Illustrierte Zeitung* of 16 September 1865, based on a drawing by Jean Hubert Reve.

5

Disappointment and Conflict (1865-71)

Musical Success and Failure

Liszt's ordination was followed by his full return to European music. His first engagement was in Pest in Hungary to give the first performance of his long-awaited oratorio, *The Legend of St Elisabeth*. He conducted wearing a Franciscan habit.[1] A Leipzig newspaper report noted how much quieter his manner of performance was compared with that of his symphonic poems. Nevertheless, Liszt's pride in his success and also his ever-present fear of failure were evident in the letter he sent to Carolyne:

> This time I cannot boast of any blow – unless it be to my obligatory modesty! The *Elisabeth* was greeted with cheers yesterday evening – the newspapers are filled with my name – I have become a kind of public event! Eduard, who has been here since the day before yesterday, will write to you about it, as will Cosima. (Pest, 16 August 1865)

The concert was in fact so successful that it had to be repeated a week later. On 20 August, the feast day of St Stephen, the patron saint of Hungary, he conducted an all-Hungarian festival concert performed by 50 choral societies from across the country. It was celebrated as a great patriotic event.

Liszt had asked Cosima and Hans to accompany him to Hungary for his concert performances. He had requested the assistance of Hans with

---

1. St Elisabeth was thought of as associated with the Third Order of St Francis.

his music making but seems to have been primarily hoping to exert a positive influence upon his son-in-law's failing marriage. Liszt had spent an unusually large amount of time with his daughter in the late summer of 1864, which was already suggestive of his need to protect her from some danger. Cosima's third daughter Isolde had been born in April 1865 and there were suspicions being voiced as to her true paternity.

After the concerts in Pest, Liszt, together with Cosima and Hans, travelled to Gran/Esztergom as guests of Cardinal Scitovszky, the primate of Hungary. Back in Pest, he gave the first public piano performance of his two Franciscan legends which he had dedicated to Cosima. Much to the annoyance of Wagner, as we know from the latter's diary, Liszt prolonged their stay into September by taking them to stay in the house of Baron Augusz in Szekszárd. Liszt was in his element. Thousands gathered outside Augusz's house and Liszt serenaded them from the window with various pieces including a four-handed arrangement of the *Rákóczy March* which he played together with Hans. Liszt would have taken his daughter and son-in-law on to Venice, perhaps hoping its magic would rekindle their love for each other, but they refused and took the train back to Munich – and to Wagner. It was, as Walker notes,[2] as if Liszt and Wagner were engaged in an emotional 'tug-of-war' over Cosima.

Back in Rome by September, Liszt wrote to thank Augusz for his friendship and support over the previous years and the inspiration he received from him to continue his composition of religious music:

> Let me thank you for it once again, for it is to your persistence of 9 years ago that I am indebted for the position made for me in Pest this present year, one which without the precedent of Esztergom would have lacked the necessary foundations. ... It was while thinking of you, of your family, of Hungary, of what I still have to do to justify to some extent the good opinion of my friends, that I returned to Rome, where I shall resume my work as soon as possible. In 6 or 8 months I hope to have finished my oratorio on Jesus Christ. (Vatican, 20 September 1865)

As he also told Augusz, the Vatican was making plans to commemorate during the following year eighteen centuries of the establishment of the See of St Peter in Rome. Liszt wanted to contribute to this assertion

---

2. Walker, *The Final Years*, p. 92.

Disappointment and Conflict (1865-71) 115

of the primacy of Rome and wrote in the same month to Brendel that he was composing a hymn, 'Tu es Petrus', in honour of St Peter and his successors as popes. At the same time, he asked both Brendel and Gille to be patient in putting on his *Elisabeth* in Jena because of the care that would be required in preparing the performance. Some weeks later he expressed the same concern to his cousin Eduard about pressure for a performance of the same work in Vienna. Despite his recent success in Hungary, he was still very anxious about the reception of his music in the wider world of European music:

> You know how much against my wish it is to put this work into circulation. And, however flattering it may be to me (the execrated composer!) to receive offers from various places about it, still I think it advisable to avoid precipitancy, and not to expose my friends so soon again to unpleasantness such as my earlier works brought upon them. (Letter to Eduard, Rome, 1 November 1865).

That his anxiety was justified was borne out by his experience at his next major concert.

At the beginning of 1866 Liszt wrote what was to be his last letter to his mother telling her that he would be coming to Paris in March for a performance of his *Missa Solemnis*, which he had written for the consecration of the basilica at Gran/Esztergom in 1856. He was looking forward to sharing with her what he hoped would be a successful performance. However, on 6 February Anna died quite suddenly of pneumonia following a short illness. Émile Ollivier organised her funeral and provided an eloquent tribute to her, in which he also took care to praise her son.[3] Liszt arrived in Paris at the beginning of March and stayed for over two months in Emile's apartment while they sorted out his mother's affairs. Émile noted in his diary that: '[Liszt] is basically sad and unhappy, and his soul is certainly not joyful; but he is very good and affectionate towards me, and I feel a genuine pleasure in seeing him.'[4]

Parisian society showed huge interest in Liszt's return to the city and he responded in public with his usual charm and wit. Unfortunately, the main purpose of his visit, the performance of the Gran Mass on 15 March in the church of Saint-Eustache, was not a success. Before the concert took place, Liszt had informed Carolyne of a major problem.

---

3. See Walker, *The Final Years*, p. 96.
4. Cited in ibid., p. 97.

Because of a recent scandal, the archbishopric of Paris would not loosen its 'regulation prohibiting women singers from performing in church' and as a result it was necessary for Liszt to replace his leading singers with three choirboys who could not provide the strong articulation needed. Moreover, there was much else to distract the audience. Liszt, as had often been his practice throughout his career, had agreed that the proceeds of the concert should be donated to charity and in this situation to the schools of Paris's second *arrondissement*. This had the effect of not only attracting a large crowd but a boisterous one: there was much rattling of collection boxes, and even a noisy band of soldiers who brought their drums along!

That the performance of his Gran Mass in Paris had been not only unsuccessful but also disastrous for Liszt's musical reputation seems to have gradually become clear to him. He wrote to Carolyne, initially approaching the subject tentatively and putting a brave face on a 'difficult situation':

> I am trying to find the right word. Success, yes – sensation even – but a difficult situation. St. Gregory will help us! One gains an idea of certain things only by doing them! … But life isn't becoming more agreeable for me, nor any easier! Nevertheless, I have no reason to complain. St Gregory and you will not abandon me – of that, I am quite certain! (Paris, 18 March 1866)

However, he then had to admit to Carolyne that he had been receiving negative reviews in the Parisian press:

> Continue to put up patiently with some stupid and unpleasant articles. … *Poco a poco*[5] my fingers will do my brains less injustice – and my celebrity will no longer stand in the way of my reputation! It's just that the transition is a little too slow! Nothing, however, prevents our putting this time to good use, by loving God and His Church – and by modestly practising the virtues taught us! It is that to which is applying himself your very humbly devoted Franz Liszt. (Paris, 29 March 1866)

He tried to rescue the situation by putting on a separate performance at a new venue of the Credo alone because, as he had written to Carolyne, this had been heavily criticised as the 'the weakest and

---

5. 'Little by little'.

most inharmonious piece'. However, perhaps because of the adverse publicity, Liszt decided not to attend himself and Émile went in his place. His report back was not positive. As Liszt told Carolyne, the performance was 'flabby and confused – the soloists had colds, the choruses were uncertain, etc.' Nonetheless, both the conductor and Émile tried at the same time to be reassuring to Liszt: 'It was not a failure, despite a few hisses which were heard. A third of the audience applauded, and a good many people even applauded warmly. ... In sum, it's a kind of success – especially in comparison with what happened to Wagner and Berlioz.' Liszt ended this letter to Carolyne with a note of hope: 'One can only progress slowly. My new public will gradually be formed – at the same time that the prejudices of hostilities of determined opponents are lessened or reduced to impotence.' (Paris, 2 April 1866)

While he was in Paris, Liszt made a last effort to convince his most critical friends including Berlioz of the merit of his new style of his musical composition. He assembled three of them in another friend's house and in a piano-duet version explained his new approach to harmony, rhythm and melody. Berlioz remained silent and later expressed his opinion that Liszt's *Missa Solemnis* was 'the negation of art'. Such a negative judgement from an old friend made the performance of the Gran Mass in Paris a particularly low point in Liszt's musical career. The press had mocked him mercilessly. Even the kindest reviews begged him to give up his clerical robes and return to being the excellent pianist he was known to be. Sadly, orchestral and church composition was not what Parisians expected or wanted from Liszt on his return to their city. The Gran Mass with its strong declamatory and prayerful character is still today hardly known outside Hungary, despite the existence of some fine recordings.

One of the most critical reviews of the first concert had been written by Marie d'Agoult's son-in-law, a person with little in the way of musical knowledge, and Liszt perhaps inevitably attributed its content to her influence. He had so far avoided going to see her. She had that very year republished *Nélida* which had been out of print for more than twenty years. It is likely that Liszt saw this as a deliberately intended hostile act towards him rather than simply an opportunity to make money from Liszt's presence in town. Nevertheless, he finally succumbed to pressure from Émile and others to visit her. Primed as he was by the insults which he perceived to have been directed against him, he responded angrily when Marie told him of her plans to publish her memoirs. He wrote to Carolyne about his response:

Countess Marie d'Agoult. Photograph taken in Paris around 1866.

I retorted that I did not believe it possible for her to write them, for what she would entitle memoirs would consist of lies and postures. In saying that, I put plainly to her for the first time the distinction between the True and the False! Those are big words – but it was necessary to use them, to do my duty. Since the continuation of a communion of minds between the two of us is now becoming an immorality, nothing was left to me when seeing her again but to lean on duty. Besides, the role of Guermann is a very silly invention once and for all with such a doctrinal sentimentalism. (Paris, 13 April 1866).

No biographer as far as I know has recorded whether Marie responded in spoken words or in her written diary to this attack upon her integrity. However, later in 1866 she wrote some words of reflection in the margins of the account of her travels with Liszt some twenty-eight years earlier: 'What has *he* done with these twenty-eight years? And what have *I* done with them? He is the Abbé Liszt and I am Daniel Stern! And, between us, how much despair, how many deaths, tears, sobs, and griefs!'[6]

If reconciliation with Marie had been Liszt's aim, it would probably have been better if on this occasion he had kept to his original instinct to avoid a meeting with Marie. The rift between them had grown deeper.

Not all went badly for Liszt on his visit to Paris in 1866. Although Berlioz's rejection of Liszt's work hurt him, he received support from other old friends in music, such as Rossini[7] and younger colleagues such as Gounod, Massenet and Saint-Saëns. Moreover, his links with Émile were further strengthened and he went to the French Chamber of Deputies for the first time to hear his former son-in-law speak. Later in April, Liszt travelled to Amsterdam for a further much more successful performance of the Gran Mass in the Franciscan church of Moses and

---

6. From Marie d'Agoult, *Mémoires, 1833-1854*, ed. Daniel Ollivier (Paris: 1927), in a passage cited by Williams (ed.), *Franz Liszt: Selected Letters*, p. 950.
7. As Liszt told Carolyne in his letter of 29 March, Rossini had been heard to quip: 'Liszt is composing masses, to get used to saying them.'

Aaron. He also took part in two other piano and orchestral concerts which included his Psalm 12/13, 'How long, O Lord, wilt Thou forget me?'. Hans came from Berlin to perform Liszt's piano music on these two occasions.

In both capitals he was received by royalty. Despite the French Emperor's ailing health and his preoccupation with the worrying political situation in Europe, Liszt was invited again to spend some time with Napoleon soon after his arrival in Paris. On his return from Amsterdam, it was the Empress Eugénie who invited him. While in the Dutch capital, he was received by Queen Sophie, consort of King Willem III of the Netherlands. He described all these invitations to Carolyne with understandable pride.

Cosima had accompanied Hans to Amsterdam and stayed at the same hotel as her father. Pocknell suggests that this can be explained by her wish 'to allay her father's displeasure' that she had recently been to visit Wagner in Geneva.[8] Wagner had fallen heavily into disfavour in Munich because of his lavish lifestyle and expensive demands on state finances but even more because of his apparent interference in Bavarian politics. Despite King Ludwig's continuing support, Wagner had been forced to leave the kingdom for the time being. Liszt had appealed to Cosima for information on what was happening at the end of the previous year and therefore was able to satisfy Agnes' curiosity on this issue. Liszt was in two minds about Wagner. His letter to Agnes in January 1866 shows his very real concern for his former friend that King Ludwig would retract from his commitment to Wagner's *Nibelungen* since such an enormous project needed royal patronage. He wrote to Carolyne from Brussels on 1 May that his main desire was for Wagner 'not to return to Munich for a long time'.

It is in his letters to his friend Baron Augusz, rather than to Carolyne, that one senses how badly Liszt was being hurt by attacks on his music in the press. This had also occurred in Vienna, although fortunately not in Hungary. He was drawing on deep spiritual resources to cope with the situation:

> If, as you tell me, Hungarian newspapers have declined to reproduce the *Freundenblatt* articles about me, then they are behaving very decently, in a way that touches me deeply. ... Far better, loftier, and worthier souls than I have been subjected

---

8. Pocknell (ed.), *Franz Liszt and Agnes Street-Klindworth*, p. 249.

to worse treatment, both now and in days gone by. This, it must be said, is no consolation; but these examples can help to bolster one's courage. A man endowed with some superiority will accomplish his task only at the cost of many sufferings. But so long as we have clear consciences, there is nothing to fear. 'If God be for us, who can be against us?'[9]

Once again, very dear friend, please do not be distressed by attacks upon me, whether spoken on or in print. *I am not going to complain*, for I have been nobly loved, far beyond what I could ever deserve. So it is from the depths of my soul that I say and often sing this psalm: 'Convertere anima mea in requiem tuam, quia Dominus benefecit tibi, quia eripuit animam meam de morte, oculos meos a lacrymis, pedes meos a lapsu. Placebo Domino in regione vivorum'!!![10] (Paris, early May 1866)

We know from Émile's diary that Liszt cried as he boarded the train on leaving Paris.[11] He had many reasons to feel emotional at that moment. After Blandine's and now his mother's death, coupled with the failure of his main Paris concert in which he had put so much hope, not to speak of his bitter encounter with Marie d'Agoult, did he also have a sense that the city of his dazzling youth no longer belonged to him?

Increasing Doubts and Worries

Soon after Liszt arrived back in Rome, Gustav Hohenlohe was elevated to the College of Cardinals and, as a result, Liszt had to leave his Vatican apartment and return for a while to the Madonna del Rosario on Monte Mario. He settled back to his theological studies as well as his work on his oratorio, *Christus*, about which he wrote with enthusiasm to various people including Augusz, Brendel, Agnes and Émile. He also wrote to Carolyne to thank her for a copy of Rubens' painting, *The Four Great Sinners*, that she was having framed for him and that he was intending to hang in his study:

---

9. Romans 8:31.
10. Psalm 114: 6-8 / Psalm 116:7-9 'Turn again then into thy rest, O my soul, for the Lord hath prospered thee. For He hath delivered my soul from death, mine eyes from tears, and my feet from stumbling. I will be well-pleasing before the Lord in the land of the living.'
11. See Walker, *The Final Years*, p. 105.

> I would almost risk a little interpretation, probably a very foolish one, of this sublime painting by Rubens. In saying that the 4 sinners loved much, I yet distinguish in St Peter, love through faith – in the penitent thief, love through hope – in David, love through contrition, humiliation and a broken heart! For Mary Magdalene, it is love quite simply and despite everything! (Madonna del Rosario, summer 1866)

Analysis of his correspondence with Agnes during 1866 suggests that he probably visited her in Brussels twice, both on his way to Amsterdam and on his way back to Paris. She is also known to have attended performances of his works in the Dutch capital. However, this was a busy year for Georg Klindworth and his daughter as the developing conflict between Austria and Prussia for dominance over the German-speaking lands was reaching its climax. Rivalry between the two had become almost inevitable since the dissolution of the Holy Roman Empire in 1806 and the consequent end of Habsburg rule over central Europe. Klindworth was involved heavily in the Austrian preparations for war and he also acted as a consultant for France, for it too feared the advance of Prussia. The Austro-Prussian war, during which France stayed neutral, began in June, lasted for only seven weeks and ended with the massive defeat of Austria at the battle of Königgrätz in Bohemia with a huge loss of life for the Austrian army. Prussia subsequently annexed a number of the smaller German states, including Hanover, which had made the mistake of allying with Austria.

During the early months of the year Liszt was still being kept informed about political developments in Europe by Agnes. In January she had sent him a report she had prepared on the protection of Belgian autonomy and territorial integrity following the death in the previous month of its first monarch Leopold I. However, by the time the Austro-Prussian war started on 14 June, she had stopped corresponding and Liszt's subsequent letters to her show that he was agitated by her silence, even though he must have guessed the probable cause. The war had consequences both for Italy and for Rome, with the loss of Austrian rule over Venice and its lands to the new Kingdom of Italy. The French army had been removed from Rome for a time and there was genuine concern about the overthrow of papal rule as the Vatican's continuing independence now depended only on promises from the new Italian government.

Over the next two years the letters Liszt wrote to Agnes are the most revealing of his mental state. Despite the enthusiasm he had expressed to others, by November 1866 he was already writing pessimistically to her about the prospects for performance of his now completed oratorio, *Christus*, and adapting himself to its likely fate:

> I have indeed finally completed this piece, after having worked on it for a couple of years; – but as for its performance, I have no idea either *when* or *where* it will be. Paris is hardly fertile ground for oratorios. ... What is more, I am personally in an exceptional and very unfavourable position in several respects. I cannot put myself either in *the van* or in the *rearguard*. What is perfectly proper and profitable behaviour for other composers is no longer fitting in my position. Organizing concerts, for example, seeking ways to have my works performed, accepting the semi-patronage of certain proposals are things which are absolutely barred to me. Therefore, through finding myself off the beaten track, I shall probably make no headway. But that does not matter. My mind is made up – and has been for a long time. ... So I enjoy declaring total disinterest in my compositions' fate. If they have some value it will be noticed soon enough, without my worrying about anything other than composing them to the best of my ability. (Rome, 24 November 1866)

In the same letter Liszt indicated his intention of staying in Rome, despite the uncertain political future there, and explained that he had been obliged to move to the centre of Rome and was now living in an apartment attached to the church of Santa Francesca Romana, overlooking the ruins of the Roman Forum. Although he again was in a room with a splendid view, Liszt soon found himself being overwhelmed by social engagements. In his next letter to Agnes in February 1867 he explained that he could not cope with the dealings he had with so many people and confided to her his feelings about the reception of his music. His recent composition, the *Legend of St Elisabeth*, had been well received but 'so much so that friends, brimming with impartiality, compliment me quite flatteringly by declaring that it is not like my earlier works and is not at all offensive to the ears'. Although he also wrote that he was training himself to 'saintly detachment', he continued to look despondently at his future prospects in the world of music:

> The predominance of coarse practices, prejudices, and every kind of ineptitude and ill-will, in the most varied forms

(pedantic, trite, puffed-up, or scatterbrained) is still far too common in the musical world. Perhaps it will decline little by little, and perhaps I shall then find *my* audience. I am not seeking it and barely have any more time to wait for it. (Rome, 14 February 1867)

Less than two weeks later he wrote to Agnes that it had been reported to him that at a recent concert in Leipzig the audience 'were pleased to hiss my poor "Gretchen"'.[12] However, if they were to do the same to his music at a forthcoming concert in Brussels, he added, implausibly, he would 'not be a whit more upset or put out'. At the same time, he told her he was 'delighted' at the reception of his former pupil, the pianist Carl Tausig, in the same concert in Leipzig. Liszt's ability to take pleasure in others' deserved success continued to shine even as his hopes for his own declined.

His subsequent letter to Agnes indicates how much he was pinning his hopes for Europe's future on the continued success of Napoleon III. This was an issue on which Liszt did not see eye to eye with Agnes. Now

Forum Romanum, Rome. Photograph c. 1850. Liszt's rooms in the Monastery of Santa Francesca Romana are marked with an arrow.

---

12. The second movement from his *Faust* symphony.

that Émile Ollivier's political star was rising in Paris, Liszt was hoping that Agnes would not try to influence him negatively in his own attitude to Louis Napoleon:

> I am delighted that you have got on good terms with Mr. Ollivier, but for goodness sake do not go and spoil him with your amiability. If ever you came to persuade him that he 'could never get on with the head of state', I should be truly upset. ... Napoleon III's genius lies in his balancing of political imperatives against the sum of progress achievable in this century.
>
> My thanks once more for your letter and a request for a sequel despite my incorrigible Napoleonism. (Rome, 29 May 1867)

At this rather low point in his life Liszt received a boost to his self-esteem from his native land. Following the positive reception of his *St Elisabeth*, he was invited by the Cardinal of Budapest to compose a mass for the coronation of Emperor Franz Joseph I in the Hungarian capital on 8 June 1867. As another consequence of its weakened position after its recent defeat by Prussia, the Austrian government had decided to accommodate Hungarian nationalist sentiment by establishing the concept of the 'Dual Monarchy', thus making the two nations equal in status. The formal invitation to Liszt was delayed because of protests from Vienna but in the end the Austrians yielded to Hungarian pressure. Within only a few months Liszt succeeded in creating a relatively short, simple and pleasing set of movements for this Mass (his *Ungarische Krönungsmesse*), which suited the situation well with its inclusion of some Hungarian elements. He was applauded by the people as he walked back from the scene of the coronation in the Matthias Church at Buda Castle over the Chain Bridge across the Danube to his apartment in Pest. He reported his success to Carolyne in a letter he wrote on 8 June: 'I believe you can be satisfied. The musical success of my Mass is complete. It surprised everyone by its brevity, its simplicity – and dare I say it, by its character.' Liszt was also able to tell Carolyne of the warm greetings he received from Prince Konstantin, the husband of Marie who was unable herself to attend because of illness. He had come from Vienna especially for the occasion.

In the same month Napoleon III, Liszt's hoped-for saviour of European harmony, received a major blow to his prestige with the arrest and execution by republican forces of the newly installed Emperor Maximilian I of Mexico, the younger brother of Franz Joseph I. Liszt wrote a *Marche funèbre* in his honour with the inscription, *In magnis et voluisse sat est*.[13] It had been French arms that had installed him in position. This coincided, unfortunately for Napoleon, with the Great Exhibition of Paris, the cultural celebration of all that he had achieved in making Paris the most beautiful, new developed city in the world. The centre of the city had been transformed by a massive rebuilding scheme, the introduction of street lighting and the creation of striking new boulevards designed by his master architect Baron Haussmann.

The one letter that survives of those Agnes wrote to Liszt shows how much she agreed with Émile Ollivier's views on the need for reform in France and how critical she was of the then French government, while showing sensitivity to Liszt's views on Napoleon:

> Mr. Ollivier understands the situation perfectly clearly; his last speech is all the proof I need; it is a masterpiece of moderation and commonsense, and above all, an accurate assessment of the present régime. Personal Government – with apologies – is in a state of severe collapse. ... The Emperor is on Olympus, and criticism cannot rise as high as him. ... And what about that disgraceful lunacy, that abominable Mexican catastrophe! But I shall stop; naturally I see things with different eyes than you, and for that reason I am truly afraid of irritating you by passing on opinions which agree so little with yours. (Agnes Street-Klindworth to Liszt, Brussels, 20 July 1867)[14]

It may be that Liszt did not receive this letter before he left Rome, which would explain his lack of immediate reply and why it happens to have survived Liszt's regular destruction of the letters he received from Agnes.

In July 1867 Liszt was in fact travelling to Germany and back to Weimar. Again, he wrote lovingly and with gratitude to Carolyne of the memories this brought back to him:

> In this place, thirteen years of joys and sorrows, of truth and poetry, press upon me, sing, weep, cry, moan, and shine! Every object – what am I saying? – every

Franz Liszt. Photograph by Joseph Albert, Munich 1867.

---

13. 'In great things it is enough to have been willing', Propertius.
14. See Pocknell (ed.), *Franz Liszt and Agnes Street-Klindworth*, p. xxi.

atom of air and of light contains a fragment of your soul! It is a glorious, ineffable, immense hymn of all the energy and all the tenderness of Martha and Mary at one and the same time! ... When I read the epistle of the office of the day, 'Who will find a strong woman? She is more precious than treasures brought from the ends of the earth', these admirable words were illumined for me by remembrance of you in Woronińce, in Weimar, and of every single day! (Weimar, 29 July 1867)

Thoughout his travels in Germany for the next two months Liszt continued to write regularly to Carolyne. He told her with regret of the increasing Prussian presence in Weimar, that rooms containing her furniture at the Altenburg would be needed by Prussian military staff, and that the former attractive green uniforms of the Duchy's soldiery would shortly be replaced by Prussian blue. On the positive side, he was able to report a successful performance of his *St Elisabeth* in Eisenach and that his cousin Eduard as well as Émile had travelled far from east and west, respectively, to be present. The Grand Duke had also decorated him with the insignia of *Commandeur*. On his return journey Liszt stayed in Munich, near to the house of Cosima and Hans, and attended performances of *Tannhäuser* and *Lohengrin*, conducted by Hans. He also took the opportunity to visit Wagner who was still at his home at Triebschen near Lucerne, before returning to Munich where he celebrated his fifty-sixth birthday with his daughter and son-in-law.

Although his letters to Carolyne contain no mention of his conversations with Cosima, Hans and Wagner, it is clear from Wagner's diary that Liszt was still aiming to prevent the breakdown of his daughter's marriage. He and Wagner appear to have spoken together for many hours but, as so often before, it was Wagner's musical talent that captured Liszt's attention. They worked together in apparent harmony on Wagner's new score, *Die Meistersinger von Nürnberg*. Liszt wrote to Carolyne from Munich on 11 October of 'its incomparable vigour, boldness, vitality, richness, verve, and *maestria*.[15] No one but Wagner could have succeeded in creating such a masterpiece'. Wagner wrote in his diary of Liszt's visit that it was 'dreaded but pleasant'.[16] Alan Walker comments how remarkable it is that in this situation of marital turmoil Liszt could

---

15. 'Mastery'.
16. Cited by Walker, *The Final Years*, p. 125.

have decided to compose his piano transcription of Isolde's *Liebestod* from Wagner's *Tristan*. At the conclusion of his musical discussion of this beautiful piece, he writes: 'It may be Wagner's music, but it is of Liszt that we think when we hear the paraphrase itself. At its centre it contains a bitterness of heart – for those with ears to hear.'[17]

In contrast to his enthusiasm for Wagner's new work, Liszt seems to have been feeling downhearted again about the prospects for his own compositions. While still in Munich he responded pessimistically to Eduard's encouragement to have his *Elisabeth* performed in Vienna:

> I do not share your rosy hopes of this work proving a success in towns where my earlier works not only met with little appreciation, but even received unseemly rebuffs. In Vienna, Leipzig, Berlin and even larger cities, the hisses of half a dozen stupid boys or evil-disposed persons were always sufficient to delude the public, and to frustrate the best intentions of my somewhat disheartened friends. In the newspaper criticisms these hissing critics are sure to find numerous supporters and pleasant re-echoes as long as the one object of the majority of my judges of this species is to get me out of their way. The improvement, which is said of late to have shown itself in regard to my position, may be interpreted somewhat thus: 'For years in his Symphonic Poems, his Masses, Pianoforte works, Songs, etc., Liszt has written mere bewildering and objectionable stuff; in his *Elisabeth* he appears to have acted somewhat more rationally – still, etc., etc." (Munich, 16 October 1867)

On his return to Rome at the beginning of November, Liszt wrote to Agnes about his travels, commenting negatively on their impact upon him. His mood was low:

> For my part it is time to coop myself up, for I have wasted almost my whole year running about. ... Besides, my sociable disposition of old is waning markedly, and there are few faces I feel pleased to see.
>
> Therefore I shall stay quietly in Rome for the whole of this year. (Rome, 8 December 1867)

---

17. Ibid., pp. 126-28.

He subsequently also expressed surprise at Agnes' suggestion, arising from an offer from Liszt's previous concert director in Paris, that he should have his music performed there again:

> What has come over you to talk to me about a performance of Mazeppa at P[as] d[e] l[oup]'s? I certainly intend that nothing should come of it, for under the present circumstances it would only lead to unpleasantness for everyone, and especially for me. At fifty-six years of age, I could not class myself among the 'young composers', and I am not dead enough for them to take a serious interest in me in Paris. (Rome, 6 March 1868)

Three months later, while continuing to give further advice to Agnes about the musical education of her son Georges, he wrote that, although he had no intention of coming to Paris, he hoped it might be possible to hear her son play the piano in Weimar the following year. For the present he remained 'tucked away in the ruins of the Forum' and hoped to stay there for the summer which was 'the good season for me because of the decrease of visitors'.[18]

The next month Liszt accepted the invitation of a friend, Father Antonio Solfanelli, his previous tutor in theology who was recovering from a serious illness, to accompany him on a pilgrimage of two months to Assisi, Loreto and Grottammare. He gave a detailed account of it in a succession of letters to Carolyne. Already, eight days into the journey, he was complaining that it 'has not increased my limited taste for travel'. Carolyne by now would have become well aware of his melancholy state:

> For the little I can accomplish in music, I am convinced it is better to do it in retirement, in my way, and without importuning others. If I had the choice, I would live in some country district far from the railway, and really removed from social relations – for I no longer delude myself into thinking myself useful to my neighbour! Were it not for a certain taste for personal independence, which I think it futile to fight – I would gladly become a Franciscan. (Grottammare, 23 July 1868)

However, by the end of his stay in Grottammare, Liszt was able to write positively of his experience of 'retreat':

---

18. Letter from Liszt to Agnes of 13 June 1868.

> I thank God and you for these two months of tranquillity and simple contentment. The chief object of my journey was to acquaint myself with the breviary – Solfanelli has rendered me excellent service in that, and I am beginning to read the offices quite tolerably. Such an occupation is enough to live well and die well! (Grottammare, 29 August 1868)

Liszt had complained for a long time about the 'unbearable' number of visitors he was receiving in Rome, so he was fortunate to be given two offers in quick succession by two friends. The first came from Carl Alexander to spend the winter in new accommodation being furnished for him in Weimar and the second from Cardinal Hohenlohe to stay at private rooms he had prepared for him at the Villa d'Este in Tivoli in the Roman countryside. It was, he wrote to Agnes on 20 November, a 'secluded life-style' which suited him perfectly and that he was intending to maintain for 'the rest of his days'. 'Only Agnes and her father', he continued, were capable of 'living as ubiquitous people ... shuttling from Brussels to Constantinople, Prague, London, Petersburg, Paris, Vienna'. Nevertheless, he expressed again the hope of meeting Agnes in Weimar.

For Carolyne, Liszt's move to the Villa d'Este must have been an unwelcome surprise since Tivoli was an uncomfortable, four-hour, coach journey from Rome. Shortly after Liszt arrived there, he wrote a puzzling short letter to her which reflected a level of strain in their relationship: 'I think I am more with you in heart and mind by keeping myself a little afar now. When what should be said can be said – call me.' (Villa d'Este, 8 October 1868)

However, he did return to Rome for his birthday towards the end of October, leaving again for Tivoli the next month from where he wrote to Carolyne to reassure her of his well-being:

> Things could not be better for me here. My rooms are very nice – there are carpets, two fireplaces, and all the comfort I could need, plus the view of the Roman Campagna with the dome of St Peter's and its *bambinello*,[19] the dome of the Madonna del Rosario, on the horizon. I see them continually from the terrace, from my turret window, and even, without having to move, from my desk. For such a view, one would give all the royal and imperial palaces in the world! (Tivoli, 17 November 1868).

---

19. 'Little brother'.

Crisis with Cosima

Liszt's continued to be withdrawn and somewhat depressed throughout much of 1867 and 1868 and his mood may also be explained by his distress at the impending breakdown of his daughter Cosima's marriage to Hans von Bülow. This is a very important area of Liszt's later life of which his own surviving letters up to late 1868 provide only small hints. To Agnes, he appears not to have mentioned the matter in his correspondence, despite his frequent mentions of both Wagner and von Bülow's musical activities. Perhaps this was because Liszt knew that she was well acquainted with Wagner and was interested also in meeting von Bülow.

Did Liszt appreciate how bad the relationship between Cosima and Hans had become? He had spent much time with his daughter, but had she been able to truly confide in him about Hans' irascible and neurotic behaviour towards her? We know from her diary that she suffered greatly around the time of the birth of her second child Blandine in March 1863 and it is probably no coincidence that later that year she began her emotional involvement with Wagner. Their first child Isolde was born in April 1865, although Hans publically accepted her as his own. It is an interesting question why Hans continued to tolerate this situation, even after the birth of another child, Eva, in 1867. Throughout this time, he remained director of the Munich opera house and conducted Wagner's work to great acclaim, including the premiere of *Die Meistersinger von Nürnberg* in June 1868. Perhaps he could not break free from his devotion to Wagner's music. Like his father-in-law, he was dazzled by the man's talent. As Liszt commented to Agnes: 'If I had to write a book on Wagner, I would happily use as an epigraph this remark by Victor Hugo on Shakespeare: "I admire everything" – "I admire like a fool".' (Rome, 13 June 1868)

The surviving letters of Liszt to Cosima give little or no indication of the situation that had developed. We know, of course, that Cosima destroyed many of her father's letters to her. However, a hitherto unknown letter from Liszt to Cosima was discovered among the papers of Cosima's half-sister Claire de Charnacé[20] in an archive in Versailles, in time to be included in the third volume of Alan Walker's biography of Liszt. It

---

20. Probably Claire had received it from Cosima with whom she had a good relationship. Claire was the second daughter of Marie d'Agoult, born in 1830 before Marie left her husband for Liszt. Claire married Guy de Charnacé in 1849.

appears that Cosima had written to her father telling him of her intention to ask Hans for a divorce and join Wagner. Liszt responded vehemently in a long letter which is included in full in Walker's translation.[21] The following citation provides only the first two paragraphs:

> Where are you going? What are you telling me? What! Everything is dead for you except a single person to whom you think you are necessary, because he says he cannot do without you? Alas, I can foresee that this *necessity* will soon be an encumbrance, and by possessing you in this fashion, you will necessarily become inconvenient, annoying, contrary to him. Although you might well only want to live for him, that would not be enough at all, and would hardly be feasible because fatal poisons would begin to seep from the rock on which you aim to rest yourself.
>
> God save me from judging you wrongly. I know that 'nothing infamous, nothing low, nothing futile is subjugating you' but you have become giddy and are dissipating the vital and holy forces of your soul by sealing an evil deed with approval. This perversion, this adulteration of God's gifts breaks my heart! ...
> (Rome, 2 November 1868)

This final intervention of Liszt in Cosima's marriage situation was ill-advised since it should have been clear to him by now that Cosima had already made her decision. Hilmes, who has written a biography of Cosima as well as of Liszt, notes that there is evidence from a later letter which Cosima wrote to a friend that she had primarily written to ask her father to provide support to Hans after the divorce and was shocked by her father's accusatory tone – as well as by the fact that he subsequently wrote to Hans to ask him to withhold his consent to the divorce.[22]

Nevertheless, the letter reflected Liszt's view of the situation at the time. He sets out his arguments against Cosima joining herself to Wagner in sufficient detail and, if it had been written four years earlier, it might have been a more convincing letter. Although Liszt had misjudged Wagner's genuine devotion to Cosima, his concerns were justified by his friend's past behaviour with women. Moreover, his worries about the couple's future were understandable in view of Wagner's unpopularity in Munich and the possible ending of King Ludwig's support for him.

---

21. Walker, *The Final Years*, pp. 135-36.
22. Hilmes, *Franz Liszt: Musician, Celebrity, Superstar*, pp. 219-20.

Equally, his worries about Hans, who had so far been the most loyal of acolytes to Wagner's career, were fully borne out by Hans's subsequent descent into long periods of mental disorder. However, his calls to respect the sanctity of marriage and provide a good model for her children were weakened by the model Liszt himself had provided.

All in all, this letter indicates that Liszt badly misunderstood his daughter. Compared to her sister Blandine, Cosima seems to have been a much more complex character. Liszt had known the risks his daughter was taking by marrying a man of Hans' psychological vulnerability and been concerned about them himself. When, in very trying circumstances and feeling neglected by her husband, she fell in love with Wagner, who in return made such a strong romantic appeal to her, she was put in the impossible situation of being thought 'necessary' to two men who, to complicate matters further, were in the closest of working relationships.

At least Liszt did his best in the following years to support Hans in his new situation, living without both Cosima and Wagner. Since he could not be expected to continue as musical director in Munich, he needed to find other work. Early in the new year of 1869 Liszt called in on Hans, his mother and two daughters in Munich on his way to Weimar, and, while in Vienna in the spring, he took the trouble to travel back to Regensburg to a concert Hans gave there before journeying on to Pest.

Return to Weimar and a Travelling Life

Carl Alexander had long been attempting to bring Liszt back to the musical life of Weimar and had designated new accommodation for him in the court gardener's house, the Hofgärtnerei, a two-storey villa backing on to the Goethe park. Its decoration and furnishing had prepared under the close supervision of his wife the Duchess Sophie. Not only would Liszt have been impressed by the care taken on his behalf but the general welcome from the people of Weimar must also have surprised him. Already in his first months there, in 1869, he received many visitors and began organising masterclasses for the pianists who wanted to learn from him. One of his first visitors was the famous mezzo-soprano Pauline Viardot-Garcia, who arrived in Weimar with her husband and family and long-term companion, the Russian novelist Ivan Turgenev. Liszt played the piano in a public concert to fill a gap in the programme and was pleased by the Weimar orchestra's performances of his own works. In all of Liszt's activity the Grand Duke took an even greater interest than before, attending many of his masterclasses.

Disappointment and Conflict (1865-71)

As Liszt's return to Weimar must have been even more disturbing to Carolyne than his move from Rome to Tivoli, he took pains to keep up a close correspondence with her in which he stressed not only his musical work but also the debt he owed to her in helping strengthen his Christian faith. He stressed that he felt her presence still in Weimar: 'Monday, 8 February[23] I spent with God and His well-loved servant – whose memory is imprinted here on everything I look at. At 8 o'clock I took communion at that same altar where after long years you made me find the God of my childhood again.' (Weimar, 12 February 1869)

He also wanted Carolyne to know that, despite the successes he had achieved both in Weimar and Pest, he was not reverting to the socialising lifestyle of his younger self. He would have realised that this would have been one of Carolyne's main concerns. He wrote from Pest about his firm intention to live differently and in a way she would approve:

> From Augusz's letters and the newspapers you know that my little run of successes is continuing. The first concert, last Monday, was a complete success – and this evening's will not fail either. On Sunday I had the honour of dining at Court, in a small gathering – and afterwards of producing for the Queen my little talents of a superannuated old pianist. ... As for my relations with society, I keep very much to myself – it being my most decided intention no longer to depend on the salons, where I expect to gain nothing. My path lies elsewhere – in Him who is the Truth and the Life! You taught me it – and I bless you for it, and pray for you with all my soul! (Pest, 30 April 1869)

Just before he returned to Rome, he wrote to Carolyne from the Italian border of his plans to compose two new works, a 'St Stanislaus of Poland' and a 'St Stephen, King of Hungary'. He asked her to assist him both in his compositions and in keeping him free from other commitments: 'My passion for composing is keener than ever. I need only remain quietly in my room – and leave three quarters and a half of visitors at the door. Help me in this, I entreat you – no greater kindness can be done me! See you Sunday!' (Sagrado, 6 May 1869)

It is from 1869 that we are able to continue reading, after a gap of almost nine years, Liszt's regular correspondence with Carolyne's daughter Marie, now for ten years Princess zu Hohenlohe-Schillingsfürst and

---

23. Carolyne's birthday.

living in Vienna. From this we know that he visited her in Vienna where he stayed with his cousin Eduard. How one wonders did Carolyne respond to news of Liszt's contact with her daughter? A clue is given by one of Liszt's first actions on returning to Rome. He corresponded with Marie about 'a plot he was hatching' to have a portrait of her mother commissioned. He had found a suitable artist, the director of the French Academy in Rome. For this he needed her to write to Carolyne saying that she wanted to place such a portrait in her salon in Vienna. Marie agreed to do this. This seems to be one of the ways Liszt was trying to bring mother and daughter closer together again. Liszt had clearly recovered, if indeed he had ever lost it, his close relationship with Marie.

Princess Marie de Hohenlohe. Photograph taken in the studio Atelier, Vienna 1870.

Liszt had also met Agnes again in Vienna while she was busy with her intelligence work on the developing conflict in Europe. Back in Rome he wrote to tell her of his intention 'to cloister myself in the Villa d'Este's turret'. Pope Pius had announced a new council of the Catholic Church beginning in December and Liszt feared an influx of visitors to Rome. He stressed his need for disengagement:

> The moment has come for me not to waste too much time any more with hundreds of old and new acquaintances. But for my firm resolve not to neglect what I hold as a *prime* duty, I would have freed myself a long time ago from the social obligations of town life and would be living in rustic simplicity, doing as I pleased in some Hungarian village. Books, music-paper, a mediocre little spinet, and a church, that is all I would need to achieve perfect happiness, which is clouded constantly by every other worldly and harassing thing. (Rome, mid-September 1869)

He showed that he did not intend Agnes to consider herself to be one of those excluded by asking her whether she too was intending to come to Rome for the Vatican Council. If so, Liszt hoped that the visit would bring Agnes 'as much pleasure as you will bring me'. He added a postscript to this letter praising Napoleon III yet again: 'You can always be sure of giving me extreme "pleasure" by speaking well to me

Disappointment and Conflict (1865-71)

of Napoleon III, whom for twenty years I have had the good sense to admire as the greatest man anywhere in this century, of which he is the crowning glory.'

His final letters of 1869 showed Liszt in a sombre mood. In a letter to Baron Augusz, confirming his plans to visit Szekszárd for a music festival the following summer, he explained his 'withdrawal' from Rome to the Villa d'Este:

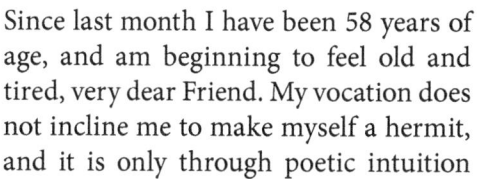

> Since last month I have been 58 years of age, and am beginning to feel old and tired, very dear Friend. My vocation does not incline me to make myself a hermit, and it is only through poetic intuition that I sometimes exclaim: *O beata solitudo, o sola beatitudo!*[24] But I feel a pressing need to live rather quietly from now on, and no longer to waste too much time with anybody and everybody. Consequently, during the remaining days that God leaves me in this world, I wish to isolate myself from common pleasures, worries, successes, and disappointments, so that I can concentrate the best of my powers on two works: our *Sz Tűz és Víz*[25] – and *St Stanislaus* (a Polish oratorio in whose text I am passionately interested).
>
> That will be my *Nunc dimittis*! (Villa d'Este, 9 November 1869)

Princess Carolyne de Sayn-Wittgenstein. Portrait by Ernest Hébert 1873.

A short while later, on 27 November, he wrote to Carolyne telling her the funeral arrangements he wished for himself: 'without any pomp', no 'summoning of friends and acquaintances', no 'eulogizing, nor speeches of any kind', no sung requiem but a low mass at the place of death and burial in a cemetery at the place where he died.

During the winter months Liszt worked on a major revision of a cantata he had first composed in 1845 for the unveiling of the Beethoven statue in Bonn. This was to be performed the following May in Weimar as part of the music festival to be held in celebration of the centenary

---

24. 'O happy solitude, O sole happiness'.
25. 'Holy Fire and Holy Water' – referring to his planned oratorio, *St Stephen, King of Hungary.*

of Beethoven's birth. The letters which he wrote to Carolyne, Marie and Augusz show Liszt in peaceful, contented and grateful. Besides telling Marie about his musical compositions, he wrote sweetly and prayerfully to her on her birthday reminding her of previous birthdays which they had celebrated together at Weimar and giving her reassurance for her future:

> You are a sincere Christian and a most worthy, infinitely charming woman. All else will come to you in good time, and in abundance. So let's not worry; and look instead, as it has been taught us to do, at the birds of the air and the lilies of the field, keeping complete faith in Our Father's goodness. (Rome, 18 February 1870)

Back in Weimar again he wrote regularly to Carolyne. On 20 April he described the reception of a carpet which she had sent to the church for Easter and which he now saw every morning laid out at the foot of the altar. Five days later he wrote thanking her for inspiring him in the right direction:

> It is 5 years to the day since I entered holy orders. I bless God for it every day, while asking Him to shower His blessings upon you – you, to whom above all I owe the fact of being able to walk on the broad and luminous path of His commandments. *Et meditabar in mandatis tuis, quae dilexi!*[26] (Weimar, 25 April 1870)

He may well have felt Carolyne needed this reassurance because later in the same letter he explained that he would not be returning to Rome as he had told her before. He needed to stay longer than planned in order to witness the performance of five of Wagner's operas in the Weimar theatre and also wanted to take the opportunity to travel to see the Passion Play in Oberammergau. He would then travel directly to Hungary to help Augusz organise the music festival in Szekszárd before returning to Rome at the beginning of October. However, he added that he would return to Rome earlier if she 'thought it advisable' – a surprising turn of phrase.[27] As events turned out, Liszt left Germany for Hungary

---

26. Psalm 118/119:47, 'And my study was in Thy commandments, which I greatly loved.'
27. Most likely Liszt was referring to issues around the political situation in Rome.

very much in a hurry at the end of July. France had declared war on Prussia and even the troops of the Duchy of Weimar were mobilising in support of Prussia.

The Franco-Prussian War and Its Aftermath

In January 1870 Émile Ollivier was asked by Napoleon III to form a government. As Alan Walker suggests, there is a strong possibility that Liszt himself influenced his son-in-law to leave the opposition in the French Chamber of Deputies and to support the policies of the Emperor.[28] However, Liszt's long-held hopes for European peace and harmony were dashed by the subsequent war with Prussia. It led to Napoleon's disgrace and the collapse of the Second French Empire, to German unification under Prussia and the threat of ever more deadly conflicts between France and Germany. Unfortunately, there seem to be no surviving letters between Liszt and Émile for this period which is perhaps understandable considering Émile's heavy involvement in affairs of state.

On 15 July it was Ollivier who told the French nation that it was at war with Germany. In an unfortunate turn of phrase, he added 'with a light heart', by which he meant, he said later, 'with a clear conscience', but it was his original expression that was remembered. Two weeks later Napoleon III placed himself at the head of the French forces assembled at Metz and sent two divisions across the new west Prussian border to take the town of Saarbrücken. However, within days the Prussian army had counter-attacked, driven French forces back across the border and advanced itself deep into French territory. By now Liszt had arrived in Hungary at the house of his friend Baron Augusz, thus avoiding being in Germany during a war in which his sympathies were fully with France. He was accompanied by some of his new pupils from Weimar. Nonetheless, he could not ignore the serious events occurring in France when he wrote to Carolyne:

> One feels almost ashamed of talking about oneself just now. Yet I must tell you that I could not feel better here – and that I hope to put my time to fairly good use by writing a few pages of music. Augusz remains, as ever, the staunch and excellent friend that you know. (Szekszárd, 3 August 1870)

---

28. Walker, *The Final Years*, p. 215, footnote 7.

Twelve days later, as the war raged on, he wrote a short note to Marie about the value of the Christian faith in times of difficulty. Perhaps he had read in the newspapers that Ollivier had already been voted out of office and his successor had placed Paris in a stage of siege:

> Even on the most troubled days, there is a certain peace for those who have the signal felicity to be Christians. It is this continuous, ineffable, indestructible peace, the summation of all the goods here below, which is besought for you from the Celestial Father by your old servant F.L. (Szekszárd, 15 August 1870)

To Carolyne his messages expressed his growing concerns:

> If the Empire were to collapse, I should personally feel extremely sad. I absolutely do not believe that the personal rule of Napoleon III has been corrupting and oppressive for France – but quite the contrary, it is demonstrably necessary, conciliatory, progressive, and genuinely intelligent and democratic in the best sense of the word. (Szekszárd, 31 August 1870)

The decisive and brutal battle of Sedan was fought on 1 and 2 September. The Germany artillery was deadly accurate, obliterating all in its path. Napoleon III was forced to surrender and himself captured by Prussian forces. His folly in deciding to lead French forces into battle in person was now obvious. Back in Paris there was revolution with the crowds demanding republican rule again. The Prussian army under General von Moltke advanced on Paris, laid siege to the city rather than attacking, and gradually starved the population into surrender four months later. There were more immediate consequences elsewhere. The remaining French troops left Rome and on 20 September troops of the new Kingdom of Italy entered Rome, and Pius IX was obliged to disband his own papal forces and surrender all his temporal power, retaining only the territory of the Vatican itself. Italian unity had finally been achieved.

German headquarters were established in the Palace of Versailles outside Paris and it was there on 18 January 1871 that King Wilhelm of Prussia was proclaimed 'Kaiser' of the new German 'Reich'. The armistice signed ten days later required the French to agree not only to a huge war indemnity plus the costs of maintaining a German army of occupation in eastern France until it was paid, but also to the German annexation of the eastern provinces of Alsace and Lorraine. To add insult to injury, a victory march of the German army was required through the Arc de Triomphe. In Paris the uprising of the 'Communards' led to civil war in the city which it took the French army four months to put down, while the German army remained camped outside the city.

All of these events must have been very distressing for Liszt and the consequences for him can be read in his correspondence. On 4 September he wrote to Carolyne: 'as Voltaire predicted, the century of the Prussians has at last arrived!' The distraction of news on the changing power relationships in Europe prevented him from working on the compositions he had previously had in mind: 'To my regret, I have not been able to begin *St Stanislaus*. I feel little in the mood for work – the greater part of my days is spent reading newspapers, books, and music.' (Szekszárd, 28 September 1870) However, he ended the same letter with reassurance about his own state of health: 'My mental and physical health is perfect – so much so, that I feel this absolute liberty, indicated by Pascal: to know how to sit quietly on a chair. Even the chair is almost too much – if it broke, one would be able to avoid falling and to remain standing!'

Liszt's relative tranquillity was also bolstered by his warm reception in Hungary. He was urged to settle in the country and invited to take on an official position in Hungarian musical life. This presented Liszt with a new challenge and a problem which he had to resolve within his own mind and heart. Had he not promised to himself to focus on composition in this the last stage of his career? He presented the dilemma to Carolyne and indicated to her that, although his mind was not made up on the matter, it was also not something he could lightly refuse:

> I have in no way desired it, and shall undertake it only after deliberation – as someone who would far prefer to remain ignored in some quiet corner. Although I am told that the press is coming out unanimously in favour of my settling in Hungary, and that in the Chamber and at the Ministry the question of funds to be obtained for the establishment of a new national Conservatoire under my direction or presidency will shortly be resolved, I am by no means persuaded of the matter, and am totally on my guard. Nevertheless, you will understand that it would not be proper for me now to quit a country where I am shown such honourable goodwill – and which is my own. (Szekszárd, 13 October 1870)

However, as on previous occasions in his life, Liszt could be swept up in the emotions of the moment. On 22 October his birthday was celebrated in style at his friend's villa. On the evening before he was greeted by the townsfolk who assembled outside and was serenaded by a gypsy band. After Liszt attended mass the next day, there was a banquet at the end of which he gave a short but remarkable speech of thanks:

> St. Francis of Assisi had a pupil who would have liked to know what his master said during his prayers. So he listened to him, but on the first morning he heard only these words: 'O my Lord!' On the following morning he heard the very same words. There is nothing I can say either, as this idea contains within itself all that is great, sublime, and noble. Therefore when I turn to my Lord I also remember my friends, for whose devotion and friendship I can only show myself worthy if I devote my activities hereafter to my country.[29]

He seemed to have come close to committing his future to Hungary.

However, a few days later he wrote candidly to Marie expressing his concerns:

> The huge events that startle the world also bear on my little existence. I had planned to return to Rome during the first days of October; but considering the actual state of things, I would be a great deal of trouble to myself, and superlatively useless to everyone else. Thus it wasn't much of a task for them to persuade me to prolong my stay in Hungary; and as you know, it's a question of keeping me there even longer. ... No matter what happens – and I still hope that nothing does happen, since I am so terrified by the prospect of being thrown back into an active career! – I have promised to go to Pest in mid-November and conduct the *Beethoven-Festival* Concert in December. (Szekszard, 27 October 1870)

On 22 December Liszt was visited by the Hungarian prime minister Gyula Andrássy, who told him that the government intended to establish a National Academy of Music and wished him to become its first director. Liszt did not give a direct answer but a short time later accepted the position, with a stipend, of Royal Hungarian Councillor. Therefore, as

---

29. Cited in ibid., p. 226.

a consequence of the Franco-Prussian war Liszt stayed a total of nine months in his native country, the longest period since his childhood. He thus avoided the events in France and in Rome which would have been distressing to him and did not have to witness Prussia's final triumph in Weimar itself. By the time the armistice was signed, Liszt had even given up all interest in politics. He wrote to Carolyne on the subject: 'After the fall of Emperor Napoleon – in whom I had unlimited faith, and whom I continue to respect and admire for the great things he accomplished – I have become totally uninterested in politics. I read the newspapers only out of force of habit.' (Pest, 17 February 1871)

Although Liszt's chosen language had been French from his youth, he had always insisted that not only he but also his children should be considered Hungarian. The disaster that befell France in 1870-71 seems to have led him to identify even more strongly with Hungary.

The war had greater consequences for a number of Liszt's family members and friends. The unfortunate Émile Ollivier had been disgraced and his home in Paris severely damaged by fire, along with many other public buildings, in the conflict between the Communards and the new republican government. His possessions were destroyed along with many documents, including Anna Liszt's early correspondence with her husband and mementoes of Liszt's childhood. By then Émile had left Paris with his son and new wife to escape the general wrath of the population and crossed over into Italy. Agnes and her father had also fled France for destinations unknown. No doubt they would have had to remain hidden for a while in the new Prussian-dominated Europe. There appears to have been no correspondence between Agnes and Liszt during this period and, even if he had wanted to write, he would have found it very difficult to trace her.

Berlioz had died the previous year and thus missed this humiliation of the French nation. Wagner by contrast had delighted in the Prussian victory and all that had led up to it. He exalted the new Kaiser with his newly composed *Kaisermarsch* and wrote a poem in praise of the German army which he sent to Bismarck. The Iron Chancellor replied telling Wagner that in his music he too had defeated the French. More surprisingly, considering her French upbringing, Cosima appears to have shared fully in Wagner's celebration of German superiority, writing in her diary of her pleasure at the progress of 'our splendid Germans' and their subsequent bombardment of Paris.[30] She had come to fully identify with Wagner's increasingly nationalistic mission. He

---

30. See ibid., p. 223, footnotes 27 and 28.

indeed may have played an important role in the German victory by having persuaded King Ludwig to abandon his neutrality and commit to the Prussian cause. It was his Bavarian troops which began the Battle of Sedan by crossing the river Meuse and attacking the French positions.

Carolyne shared in Liszt's distress and witnessed at first hand the end of more than a millennium of papal rule over Rome. Liszt was pleased when she wrote to him in praise of Emperor Napoleon III but did not feel able to share her hope in the restoration of monarchic rule in France. Above all, he lamented that the war had dashed his hopes for the early dawning of a more pacific Europe:

> What a dreadful and heart-rending thought: that 18 centuries of Christianity, and a few more centuries of philosophy and of intellectual and moral culture, have not delivered Europe from the scourge of war! How much longer are we going to go on cutting one another's throats? When will the precepts of religion and the dreams of humanity succeed in achieving something positive? ... Oh! may God take pity on future generations, and may duels, wars, and the death penalty be abolished for ever! (Pest, 4 March 1871)

A casualty of the war amongst Liszt's younger friends was one of his early Parisian pupils Hermann Cohen, now Father Augustine of the Carmelite order, whom Liszt had last met in Rome in 1862. The huge number of French soldiers taken prisoner in the war had been sent to various prisons in Germany. Heroically, Father Augustine volunteered to go and tend the sick and dying Frenchmen in Spandau prison in Berlin. He died there in January 1871 as a result of typhoid which he had contracted from the prisoners. Although his death remained unknown to Liszt, his life witnessed the Way of the Cross that Liszt honoured.

6

Pursuing Divergent Goals (1871-76)

'The Three-Branched Life' – Rome, Weimar, Budapest

Despite Liszt's repeated appeals for a quieter existence, he was in his sixtieth year starting on a demanding lifestyle, more akin to the travelling days of his *Glanzzeit*. Ten years before he had taken a gamble in leaving the comparative security of his musical directorship in Weimar and beginning a new life in Rome. Although he had been faced by an immediate crisis with the last-minute refusal of the Vatican to allow his planned marriage to Carolyne to take place, he had been welcomed in Rome, including by the Vatican itself. Four years later he had partially realised his own long-nurtured vocation to the priesthood and entered the ranks of ordained clergy. At the same time, he had continued to be creative musically, writing for the most part music of a religious character. Nevertheless, despite his continued commitment to his religious status, he had decided against further advancement and was no longer sure that he wanted to remain living in Rome. Any musical interest the city had offered him had by now waned and he felt strongly the need to return to the centre of European music making. It must have been painful for Carolyne to realise that he now only came to Rome because of her.

Liszt's experiences in the years since his ordination had troubled him greatly. There had been the rejection of his music in Paris, where his career as a pianist had begun. More recently, there had been the violent and humiliating ending of Napoleon III's Second French Empire whose ideals Liszt had strongly supported. He had been compensated to a large degree by the interest and warmth shown him by his native country.

He was now well established there and had developed deep friendships. However, to commit himself to a new position of responsibility for the development of music in Hungary was not what he desired since his prime wish was to continue composing. Moreover, he had recently agreed to the invitation from his friend the Grand Duke Carl Alexander to return to Weimar and take a more active part again in musical events there.

Personal worries must also have been uppermost in Liszt's mind. He had distanced himself from Cosima, his only surviving child, by persistently refusing to accept her wish for divorce from his former pupil Hans von Bülow and remarriage to another close friend of his, the highly creative but egocentric Richard Wagner. He now probably regretted his harsh letter of 1868 and wanted to make peace. Indeed, he had taken a first step by sending a telegram to greet Wagner on his birthday on 22 May 1870.[1] However, he was disappointed not to be told in advance of Wagner's marriage to Cosima later that summer in a Protestant church soon after Hans had been granted a divorce. Liszt as always had welcomed Wagner's success, most recently in persuading the town of Bayreuth in northern Bavaria to grant him land to build a theatre large enough for him to have his Ring cycle of operas, the *Der Ring des Nibelungen*, performed to his original intentions.

Liszt would have had major concerns too about Carolyne, his loyal partner for more than 20 years, and still the most important person in his life. She had given up so much to follow him in his career move to Weimar, been cruelly disappointed by the machinations of others which had prevented the annulment of her first marriage, but had now achieved a level of serenity living in Rome. Even though Liszt and Carolyne had decided not to marry after her husband died in 1864, they remained partners and each had granted the other authority to execute their wills. Carolyne had encouraged Liszt in his initial moves towards the clerical state but perhaps by now would have been disappointed that he had decided not to proceed towards the actual priesthood. She would certainly have been very concerned that he was seeking to return to his former travelling lifestyle. She may have also felt some resentment that he had agreed to live outside Rome in Tivoli in the residence of Cardinal Hohenlohe, the man who had done more than anyone to block their marriage. She would have also had some doubts about how Liszt's musical career would develop in Germany and Hungary, especially without her direct guidance.

---

1. Cosima's diary entry shows that she welcomed her father's telegram.

Europe in 1870 and the principal
destinations of Liszt's 'Vie Trifurquée'

Piano concert by Liszt in the Redoutensaal in Budapest, attended by Emperor Franz Joseph, 18 March 1872. Oil Painting by Schams and Lafitte.

Liszt had begun what he came to refer to as his *vie trifurquée*,[2] alternating between residence in Weimar, Rome and Budapest. In all three places he was admired and fêted. His reception the previous year in Hungary had given him particular pleasure and he looked forward to further visits there. He was happier, too, in Italy now that he had place in the countryside where he could work on his compositions in relative tranquillity. Moreover, the Grand Duke and Duchess in Weimar had gone out of their way to welcome him back and encourage his musical presence in their Duchy. Nevertheless, there would have remained many question marks in Liszt's mind about exactly what would be expected of him in each of his three destinations.

That Liszt had made a definite decision to spend much less time in Rome is indicated by his letter written in early 1871 to his manservant Fortunato Salvagni to release him from his service after nine years. He understood that he could not expect Fortunato to follow him on his travelling life as he needed to remain living near his wife in Rome. Liszt thanked him sincerely for his years of service but also took the opportunity, as he often did with fellow Christians, to strengthen his religious practice:

---

2. 'Three forked/branched way of life'.

> Man's real happiness and high dignity are found only in the observance of the precepts of our holy religion, whose rewards and promises are the only desirable and certain ones. Let us remain firmly attached to it until our last breath, my dear Fortunato, and count on the sincerely affectionate feelings of your old *padrone,* who knows no profitable satisfaction in this world other than that of humbly serving our Lord Jesus Christ! (Pest, 22 January 1871)

Correspondence would from now on become the main source of communication between Liszt and Carolyne. This was something that they had done a lot of in the past. However, composition of a letter needs more care and consideration of its impact on the receiver. Remarks made in conversation can more easily be corrected if they are seen to arouse discomfort. Moreover, delays in correspondence can also be misinterpreted. A small early hint of unease is the concern Liszt expressed at the absence of a reply from Carolyne when he decided to travel back to Weimar from Hungary via Vienna, where he stayed with his cousin Eduard, and Prague, rather than coming back to Rome first. In the past Liszt had been used to sometimes daily correspondence with Carolyne and was worried that she had not replied for more than a week:

> I sent you a telegram from Vienna yesterday to say that I had received no letter from Rome since 22 April, the day of my departure from Pest. Although I profess permanent satisfaction and tranquillity, I admit that I couldn't understand this unusual silence. … The last time I spent a week in Vienna, it was only a convenient stopping-place. After having spent the entire winter in Pest, I thought it absurd not to make a few visits in Vienna. Magne[3] invited me to dinner, and a very brilliant soirée – on Tuesday and Wednesday. Eduard was invited to both dinner and soirée. I played the *Glanes de Woronińce,*[4] a Nocturne by Chopin, at the request of Prince Konstantin. (Prague, 2 May 1871)

---

3. Liszt and Carolyne's pet-name for her daughter Marie.
4. The 'Harvest at Woronińce' was composed by Liszt and dedicated to the young Marie in 1847 while staying at Carolyne's estate in Woronińce (Voronivtsi). The music included three elements: (1) a *Ballade d'Ukraine;*

He had presumably wanted to be reassuring but his closeness to Marie and her husband could well have been still troubling to Carolyne who had not recovered her earlier close relationship with her daughter.

Liszt also had to face some discomfort from his hosts on his return to Weimar as he was asked to explain his position on the recent Franco-Prussian war. He explained to Carolyne:

> Reaching Weimar at 5.00pm on Wednesday, I was on Friday received by Their Highnesses with the most perfect grace – and a little more! It seems I have been reported as guilty of anti-German feeling. I had it out straightaway with the Grand Duchess and Monseigneur, without hiding from them that the fall of Ollivier's government was a personal sorrow for me. I stood firm by my grateful admiration for the Emp. Napoleon – despite his terrible final blunder, the culmination of everything that had gone on before – alas! – and made still worse by France's faults! (Weimar, 7 May 1871).

Carolyne did reply to him once he arrived in Weimar and in so doing provided one explanation for her previous delay in writing, as Liszt acknowledged in his reply: 'Thank you for the dear little picture of my Patron Saint – and for every line of your dearest last letter of 1 to 4 May, written despite rheumatism in your arm.' (Weimar, 10 May 1871)

As spring turned to summer, Liszt regularly shared with Carolyne his news from Germany. These included the invitation that came to him from one of Wagner's friends to be part of the group seeking to fund a performance of the complete Ring in Bayreuth; the tragic early death with typhoid of his brilliant pupil Carl Tausig, which had affected Liszt greatly; and his attendance at a meeting of the Society of Saint Cecilia in Bavaria for the reform of church music and its better integration with liturgical worship. He also wrote to Baron Augusz to thank him for finding him a suitable abode for his future stays in the Hungarian capital and took the opportunity to express his appreciation for all he had done for him over many years. There was, Liszt noted, a special harmony between the two of them. Liszt returned at last to Rome in September where on 22 October he celebrated his sixtieth birthday with a dinner at Santa Francesca Romana. Princess Marie arrived especially for the occasion and was thus united with her mother. His past pupils

---

(2) two Polish folksongs, the second of which had been written by Chopin; and (3) a *Complainte*.

Hans von Bülow and Giovanni Sgambati both came too, as well as Father Agostino Theiner and other ecclesiastical and diplomatic figures in Rome. Liszt described to Augusz how pleased he was to see Hans again and that his health and career had recovered. Both Hans and Sgambati accompanied Liszt in duets on a second piano which Sgambati arranged to be brought to the building.

On his return to Pest in November, Liszt experienced a major scare when his life was threatened by a tempestuous and unstable former Ukrainian pupil, Olga Janina, who burst into his apartment with a revolver in hand. She claimed to be a countess and had first come to Rome to study with Liszt two years earlier. She had also been part of the student group which the previous winter had accompanied him to Weimar for the Beethoven festival and then to Pest. Unsurprisingly, many of Liszt's biographers have given a lot of attention to Olga Janina, but it seems improbable that he bore a major responsibility for her disturbed behaviour on this occasion. No doubt he had been too indulgent to her because of her pianistic talent and misjudged where her fiery and unstable character might lead her. Obsessed with Liszt, she had begun to feel abandoned by him when her career in the United States, where she had travelled at his suggestion, failed to flourish.[5] His subsequent rejection of her appeals for help provoked ideas of vengeance which she had made plain in letters to him.

That he was already highly concerned about Olga is revealed in Liszt's correspondence earlier in the year both to Carolyne and to Baron Augusz. She had, he wrote, been 'nourishing her mind' on the anarchist theories of Proudhon and the poetry of Baudelaire's *Fleurs du mal*. To his credit, Liszt appears to have reacted calmly to the dangerous situation with which he was confronted and he managed to pacify her. Augusz and another musician friend came to Liszt's aid and insisted that Olga leave Pest. Nonetheless, his letters show that he was clearly shaken by this episode, asking Carolyne 'not to talk about it – even to me.'[6]

Most of Liszt's correspondence with Marie between 1871 and 1872 appears to be missing, perhaps because Marie lost some letters following the death from diphtheria of her eldest son Franz Joseph, aged ten years, at the end of November. We know from his letters to Carolyne that he wrote a letter of condolence to Marie from Pest and that he also visited her at the end of December when he travelled to Vienna. He came to hear

---

5. See Hilmes, *Franz Liszt: Musician, Celebrity, Superstar*, pp. 236-37, and also Walker, *The Final Years*, pp. 171-90.
6. Letter from Liszt to Carolyne 29 November 1871.

a performance of the first part of his *Christus* oratorio, which describes the Gospel scenes concerning the Nativity of Christ. This took place on New Year's Eve and was conducted by Anton Rubinstein with Anton Bruckner on the organ. His friends praised it and he too was pleased with the performance. However, the musical critics in the Viennese press were as usual less kind, praising his personal qualities but without 'the gifts necessary for a high-ranking musician'. He responded in religious mode in his letter to Carolyne:

> So be it! I shall remain in better company with the shepherds who heard the voice of the Angel – announcing peace to men of goodwill! During their journey the Three Kings will admit me to into their retinue. ... We shall thus proceed by the light of the Star of Bethlehem, and shall ascend the stations of Golgotha while blessing the God of Truth and Mercy! (Vienna, 6 January 1872)

Liszt's *Christus*, considered by present day experts to have been the composer's greatest artistic creation, is still insufficiently known and rarely performed. Why this should be so is difficult to explain. It is a long work lasting almost three hours. However, even excerpts from it are little heard, despite their great beauty. For example, 'The Three Kings', the last section of the 'Christmas' part of the oratorio contains one of Liszt's most majestic and memorable orchestral melodies. Once heard, never forgotten.

Olga von Meyendorff – A New Correspondent and Confidant

Liszt's sixtieth year marked not only the beginning of his 'three-pronged' life but also the beginnings of his correspondence with an important new confidant, named Olga von Meyendorff.[7] Liszt and Olga had first met during Liszt's early years in Rome when he was invited to musical events at the home of husband, Baron Felix von Meyendorff, the Russian ambassador to Rome. Olga herself came from a noble family; she was the daughter of Prince Mikhail Gorchakov, who had successfully defended Sevastopol in the last days of the Crimean war, and was more distantly related to the current Russian foreign minister,

---

7. See Tyler (ed.), *The Letters of Franz Liszt to Olga von Meyendorff, 1871-1886*.

Prince Alexander Gorchakov. She was a talented pianist whom Liszt had already mentioned in a letter to Agnes in 1863. Three years later Baron Felix was expelled from Rome after a quarrel with Pope Pius IX over Russian actions in Poland. He then worked for a period in the Russian Embassy in Weimar, where Liszt again met the couple when his *St Elisabeth* was performed in 1867, before being appointed ambassador to the court of Baden in Karlsruhe. He died suddenly in the beginning of 1871 leaving his widow, aged 32, with four small sons to bring up. At this very difficult and critical point in her life, she turned to Liszt for advice as she wanted to continue living in Germany.

The alacrity of Liszt's response implies an already closely developed sympathy and affinity of outlook. Indeed, the first letter we have from Liszt to Olga indicates a strong emotional bond between the two of them, even when one takes into account Liszt's often poetic and romantic style of writing:

> Your words penetrate the depths of my soul – and awaken in it more than merely a memory. Will I be worthy of the sentiment, enigmatic but overflowing with conviction and loyalty, which you have vowed to me? I know not, and hardly dare think so. Since our last meeting in Rome my inner sorrows have deepened. To make others share them would weigh on me as a wrong, and for the years still allotted to me I feel capable only of a kind of passive perseverance in conformity with Christian precepts. (Pest, 31 January 1871)

Olga von Meyendorff (1838-1926).

In understanding Liszt and Olga's relationship we are hampered by having almost no further information on Olga's attitudes and activities other than what is suggested by Liszt's answers to her. His second letter, written only one week later, show that Olga had swiftly made the decision to move with her children to Weimar. Liszt expressed his approval and immediate support, and his willingness to be of service to her there, and continued to write regularly to Olga during his travels between Rome, Pest and Weimar for the rest of 1871. Many of the subjects are the same as those in his letters to Carolyne, such as Wagner's plans in Bayreuth, the death of Carl Tausig, and Liszt's interest in the future of church music, but there are also differences. For example, he and Olga also regularly corresponded on church affairs but in this year particularly on the conflicts within the Catholic Church in Germany following the Vatican council. Olga seems to have shown special interest in these matters. She attended a meeting in Munich in the spring of 1871 at which the 'Old Catholic Church', which refused to accept the new doctrine of papal infallibility in teaching on faith and morals, was established.

Liszt also gave advice on accommodation in Weimar and, as with Agnes, the choice of a suitable piano teacher for her children. He asked for news about Weimar, as well as Bayreuth, and they regularly shared views on literary and philosophical subjects. These included Nietzsche's *Die Geburt der Tragödie aus dem Geiste der Musik*, a copy of which the author had sent to Liszt with a note saying that he saw him (Liszt) as a 'remarkable exemplification of the Dionysiac phenomenon'! As Liszt commented to Olga in January 1872, it would be 'fairly hard for me to reply to the author so as to please him' and that she was correct in commenting that much of the book ran 'counter to my feelings and to my manner of thinking and acting'. Liszt did in fact write a tactful letter[8] back to Nietzsche the following month praising him for the quality of his writing and thought but also making clear that his own focus was on 'Tabor and Golgotha' rather than 'Parnassus and Helicon'.[9]

Of particular interest are Liszt's personal remarks about himself. He refers with regret to his lack of 'epistolary talent', urges her not to pay attention to most of the things said about him, and confides in her the closeness he feels towards Hans von Bülow, describing him as 'practically my son'.[10] What is already striking is that Liszt seems more prepared to disclose his own negative, painful and depressive feelings with Olga than with others. Referring to a recent letter he had received from Cosima on Wagner's Bayreuth development, he contrasted the new theatre director's optimism with his own more pessimistic outlook:

---

8. Letter from Liszt to Friedrich Nietzsche in Basel on 29 February 1872 included in Williams: *Franz Liszt: Selected Letters,* p. 742.
9. Liszt names important mountains in Classical Greece, as well as the sites of Christ's Transfiguration and Crucifixion, and indicates that 'his soul turns unceasingly' to the latter rather than the early Greek thinkers and writers who fascinated Nietzsche.
10. Letter from Liszt to Olga von Meyendorff on 23 October 1871.

> He has the advantage of not being unduly awed by the difficulties of the Bayreuth undertaking and of 'seeing things through rose-coloured glasses', an advantage I appreciate all the more in that I have it so little. I am usually given to seeing things neither in rose nor in black, but in grey – half in mourning: and even so I have to make a certain effort of will not to see things more sombrely still. (Rome, 23 October 1871)

After his confrontation with Olga Janina in Pest in November, he wrote to Olga von Meyendorff in a similar vein as he had written to Carolyne 'to spare him the pain of a more detailed account'. His comments to her after he received less than complimentary reviews of his *Christus* oratorio in Vienna are also similar to those which he sent to Carolyne. They confirm his Christian response to disappointment, but he also expresses himself in a less serene and less secure manner: 'As for me, I have only reached the stage of a kind of sad resignation regarding men and events, sometimes tempered and as though illumined by faith in divine providence, and invincible hope in Christ's redemption!' (Budapest, 28 February 1872)

Liszt had clearly found a new soulmate in Olga who reciprocated his need to share mutual concerns. We are very fortunate that Olga, like Carolyne and Agnes, preserved his correspondence. It provides an insight into Liszt's mental state in his last fifteen years which is distinct from that provided by his letters to his other long-established correspondents. The letters passed into the possession of her youngest son Alexander after Olga's death. After he sold them to come to the financial help of one of his brothers, the correspondence was lost from sight until it fell into the hands of a wealthy US collector in the 1950s, who in turn donated it to Harvard University as part of the Dumbarton Oaks collection held in Washington, DC. The letters still await publication in their original French, existing in book form at present only in William Tyler's translation into English, published in 1979.

The publication of Liszt's correspondence with Olga von Meyendorff had a major influence on attitudes to Liszt's character, correcting the damaging stereotypes spread by earlier biographers. Robert Craft, the distinguished American musician and conductor, provided an early review, in which he drew a comparison with the attention Liszt biographers had been giving to Olga Janina and that which should now be paid to this 'new Olga':

> The book alters the received notions of Liszt's character and personality, and wholly reverses the portrait of his later years

as drawn in Ernest Newman's anti-hagiography.[11] ... The only Olga in his biography is Janina, the young 'Cossack' Countess, whom Liszt had seduced and who, in 1871, pursued the sixty-year-old composer from New York to Rome, and from there, pistol-packing, to Budapest. Rebuffed, and smarting from the humiliation, she avenged herself in two scarcely readable books, among the many by women who had known Franz Liszt. The story of the Baroness von Meyendorff could not offer greater contrast, for though the relationship of this attractive young widow to Liszt can only be assumed by his behaviour patterns, she never broke her silence about him.[12]

For Liszt's psychology and attitudes over the last sixteen years of his life, the correspondence with Olga von Meyendorff is a major source of understanding, of equal if not more importance than that of his letters to Carolyne. Liszt appears to have written to Olga from the very beginning of their relationship with an unpretentious honesty, revealing his current mental state without evident reserve or ulterior motive. Crucially, his letters to Olga provide an alternative self-presentation to the one provided in his letters to the other important women in his life.

Reconciliation with Cosima and Wagner

The year 1872 saw Liszt's reconciliation with his daughter and Wagner, but a corresponding deterioration in his relationship with Carolyne, who appears never to have accepted Cosima's divorce nor her conversion to Protestantism. Carolyne had expected Liszt to remain firm in his disapproval and, initially, he had appeared to remain distant from the new couple. He indicated in his letter to her of 21 April that, despite encouragement from friends, he would not be attending Wagner's concert to mark the laying of the foundation stone of the new concert hall in Bayreuth in May. However, although Liszt kept his promise to Carolyne not to attend, when Wagner sent him a warm personal letter of invitation, he wrote back equally warmly in a letter that he entrusted to Olga to deliver personally to the Wagners in Bayreuth. In it, he clearly acknowledged, probably for the first time, acceptance of Wagner's marriage to Cosima:

---

11. E. Newman, *The Man Liszt: A Study of the Tragi-Comedy of a Soul Divided Against Itself* (London: Cassell & Co., 1934).
12. R. Craft, 'The New Liszt', *The New York Review*, 5 February 1981.

> Profoundly moved by your letter, I am unable to thank you in words. But it is my ardent hope that all shadows and considerations which bind me at a distance will disappear – and that we shall soon see one another again. Then it will become clear to you, too, how inseparable my soul remains from *both of you* – living again in your 'second higher life', in which you can achieve what you could not have achieved alone. Therein I see Heaven's amnesty! God's blessing be with both of you, as all my love! (Weimar, 20 May 1872)

However, he now had the problem of explaining his change of attitude to Carolyne. Initially, he avoided the subject but eventually had to be honest with her:

> My old bruises have prevented me from speaking to you in detail about the Bayreuth question. Here is a copy of Wagner's letter and of my reply. One always falls in the direction in which one is leaning – God will forgive me for coming down on the side of mercy, while beseeching his and wholly committing myself to it! (Weimar, 21 June 1872)

Liszt wrote in successive letters to Carolyne, begging for her understanding, denying that he no longer paid attention to her views, expressing his continuing devotion to her and his attempts to be in accord with her wishes for him, including going to mass every day. He pleaded for understanding of how busy his musical and social life in Weimar was and asked her again whether she would be prepared to join him there as before. He urged her to share her writings with him and stressed that he was close to her in spirit:

Richard Wagner with his wife Cosima. Vienna, 9 May 1872. Photograph by Fritz Luckhardt.

> Won't you communicate some few fragments of them to me – or do you regard me as too inept? Unfortunately I have scarcely any time left to read – however, the amount I give to sleep I shall gladly reduce in order to absorb your thoughts more thoroughly. Do believe and be aware that the physical distance between us does not remove me from you

> in spirit. It weighs on me a lot, it is true – and sometimes I think of ways of ridding myself of it. (Weimar, 30 July 1872)

He told her that, when he saw her again in Rome in September, he would be able to tell her 'everything I have on my mind. It will be a general confession, impossible to make in writing – after which I shall serenely await death!' It would be well over a year before Liszt returned to Rome.

At the beginning of September Wagner and Cosima came to visit Liszt in Weimar. On 8 September Liszt wrote to Carolyne to explain. Wagner had written beforehand to ask whether their visit would be 'an annoyance' for him: 'I had not written a word either to Wagner or to my daughter. In such circumstances I could not refuse him: it would have been contrary to my character.' As a consequence of their meeting, Liszt agreed to go to stay with them in Bayreuth. Liszt went on in his letter to remind Carolyne of how she had cared for his three children in the past and thanked her again for this. Cosima was still his daughter, he stressed, 'altogether worthy of the feelings of admiration she inspires in those who know her'. She had dedicated herself absolutely to Wagner and would be 'the saving of him'.

Carolyne remained unpacified and wrote back letters implying that Liszt was acting selfishly for choosing the attractions of Wagner's music over Carolyne's love for him: 'You want it, whatever the cost – and in wanting it you trample my heart underfoot.'[13] She went further in accusing him of betraying his Christian vocation and associating himself with Wagner's 'anti-Christian dogma'. Liszt stood firm, even indicating that he was intending to visit Bayreuth on his birthday, which provoked a further verbal attack from Carolyne. In fact, he visited the Wagners a few days earlier and he confided in Cosima the arguments with which Carolyne was trying to prevent him from seeing them. Cosima noted in her diary how 'torn apart' her father seemed.[14]

Liszt spent 22 October alone, the first time for many years, in a hotel in Regensburg, en route from Bayreuth to Vienna. From the hotel he wrote to Carolyne, telling her that he had attended mass where he had 'prayed for you with all my soul'. He also described his recent experiences in Bayreuth, the rise of Wagner's new *Nibelung* theatre and how he had shared the family life of the Wagners with their five children. He praised

---

13. Cited by Hilmes, *Franz Liszt: Musician, Celebrity, Superstar*, p. 249.
14. Cited in ibid., pp. 249-50.

his daughter: 'Cosima surpasses herself! Let others judge and condemn her – for she remains a soul worthy of the *gran perdono* of St Francis and admirably my daughter.' (Regensburg, 22 October 1872)

He also took pains to defend Wagner from Carolyne's accusations of being anti-Christian. A week later he described the sketch of Wagner's *Parsifal* which he had been shown, explaining to Carolyne that it was 'stamped with the purest Christian mysticism' and he regarded it as superior in religious feeling to several of our poets 'deemed religious and Catholic'. Liszt took care in this letter to express his admiration also for Carolyne's own writings on spirituality, while noting that their creative efforts diverged, and asked for God's blessings on her own 'chosen path'.

Liszt's aim of maintaining closeness both to Carolyne and to his daughter had come under severe stress, and he was fortunate to have someone else to whom he could confide his troubles. At the beginning of June, he complained to Olga of feeling confused and compared himself with the incompetent judge Don Guzman Brid'oison in Beaumarchais' *The Marriage of Figaro*: 'No knowing what to say was Brid'oison's mode of thinking. I'm just about at that stage myself, and on the verge of completely losing the use of words which correspond to my mode of thinking and feeling.' (Weimar, 4 June 1872) In the same letter he told her that he had acquired a cross to place at his bedside and that the Cross was part of his regular practice of prayer:

> I often repeat to myself the words of St. Paul: 'We must place our glory in the Cross of Jesus Christ', and in Rome I used to repeat in St. Peter's Square this prayer: 'O crux, ave, spes unica',[15] ... grant to the just increasing grace, and to sinners forgiveness of their faults.'

In October he wrote to Olga consoling her for own concerns. She had worries about her third son Clement's health and encountered difficulties with her accommodation in Weimar:

---

15. 'Hail to the Cross, our only hope.' An important Christian expression, added in the 10th century to the ancient Latin hymn 'Vexilla Regis' ('the Royal Banner') and exemplified in the Feast of the Exaltation of the Holy Cross, 14 September (the day on which Liszt had written his will in 1860). Liszt's setting of 'Vexilla Regis' was to provide the opening of his last major religious work 'Via Crucis'.

> You err in saying that sorrows do not make people kind. I am in love with yours, and being unable to rid you of them, I feel drawn to them and share them. If I could deliver homilies I would dedicate one to you on this text: 'prosperity was the blessing of the Old Testament and afflictions is that of the New.' (Schillingsfürst, 10 October 1872)

Later in the month he confided to Olga, a little self mockingly, his experience of women's complaints against him. This shows that she must have already been rather well acquainted with his life story:

> I have always had the misfortune of hearing those I love best tell me that I did not love them much. In Geneva Mme d'A[goult] felt that the Conservatoire Helvétique ... was closer to my heart than she; and she it was who was convinced of the absolute truth of the advice given her by one of my friends, never to count on me should any fad or any occasion to shine attract me elsewhere. Later, when I published the *Symphonische Dichtungen*, Princess W[ittgenstein] accused me of thinking only about Härtel [Liszt's publisher], and now you sweetly insinuate that I write to you 'as I do to Riedel'.[16] (Vienna, 28 October 1872)

Back working in Hungary for the winter, in the now conjoined city of Budapest, Liszt wrote regularly to Carolyne, Olga and Marie. The characteristic tone of these letters varied with their recipients. To Carolyne, he wrote to reassure her both of his continuing links to her in her daily life and of his attention to his religious duties. He also asked understanding for his busy life and his slowness in writing:

> It grieves me to write to you so little. Today, however, my conscience is not too bad, for I have written several pages of music this week. Now, you know that to express myself through letters is not easy for me – I attempt it only in certain hours, of which I always need several to stitch together forty lines or so. The fault lies in my very neglected early education – and in the long years of my anti-literary habits. I write to you as I pray and work: conscientiously, slowly, and with humility. Kindly take account of this frailty of my nature, which worsens with

---

16. Brendel's successor as president of the Allgemeine Deutsche Musikverein.

age. Perhaps I am more to be pitied than condemned! Besides, nobody is less acquainted with leisure than I – my days and years are wasted in not finding the hours I would seek! The happiest of my hours is now that in which I kneel near a few poor old women in my parish church, or in the Franciscan Church, during morning mass. Lighting my *cerino*,[17] I share it with a royal joy – while blessing the gentle yoke and light burden of Our Lord Jesus Christ.

The evening of Christmas Eve I spent *en famille* at the Auguszes'. No other guest but myself. (Budapest, 27 December 1872).

To Marie, Liszt explained his need for disengagement. He asked her particularly for help in excusing him from becoming involved in the forthcoming Beethoven commemoration events in Vienna. He felt it inappropriate to repeat what he had already done for the Beethoven statue in Bonn in 1845. He was also still concerned about subjecting his own work to public scrutiny in Vienna. As always, he expressed appreciation of the understanding Marie typically showed him:

Your kind words concerning my answer to the Beethoven Committee calmed me. In stopping myself at the preamble to what I wrote Mosenthal [the Beethoven events organiser] in July, I do not claim to exclude myself completely from the affair; it is only that I feel neither the age nor the inclination to draw my sword. Others younger and more sound than I ought to take this chance to advance themselves. (Budapest, 10 December 1872)

However, it was only to Olga that he expressed the depth of his concerns and his depressed moods during this period. He had written to her of feeling so 'crushed' that it was 'becoming almost impossible for me to raise himself up a little'.[18] He was struggling to find time to compose music and felt distraught at the number of letters he had to write. Early in January of 1873 he wrote to her using a musical analogy: 'My middle note, the one which tied me to life, has disappeared – there remains for me only the tonic and the dominant, which becomes a terrible dissonance when it rises to the augmented fifth.' (Pest, 7 January 1973)

---

17. Wax paper or candle.
18. In an undated letter of 1871-72, in Tyler, *The Letters of Franz Liszt to Olga von Meyendorff*, p. 68.

This was the month that he received news of the death of Napoleon III in exile in England. He composed a long and eloquent tribute to his fallen hero in a letter to Carolyne which she subsequently showed to several members of the Bonaparte family who lived in Rome. In it he expressed the wish that one day Napoleon III's coffin would rest alongside his uncle's in Paris. Olga sent Liszt a photograph of the ex-emperor on his deathbed which he framed and placed near his writing desk in Pest.

His correspondence over the following months emphasised his wish for withdrawal from the world. All he wanted, he wrote to Olga, was to attend mass regularly and on important feast days to 'go to confession in order to draw near to the sacrament of Communion in Jesus Christ our Lord'.[19] To Carolyne's question about his will, he wrote that he wished to be clothed in his coffin in the habit of the tertiary order of St Francis, as his 'last homage to the great saint who carried out his apostolate as a "madman of the Cross"' and repeated that he wished to be 'spared the honours of an ostentatious funeral'.[20] That there was now a strong depressive element in his moods is clearly evident from the closing paragraph of a letter to Olga: 'Forgive me for not writing longer. I am not sick and am doing almost nothing; nevertheless it is becoming sometimes rather difficult for me to continue living here below. ... While this lasts, I beg you to grant me your indulgence and compassion.' (Pest, 19 March 1873)

A psychological question that arises is whether Liszt was suffering from what is now called seasonal affective disorder. His previous episodes of low mood had also tended to occur in the wintertime.

In the spring Liszt began his travels again, first to Vienna, where he stayed with his cousin Eduard, and then on to Weimar where on 29 May he conducted the first complete performance of his oratorio *Christus* in the presence of both his daughter and Wagner. There is no sign of depression in his correspondence in this period, although, of course, he was not writing to Olga but seeing her regularly. It does seem that the spring and summer of 1873 were rewarding times for him with further major performances of two of his other major religious choral works the *Gran Mass* and the *Missa Choralis*. Later, in July, he went to stay with the Wagners in Bayreuth and in September played the piano at the celebrations for the wedding of the Hereditary Grand Duke in Weimar.

---

19. Letter from Liszt to Olga on 22 January 1873.
20. Letter from Liszt to Carolyne on 6 March 1873.

Attending to Carolyne

In October 1873 Liszt finally returned to Rome after an absence of two years and, as he told Olga, spent most of his time 'talking with Princess W.' They had much to talk about. Carolyne was displeased that Liszt was now living much more of his life in Budapest and in Weimar rather than closer to her in Rome. As a consequence, she had begun to exclude him from her own intellectual life. However, earlier in the year she had sent him drafts of the first two volumes of a major critical work she was writing on the state of the Catholic Church. Alan Walker suggests[21] that taking up this task helped her to come to terms with the frustrations arising from her battles with and eventual defeat by the Church's authorities over the annulment of her marriage. In this work Carolyne argued that the Church had made a mistake in disengaging from modern society rather than attempting to shape it. Although she was well qualified by her education and intelligence to undertake such a task, one which would remain an important issue for the Roman Catholic Church right up to the present day, she was writing at a particularly sensitive time. There was virtual warfare within the highest ranks of the clergy between the liberal 'whites' who supported separation of church and state power and the conservative 'blacks' who rejected acceptance of the loss of papal influence in the new Italian state.

Liszt understood these dangers better than Carolyne. He had always been sympathetic to those like Lamennais and Rosmini who had argued for a greater engagement by the Church in social and political affairs. Indeed, his growing friendship with Cardinal Hohenlohe, who had become one of the major internal critics of current Vatican policy, was probably based in part on their shared wish for greater rapprochement between the Church and civic life. However, Liszt was also a loyal Catholic who accepted the Church's requirement of obedience to papal authority. He was no longer the young idealist who had taken up with the Saint-Simonist movement and later with Lamennais. In his letters to Carolyne during the preceding months Liszt had demonstrated increasing concern about what he had read in her latest writings. He had cautiously approached the subject with Carolyne, expressing 'admiration' mingled with 'amazement' and 'even ... fear', and advised her that distribution of copies should be done 'only with much prudence'.[22] He had queried the

---

21. Walker, *The Final Years*, p. 323.
22. Letters from Liszt to Carolyne of 7 and 8 August 1873.

title of the work. Nonetheless, Carolyne had gone ahead and published the first two volumes of *Des causes intérieures de la faiblesse extérieure de l'Église*[23] in July. Initially, it attracted much praise from liberal quarters but Liszt still remained concerned. As with his earlier doubts in 1861 about Carolyne's annulment, he appreciated that dominant forces in the Church had yet to fully show their hand.[24]

After celebrating his birthday with Carolyne and attending a personal audience with Pope Pius, he returned to Hungary by way of Vienna. Back in Budapest he began preparing for the splendid celebratory events which the Hungarian authorities organised to mark the fiftieth anniversary of his public career. This was dated to the 'legendary' occasion in 1823 when Beethoven came to see the talented young pianist play in Vienna and kissed him on the forehead. This culminated in a court reception, the award to him by Emperor Franz Joseph of an honorary stipendium of 4,000 florins a year, and his performance at the Emperor's charity concert in Vienna.

During this period, he wrote a series of letters to Carolyne reflecting on the success he had achieved with *Christus* but, more importantly, that this had allowed him to demonstrate the continuity of his religious feelings and fidelity to the Catholic faith, shown also in his taking of religious orders in the Vatican. He stressed to her that he was not seeking merits but was only pleased that he had gained 'the reputation of being a man of trustworthy character'.[25] His speech at the event in Budapest came spontaneously and had been well received: 'It seems, however, that I made a good impression – and even several newspapers which usually praise only my talent as a pianist vouch that I displayed neither vanity nor ridiculousness.'[26]

He told Carolyne that the golden laurel wreath he had received, together with previous gifts kept in Weimar, including a gold baton for conducting that she had given him, he intended to place in the National Museum in Budapest.

However, as the winter progressed Liszt again began to show signs of weariness. He had started January positively with an upbeat reply to Carolyne's New Year telegram suggesting to him that they once again live together. He replied immediately and positively that it 'expresses

---

23. 'The Internal Causes of the External Weakness of the Church'.
24. In July 1877, Volume 5 of Carolyne's work was placed by the Vatican on its Index of Forbidden Books, followed by Volume 3 in February 1879.
25. Letter from Liszt to Carolyne of 19 November 1873.
26. Letter from Liszt to Carolyne of 19 November 1873.

the supreme wish of my heart' and 'I pray to God to grant it'.²⁷ Could he have really meant this? It is hard to know since he seems often to have submitted to others' requests in the passion of the moment. He also wrote with enthusiasm of his composition plans, including his ideas for a *Via Crucis*: 'they will by no means be works of learning, or of display, but simple echoes of the emotions of my youth – these remain indelible through all the trials of the years'²⁸. Two weeks later, however, he told her that he was feeling 'extreme mental fatigue' and expressed amazement at receiving a further volume from her in which she formulated 'an entirely new constitution for the Church'.²⁹ Having read it more carefully, he wrote again a week later to repeat his concern:

> It is repugnant to me to tell you lies, or to write to you in the rather meaningless way that I do often enough to other people – and so all that remains to me is to vex you more often than I would wish.... There is no point in my saying to you once again that several of your ideas strike me as unsound. ... Nevertheless, in reading the 3rd volume of your *Causes intérieures* I admire from the bottom of my heart your great militant spirit, while following it timidly and not without some terror. (Horpács, 23 January 1874)

The next month he wrote to her in emotional terms, perhaps relieved by her response to his previous letter, thanking her in the strongest terms ('rapturous gratitude') for the letter she had recently sent him, praising her intelligence, assuring her of his strong religious belief, and expressing modestly his own ambitions for the future. There is a strong integrity of expression to the wording he uses in this letter – his aim as a musician has been 'to hurl my spear into ... the future' – which has been rightly seized upon by Liszt biographers:

> Yes, dear holy Carolyne, I am a sincere believer and man of religion, and shall remain so to my very last breath. Believe me, accordingly, when I say that I pursue neither decorations, nor performances of my works, nor eulogies, distinctions, and newspaper articles, anywhere at all. My sole ambition as a musician has been, and will be, to hurl my spear into

---

27. Letter from Liszt to Carolyne of 1 January 1874.
28. Letter from Liszt to Carolyne of 1 January 1874.
29. Letter from Liszt to Carolyne of 16 January 1874.

> the undefined void of the future. ... So long as this spear be of good quality and fall not back to earth, the rest is of no importance to me whatsoever! ... I kiss your hands. (Horpács, 9 February 1874)

However, underneath this positive surface, Liszt was suffering considerable strain and depression is evident in his regular correspondence to Olga: 'you know how harassed I am from all sides' (2 January); 'I am swamped by my epistolary task, which grows daily. If things go on like this, ... I don't know what will become of me' (8 February); 'I beg my friends on the banks of the Ilm [in Weimar] to think of me as dead. This will inconvenience no one and will be a relief to me' (3 March); 'In May, I shut myself up in the Villa d'Este; if people make my stay there uncomfortable, I shall think about shutting myself up elsewhere' (30 March); 'various minor tasks preoccupy and disturb me all the time. I need still another month before I can fully turn into my sad self again' (7 April).

Yet, at the same time, he was also making efforts to support Olga with her own personal problems, encouraging her to confide in him, and giving her much spiritual advice. He urged her to have trust in God and not to despair, referring repeatedly to the importance of praying to 'Our Father': 'Ah, believe me, I beseech you, we must kill the hateful ego within ourselves; and then divine mercy and its truth will shine once again within us when we ask Him to "forgive us our trespasses as we forgive those who trespass against us".' (Horpács, 8 February 1874)

In April a resurgence in conflict between Carolyne and her daughter over Marie's husband's family brought Liszt further pain. He wrote to Marie about it:

> Several passages in the letter from Rome have upset me, without surprising me: last October, I was told almost the same thing *orally*, so that my conscience caused me to drop a few hints to you. ... I do hope that these frightful shadows will disappear, and that it will be given me to help bring about the return to Christian clarity and serenity. (Pest, 14 April)

Liszt clearly sympathised on these matters with Marie and he praised her for her 'admirable restraint, worthy of the noble, tender daughter who understands how to be both a wife and a mother'. A few days later, having spoken to Marie and to her husband in Vienna, he wrote to Carolyne to try to mediate:

> Lately my relations with Marie have taken on the character of a new, serious intimacy on account of you. In a few words, she had privately expressed to me, and has made me understand her filial affection – true, deep, and tender. On his side, Prince Konstantin has taken me into his confidence by speaking of you without any false verbosity. He has assured me that he would be quite ready to display his devoted gratitude to you by coming to Rome, if it were necessary. (Vienna, 17 April 1874)

By now Liszt had recovered a sense of purpose and had come to realise that he needed to spend an extended time in Rome in order to support Carolyne in her increasingly troubled life. He explained this both to Olga and to Cosima and that as a result he would not be coming to Weimar or attending Bayreuth this year. It was not primarily, as he had suggested before, that he wished for a period of 'rustication' at the Villa d'Este, but that he needed 'to have several lengthy talks with Princess Wittgenstein on matters relating to my will, of which she is to be the executrix, and on two other no less serious topics'. He went on to explain that he wished to be able to help Carolyne bear her difficulties, stemming from her 'loss of all civil rights by the Russian government':

> Since then, something more sacred has merged with my deep love for and inexpressible gratitude to her. She has revived my conscience and kept alive the few good qualities with which I have been endowed. (Letter to Olga, Pest, 10 April 1874)

Olga's subsequent letter greatly displeased Liszt by, presumably, commenting on Carolyne's excessive influence over him. He replied insisting on his independence and that, contrary to what others had said, it was his decision to enter religious orders. He strongly defended Carolyne to Olga. He also pointed out to her how pained he was by the fact that the Grand Duke and Duchess never mentioned Carolyne in his recent visits to Weimar, despite the fact that she had lived there with Liszt as court musician for thirteen years. He reiterated that 'in the present situation it is absolutely my duty to go to Rome, and that it is entirely of my own accord, without anyone else "prescribing" it, that I go there'. He had already agreed with Marie that together they should encourage her mother to move from her present apartment. However, he ended this letter on an encouraging note while referring to both his and Olga's 'sorrows': 'To your sorrows, I could, alas! only reply with my own, which are better left unexpressed. Inertia and despair are false remedies, and too pagan; let us scorn them.' (Budapest, 27 April 1874)

Liszt resisted pressure to contribute to various music festivals in Germany and elsewhere and succeeded in arriving in arriving in Rome on 21 May. He was happy to be back at the Villa d'Este, as he wrote to Augusz, Olga, Marie and (in the following excerpt) to Carolyne:

> Having arrived at the olive grove, I made my way to the Villa on foot, in a beautiful sunset – tranquilly thinking back on many things. For many years the belief that the end of my life will be a good, sweet one has been familiar to me. It does not grow weaker, and I am far from treating it as illusory. May I only finish my journey while fighting the good fight and serving the faith! For the moment, it suits me extremely well to stay here at the Villa d'Este. Everything pleases me here: landscape, atmosphere, trees, bells, rooms, memories – and there is nothing in any of them to bother or disturb me! This morning I enjoyed arranging my books and music on the shelves; soon I shall reread *St Stanislaus* and set it to music. (Villa d'Este, 8 June 1874)

His peace was not to last long. Carolyne's health condition was worse than he had expected. He wrote to Marie in confidence:

> I have something on my mind to speak to you openly about, and to you alone, concerning M. ['Minette']. ... She is very tired, bowed down by her excessive work, troubled so badly by her eyes that she can scarcely read without effort; encumbered morning and evening with correcting proof, sickly, given to homeopathic doses, worried by the onset of a serious illness, extremely discontented with the two persons working for her, whom she scolds continually for their lack of brains and care: – to sum up, she is in a very distressing nervous condition.
>
> She insists that she finish, without interruption, the 4th big book of her last work; 'following that', she says, 'I'll give myself one month of rest away from Rome'. She hasn't left Rome for the past 14 years, and has stayed as if locked up in her room, and never leaves it for a walk. You know how incapable she is of accepting any ideas save her own; I don't dare risk suggesting anything to her, having so often failed. Up to now she hasn't picked out a place for her intended

Pursuing Divergent Goals (1871-76)

> country holiday, and she talks vaguely of Siena, Assisi, or of any small village whatsoever near Rome; but I'm afraid that it will be the same with this trip, as it is with all her plans for changing her residence. At the last minute she'll change her mind ... and won't budge. The only promise I've obtained from her, is that she will come to Weimar next May. This *initial* success has given me hope again for the future. (Villa d'Este, 10 June 1874)

Olga also caused Liszt pain by continuing her accusations and there was a critical exchange in which his painful memories of 'Nélida' resurfaced:

> In this noble zeal, Princess, Daniel Stern anticipated you by more than a quarter of a century. Her novel of indictment, *Nélida*, condemns me to loss of civil rights for possessing only 'sham' lofty sentiments and even genius. Consequently, I should be relegated to the company of the menials of Princes, and 'dine' with the scullions and broomsweeps who, contrary to the holy Christian law, are quite wrongly despised, in the servants' hall of Monseigneur the Grand Duke of Saxony. (Villa d'Este, 22 June 1874)

Liszt was clearly very angry as shown by the abrupt ending to this relatively short letter which he signed in his most formal way. Fortunately, postal services within Europe were so good that he could receive a reply and write a different letter two days later, although it was again expressed in rather strong terms for Liszt:

> Your last letter makes it again possible for me to write to you. So let us together celebrate the fifty-sixth anniversary of the birth of the Grand Duke of Saxony [Carl Alexander]. June 24 is moreover a great Catholic feast day: that of St. John the Baptist of whom Our Lord said, 'Among the children of men there has been none greater'.[30] It used to be the custom in Italy to celebrate this feast with magnificent fireworks. If this is still the case, I shall today burn there in my mind the whole file of my crimes together with that of your worries, torments, sacrifices, objurgations, and minatory ukases [edicts of the

---

30. Matthew 11:11.

> Russian Tsarist government]. For pity's sake, do not ask that I become an epistolary poodle. (Villa d'Este, 24 June 1874)

At least he had learned to be firm with Olga. Could he apply the same lesson to Carolyne?

To add to Liszt's stress, he had to answer a complaint by Carolyne's that he had not received an appropriate musical appointment in Rome. He patiently explained that, although he would have accepted such an invitation from the Pope, this would have been a difficult task and certainly not one which he wished that he possessed now. He was content with the way he had been received and treated in Rome. In successive letters he repeated that he was happy with his retreat at the Villa d'Este. Later in August, however, he became concerned that Carolyne had not recently replied to him and wrote a letter, again frequently quoted by Liszt biographers, reflecting on the difficulties he had experienced with women in his life:

> Are you perhaps unwell – or have I committed some new misdeed? If you do not send me a line, I shall not dare to come to Rome on Saturday as I was planning. The day before is the anniversary of the death of my father. On his death-bed, at Boulogne-sur-Mer, he told me that I had a kind heart and did not lack intelligence –but that he feared my life would be troubled, and I dominated, by women. Such a prediction was remarkable, for at that time, aged 16, I knew nothing about women, and naïvely asked my confessor to explain God's 6th and 9th commandments to me, fearing that I had perhaps broken them unwittingly. Later, my *amours* began only too sadly – and I resign myself to seeing them finish in the same manner! Even so, I shall never abjure Love, for all its profanations and false pretences! (Villa d'Este, 26 August 1874)

It is probable that Carolyne's silence on this occasion may have been caused by her deteriorating health. Liszt later wrote to Marie that her mother had been bedridden for two weeks and, in addition, had picked up 'the Roman fever' (a term used for malaria) and was so weakened that she could not bear a long conversation. He stressed that she could not bear to be contradicted and urged Marie to be careful how she wrote to her mother and that it would be best if she did not come to visit her in Rome until Carolyne was better. However, it seems that it was again only to Olga that he conveyed the depths of his low mood at this turn of

Pursuing Divergent Goals (1871-76) 169

events. In previous months he had repeatedly asked her not to enquire about his health nor to worry about him and she had written less to him as a result, but by mid-September he felt the need to confide in her: 'Thank you from my heart for what you have written since then, and especially for the adorable letter I received this morning. It finds me in a state of deep depression, and although I refuse to let myself worry, I feel nonetheless overwhelmed.' (Rome, 15 September 1874)

He went on to describe his very real concerns for 'Princess Wittgenstein', her long history of illness, painful physical condition aggravated by her long hours of sedentary work, lack of outdoor exercise, and refusal to change her way of life.

Unbeknown to Carolyne, Liszt travelled to Duino on the Austrian border for a short meeting with her daughter and to seek her advice. He then remained in Rome rather than returning to the Villa d'Este to keep an eye on Carolyne's condition. Throughout October Liszt gave Marie regular reports on her mother's health. At last, two months after the onset of the illness, he was able to tell Marie that Carolyne was sufficiently recovered to enter her 'encyclopaedic' working and living room. During her illness Liszt and Marie had made arrangements for Adelheid von Schorn[31] to come from Weimar to Rome to be Marie's 'representative' in caring for her mother. The plan was a success, with Liszt telling Marie that Carolyne approved of Adelheid's 'bearing and manners'.[32]

However, in the meantime, yet another blow had landed on Liszt. The other Olga, Olga Janina, had published her fictional reminiscences, *Souvenirs d'une Cosaque*, including detailed accounts of an affair with Franz Liszt. This was the revenge which she had promised on her teacher and mentor. She sent copies to Pope Pius, the Grand Duke Carl Alexander and other friends of Liszt, and subsequently wrote another book, *Souvenirs d'un pianiste*, under a fictitious name, which purported to be the response of the cited musician to his 'crimes'. Liszt first heard of the publication from Olga in July and seemed initially more amused than disturbed by the news: 'What horrors has the "Cosaque" then written? Were it not for my total lack of curiosity with regard to low deeds, what you tell of the slander by the "Cosaque" (whom I did not suspect at all of

---

31. Adelheid's mother Henriette von Schorn, a lady-in-waiting to the Grand Duchess, had been the one woman in Weimar who had befriended Carolyne in her difficult years living there.
32. Letter from Liszt to Marie of 10 December 1874.

sporting this pseudonym) would almost make me want to read it.' (Villa d'Este, 8 July 1874)

Perhaps it seemed to him a repeat, although on a more ridiculous scale, of Marie d'Agoult's *Nélida*. Nevertheless, enquiries from friends and acquaintances made him realise the seriousness of the situation and obliged him to issue a statement of defence.

News of the scandal also came to Carolyne's ears. She was more ready to believe the 'Cosaque's' account and told Liszt that she was not wholly satisfied with his explanations. She wrote to him that she 'prayed to God that reading the book does not cause you as much pain as it has caused me'.[33] Oliver Hilmes also describes how Carolyne wrote a confidential letter to Eduard in Vienna the following May telling him how offended she was by Liszt's persistent erotic affairs with women and that he Eduard should try to bring his cousin back to the path of honour. Confession of his sins to a priest in church was evidently not sufficient to change his behaviour.[34] Was Carolyne correct in her accusations about Liszt at this stage of his life? This has been an important topic of Liszt biographers and it will be discussed further in Chapter 9.

Around his birthday Liszt enjoyed welcoming his former son-in-law Émile Ollivier and his new wife to Rome. He also showed appreciation to Olga both for her increasingly friendly relations with Cosima as well as her support for Wagner's Bayreuth project. Yet it was clear he was struggling with himself even while living in the favourable circumstance of the Villa d'Este. Evidence for an underlying depressed mood is clear in his explanation to Olga of his delay in writing to Cosima as he wished: 'Unfortunately I can no longer hold a pen in the evening, and I don't really spend my days as I would like to. Do not ask me to explain; to go on living is enough … without any further explanation.' (Villa d'Este, 11 November 1874)

Later, in the same letter, Liszt restated the beliefs that sustained him. It was not to 'the man', depicted by modern thinkers such as Nietzsche, that he wished to become converted but to the God of Christian belief:

> Ah! believe me, dear beloved soul, let us leave to others more learned than we the perilous paths of thought, and let us remain united in heart to our heavenly Father and His Son Jesus Christ our Saviour! … We will breathe more easily

---

33. Cited by Hilmes, *Franz Liszt: Musician, Celebrity, Superstar*, p. 243.
34. Ibid., pp. 243-45.

there, and be better comforted than in Schopenhauer or Goethe, without diminishing ourselves or depreciating the higher intellects which are drawn to an ideal other than that, infinitely sublime and practical, of humility and Christian charity. Alas, eighteen centuries of Christianity have still imbued us very little with its truth and invigorating spirit!

Early in the new year Liszt was able to write to Marie to tell her that her mother was 'noticeably better' and that Adelheid was looking after her 'in the most perfect fashion' and instructing her carers in their duties 'with much tact and concern'[35]. Liszt was still hoping that Carolyne could be persuaded to come for a visit to Weimar in the summer and that Adelheid would accompany her on the trip. His own plans were to return to Pest in February, where among other commitments he had concert engagements together with Wagner, and after Easter to go to Weimar and await Carolyne. First, however, he had the problem of explaining to Olga why she should not come to Rome to visit him. Clearly, she was not satisfied with his explanation – 'your stay in this town would be aggravated by many sorrows, perplexities, and tribulations against which I could not defend you, nor could I find a remedy for them' – because Liszt had to write once more to reassure her that he had her best interests at heart.

Nonetheless, Olga did come to Pest in March and accompanied him to meet Richard and Cosima Wagner on their arrival in Hungary. At the concert in Pest on 10 March there was a performance of Liszt's recently completed cantata, *The Bells of Strasbourg Cathedral*,[36] together with excerpts from Wagner's Ring Cycle, both conducted by their respective composers. In addition, Liszt was the pianist for Beethoven's Fifth Piano Concerto and gave a performance which greatly impressed the Wagners. On 30 March he was presented with his appointment as President of the new Hungarian National Academy of Music. He then continued his travelling life of fulfilling various musical commitments throughout 1875.

In April he visited Vienna and Munich, for a performance of *Christus*, before returning to Weimar which would be his base until September. Visits to Hanover to hear a performance of his *St Elisabeth* and to play his Variations on Bach's *Weinen, Klagen, Sorgen, Zagen* at a concert in Eisenach were followed by a journey to the Netherlands to be a guest

---

35. Letter from Liszt to Marie of 18 January 1875.
36. With lyrics taken from a poem by Longfellow.

of King Willem III at the palace of Loo near Apeldoorn. Later in the summer, after visits to Wilhelmsthal and Nuremberg, he stayed with the Wagners in Bayreuth. Finally, he travelled to Leipzig to play at a private concert of his works, organised by the piano manufacturer Julius Blüthner, before returning to his third 'home' in Rome at the end of September.

Throughout this period his correspondence shows him determined to maintain his responsibilities but with little experience of joy in his personal life. To Marie on 30 May, he quoted Frederick the Great, 'one must find one's pleasure in doing one's duty', and told her that 'if it were up to me, I wouldn't budge from the place [Villa d'Este] except to be buried near by'. To Carl Gille, his long-standing friend and legal advisor in Jena, he wrote that his life was becoming if anything even more complicated: 'The *fourfold* division of my little life between Pest, Weimar, Rome, and the rest is very tiring and troublesome. And yet I have no reason to complain – rather to rejoice at my friends' kindness; and first of all at your devoted, long-standing, and loyal trustworthiness.' (Weimar, 23 June 1875)

Although Carolyne would not agree in the end to travel to Weimar in 1875, as he had originally hoped, Liszt continued trying to involve her in his life: asking her help in developing the texts for his planned *St Stanislaus* oratorio, sharing with her his enthusiasm for Wagner's genius and amazing achievements, still with the hope no doubt of changing her attitude to the composer, wishing her well with her own writing, thanking her for all the 'sweet things' in her letters, and admiring her steadfast remembrance of the artistic plans they had developed beginning with their original time together in Poland: '*Orare et laborare* – without respite!' Back in Rome, again, in September, he was able to write to Marie that her mother was in 'fairly good health' and involved again in 'her constant, prodigious intellectual labour'.

Liszt for himself was relieved to be back at the Villa d'Este and told Olga of his gratitude to Cardinal Hohenlohe:

> Since Saturday evening, here I am settled down again in solitude at the Villa d'Este. This spot pleases me above others, and I am deeply grateful to Cardinal Hohenlohe for having put me here – like the solitary sparrow in the Psalm. Music, the most communicative of the arts, is also the most lonely for those who plumb its depths. Beethoven tells us this sublimely in his last years. (Villa d'Este, 7 October 1875)

He also told her that he was not going enter religious controversy and would remain a 'timid and peaceful sheep' in the 'fold of the Holy Roman Church ... without a bleat'.

By mid-November he was complaining to Olga again about the burden of responding to the correspondence he received, which disturbed 'the little musical work' he wished to pursue. He was receiving 'nearly fifty [letters] a week', not counting shipments of manuscripts: 'the time required to peruse them, even casually, deprives me of the time needed to answer them. ... I don't know what will become of me in such a purgatory.'[37] He also, perhaps surprisingly, since she had discouraged his involvement, confided in Carolyne that the Budapest Music Academy had become both a 'millstone around the neck' and, mixing his metaphors, 'an appalling collection of swords of Damocles' as well. However, he added a note of resignation to his complaint: 'Fortunately another Greek, Euripides, has given us this good advice: "There is no point in getting angry with things, since that has no effect on them." We'll meet in Rome on Sunday evening. Like mahogany and violins, I hope in ageing to improve a little.' (Villa d'Este, 17-18 November 1875).

He was finding consolation in his regular correspondence with Marie:

> I am often reproached for writing too seldom and too little; I hope that You won't accuse me of the opposite. Your last lines calmed me again so well, that I couldn't delay thanking you from the bottom of my heart.
>
> May all the maternal 'wounds', with their accompanying procession of misunderstandings, disappear: this is my humble prayer to the Holy Father. ... I shall come to the Augarten [Marie and Prince Konstantin's palace in Vienna] to seek your kind and very helpful aid promised me for the *St Stanislaus*; and you will decide for me how to end this *Oratorio*. (Villa d'Este, 26 November 1875).

On 1 January 1876 he thanked Carolyne for her presents of flowers and fruit and also for the new watch which, he wrote, 'exhorts me to make good use of my time, in a way that will please you, and to make progress in the practice of the Christian virtues'. He also wrote enthusiastically about the idea they had formed together of publishing a second edition of their earlier biography of Chopin. Again, however, it was in his letters

---

37. Letter from Liszt to Olga of 20 November 1875.

to Olga that he showed that he was not as content as he often pretended to others. He complained of the amount of time he spent 'concocting tedious letters' and 'revising the manuscript of the big catalogue of my poor compositions'. His *Via Crucis* was still 'more in my head than on paper'. His surprisingly negative view of his creative work suggested his self-esteem had also reached a damagingly low level:

> To tell the truth, I have an increasingly poor opinion of my things, and it is only through my reaction to the indulgence of others that I manage to find them acceptable. On the other hand, I greatly enjoy many of the compositions of my colleagues and masters. They amply repay me for the tediousness and shortcomings of my own. (Villa d'Este, 4 February 1876)

In February he left for Budapest where, as he had told Olga, he realised he needed to spend more time in order to properly fulfil his obligations to the new Musical Academy. It was there that he read in the newspapers of the death of Marie d'Agoult. Her last years had been difficult ones with regular bouts of mental illness, including psychotic behaviour which had required her to be forcibly restrained. However, she had still continued to write, including fierce attacks against Bismarck after the Franco-Prussian war. Liszt would have probably known about Marie d'Agoult's last years via Cosima, who kept in contact with her mother through her half-sister Claire. His reaction to her death appears distant, cold and condemnatory, especially when one takes into account his normal generosity of spirit when judging others. He wrote first about her death to Carolyne:

> Mme D'Agoult possessed to a high degree a taste, and even a passion, for the false except at certain moments of ecstasy, of which she could afterwards not bear to be reminded! At my age, moreover, condolences are no less embarrassing than congratulations. *Il mondo va da sè*[38] – one exists in it, keeps oneself busy, frets, worries, deludes onself, thinks better of it, and dies as one can! The most desirable sacrament to receive, it seems to me, is that of extreme unction! (Budapest, 14 March 1876)

---

38. 'The world goes by itself.'

Pursuing Divergent Goals (1871-76)

Liszt also wrote to Olga, thanking her for having written to offer condolences to Cosima: 'As for me, the only thing to do is to keep quiet and to bury in silence the strange behaviour of Mme d'A. toward her children.' (Budapest, 15 March 1876)

His children with Marie were also uppermost in his mind when he wrote to Émile, who had remained close to his former mother-in-law and helped to edit her papers after her death:

> Thank you for having copied out for me Ronchaud's lines on the death of Madame d'Agoult. To make phrases does not become me: the memory I retain of Mme d'A. is a sorrowful secret; I confide it to God while asking Him to grant peace and light to the soul of the mother of my three dear children. (Budapest, 27 March 1876)

These comments are kinder but also demonstrate that Liszt had not come any closer to healing from the breakdown of the major relationship of his early adulthood. He seemed to cope principally by not engaging.

Clockwise from top left: Title page of Liszt's piano piece *Aux Cyprès de la Villa d'Este*; Contents of Liszt's *Années de Pèlerinage, Troisième Année*, 1883; Garden of the Villa d'Este, photograph taken c.1880, with a dedication in Liszt's own hand dated 1 January 1886 and addressed to his pupil August Stradal.

7

Bearing a Heavy Burden (1876-80)

Carolyne's Suspicions Become Intolerable

In his sixty-fifth year Liszt was struggling greatly. Moods of intense depression were now a regular occurrence and not only in wintertime. The demands on him had become greater and at times he seemed to be functioning at the limit of his own psychological resources. He had taken on major new musical commitments involving regular travel and, although he complained, he had no intention of reducing them. His sense of personal obligation would not allow him to withdraw from commitments he had accepted. Moreover, he had developed a passion for supporting original music wherever he felt it to be deserved. A letter he had recently sent to Olga illustrates that he had become interested in promoting the new music being created in her homeland:

> By the way, I have written to Riedel ... to say that I particularly want one or two orchestral works by the new Russian composers – Rimsky, Tchaikovsky, Cui, Borodin – to figure on the programme of the *Musikfest* at Altenburg next May. Should they fail to please at the first hearing, we will play them again – until people understand and applaud them. (Rome, 27 September 1875)

One task he would have gladly given up was answering correspondence but this, of course, was also impossible for the same reasons of duty. Letter writing seemed to tire him considerably and he attributed the difficulties he experienced to his lack of education when he was

Franz Liszt. Photograph by Friedrich Hertel, Weimar 1876.

young. Nevertheless, he seems to have enjoyed composing the long letters he often wrote to his closest friends and confidants. The many people who preserved his letters and subsequently assembled them bear witness to the quality and value of his letter writing. In this respect, as in so much else, Liszt demonstrated a poor self-evaluation.

As a result of his return to a more public musical lifestyle, he had been composing less in recent years. Since the completion of his *Christus* oratorio he had produced mainly small works for piano and also for voice. He had become frustrated by his lack of progress with projected larger works such as his long-planned oratorio on Stanislaus, the Polish saint. Carolyne had warned him that his composing would suffer as the result of his return to Weimar, as well as his taking up of new duties in Budapest, but her constant fault finding with Liszt was now the major cross in his life.

Carolyne's questioning of him had become very burdensome. When she asked him why he was breaking his journey from Budapest to Weimar by staying in Vienna on 2 April – perhaps suspicious that he would be seeing her daughter Marie on that day – he replied sternly:

> I was here on the same date last year and the previous years. During the sad variabilities of my life, I am happy to retain some fixed point of affection. My cousin Eduard being content with me, I most gladly celebrate with him on 2 April the feast of my patron saint, Francis of Paola, founder of the Order of Minims. (Budapest, 14 March 1876)

Carolyne made amends by sending a letter and bouquet to Eduard's house for Liszt to receive when he arrived, and he wrote back graciously, ending with a delicate reference to Carolyne's Polish background:

> I shall repeat with all my heart, and also my lips, the beautiful Polish prayer for all those I have caused to sin or have been unable to keep from sinning. As for my reply to your letter 'to be read on the train' – it could be written only in sobs! May the good angels protect you! (Weimar, 8 April 1876)

Liszt continued to travel a great deal, first to Düsseldorf to attend concerts and then to Hanover to visit Hans, who had become seriously depressed again after an exhausting American concert tour. From Hanover he complained to Olga of feeling 'stupidly melancholic'.[1] His low mood, he wrote, had been exacerbated by seeing the condition of his former son-in-law. Back in Weimar he wrote to Carolyne telling her of his travels and the honours bestowed on him by King Willem of the Netherlands. He also encouraged her to 'speak to me again of your "*Causes*"'.[2] Carolyne had stopped sending him her writings and, although Liszt might have been relieved not to have to read them, he would have interpreted her withdrawal from involving him in her work as a lessening of trust. Carolyne replied, asking him not to refer again to her work. He accepted this calmly acknowledging his 'ignorance of theology and politics'.[3] In August he wrote on three occasions[4] to Carolyne from Bayreuth, extolling 'Wagner's immense genius' displayed in *Der Ring des Nibelungen*. He had met there unexpectedly the reserved and withdrawn King of Bavaria, without whose support, he told Carolyne, 'Wagner would be reduced to experiencing only the depressing difficulties of a great genius'. He thanked Carolyne for completing the work on their second edition of *Life of Chopin* which he hoped that they would soon reread together 'remembering our beautiful days of struggle and of hope!' He told her of his intention to return to Rome at the end of September.

It was at this point that whatever peace of mind Liszt had been able to attain was shattered by a letter from Carolyne that deeply shocked him. She had persistently criticised him for his reconciliation with the Wagners, but on this occasion she had gone further. The letter does not exist in the Weimar archives of Carolyne's correspondence with Liszt as he returned it to her, but it clearly referred to Liszt's relationship with both Cosima and Marie:

> In all humility I do not think I deserved the letter you administered to me today. With the most sorrowful sincerity I maintain what I told you in Rome – you are seriously mistaken about your daughter, about mine, and about me. God knows that lightening your suffering was my only care

---

1. Letter from Liszt to Olga of 11 May 1876.
2. Letter from Liszt to Carolyne of 26 May 1876.
3. Letter from Liszt to Carolyne of 2 June 1876.
4. Letters from Liszt to Carolyne of 10, 19 and 28 August 1876.

for many years! I did not have much success it seems! As for me, I want to recall only the times when we wept and prayed together, with a single heart! After your letter today I am abandoning my trip to Rome. (Weimar, 6 September 1876)

Hans von Bülow (1830-1894).

Realising the damage she had done, Carolyne wrote back attempting to save the situation: 'no one will ever understand you as I understand you, and no one will love me as you have loved me. ... Come, for I await you with open arms.'[5] However, Liszt, whilst thanking her for her letter, stood firm: 'Your latest letter is full of kindness and indulgence. I thank you for it with all my heart, which is still bleeding from recent wounds. Allow me to cure myself alone, without further discussion of my faults and wrongdoings!' (Weimar, 16 September 1876)

Carolyne tried again to persuade him to come back to Rome for his birthday. Again, he refused but indicated he would eventually return: 'Don't ask me to [return to Rome in October] – to heal within, I need several months elsewhere – and before that I haven't the courage to present myself in your home.' (Hanover, 26 September 1876)

He had gone from Weimar to Hanover to support Hans von Bülow. To see his friend in such a state of mental distress added to Liszt's pain. He himself was now experiencing states of depression which could last throughout the day, as he wrote to Olga: 'It is something of an effort for me to live through certain hours and days. Sometimes sadness envelops my soul like a shroud. This was the case last Saturday from morn till eve.' (Hanover, 27 September 1876)

As he had given up his immediate plans to go to Italy, Liszt decided to travel to Hungary for his autumn and winter obligations there. On the way, he wrote to Olga from Vienna advising her to put up with the 'local boredom' of life in Weimar:

> You have to spend a certain amount of time there for your children's sake, and hence to put up with local boredom, which is fairly benign, while reflecting that the essence of

---

5. Walker, *The Final Years*, p. 344.

human life is nothing but inexorable boredom. Bossuet,[6] the eagle of Meaux, expressed this most eloquently from his episcopal throne; and many centuries before him, Master Job asked the Lord: 'Why hast thou set me as a mark against thee, so that I am a burden to myself?'[7] (Vienna, 12 October 1876)

For his sixty-fifth birthday Liszt was again a guest of his old friend Baron Augusz in Szekszárd. Carolyne was clearly now remorseful about her words to him and on Liszt's birthday she reminisced how 29 years before in Woronińce, 'in the oak-wood where there was the big celebration for the peasants', she had presented Liszt with:

your gold conductor's wand! ... I would have liked to own a fairy's wand to evoke before you here below everything the sky above contains! I was not granted the wish to be a fairy, but I am a Christian and, even if I have no wand, I have prayer. May God grant that we meet each other next October to celebrate together our thirtieth anniversary of October 22.[8]

Liszt wrote back graciously:

The functions of the good fairies are not opposed to those of the good angels – they both have their hours in poetry as in real life. I should regret it if you abandoned 'Minette's' gracious wand entirely, to hold only the angels' censer! ... Your admirable letter of 22 October makes me hope that we shall celebrate our thirtieth anniversary together in Rome, in '77 – Amen! (Szekszárd, 26 October 1876)

Despite the kind words exchanged between them, this was a tragic moment in the relationship between Liszt and Carolyne. Only two years earlier Liszt had chosen to come to Rome for an extended stay in order to help Carolyne in her difficulties and, together with her daughter Marie, had made arrangements for more permanent support for her. Now he was refusing to come to Rome in the face of Carolyne's

---

6. Jacques-Bénigne Bossuet (1627-1704), a French bishop and theologian, renowned for his sermons and considered a brilliant orator.
7. Job 7:20.
8. Cited in Walker, *The Final Years*, p. 344.

pleading. In this situation one can only sympathise with Liszt. He was caught in an impossible dilemma. He had disapproved of Wagner's role in the breakdown of Cosima's first marriage and promised Carolyne he would continue to stand aloof from them. However, this stance was impossible for him to maintain in the long term. Not only was Cosima his only remaining child but Richard Wagner was also an old friend whose music he appreciated more than that of any other contemporary musician and whom he genuinely saw as the leading light for the music of the future. He had been hugely relieved to have become involved again with Wagner's career and to have renewed their friendship. He had also succeeded in becoming reconciled with his daughter Cosima, while retaining close ties with her former husband Hans.

All of these seem highly commendable actions on Liszt's part. He had also tried hard to make Carolyne understand why he had found it necessary to seek reconciliation with Cosima and Wagner. He had tried to bring Carolyne back to Weimar. He had reminded her of the care she had shown for Cosima over so many years. He had tried to persuade her of the spiritual qualities in Wagner's recent compositions. He had spoken of the importance of mercy and forgiveness but all to no avail. In Carolyne's mind, Liszt had put others before his love for her, something she would never have done if she had been in his place. Moreover, the fact that Liszt's relationship with Carolyne's daughter Marie remained excellent, instead of being a source of harmony between Liszt and Carolyne, tended to deepen the conflict, for mother and daughter remained semi-estranged because Marie was part of the family that had stood in the way of Carolyne's marriage to Liszt.

Experiencing Worse Distress

Liszt's correspondence in the winter months of 1876-77 while living in Budapest show him repeatedly succumbing to depressive moods. This was understandable, given the intensity of his conflict with Carolyne. Their exchange of letters around the time of his birthday in late October had given promising signs of a new beginning to their relationship but by the next month Liszt was already becoming concerned about Carolyne's negative attitude to her own life:

> In your letters a tone of bitter desolation can often be heard! Can I not sweeten it by pruning away the doleful reasons which cause it? ... However, I fail to understand how you can feel yourself to be surrounded by the emptiness of indifference; to

Bearing a Heavy Burden (1876-80)

be isolated, dying, alone with Jesus Christ on the Cross! Are you, then, forgetting your daughter, who loves you deeply? Are you taking no account of your very numerous friends and admirers? (Budapest, 18 November 1876)

Early in January he again felt challenged to defend himself against renewed criticism of his spiritual life, in addition to his behaviour towards her:

> Let's argue no more about devotional practices! You have often recommended to me the narrow way of the Gospel; to make it easier for me you have also often tried to lighten the heavy crosses imposed upon me by my faults. Have I aggravated these still further by the least ingratitude towards you? I think not. The 30 years of our close relationship are full of the respect, admiration, and keen gratitude I have shown to you. As for the good crosses – I have always regarded them as a propitious means of penitence and salvation. In that, I associate myself with the sentiment of the penitent thief, who recognized that he had deserved his punishment, and put his trust in the promise given him by Our Lord Jesus Christ! ... What is most depressing for me in my old days is to find our opinions at variance. It was not thus from '47 to '62! Apart from a few disputes about literary requirements, and my follies, we were in total agreement on all essential matters. Rome and your transcendencies of mind have changed all that – but even now I acknowledge only the differences of opinion, not any disagreement of the heart – to which I shall *never* subscribe. (Budapest, 10 January 1877)

However, Carolyne continued with her accusations and provoked more intense complaint from Liszt two months later:

> I am greatly distressed to find you accusing me of ingratitude. If I thought I deserved this reproach, nothing would be left to me but to die at the very earliest. Having to bear the shame of ingratitude seems to me to be a fate worse than the forced labours of galley slaves! You also take me to task for not writing about what I am doing. Alas! I am hardly interested in my existence anymore, and do not find that its details make an agreeable communication! During the last 4 months my time has been spent in reading about a thousand letters and

notes – and in replying somehow or other to the most urgent. My best hours are those of my professorship at the new Academy of Music. (Budapest, 7 March 1877)

Walker points to the correspondence that Carolyne engaged in with Antal Augusz in the spring of 1877 as evidence of distortions in her thinking about Liszt. Augusz had written to Carolyne to express concern about learning of the near breakdown of his friend's relationship with her. She responded angrily and made a number of false statements not only about Liszt but also others. She even blamed the Pope for appearing to offer him a musical appointment but in the end giving nothing even after Liszt had taken holy orders. She also wrote that Liszt had then decided to leave Rome for Budapest and other places but this had not turned out well for him. Now that he was far away from her he was not writing anything worthwhile. In short, he was 'sterilising his genius before his time'.[9] This was clearly not Liszt's impression of events nor that of his other friends. Carolyne was unnecessarily traducing Liszt, as she had done in her letter to his cousin Eduard two years earlier, following the publication of Olga Janina's *Souvenirs*.

Liszt's distress at this point in his life is clearly reflected in his correspondence with Marie, Cosima and Olga. In his November letter to Marie he had been optimistic about improvements in her mother's attitude and told her of his plan to make a surprise visit to Rome in Holy Week.[10] By February, however, he admitted that he was 'stunned' by the letters both Marie and he had received from Carolyne, and concerned about the impending condemnation of her writings by the Vatican. He wished he had been more direct in his previous warnings to her to avoid criticism of the organisation of the Church itself. Nevertheless, his correspondence to Marie was marked as usual by a light touch:

> In this turn of events, a good spell of silence would seem to be necessary. To sound the note of the Penitential Psalms would scarcely be suitable. As you so aptly noted, you can't claim to repent of sins which, in the depths of your soul, you don't believe you have committed; and 'humility is too holy a virtue to be hypocritically employed'. (Budapest, 14 February 1877)

It is also striking that he shared with Cosima his criticisms, as well as admiration, for Carolyne, and admitted how serious his disagreements

---

9. Ibid., p. 337.
10. In the event he spent Easter with his daughter and Wagner in Bayreuth.

with her had become. He even made a comparison between Carolyne and Cosima's mother:

> Your comparison of the 'heroic and brilliant' nature of the Princess W. with the beautiful mirrors of the 17th and 18th centuries embellished with flowers, and small genies and angels, painted by skilful artists, but whose talent did not allow the mirrors to properly reflect the objects – this comparison is perfectly correct. ... As you know for many years I have been painfully led to having a different opinion to hers regarding the major issues of our existence. Not less than Daniel Stern, although in another way, much more nobly and bravely, she also swims in the river of illusions, and I find myself high and dry quite unable to follow. (Budapest, 22 February 1877)

However, it is again only in his writings to Olga that Liszt indicated that he was suffering from severely depressed moods. In December he had repeated to Olga that he no longer wished to involve himself in the performance of his works, of which even the shortest were regarded as too long, and that he was urging even his friends to ignore them. The next month he told her that his depression was becoming worse:

> Writing is becoming more and more onerous and sometimes odious for me. Banalities repel me no less than affectations. It is indeed difficult for me to make my way between them with my pen. So long as there is work to be done, I still feel relaxed and in fairly good form. For the rest, I am overcome by indescribable depression and have reached the point where Carthusians and Trappists often seem garrulous to me. ... From Rome I receive nothing but superb admonitions in the finest style. I answer these by an increasing devotion to the repentant thief ... [who] administered justice to himself with the words: 'I deserved my punishment.' (Budapest, 28 January 1877)

A couple of weeks later, Liszt wrote to Olga: 'This is a very mild winter, but I am suffering physically and mentally. I beg you not to tell anyone.' (Budapest, 12 February 1877)

He wrote next, presumably in response to Olga's expressions of concern for him, to reassure her that he was managing to cope. His comments are of particular psychological interest because they suggest that Liszt was still able to put his negative moods into perspective and that he could evaluate his life in a broader context. He referred again to Pascal:

> I don't know who said: 'Were it not for me, I would be in very good health.' Were it not for the *moi*, which Pascal denounced as hateful, and which to me seems to be chiefly a nuisance to each of us, one would also be fairly happy in this world of ours. ... [R]est assured that my health is adequate, my nerves and my mood are holding their own fairly well, and that I would be an arch idiot not to recognize the fact that Providence has placed me among the most favoured. (Budapest, 23 February 1877)

In the spring of 1877 Liszt resumed his musical position in Weimar and travelled from there to concerts elsewhere in Germany, including the *Musikfest* in Hanover from where he wrote to both Olga and Carolyne. Liszt was very pleased with the performances and their reception. The successful playing of Cornelius' *Barber of Baghdad*, he told Carolyne, helped remove the 'scandal' of its Weimar performance and reception in 1858 which had sparked Liszt's resignation as musical director. Among the most well received performances were that of Berlioz's *Symphonie fantastique*, conducted by Liszt himself, and the Andante and Finale of Tchaikovsky's Symphony No. 2, which gave Liszt particular pleasure, as it had been on his insistence that the Russian's music had been included in the programme.

However, painful notes of depression continued to appear in his letters. He admitted even to Carolyne his difficulties in settling down to work and even on occasions being unable to rouse himself in the morning. Even a short letter could take him many hours: 'Correspondence has become my purgatory here on earth! Sometimes, after having foolishly spent the day pen in hand, I feel an absolute need to get my breath back a little, to sleep – and to dream of my old companion, music.' (Weimar, 25 April 1877) Yet, the next day he was able to write to her again in praise of Wagner's *Parsifal* and to express his regret once more that she now excluded him from her writings:

> You are wrong to deprive me of them. If my ignorance justifies your excluding me from your literary and philosophical works, I resign myself to this humiliation only with deep sorrow! In earlier and better days, in Weimar and even in Rome, you were more generous towards me and did not entrench yourself so

much in a kind of Tabor, inaccessible to simpletons of my sort! (Weimar, 26 April 1877)

In June he referred to the sad state of his 'soul', while at the same time reiterating his gratitude for Carolyne's support of him over many years:

> Without complaining, I often suffer from living – health of the body remains to me, that of the soul is lacking. *Tristis est anima mea*![11] However, to my numerous real and alleged faults will never be added that of ingratitude, the very worst of all! From the bottom of my heart I bless you for persevering for 30 years in actively wishing for me the Good, the Beautiful, and the True. In this, you are heroic and sublime – and I feel unworthy to unlace your shoes! (Weimar, 15 June 1877)

As Walker notes,[12] Carolyne would have known only too well the continuation of the Latin phrase from the passage in St Mark's Gospel – ... *usque ad mortem*.[13]

Ten days later, while thanking Carolyne for the present she had sent him, a copy of a work by Titian, he repeated his regret at her refusal to return to Weimar:

> I can only add my profound regret about your remoteness from Weimar – your undue remoteness, it seems to me. But I have to get used to the fact that my words, whether spoken or written, no longer count for much! I am wrong to write that – but one quiet evening in the Babuino[14] you will grant me permission to explain myself at greater length. (Dornburg, 25 June 1877)

Despite Liszt's appeal to her one can understand how hard it would have been for Carolyne to return to Weimar. Besides her disinclination to travel anywhere outside Rome, she would have had to overcome her memories of the exclusion she had suffered during her ten years of living in Weimar. Moreover, many people there would remember that she had left in order to fight for her remarriage to Liszt in Rome and had failed in

---

11. 'My soul is sorrowful ...'
12. Walker, *The Final Years*, p. 369.
13. Matthew 26:38, '... even unto death'.
14. Via del Babuino was the street in Rome where Carolyne lived.

this quest. She would have needed much courage to face those who had previously condemned her and, perhaps even more so, those who might pity her because she was still not married to Liszt.

As always, Liszt was buoyed by Wagner's success. In July he visited Berlin and stayed with friends of Cosima and was received at Potsdam Palace by the Crown Prince Friedrich and Crown Princess Victoria. ('Vicky' wrote to her mother Queen Victoria in London to tell her how much she was looking forward to hearing Liszt play again.) He played for them and told Carolyne how much he enjoyed their company. He also made a point of stressing to her how they had shared his admiration for Wagner:

> The Prince and his wife openly admire Wagner, which at once put me at ease in their presence. I remember that, at the Villa d'Este, Queen Olga of Würtemburg told me that no sensible person thought anything of the *Ring des Nibelungen*, an absurd work and impossible to perform according to the most learned professors of aesthetics. I permitted myself to observe very humbly to Her Majesty that infallibility was not the attribute of professors! The Bayreuth performances are a *fait accompli* – the condemned work exists and nobly makes its way to the honour of art; the name of Wagner is at once most glorious and very popular, above all the scowlings, stupidities, and insults of the critics! (Weimar, 14 July 1877)

Liszt never stinted in his advocacy of Wagner to his critics, not even to Carolyne.

Two weeks later he told Olga that Cosima had been to stay with him in Weimar: 'She read me *Parsifal* Sunday evening. In the third act there is a sublime religious page. I don't know whether it's possible to stage this miraculous work. No matter; Wagner's genius overcomes even the impossible.' (Weimar, 1 August 1877)

However, before returning to Italy, he admitted to Olga in successive letters that his nerves were 'seriously out of order' and that perhaps he should consult a doctor. He thanked her for the journals she sent him which distracted him from his 'sombre' and 'sterile' thoughts. He also continued to describe himself as resigned to rejection of his musical compositions. The best description he could give of himself was as 'impassive': 'Fortunately, FL has become quiescent to the point of impassivity, and though not exactly enjoying either the refrain or its variations, he puts up with them in a penitent spirit.' (Munich, 17 August 1877)

Liszt arrived in Rome in an exceptionally hot summer. He was pleased to move soon to the Villa d'Este where he described the heat as less suffocating. Here he began in the evenings to play the piano again and enjoyed conversation with his 'padrone' Cardinal Hohenlohe. He complained to Olga of the demands on his time of writing letters of introduction which many people continued to ask of him. However, at the same time, he was also beginning to compose some of the greatest piano works in his latest years, eventually published as a collection entitled, *Années de pèlerinage, troisième année*, returning therefore to the same title as his successful collection of pieces from his younger travelling days with Marie d'Agoult. The fourth piece, *Les jeux d'eaux à la Villa d'Este*, is the most well-known of the set, a remarkable composition depicting the play of water in the famous sixteenth-century fountains constructed adjacent to the villa. It set the precedent for the subsequent depiction of water in music. For Liszt, this water had a religious meaning, it was 'the water springing up into eternal life'. He set, as an inscription in Latin above this piece of music, the famous lines of Jesus to the Samaritan woman he met at a well, as recorded in the Gospel of St John: *Sed aqua quam ego dabo ei, fiet in eo fons aquae salientis in vitam aeternam.*[15]

However, Liszt does not appear to have referred to *Les jeux d'eaux* in his correspondence. Instead, the two pieces from the set that he often refers to in his correspondence with Carolyne and Olga both concern his attempts to describe the impressions made on him by the grand cypresses in the gardens of the Villa d'Este. He mentioned the subject in a letter to Olga for the first time two weeks after his arrival there:

> Though I have not yet gone back to work, I have just written a hundred or so measures for the piano. It is a fairly gloomy and disconsolate elegy; illumined towards the end by a beam of patient resignation. If I publish it, the title will be: *Aux cyprès de la Villa d'Este*. (Rome, 13 September 1877)

In its movement towards atonality this piece illustrates the radical and disturbing – at least to his contemporaries – way in which Liszt's musical thinking was moving in his later years of composition.

To Carolyne he wrote ten days later of the progress he was making:

> These 3 days I have spent entirely under the cypresses! It was an obsession impossible to think of anything else, even church. Their old trunks were haunting me, and I heard their branches singing and weeping, bearing the burden of their

---

15. John 4:14, 'But whoever drinks of the water that I shall give him will become in him a spring of water welling up to eternal life.'

> unchanging foliage! At last they are brought to bed on music paper; and after having greatly corrected, scratched out, copied, and recopied them, I resign myself to touching them no more. They differ from the cypresses of Michelangelo by an almost loving melody.
>
> May the good angels make the most beautiful inner music for you – the music we shall hear fully, in its boundlessness, there above! ... Thank you for the information about Michelangelo's cypresses, and the small photograph showing them. ... If he took a little trouble, Hohenlohe could play the *Cyprès* – for they are quite easy to play, technically speaking. Zaluski will play them fluently *a prima vista*.[16] (Villa d'Este, 23 September 1877)

In his letter to Olga four days later, Liszt elaborated on his interest in Michelangelo, who, he thought, had planted cypresses in the cloister of a monastery he had been constructing in Rome. However, he also expressed his own lack of 'worldly' interest in the results of his efforts:

> For the last two weeks I've been absorbed <u>in cypresses</u>. Those of the Villa d'Este have taken me back to Michelangelo's cypresses at the Carthusian monastery in Rome – *Santa Maria degli Angeli* (in ancient times the Baths of Diocletian, near the main station of the present railroad). Michelangelo built the cloister with its hundred travertine columns and the sublime church. He also planted the cypresses which bear his name and near which his dead body lay for some time (until it was moved to Florence, I'm told). ... Thus, I have composed two <u>groups</u> of cypresses, each of more than two hundred bars, plus a *Postludium* (*Nachspiel*) to the cypresses of the Villa d'Este. These two sad pieces won't have much success and can do without it. I shall call them *Thrénodies*, as the word *élégie* strikes me as too tender, and almost worldly. (Villa d'Este, 27 September 1877)

Two weeks later he told Olga that his 'cypresses' had 'grown taller' and that he had been working on them without interruption for a further ten days and started on other compositions, none of which he thought would have any success:

---

16. 'At first sight'.

> Having once started blackening music paper, I wrote four more pages which will have as their epigraph: *Sursum Corda*.[17] These pieces are hardly suitable for drawing rooms and are not entertaining, nor even dreamily pleasing. When I publish them I'll warn the publisher that he risks selling only a few copies.

He continued this letter by referring again to Michelangelo and his disappointment that Olga had not been able to find further support for the story that the cypresses Michelangelo had planted had sheltered his dead body. He drew a comparison between himself and the great artist: 'No one, perhaps, knew and experienced the loneliness of human genius as much as he in the course of a long life. Before this great figure I feel a sad modesty combined with shame. This too is a form of vanity!' (Villa d'Este, 14 October 1877).

Nevertheless, despite his enthusiasm for his 'cypresses', Liszt remained dissatisfied with his recent compositions. Two weeks later he wrote again to Olga:

> I have spent this week here very much absorbed in the silly things I am writing on music paper – continually scraping, changing, and re-changing, without managing to express what I feel, and yet would like more or less to express musically. ... Forgive the lack of interest of my letters, as well as of my whole melancholy self. (Rome, 27 October 1877)

A further two weeks on, Liszt was showing clear symptoms of clinical depression, but persisting with his work. It was again to Olga that he wrote:

> I am desperately sad and completely incapable of finding a single ray of happiness. I'm in a kind of mental depression accompanied by physical indisposition. I've been sleeping badly for weeks, which doesn't help to calm my nerves. Nevertheless I pursue my labours while trying not to become too much discouraged in my musical work, which I have resolved not to give up short of either total infirmity or death.
>
> A few more leaves have been added to the cypresses – no less boring and redundant than the previous ones! To tell the truth I sense in myself a terrible lack of talent compared

---

17. 'Lift up your hearts'.

> with what I would like to express; the notes I write are pitiful. A strange sense of the infinite makes me impersonal and uncommunicative. In 1840, M. Mignet in speaking of me said solemnly to Princess Belgiojoso: 'There is great confusion in that young man's head.' The latter is now old, but not at all confused. (Rome, 9 November 1877)

The self-denigratory statements which Liszt makes about his compositions appear as symptoms of depression. However, there are also other elements in this self-description – 'a strange sense of the infinite makes me impersonal and uncommunicative' – suggestive of a state of ageing which some contemporary writers on ageing describe as 'gerotranscendence'. This term has been used to refer to potential spiritual development in later life in which the personal self is outgrown and replaced by a sense of self which is broader and more universal.[18] Were Liszt's difficult experiences leading him to transcend his previous self-centred focus?

Liszt's misery appeared to reach a peak on his return to Budapest in late November. He had brought a bad cold with him from Rome. Writing to Olga, he denied the newspaper reports that he was sick but confided in her that he felt that he was 'reaching the end and even succumbing – and no longer wanting an extension'. In a later paragraph he was even more explicit about his state of mind:

> Let me tell you once again that I am extremely tired of living; but as I believe that God's Fifth Commandment, 'Thou shalt not kill', also applies to suicide, I go on existing with deepest repentance and contrition for having formerly ostentatiously violated the Ninth Commandment,[19] not without effort or humility.
> Forgive me these intimate and too gloomy maunderings. (Budapest, 28 November 1877)

There is no record of him referring to suicide in his correspondence in the remaining nine years of his life, and it appears as if from this point on he learned to cope better with his negative thoughts and feelings.

---

18. See P.G. Coleman and A. O'Hanlon, *Aging and Development: Social and Emotional Perspectives* (London: Routledge, 2017), pp. 22-26.
19. In Roman Catholicism, the Ninth Commandment is 'Thou shalt not covet thy neighbour's wife'.

Asserting His Independence of Carolyne

On 19 January 1878 Liszt wrote a bold letter to Baron Augusz expressing his independence of Carolyne. We know that she had been writing in the previous years both to Augusz and to Liszt's cousin Eduard in Vienna about Liszt in very critical terms, even asking them to upbraid Liszt for what she saw as his immoral behaviour. Liszt had been very direct and to the point in his reply to Augusz. He wrote that he greatly admired Carolyne to whom he was 'indebted' but this did 'not compel me to run my little household in Budapest, Weimar or elsewhere according to her ideas'. Nearly three weeks after his letter to Augusz, he wrote an impassioned plea for mercy to Carolyne herself:

> On the day of your birth I very humbly repeat to you all the blessings and eulogies of my heart! You are ruled by a holy passion for the Good and the Beautiful – consumed by an evangelical hunger and thirst for justice – St Teresa of Ávila and St Catherine of Siena are your sisters! My fault, my very great fault, lies not in any failure to understand your sublime virtues, but in my unworthiness in following them! Nevertheless, please believe that my errors are quite involuntary and do not spring from obstinacy. Will you eventually grant them some mercy? Will you find that contrary to justice? Perhaps not. In any case, I shall persist in revering you as my good guardian angel! For 30 years you have been unceasingly good to me, and desire to go on being so – it would really be too despicable of me not to recognize this with the loving gratitude which alone is admissible. Our God remains, everlastingly, Truth and Mercy! This is already revealed in the Old Testament – how much more in the New! And so let every knee, in Heaven, on Earth and in Hades, bow before the Name of our Redeemer, Jesus! (Budapest, 8 February 1878)

Unbeknown to Liszt, Pope Pius IX, aged 85 years, had died the day before his letter. Carolyne responded by wearing black for a very long period of time. The Pope's death seems to have brought back pain at the memory of the marriage to Liszt that Pope Pius had at first granted so many years before but which did not take place. She sent a painful letter to Marie, probably reproaching her for that final failure. Liszt wrote a consoling letter to Carolyne, and one also to Marie with advice on dealing with her mother: 'The best thing is to content yourself with a tender and *genuine* telegram, and to accept the letter as a cross to bear – and one of the saddest ones ever. I pray God to remedy this affliction for both sides.' (Budapest, 24 February 1878)

Liszt's subsequent letters to Marie are unusual in that he began repeating many of the same depressed themes as in his letters to Olga and Carolyne: 'I find that my life had lasted too long'; 'my extreme fatigue from trips, either short or long, which my *triangular* existence (as Wagner calls it) between Pest, Weimar and Rome inflicts upon me'.[20]

He made no mention of his own compositions to Marie; but repeatedly to Olga and also to a Hungarian singer and admirer, who wanted to continue promoting his work in Budapest, he insisted, unusually harshly, that he did not wish 'to play the piano in public', tried to avoid hearing his works played in concerts and even wanted his 'compositions to remain unperformed'.[21] Perhaps this outburst was related to criticism he had received in Budapest which Walker[22] indicates had deeply shocked him. Liszt had tended to assume that Hungary was one country where he was universally admired. However, the editor of a journal had recently accused him of attributing the Hungarian folk-music tradition to the gypsies and gone further in declaring that Liszt, like the gypsies, had little talent for creating melody. Augusz and other friends, including the young Count Zichy, rallied around Liszt but the shock remained.

Liszt continued with his life of travel, first to Weimar and then Hanover to see Hans in his new position as musical director. He was greatly encouraged to see how boldly and successfully he was conducting his new orchestra and with Wagner's music, in particular. He told Carolyne that Hans had recovered his previous lively and witty conversation style. After visiting Wagner and Cosima in Bayreuth, he kept his commitment, despite his previous protests, to be part of an international music jury in Paris, where he also dined with Émile and his grandson Daniel, and was invited to visit Victor Hugo, whom he had admired since his youth. He also seems to have taken the opportunity to meet Agnes Street-Klindworth because their correspondence resumed again shortly afterwards. His letters to her were now shorter than before; although they were still affectionate and showed Liszt's genuine interest in the musical career of her son Georges, they indicated nothing about his

---

20. Letters from Liszt to Marie of 12 March and (undated) mid-May 1878.
21. Letter to Mme Katalin Engeszer of 8 March 1878, cited by Williams, *Franz Liszt: Selected Letters*, p. 827 (see also p. 964).
22. Walker, *The Final Years*, pp. 375-76.

state of mind and mood which were still depressed, as evidenced in his letters both to Carolyne and Olga.

He wrote to Carl Riedel recommending the inclusion of another Russian composition, Borodin's Second Symphony, in the year's music festival, offering to pay himself for the additional expenses involved and asking for some of his own works to be excluded. He wrote to Carolyne in July that he had told Lina Ramann[23] he attached 'no importance to my biography'. It would have been better if in writing about him she had concentrated solely on a 'musical and aesthetic analysis' of his works as in her previous study of his *Christus*:

> I have lived only too much, and not well enough, in my opinion! What's the good of sifting the details of the past? Had she listened to me, her volume would have been limited to a musical and aesthetic analysis of my works – very defective, doubtless, but numerous enough to provide material for 100 or so pages of criticism, favourable or otherwise. (Weimar, 26 July 1878)

He learned of Baron Augusz's serious illness in time to write him a letter before his old friend's death on 9 September: 'so you have been ill for six weeks! And you still show me your unwearying and most attentively kind friendship. May God reward you!'[24] He reassured him that the new building for the music academy in Budapest would be realised. Augusz's death was a heavy blow to Liszt, the loss of his most loyal and generous supporter in Hungary who had stood by him gladly in good times and bad.

As he left for Rome at the beginning of September, he was in a serious mood, signing his letter to Olga 'your melancholy FL'[25]. On 12 September he followed this letter with a brighter message from Rome: 'This evening I return to the Villa d'Este. The cypresses and the wonderful clouds at

---

23. Lina Ramann was a German musicologist whom Carolyne had personally selected to write a biography of Liszt. In Alan Walker's intriguing prologue to his three volume biography of Liszt he describes the history of Liszt biography including the influence Carolyne exerted on this the first major biography of Liszt and its unforeseen consequences on later biographies (Walker, *The Virtuoso Years*, p. 3-29).
24. Letter from Liszt to Baron Augusz of 28 August 1878.
25. Letter from Liszt to Olga of 1 September 1878.

sunset will be lovely company.' He also wrote to Agnes on the same day sending a rosary blessed by the new pope Leo XIII and congratulating her sons on their achievements. Most significantly, Liszt had found a new focus for work. He wrote to both Carolyne and Olga on 22 September, telling them he had resumed work on his *Via Crucis* project, for which Carolyne had selected the texts, and that he was 'absorbed' in it. He used the same expression a month later writing to Olga. However, he also referred to the fact that the process of composing could be a disturbing experience:

> These last two weeks I have been completely absorbed in my *Via Crucis*. It is at last complete (except for the indications of the *fortes*, *pianos*, etc.) and I still feel quite shaken by it. Day after tomorrow I will go back to writing letters, a task impossible for me to undertake so long as music torments my brain. I am barely able to keep up a few indispensable though brief conversations during pauses in my work; and in the evening I feel very tired. I go to bed at 9:30 and read for another half an hour; then the wretched notes of the morning and of the day to come enter my mind and disturb my slumber. In music as in moral matters one rarely does the good one would wish, but often the evil which one would not wish. (Rome, 23 October 1878)

In fact, the *Via Crucis* was not yet finished. Both it and other ideas continued to occupy his mind. He apologised to Olga for his delay in writing:

> As I told you, my Via Crucis has become longer than I expected; and scarcely had I reached the Thirteenth Station when I was seized by an old idea. There was no other way of ridding myself of it than to write a hundred or so bars for each of the Seven Sacraments. ... My compositions are extremely simple. They limit themselves to expressing musically a few texts of the Holy Scriptures. Perhaps they can be adapted for use in church during the communion. (Villa d'Este, 17 November 1878)

With the *Via Crucis* Liszt had broken new ground in Church music by breaking with traditional harmony. The effect is the more startling for his use of plainchant in its opening movement ('Vexilla regis prodeunt').

Alan Walker imagines how Liszt's listeners would have experienced discomfort:

> It is safe to say that never before had the traditional story of the Crucifixion been clothed in such innovative sounds. The piece contradicts all our expectations of what the Passion is supposed to represent. Even Liszt confessed that he was 'quite shaken by it'. He wanted to bring home to his listeners not only the agony of the Cross but the pain of those in Christ's circle who witnessed it. In order to do that, he had to jolt his listeners from their complacency and use a harmonic language that would have been quite literally shocking to those who hear it.[26]

Liszt offered *Via Crucis* along with *Septem Sacramenta* and *Rosario* to the publisher Friedrich Pustet of Regensburg who turned the pieces down. Liszt had not even asked for payment: 'I do not write such compositions for monetary gain, but from the inner necessity of a Catholic heart.'[27] Liszt accepted this rejection without complaint, as he wrote to his friend and admirer, the musicologist Marie Lipsius (La Mara), who, like Lina Ramann, was recording details of his life and compositions. She would later expend great effort in assembling and publishing his letters:

> There [Villa d'Este] I wrote the 'Christmas-tree', the 'Via Crucis', the 'Responses to the Seven Sacraments', etc. These three works are quite ready, and indeed beautifully copied, as well as the 'Cantico del Sole' of the marvellous St. Francis of Assisi. Their publication troubles me little, for they are not suitable to the usual musical customs and trade. ... So why bargain with them? (Budapest, 2 March 1879)

In fact, *Via Crucis* did not receive its first performance until fifty years later on Good Friday 1929 in Budapest. To quote Walker again: 'A work of outcries and asides, whispers and laments, it has meanwhile come to enjoy a high status among students of Liszt's later music. When it is placed in a sacred setting and given a performance of high calibre, the effect can be stunning.'[28] Musicians still marvel at the new ground Liszt

---

26. Ibid., *The Final Years*, p. 382.
27. Cited in ibid., p. 383.
28. Ibid., p. 384.

was breaking in musical expression, including its use of what are now called 'tone-clusters'. Reinbert de Leeuw, in one of his last recordings before his death in 2020, produced a second version of Liszt's *Via Crucis* after an interval of 30 years. His reflections led him to present the piece in a much more austere form with just sixteen voices (four to each part) and a piano (rather than organ) solo, underlining in its slower pace its personal, painful and resigned character.[29]

There was to be another difficult exchange for Liszt with Carolyne before Christmas 1878. She wrote him a critical letter urging repentance for his actions in regard to her in recent years. She also took the opportunity to object to the social life he led in Rome when he came to visit. She had probably heard that Liszt had received a large group of unexpected visitors at the Villa d'Este. They included old friends, artists and diplomats, all of whom Cardinal Hohenlohe had been pleased to host and dine. Liszt was again firm in his rejection of her criticism, told her the importance of forgiveness, and scolded her for her intransigent attitude to the way of life he had chosen for himself in recent years:

> You advise me Penitence – the practice of it is not unknown to me, first and foremost in the sacrament of the Church, infinitely sweeter than the unsought penitences inflicted elsewhere! But he who talks of penitence talks at the same time of full and complete reconciliation! Otherwise. the dissonance, to put it in the language of music, would not be resolved. ... Your Roman habits have given you a measure of absolutism which brooks no argument. The most discreet and respectful observations you regard as slights, and even as outrages! You no longer take any account of the logical honour of my life. It is by no means the salons which cause the divergence in our points of view, but your daughter, and to some extent mine too! When I am dead you will realize that my soul was and remained always deeply devoted to yours!
>
> I shall probably not return to Rome until 2 January '79. Reply to these lines then, *viva voce, con un parlare vero ed amabile*.[30] (Villa d'Este, 22 December 1878)

Carolyne's response to this letter led him to apologise himself to her, on Christmas day itself:

---

29. Reinbert de Leeuw & Collegium Vocale Gent, *Liszt: Via Crucis* (Alpha, 2019).
30. 'Face to face, in a tone sincere and loving'.

> When having my supper yesterday evening, I found your very dear and consoling letter, surrounded by an admirable assortment of flowers. It made me almost ashamed of the lines I sent you the day before – forgive me for them, and for anything else which might seem like a diminution in my deep devotion to you! ... At the midnight mass this morning I prayed for you with all my heart – and asked God to make me worthy of your supernatural sentiments! (Villa d'Este, 25 December 1878)

He continued by assuring her of the kind confessors he had not only in Tivoli, but also in Weimar and Budapest.

Ever Upward!

Liszt's correspondence in the winter months of 1879 suggests that he was without depressive moods for the first time in many years. He did not complain and referred more to his successes. Indeed, both this period and the following year were outwardly very pleasant ones for Liszt, years in which he was almost universally honoured and praised wherever he went. On 12 January he was invited to the Vatican for a private audience with the new pope Leo XIII. Although he was not to have the same warm relationship as he had had with his predecessor, the invitation was an acknowledgement of Liszt's valued status in Rome.

In his letters from Budapest both to Carolyne and to Olga he gently reminisced. To the former, he praised a former patroness, the Marchesa Martellini: 'I have always remained very grateful to her for her kindnesses in times past. In 1838, my too long hair and irregular behaviour notwithstanding, she had the more than daring idea of getting the Grand Duke of Tuscany to bestow a decoration upon me.' (Budapest, 19 January 1879)

To the latter, he wrote of being charged with 'affectation' when frequenting the Paris salons of his youth, something of which he 'hardly thought it possible to be accused'! His real 'faults and mistakes' were different. He appreciated the increasing affection he was receiving from his new compatriot-friends in Hungary. He also reflected on the meaning of wisdom:

> King Solomon[31] himself doesn't impress me much with his pompous *Vanitas Vanitatum*! Confidentially speaking (for

---

31. The writer of the book of *Ecclesiastes* according to the rabbinic tradition.

my ignorance forbids me to argue philosophy or politics with others), to consider everything as being in vain seems to me the worst of vanities. From a Christian point of view every action, every word and thought has its own value, according to whether these draw us nearer to, or farther away from Heaven. ... Scientists will make new discoveries, soldiers will shed their blood for the sake of honour, artists will produce works of beauty, etc., etc. All this is not vanity, with all due deference to King Solomon and to his glib imitators. There is, and there will ever constantly be something <u>new</u> under the sun; and in the end the Father of heavenly mercy will reward the long and persevering <u>labour</u> of mankind. This is our hope! (Budapest, 31 January 1879)

He corresponded regularly also with Marie in the first months of the year, appreciating her encouragement with performances of his religious music:

The best part of my religious compositions is the emotion evoked by them in a few fine souls. Your lines concerning the Coronation *Mass* are the most precious of rewards for me: they have also led me to make an exception to my rule of not appearing in public activity. In this regard, several flattering proposals have again recently arrived to me from London, Aachen, and Berlin. I excused myself on account of my age and for other very solid reasons; nevertheless I did not answer negatively to Bösendorfer's *prelude* – in case the Vienna 'Friends of Music' show themselves favourably inclined toward the Gran Mass and perform it at the end of March or on the first Sunday in April – since I ought to be back at Weimar on Easter. (Budapest, 26 January 1879)

In his next letter he thanked her for her letter of condolence on the death of his cousin Eduard in Vienna in early February and told her of his regret at not attending the funeral:

You have a charm bred of compassion. Profoundly moved by the real and delicate kindness of your last letter, I am reproaching myself for not going to Vienna as soon as the sad news reached me. Petty affairs kept me here; had I arrived the following day, it would only have been in time to accompany my beloved Cousin to his last earthly dwelling. My soul remains in communion with him. (Budapest, 15 February 1879)

In the same letter he gave her a detailed account of the plans for the performance of his Gran Mass in Vienna on 8 April and was able to give her the good news that he was receiving pleasant letters from her mother:

My letters from Rome are full of sublime things; before them I kneel with devotion, even while I stay in this area governed by the way of the poor world, which is not that of the Thrones, Dominions, Powers, and other Archangels! ... My humble attitude in this regard is the same one you have known for the last fifteen years.

As a postscript he told her that he would be bringing to her a copy of his song, 'Ihr Glocken von Marling', that he had composed five years earlier and dedicated to her.

In March he made his first visit to Transylvania for over thirty years. It was with his new friend Count Géza Zichy to whom he had been offering much encouragement in his musical career. Zichy had lost his right arm in a hunting accident when young but had worked hard to become a piano virtuoso and composer. After they arrived, they heard of the disastrous flood in the southern Hungarian city of Szeged: the whole city centre was destroyed, with huge loss of life, after the river Tisza overflowed and crashed through the dam protecting the city. Walker narrates their immediate response.[32] In Zichy's memoirs, his friend quotes Liszt as saying: 'nothing will be achieved by lamenting, we must do something to help'. They hastily drew up a programme for a charity concert and advertised it in pamphlets distributed throughout the city of Klausenburg.[33] At the close of the concert, the exuberance of the crowd was such that a group of students ran to Liszt and lifted him up onto their shoulders. He commented to Olga on the 'special quality of nobility and cordiality' in Transylvanian hospitality.

---

32. Walker, *The Final Years*, p. 387.
33. Present day Cluj-Napoca.

Liszt continued with further concerts for the Hungarian flood victims in Budapest and the following month in Vienna. He was universally applauded in every concert hall, even when he was not a performer. Moreover, even his long-term Viennese critic Eduard Hanslick was moved:

> It was a delightful, unforgettable moment. We know of no other instance when an artist has entered a concert hall, neither as a composer nor as a performer but merely as a listener, and been welcomed as loudly and as unanimously by the entire assembly. ... What magic still surrounds the elderly man![34]

Franz Liszt and Count Géza Zichy. Photograph by Ede Kozics, Pressburg (present day Bratislava), 4 April 1881.

Although this was one of the most successful visits Liszt had made to Vienna since his childhood, it was also a sad occasion for him to be without his cousin Eduard. However, he was still able to stay with Eduard's widow and their two young children. Eduard's death had been another painful bereavement for Liszt: Eduard had been a major living link with his childhood and the person who had done so much to support both him and Carolyne in their years of financial worries.

Nevertheless, Liszt carried on with his travels in a positive frame of mind. Besides attending concerts in Weimar, he visited Hanover, where he was again impressed by what Hans von Bülow was achieving with his orchestra. He also noted with admiration Hans' piano performance of all five of Beethoven's last piano sonatas in one evening. He then travelled to Frankfurt am Main for a performance of his own *Christus* oratorio. He was then surprised and 'touched deeply', as he wrote to Carolyne, to have been told in July that he had been elected to become a canon of the cathedral of Albano, south-east of Rome, where Cardinal Hohenlohe had been appointed bishop. This led Liszt to reflect again on his religious vocation:

> Had it not been thwarted in its first ardour by my dear mother and by my confessor, the Abbé Bardin, it might well have led me to the seminary in 1830, and later to the priesthood. ... Would I have been worthy of such a calling? Divine grace

---

34. Cited in Walker, *The Final Years*, p. 388.

alone could accomplish it! The fact remains that my mother's loving tenderness, and the Abbé Bardin's prudence, left me at grips with temptations that I have been able to overcome no more than inadequately! Poetry and music, not forgetting a few particles of innate rebellion, have subjugated me for too long! *Miserere mei, Domine*! (Weimar, 18 July 1879)

Liszt continued to support strongly not only Wagner's music but also the new Russian composers, who, he told Carolyne, were still not receiving the attention they deserved even in St Petersburg but, he believed, were 'ploughing a more fruitful furrow than the belated imitators of Mendelssohn and Schumann'. Writing from Bayreuth to Olga in August, he described the third act of *Parsifal* as 'absolutely sublime' and that it made 'the soul quiver and weep'. She had joined him for the Wagnerian festival in Bayreuth for some days and he wrote lovingly to her after she left:

FL would have to be completely heartless not to feel your absence deeply. I am sad and cannot dispel my sadness, but as it does not serve to lighten yours I conceal it and keep it unexpressed. Yesterday morning early I walked along the little river where we had dreamed together the evening before. For me there was left only prayer. (Bayreuth, 22 August 1879)

I have not noticed any Liszt biographer comment on this letter but, taken together with other evidence from Liszt's correspondence to Olga, they do suggest that she would have liked her relationship to Liszt to be even closer than the confidant, friend, secretary and general assistant to him that she had become.

Back in Rome in September, he good humouredly chided Olga for her 'quasi-criminal' mistake in confusing Carolyne's address in Via del Babuino with his own and thus writing to him there! He also corresponded enthusiastically with both Marie and Agnes, extolling Wagner's talent to the former and praising the music coming out of Russia to the latter. He wrote to Rimsky-Korsakov in St Petersburg expressing his thanks for the Russian composer's interest in his music and his own admiration for the 'new musical Russia'. The ceremony for Liszt's induction as a canon took place in the cathedral at Albano on 12 October. That autumn there had been a disastrous harvest in the nearby Sabine mountains and there was widespread famine. Together, Cardinal Hohenlohe and Liszt organised a benefit concert which eventually took place on 30 December in the

Villa d'Este and included Liszt's pupils and other musicians. It attracted a huge audience and was another huge success for Liszt, who himself contributed a fantasia on his setting of *Ave maris stella*.

Carolyne had become very weak again, probably as a result of her constant work of study and writing, and as a result Liszt discussed with Marie the advisability of her again making a visit to Rome. The conclusion was that Marie should come but without telling her mother in advance. It is interesting that Liszt also consulted Marie's brother-in-law Cardinal Hohenlohe on this matter and thus was able to tell Marie that they both agreed that Carolyne 'secretly wished' her daughter to come. Liszt came to stay in Rome for Marie's visit later in October and was able to celebrate his sixty-eighth birthday together with her mother. After Marie's departure Liszt wrote consolingly but also confidently to Carolyne, beginning now to sign himself regularly as 'Dismas', the traditional name for the repentant thief who was crucified besides Jesus on Golgotha:

> We are extremely sad, are we not, very dear and adorable superhuman? But it is written: 'They that sow in tears shall reap in joy'! May the Father of mercy and of all consolation grant us here below His peace, which passeth all understanding! Let us not examine the faults of others, and let us hope, from the sole true, good, just and supreme Judge, for the loving forgiveness of our own! Dismas (Rome, 3 November 1879).

Nevertheless, a negative tone was again beginning to enter Liszt's correspondence. Writing to Olga on 8 November, he recalled a memory that was particularly bitter for him. Mention of the only major Paris newspaper that had commented favourably on the performance of his Gran Mass in 1866 brought to mind the pain of that experience and, in particular, the rejection he received from his old friend Berlioz. Succeeding letters to Olga were also negative, stressing the burden of his 'musical paperwork', his lack of creativity ('a few sheets of useless music') and the 'weariness' and 'harassment' he felt as he composed and revised music. He was still, however, able to write before Christmas with encouragement to Géza Zichy who was recovering from a serious injury to his foot. He emphasised, as he did in his letters to so many others, the value and importance of the Christian faith, to be expected perhaps from his position as an 'Abbé', but nevertheless always consistently and sincerely expressed: 'Poetry and music try, as best they can, to remedy the irremediable sufferings of our earthly lives. Consolation and strength, however, are given only by the Cross of Jesus Christ!' (Rome, 22 December 1879)

Despite the warmth of Liszt's reception at his previous visit to Vienna, he remained cautious in replying to Zichy's suggestion of a repeat concert in the imperial city the following winter. In his New Year letter to Marie, he made plain his view that the music he was at present writing – *Ossa arida* for male chorus and accompaniment – was difficult and new and probably not for present public consumption:

> The vision of Ezekiel would be revolting to all the reigning critics; I don't know whether I'll ever risk showing these 'dry bones' at a public concert. It's only 50 or 60 slow measures; but they are frightful, and move in a progression of dissonant chords such as have never been written before. (Villa d'Este, 1 January 1880)

Eventually, however, Liszt did agree to another concert in Vienna featuring his own work, although he continued to dislike the idea, as he confided to Carolyne:

> To tell the truth, I would prefer it not to take place – the weariness of age, and some inner sadness or other, fruit of a too long experience, are making it increasingly distressing for me to show myself in public. And so I have refused several recent and flattering invitations. My bit of celebrity weighs on me singularly – it is a tyrannical blind alley from which there is no escape! I should like to do nothing more but work, and pray in my corner – unattainable, it seems! (Budapest, 14 February 1880)

Liszt's letters to Olga from Budapest in the winter of 1880 showed him generally in a contented mood and he eventually agreed to a concert of his work in Vienna on 23 March. This contained his cantata, *The Bells of Strasbourg Cathedral*, his symphonic poem, *Die Ideale*, and his Szekszárd Mass for male voices (*Missa quatuor vocum ad aequales*). Experience had taught Liszt to be more wary of how his actions could be interpreted and so he took pains to stress that the first piece had no relation to the present political situation in Strasbourg. There was still popular unrest after the border city and most of Alsace had been ceded from France to Germany following the Franco-Prussian war and Germany unification in 1871. Liszt was able to report to Carolyne that the concert went well, although his critics in the press, while acknowledging his success, had attributed it to his 'likeable personality': 'Let us leave our adversaries to grouse, growl, and grimace as they find fit – and ourselves quietly follow the motto 'Do what must be done, come what may'. *Excelsior!*' (Vienna, 1 April 1880) 'Excelsior!' – 'ever upward!' – had by now become one of Liszt's favourite watchwords.

Back in Weimar again, his intention was to continue working on his long proposed Polish oratorio, *St Stanislaus*. Princess Marie had become an active collaborator on this project. He wrote to her on five occasions in the spring and summer, indicating his determination to make progress with *St Stanislaus* and thanking her for her assistance with improving the libretto which her mother had originally prepared. It was a noble idea on Liszt's part to have seen this as an important common project which would help to bind the three of them together again. The planned oratorio honoured the heroic Polish saint, who as Bishop of Kraków had dared oppose a tyrannical king and died a martyr's death. Liszt had first conceived of writing an oratorio on the subject more than ten years earlier and had developed a clear conception of the various scenes it would depict (as in his previous oratorios). Carolyne had urged him on but progress in realising the project had slowed down. Marie's recent contribution was to have engaged the help of a historical scholar in Vienna and, on his return to Rome in September, Liszt thanked her and expressed himself content with the libretto:

> The last sheets of St Stanislaus have arrived for me. I am extremely pleased with each of the six scenes and with the whole effect, concluded so well by the Kraków hymn. From the start to the finish of this Oratorio text, the two great *strains* of the Catholic religion and of Poland are nobly upheld according to my wishes. The Bishop maintains his holiness; the King never grows contemptible, although his fit of passion drives him almost to transgression; and the *voice of the people* expresses their role of suffering and hope blended with patriotism and piety.
>
> May my composition do credit to your benign concern! (Villa d'Este, 10 September 1880)

Sadly, Liszt did not advance far with *St Stanislaus* that autumn and winter. His correspondence with Marie from Rome became focussed on how to find the best way of encouraging her mother to accept a support chair or 'cot' which would allow her to rest more comfortably.

By November Liszt reported back that their gift had been a 'complete failure'. It had been refused and they would have to find another recipient! By the end of the year Carolyne had become bedridden again and Liszt told Marie that they would have to be patient:

> I've just spent three days in Rome. M. is bedridden, and predicts that she will stay the same until the month of February. Happily she can work without respite. The last chapters of her new volume satisfy her; her frame of mind is quite calm, except in the matter of the poor service of her help and their ineptitude in fulfilling the simplest offices. We spoke again about the *Cot* in a friendly way: perhaps Your most illustrious brother-in-law will profit by it at Saint Mary's or at Albano, since M. had the idea of favouring him with this delightful piece of furniture on his birthday (February 26th). Thank you for the 80 florins received last week. It was only half-successful; certainly no defeat. Complete success will come later. To be patient and to live is one and the same thing. (Villa d'Este, 12 December 1880)

Despite his positive manner with Marie, the letters which Liszt wrote to Olga from Rome showed him to be in a low mood, referring often to his sadness and weariness. Arriving in Rome at the beginning of September, he had already sounded down: 'Tomorrow I return to the Villa d'Este. Here I have seen only the one person for whom I came in 1861and for whom I continue to return.' (Rome, 3 September 1880)

Later in the month he enjoyed a brief stay with Cosima and family outside Siena at the Torre Fiorentina which Wagner had rented for a short period. He wrote to Carolyne and Olga praising Cosima and Wagner's children and Wagner's continued progress with *Parsifal*. However, on his return to Rome, he expressed to Olga both his sense of fatigue and his efforts to combat it: 'My mood is not such as to soothe yours. I suffer from extreme mental fatigue against which I struggle by praying and working.'

In the same letter he reflected on his career, comparing himself with the ambitions of contemporary younger composers and performers: 'I sometimes envy them certain illusions with which I have never been afflicted. What people term my artistic career developed entirely on its own without any pretension on my part. If I pursue it this is solely from a sense of duty. My aspirations and dreams lie elsewhere.' (Villa d'Este, 12 October 1880)

His subsequent letter to Olga after his birthday contained a mixture of weariness, resolve, and reflection. He began by commenting on the current debates about the recovery of the Catholic Church's 'temporal power' in Italy and Europe:

> Fortunately, I am not involved in these great issues in which the cleverest people have so often failed. Simple faith, like that of the 'poor in spirit', suffices for my prayers and musical work in which I persevere despite the fatigue of age. Last Friday I entered my seventieth year. It might be time to end things well … all the more since I have never wished to live long. In my early youth I often went to sleep hoping not to awake again here below. (Villa d'Este, 30 October 1880)

He then went on to answer Olga's query about a passage about his mother in the first volume of Lina Ramann's biography of Liszt which had just been published:[35]

> You ask me whether the passage from the Ramann biography concerning my mother is accurate. Yes, it is. She loved me, and in order to please her I did not enter a seminary (in 1830), for her sincere and naïve piety did not consider my vocation for the priesthood to be necessary. Thus because of her I remained a layman and have lived only too secularly. My comfort is that her benediction was vouchsafed to me until her last hour. She liked to say: 'Whatever people may say against my son doesn't offend me in the slightest, for I know what he is.'

His letters in the same period to Carolyne also contain reflections on Ramann's book which he was reading slowly, 'not without sadness', feeling grateful to the biographer but also feeling her 'sentiments' towards him to be 'too favourable'. There was again a note of 'gerotranscendence' in his self-description: 'No one will believe me if I say that I am becoming more and more impersonal! Yet it is the simple truth – to the point that to hear myself spoken of, even to be praised, often pains me.' (Villa d'Este, 29 October 1880)

He repeated the comment about becoming impersonal in his following letter to Carolyne: 'My conscience often pains me – but not always

---

35. L. Ramann, *Franz Liszt: Künstler und Mensch* (Leipzig: Breitkopf & Härtel, 1880).

according to what other people like to say! That is why I have become absolutely impersonal!' (Villa d'Este, 10 November 1880)

His subsequent letter to Olga is in strong contrast to this. In it he admits that he is in a depressed state, but also attributes it to the state of his relationship with Carolyne, and repeats in similar form of words his negative comment of two months earlier: 'I'm writing a little poor music, but in a state of extreme depression because of my permanent conflict, for some fifteen years, with the only person who is the cause of my annual trip to Rome where I scarcely spend any time any longer.' (Villa d'Este, 13 November 1880)

His final brief letters up to the end of the year continue to show him 'displeased with himself', struggling to compose in a new way ('protesting against outmoded things') and comparing himself with Flaubert in his eager search for the *mot juste*: 'I know similar torments in music. This or that chord, or even pause, have cost me hours and numerous erasures. Those who know the meaning of *style* are a prey to these strange torments.' (Villa d'Este, 25 December 1880)

Franz Liszt. Pastel Portrait by Franz von Lenbach, Munich,
1 September 1884, with a dedication to Liszt's granddaughter. One of seven
portraits of Liszt (see also cover portrait from c. 1870) completed
by von Lenbach, who was a friend of Liszt.

8

Through Triumph and Disaster (1881-86)

A Fall in Weimar and an Unnecessary Accusation

Liszt appeared to be in relatively good physical health as he entered his seventieth year. For many years he had maintained rather well the slender body of his youth. He had no problems with mobility, and his eyesight and hearing were good. Indeed, observers had commented on how his sight-reading from musical scores was exceptional. However, his face had changed. The American sculptor Moses Ezekiel, who had acquired a studio in Rome and produced a bust of Liszt at the end of 1880, provides evidence of this in his memoirs. He had last met Liszt ten years earlier in Weimar and been impressed then by both Liszt's height and slim build. Now he was struck by how his face appeared heavy and deeply lined, although at the same time 'jovial and lion-like'. He reproduced these features in the bust he sculpted of Liszt.[1]

More significantly, Liszt was expressing feelings of extreme fatigue on a regular basis. This was understandable in terms of the huge distances he regularly travelled by train and coach, which were quite exceptional for the time and even more so for a person of Liszt's age. Yet, he continued with this exhausting schedule of activity. As Walker has calculated, the distances he covered in the spring and early summer of 1881 were exceptional, even by Liszt's recent standards.[2] In addition to his regular movement between Rome, Budapest and Weimar, he travelled an additional two thousand miles in just a few weeks between

---
1. Walker, *The Final Years*, p. 396.
2. Ibid., p. 401.

April and May, mainly to attend concerts of his own music, in Berlin, Freiburg, Karlsruhe, Baden-Baden, Antwerp and Brussels.

All these concerts seem to have been successful. As Liszt wrote to Carolyne from Antwerp, he sensed that he was at last being recognised as a composer. He contrasted the reception of the Gran Mass with his disastrous experience with the same work in Paris in 1866:

Franz Liszt. Photograph by H. von Langsdorff, Freiburg 1881. With a dedication in Liszt's hand on the rolled-up sheet of music. 'Poor composer. F. Liszt.'

> Rarely have I encountered such lively and general goodwill as here in Antwerp. It takes my work more seriously and is not limited to my *liebenswürdige Persönlichkeit* ['amiable personality'], esteemed in several countries – nor to my celebrity as a pianist, which I have not yet had occasion to display here. The Gran Mass was performed and heard with enthusiasm yesterday – I dare use this word, which is the appropriate one! In Paris, in '66, this same work failed – it was brilliantly revived in Vienna last year, and even more brilliantly here in Antwerp, before an audience of at least 3,000. I am sending you the programme of the Liszt Festival of Antwerp, and will shortly write some details.
>
> In Brussels tomorrow, for another big Liszt concert, will be your most humble old Sclavissimo. (Antwerp, 27 May 1881)

From 9 to 12 June he attended the annual German music festival which in 1881 was held in Magdeburg. There, he met again the Russian composer Alexander Borodin who was grateful for Liszt's advocacy of the inclusion of his own work in the previous year's festival. In appreciation for Liszt's help, he had dedicated to him his own 'orchestral picture', *In Central Asia*, which has become one of the most popular examples of the symphonic poem genre which Liszt had originated.

However, the many journeys may have weakened Liszt's general health and mobility and could help to explain a serious accident he incurred a few weeks later. On 2 July he fell down the steps of the Hofgärtnerei, his residence in Weimar, while his granddaughter Daniela von Bülow and her father Hans were visiting him. Although Liszt did not break any bones, and he himself minimised the importance of his fall in communications with both Olga and Carolyne, it was to have major consequences. His mobility was permanently impaired and he was never able to return to the Villa d'Este and his beloved cypresses because of the difficult terrain and problems of access to the building. Liszt remained in bed for nearly two months and he was forced to limit his activities, although he tried to continue composing and giving music lessons. Apart from regular letters to Carolyne and brief notes to Olga (who, of course, would have been a regular visitor), his only surviving other correspondence appears to have been short letters of condolence to Géza Zichy (on the death of a brother) and to Émile Ollivier (on the death of a son).

Liszt continued to work at his compositions. A main concern as always was his need to respond to so much correspondence, as he wrote to Carolyne:

> You know my aversion to advice and condolences about my health. These last two weeks I have been overwhelmed with both – I am touched by them, but very tired. Fifty or more letters and telegrams are on my table. How to cope with the replies! I should find it more expedient to quit this earthly existence! All the same, I shall never be guilty of ingratitude. And so I shall remain as I am, with all the defects of my nature – which, I venture to say, is not an ungrateful one. (Weimar, 4 August 1881)

Liszt also told her that he was putting the finishing touches to his *Cantico del sol di San Francesco d'Assisi*, which reflected his own devotion to the saint, 'God's great madman':

> I have just done some more work on 'Messer il frate sol, suor luna, suor acqua, frate vento e frate fuoco'.[3] How happy the world would be if we were living in it as in a monastery, in loving communion with St Francis – under the sweet and gentle yoke of Our Lord Jesus Christ!

However, he did not post this letter to Carolyne until eight days later when he added a postscript detailing all the tasks that faced him: music to dispatch, pupils to teach, other visitors, and many letters to send off. He admitted that he was in a difficult situation and lacked the 'aptitude for living like this'. It appears that it was during this month that Liszt

---

3. 'Sir Brother Sun, Sister Moon, Sister Water, Brother Wind and Brother Fire.'

composed the short piano piece, *Nuages gris* ('Grey Clouds'), since the manuscript has the date 24 August 1881, but he seems to have told no one about it. Sinister and full of foreboding, it may reflect something of his mental state at the time, although it is also much more than this. Liszt, as he often did at difficult moments of his life, was experimenting with new forms of music. Although put aside as an unpleasant oddity in Liszt's lifetime, it has come to be recognised as the 'gateway to modern music',[4] as a result of its keyless character and impressionistic use of augmented triads.

A month later he wrote to tell Marie that his 'silly accident was still dragging along'. For an older person a major fall can herald the beginning of physical decline, and this seems to have been the case with Liszt. Alan Walker has examined[5] the reports of the doctors involved, including a surgeon in Halle consulted by his local physician. These show that Liszt suffered two fractured ribs, possible bruising of the lungs and pleurisy. However, the investigations also revealed that, in addition, he was suffering from oedema (or dropsy)[6] and associated heart disease, as well as a cataract of the left eye.

Nevertheless, as Liszt prepared to make his long-delayed trip to Bayreuth, his correspondence with Carolyne shows that he was in a creative and optimistic mood:

> This last fortnight I have been working enthusiastically at my *Cantico di S. Francesco*. Such as it now finally is, improved, expanded, ornamented, harmonized, and finished in full score, I consider it one of my best works. I shall have it performed again at some *Musikfest* next year – despite the antipathy of the critics, and of the public influences by them, to religious works outside the conventional forms. I am going to write the arrangement for piano and organ of the new definite version of the *Cantico di San Francesco* – and at Bayreuth shall finish scoring the symphonic poem *From the Cradle to the Coffin*. ... Just imagine, Monseigneur, to whom I played my Second Mephisto Waltz, sketched at the Villa d'Este and finished here, finds it a masterpiece, filled with spirit, originality and youthful vigour! I am dedicating it to my friend Saint-Saëns. ...

---

4. Walker, *The Final Years*, p. 440.
5. Ibid., pp. 403-4.
6. Swelling of the ankles, feet and legs.

For ever, beyond the coffin, your faithful sclavissimo. D.[7]
(Weimar, 6 September 1881)

Carolyne suggested in reply that *From the Cradle to the Grave* would be more appropriate. Liszt agreed: 'I am adopting it with thanks; indeed the coffin remains only a piece of furniture, whereas the grave becomes a metaphor.'

Liszt travelled to Bayreuth in October, where he also took the opportunity to benefit from taking the warm baths, enjoyed visits to Verona and Venice before arriving back in Rome in time for his seventieth birthday, on which he attended a gala concert organised in the German embassy, the Palazzo Caffarelli near the Capitol. He had travelled to Rome with his granddaughter Daniela and was staying with her in the Hotel Alibert in the centre of the city. He told Olga that Marie had also arrived with her eldest son, now seventeen, and her daughter. Carolyne, he wrote, had been delighted to see her grandchildren. Liszt's new physical limitations meant that for the rest of his stay in Rome he stayed in the new hotel he had found close to Carolyne's apartment. During this time, he continued to engage in a lively correspondence with Olga, particularly on philosophical matters. She had sent him a book on the Roman emperor Marcus Aurelius and his practice of 'stoical non-involvement'. Liszt thanked her but expressed his disagreement with the emperor's teaching:

> I admire its heroic aspect but do not feel up to practising it sincerely. Pain is not to me the same thing as pleasure, or even peaceful absence of suffering. Everything passes, as we well know, but until this happens one is either at ease or ill at ease. As for a certain contempt of things and men, I only understand this within very narrow limits, beginning with one's self; but the gentle and wise Marcus Aurelius seems to me to have uttered a truly imperial stupidity in counselling us to *divide* up each thing in our thoughts so as to become imbued with the emptiness of everything. To reduce music to single sounds, to isolate the features of a beloved person, is this to philosophize? Away with this method; let us look for the whole, the harmony. It is there we will find beauty and truth. I far prefer Job's heart-rending lamentations and resignation to the vanity of Solomon's *Vanitas Vanitatum*, and especially

---
7. For 'Dismas'.

the sublime gentleness of the Sermon on the Mount, which sheds a divine light on our sufferings here below. (Rome, 29 November 1881)

There is another letter that Liszt wrote in Rome in this period which gives insight into his current thinking about his compositions and his need to compose. This was to his friend and fellow-composer Camille Saint-Saëns, to whom he had dedicated his recent Mephisto Waltz No. 2 and who had suggested to Liszt that he should think of returning to the city of his youth: 'No one feels more than I the disparity in my works between good intentions and what is actually achieved. Yet I go on composing – not without fatigue – from inner necessity and long habit. We are not forbidden to aim high: whether one has attained one's end remains the question.' (Rome, 6 December 1881)

He told Saint-Saëns that the pain of the insults Liszt had received in Paris in 1866 still weighed heavily on him but he nevertheless hoped it might be possible to change public attitudes there. He did not want 'to be classed among those celebrated pianists who have gone astray in composing failures'. He asked whether, if he were to return to Paris, his friend would be prepared to conduct a few of Liszt's works.

The signs were encouraging that Liszt would receive increasing acknowledgement as a composer even in Paris. However, a new blow to his reputation came from an unexpected direction. In November 1881 a revised version of his book on *The Bohemians and Their Music in Hungary* had been published. The inclusion of a new chapter on 'the Israelites'[8] had led to accusations of anti-Semitism. Most sadly, this accusation came to be attached to Liszt's name and the stigma of it lasted for the best part of a century. For example, as late as the 1950s, Howard Hugo, in his translation of Liszt's letters to Marie zu Sayn-Wittgenstein, described his negative comments on Jews, in comparison to gypsies, as 'appalling' for 'any admirer of Liszt' and explained why: 'Liszt describes the entire Jewish race as sullen, servile, cruel, and the avaricious inhabitants of cities alone – all in contrast with the Gypsies.'[9]

However, we now know that the damaging material included in the second edition of his book on music in Hungary was not written by Liszt but by Carolyne. As with his earlier book on Chopin, he had asked for Carolyne's collaboration and he appears in the case of *The Bohemians* to have handed the whole revision over to her. It was Carolyne who had

---

8. A common term in the later nineteenth century for the Jewish people.
9. Hugo (ed.), *The Letters of Franz Liszt to Marie zu Sayn-Wittgenstein*, p. 238.

Through Triumph and Disaster (1881-86)   217

taken the initiative to include a comparative chapter on the 'Israelites' compared with 'gypsies'.[10] Of course, Liszt was at fault in not checking the final result. Indeed, there were some Hungarian commentators at the time who guessed that another hand had been at work since the attitudes expressed seemed so 'un-Lisztian'.

Liszt hid his distress at what had happened. In his letter to Olga of 29 November 1881 from Rome, he told her that he was 'tormented by a great worry', asked her to find correspondence from Carolyne that could be found in a wallet in the drawer of his desk in Weimar, and to send it to him 'with the seals required for registered mail'. He must have known Carolyne's anti-Semitic views which makes it the more remarkable that he did not examine the final product of her work. It seems to reflect his tendency to over commit himself to new projects without due attention to the consequences, as well as his understandable aim of continuing to involve Carolyne in his musical life. Was he also still in awe of Carolyne's intellect and breadth of knowledge and as a result insufficiently critical of her writing? As a consequence, even when the truth came out and Liszt was excused of anti-Semitism, questions began to be raised about the genuineness of Liszt's authorship of all of his published writings.[11]

Liszt must have spoken about this matter with Carolyne while he was in Rome but there is no further sign in his correspondence until he wrote to her from Budapest, a little over two months later, asking her advice on the accusations that were being made against him, but also indicating his own preference 'to keep silent'. However, there had already been very negative consequences for Liszt in Budapest: a performance of his Faust Symphony had to be cancelled because of public unrest and he had been threatened with physical violence. He was pilloried as well in Vienna. Walker cites[12] an article published in a satirical journal there on Liszt as the 'newest Messiah of the Jews' accompanied by a cartoon on the cover showing a caricature of the 'Entry into Jerusalem' with Liszt as the Messiah seated on a donkey, Wagner and von Bülow at his side.

Liszt did not confide these problems even in his letters to Olga. He admitted to having concerns but indicated that he was coping with them well. He wrote that he was busy with his teaching commitments and so had less time and energy for composition.

In fact, it was during this difficult period that he continued to debate with Olga the values of secular philosophy when set against Christian

---

10. Walker, *The Final Years*, p. 405.
11. Walker, *The Weimar Years*, pp. 368ff.
12. Walker, *The Final Years*, p. 407.

teaching. His replies give further evidence on the importance to him of a strong Christian belief in coping with adversity. The writings of Arthur Schopenhauer had become popular and influential since the philosopher's death in 1860. Wagner had applied some of his ideas on music and discussed them with Liszt. Olga was now intently reading Schopenhauer's works and seems to have been attracted in particular by his turn to Eastern thought as a way of coping with the disappointments of life. Liszt was firm again in rejecting this approach and in a long passage urged her to reconsider her own Christian faith:

> If Buddhism is but a form of Christianity 'minus the hope of a better life' in the hereafter, I confess that all its subtle, benign, compassionate, and soporific philosophy is to me something like an embalmed corpse. ... I am astonished at your finding 'conclusive arguments' in Schopenhauer against immortality of the soul. To say that it is not possible to demonstrate *ex professo*[13] the nature of life in the hereafter amounts to not saying anything at all, for our end as well as our beginning does not fall within the competence of man. But who would be qualified to determine on the basis of the blindness of the comprehension of the mortal race the supreme rights of God's mercy? It remains eternal! What do our lapses, our malignity, our faults and sorrows matter, which sometimes lead us to wish for the annihilation of our being, by God's grace created immortal? Ah! Let us not abjure our heavenly heritage; this would be infamous. 'Conclusive arguments' against the infinity of the divine breath which animates us are hateful delusions. Believe me on this point, very dear Lo, without further vain inquiry, and do not let yourself be led astray by, or fall into false doctrines which are, alas!, all too fashionable. Night shall never prevail over day, nor evil against good. Let us hope and love in Jesus Christ, God crucified. This is the real truth. (Budapest, 14 February 1882)

Liszt also reiterated to Olga his strong moral rather than cynical stance towards life's achievements and setbacks. The evidence suggests that he was coping much better with the difficulties that life was throwing against him. In the winter of 1881-82 there were no signs of depression in his letters despite the accusations being made against him. Correspondence

---

13. 'With certainty'.

with Agnes provoked a particularly enthusiastic response. He had written offering his condolences for her father's recent death and in praise of his political understanding, expressing the hope that his memoirs would be published. Agnes had replied in a way that had touched Liszt deeply and he praised her with obvious sincerity:

> Your letter moves and enchants me. Keep your precious friendship for me, and mine, which is unchanging, is at your service. With you one need fear no *brodo lungo*.[14] You understand and express things at a wonderful tempo. ... The publication of your father's memoirs will not suffer from the delay, since you will edit them. Georges will be of good assistance to you. There is no pride more noble and legitimate than that which allows you to say of your sons: 'I have made men of them.' Your 'exceptional position' results from your very exceptional intelligence. (Budapest, 17 February 1882)

In April he began his regular season of travel, seemingly undeterred by the consequences of his accident the previous summer. First, he spent Holy Week in Kalocsa, south of Budapest, as a guest of Cardinal Haynald, a previous head of the Catholic Church in Hungary, before moving on to Vienna. From there he indicated to Olga that he was in an unsettled state of mind, troubled by past memories and sarcastically referring to his musical critics, but showing his determination to continue pressing on and telling her he would soon be seeing her:

> I ought finally to follow one of your old pieces of advice and compose *The Lamentations of Jeremiah*. The lamentable state of mind for this would hardly be lacking. Unfortunately Palestrina has written songs on these texts which have been consecrated by the Sistine Chapel and by universal admiration, and it would be improper to follow these with a new version condemned and vilified by all good judges, especially by those who hardly know the texts.... For my part I'll fall back on Job who has the additional

Agnes Street-Klindworth (1825-1906)

---

14. 'Thin broth'.

advantage of conversing personally with God, not in the name of a devastated city.

What's all this about? the most wise Lo will ask. So I'll say no more and only warn you that your very humble FL will be back in Weimar next Wednesday. (Vienna, 16 April 1882)

Perhaps Liszt was intending to tell Olga the whole story of the anti-semitic accusations that had been made against him, before starting his travels for the new concert season in Germany. This culminated in his attendance at the first performance of Wagner's *Parsifal*, which for Liszt and many other observers was to constitute the peak of the composer's achievements.

Wagner's Death and Its Aftermath

For more than thirty years Liszt had steadfastly supported and promoted the music of Richard Wagner, even through the years when they quarrelled about Cosima. At times Liszt's support had been to the detriment of his own music and also to his relationship with Carolyne and other friends such as Berlioz. However, there seems never to have been an occasion when he regretted his promotion of Wagner, attributing to the German composer a very particular genius which had merged music with story and art to form a new kind of theatrical presentation. They had been together on the same side in the musical 'wars' of the mid-nineteenth century. Their lives had then become even more intertwined, painfully for a while, through their conflict over Liszt's daughter Cosima and her first husband Hans von Bülow. Nevertheless, Liszt's belief in the eventual recognition of the musical art form which his friend, and now son-in-law, had created never faltered. He deserved his share of enjoyment in Wagner's final success.

Despite impaired mobility, Liszt continued to travel to concerts of his music in Brussels, Jena, Freiburg and Baden-Baden, and arrived again in Bayreuth in July. He described his impressions to both Carolyne and Olga. After he had attended the first dress rehearsal of *Parsifal*, he wrote to Olga that '"masterpiece" is an inadequate word. From the opening to the final bars it progresses from the sublime to the more sublime. He encouraged both her and her oldest son Peterle to come and experience the work for themselves[15]. Two weeks later, in a letter to Carolyne, his praise soared even higher:

---

15. Letters of Liszt to Olga of 20 and 21 July 1882.

> *Parsifal* is more than a masterpiece – it is a revelation in music drama! It has been said, justly, that after the song of songs of earthly love, *Tristan und Isolde*, Wagner has in *Parsifal* gloriously depicted the supreme song of divine love, as allowed by the restricted possibilities of the theatre. It is the miracle work of the century! (Bayreuth, 2 August 1882)

Some days later Liszt provided Carolyne with an even more explicit defence of the way of life he had chosen for himself in the face of her complaint that he would have done better to stay in Rome and concentrate on composition:

> My last letter had grown so long that I omitted the postscript: why am I in Weimar? Is that an error, a fault or a folly? Perhaps all three at once! Nevertheless, for more than thirty years now I have been, as it were, adhering to the house of Weimar. Musically, by works, teaching, publication, I make use of it myself as a base of operations in Germany – where more than elsewhere instrumental, choral, and serious music has taken root through Bach, Haydn, Mozart, Beethoven. Mendelssohn and Schumann have continued along this path. Italy invented opera and caused it to make brilliant progress, aided by numerous talents, composers and singers – and one great genius, Rossini, who for more than half a century dominated the theatres and salons of Europe. In his last years he poked friendly fun at the discovery of infinite melody! Nevertheless, Wagner, with the *Nibelungen* and *Parsifal*, is making it prevail! To understand one another well, too many explanations should be avoided! I have reached the point of keeping silent a good deal. (Weimar, 10 September 1882)

He explained more what he meant by 'keeping silent' in his following letter to Carolyne:

> I attach no value to my opinions, other than in music – and even in that I generally take care not to express them. On other subjects – which I have not had the means of studying in depth – I find it more convenient, and more agreeable, to remain silent, as one uninformed. In my youth I often spoke without rhyme or reason. Nowadays I profit more from listening and reading than from speaking – and take more

pleasure in turning my tongue over a few times than in using it for conversation. I submit to it when the topic concerns matters of no importance, by which it is sometimes necessary to embellish one's dealings with friends and acquaintances. (Weimar, 25 September 1882)

Fortunately, the following month Liszt found a subject on which he could ask Carolyne's help again, to find the right image to accompany his *Cantico* in St Francis' honour.

Liszt had accepted Wagner and Cosima's offer to stay with them during the late autumn and over Christmas in Venice at the splendid late-fifteenth-century Palazzo Vendramin on the Grand Canal. Its whole *piano nobile* ('principal floor') had been rented by Wagner. He gave Liszt a suite of rooms of his own where he could work on composition undisturbed. Detained by some persistent health problems, most likely linked to his fall the previous year, Liszt did not arrive until late November. From there he wrote to many of his usual correspondents. To the Grand Duke Carl Alexander, he described his experience of travelling through the recently completed St Gotthard tunnel: 'one is proud to belong to the human race when the enormous intellectual and material achievements of our century are considered. Each of us should contribute to them as much and as well as he can.' He also admired the new Galleria Vittorio Emanuele in Milan and its contribution to making the cathedral square 'among the most glorious in modern Europe'. He also gave a revealing comparison of himself with Wagner:

> He neither makes nor receives visits, and goes out solely to take the air. For thinkers and labourers alike that is a good example, and I regret that I can follow it only rarely. The pincers of daily life hold me in a kind of worldly grip, one which often runs counter to the Ideal I dream of and sometimes strive to express in music. (Venice, 24 November 1882)

The same day he also wrote to Marie, telling her that he had completed his symphonic poem, *From the Cradle to the Grave*, and thanking her for the encouragement she had given to the piano improvisation on the 'cradle' theme that he had played for her when they met in Rome. He also confided in her that he had been unwell:

> When your very kind lines came to me (at Weimar), I was suffering from a twitching of the nerves that kept me from

writing for a week. I waited for an hour of relief – which I only found today – in order to thank you at length for your continual favour. (Venice, 24 November 1882)

Wagner was also unwell. Liszt told Olga that he suffered 'from the same nervous ailment' as himself 'and more often'. Of his own health, Liszt wrote that he had been feeling 'really very low for almost a week' but as so often before told Olga not to worry about him: 'for the thirtieth time I repeat that there is never any reason to worry about me, and beg you earnestly to refrain from so doing'. He stressed how he was looking forward to the scenic designer and writer, Paul von Zhukovsky coming to stay with the family. Zhukovsky had worked on the stage sets for *Parsifal* and had also recently painted a portrait of Liszt which pleased him and which he thought could stay in Weimar as a memorial of his time there.

His stay in Venice led Liszt to become enthusiastic again about composition, including completing his long planned but continuously delayed *St Stanislaus* oratorio. He had become so 'entirely absorbed', he wrote to Carolyne on 28 December, that he had 'formed an extreme aversion to corresponding by letter ... so I have written only lines of music, much scratched and crossed out – no others!' The knowledge that Liszt was intent on finishing the work he had originally planned with her in honour of the great martyred saint of Poland would have greatly pleased Carolyne, but it was in fact to her daughter Marie again that he explained in detail his ideas for this composition. In successive letters, over the first months of 1883, he made it clear that he regarded her as a most valued assistant in this project. She had secured the services of a poet for the libretto, and she had recently provided a vital clue to help Liszt find a fitting ending to this medieval story of church/state conflict:

Thus we have found the conclusion for our St Stanislaus. I looked for it in vain until now. King Bolesław II, whom I would not want to disparage, since he was a brave warrior, ought to sing his 'out of the depths' as a penitent at the Ossiach convent in Carinthia – according to the recent historical and archaeological findings. To end it, he will cry out softly the 'Holy Poland', as if an interjection. The chorus then starts and ends it. I have already written the 'Out of the depths' and the 'Holy Poland': also the two preceding polonaises, – the one strongly lugubrious, the other triumphant. (Venice, 11 January 1883)

It was also in these weeks in Venice that Liszt was composing more of his striking and musically advanced later work, including two versions of *La lugubre gondola*, inspired by the sight of funereal gondolas taking the bodies of the deceased along the canals of Venice. Once back from Venice he wrote to Carolyne asking her to thank his previous pupil Sgambati for his intention to play this new work in Rome:

> I doubt that it will obtain any success at concerts – in view of its sad, sombre character, scarcely mitigated by a few dreaming shadows. The public demand other things – and if they were wrong, that would not worry them! Nevertheless, I shall have the *Lugubre gondola* published. It will appear after Easter, and I shall send it to Sgambati without delay. (Budapest, 14 January 1883)

La lugubre gondola, in both its versions, is now part of the standard concert piano repertoire but it has taken a whole century and a number of intervening generations of pianists to reach its present fame.

Cosima reported in her diary that Wagner did not like Liszt's new compositions: 'Today [Wagner] begins to talk about my father again, very blunt in his truthfulness; he described his new works as 'budding insanity' and finds it impossible to develop a taste for their dissonances.'[16] Wagner's poor health had made him irritable, even with Cosima, who was extremely worried and agitated by any symptom he showed of his worsening heart condition, so his disturbance at Liszt's pianistic 'experiments' is not surprising. Indeed, despite their attempts to be joyful, it must have been an emotionally painful few weeks for all of them, although the two old friends embraced warmly before Liszt departed. Liszt's steady affection for Wagner is shown in the piano transcriptions he had made of many of his musical works. Only recently he had completed a mesmerising arrangement of the 'Feierlicher Marsch zum heiligen Gral' from *Parsifal*. This piece at least shows the two composers walking again in perfect harmony.

Liszt's correspondence from Venice with Olga, Carolyne and Marie had many common elements, how he was spending his time with Wagner, Cosima and family, how popular Zhukovsky had become with them all, and especially how absorbed he had become in composing music. However, once he arrived in Budapest, although he told Olga on his arrival that he was 'again suffering from the fever of writing music'

---

16. Cited in Walker, *The Final Years*, pp. 427-28.

(adding, 'is this senility? let others decide')[17], and indicated to Marie his intention of working on *St Stanislaus*, this soon became impossible for him. He explained his position most clearly to his biographer Lina Ramann:

> My winter existence in Budapest this time is very much like that of previous years: every day at least 4 hours of letter-writing; visits – business and other – then await; proofs to attend to; in the afternoon, three times a week, several hours of piano lessons with a dozen pupils, some of whom acquit themselves in masterly fashion; in the evenings, sometimes concerts to attend and, for recreation, a game of whist.
>
> Here, I can hardly get down to my *real* work. It was easier for me in Venice. There, I wrote various things, among them a *third* elegy, dedicated to Lina Ramann. Don't be frightened by the title, *Die Trauer Gondel* (*La gondola lugubre*). As you know I bear in my heart a deep sorrow; now and then it has to break out in music. (Budapest, 9 February 1883)

It was at this point that Liszt decided at long last to make a public reply to the accusations of anti-Semitism in his publication on the music of gypsies in Hungary. He explained to Carolyne why he had made this decision:

> Local circumstances, difficult to appreciate elsewhere, have made me decide to have published in the *Gazette de Hongrie* a letter relating to the criticism of the Israelites which is wrongly attributed to me. To publish this letter last winter seemed to me to be timorous – and the foolish courage of fear is not known to me! – I incline rather in the other direction! I now think I shall not be committing a shameful retraction. Kindly let me know your opinion, without any reserve whatsoever. You quote to me Sainte-Beuve's just remark in 1833 [1834] on Lamennais, after the fulgurating publication of *Paroles d'un croyant*: 'He has changed his public, but will not gain by the change.' For my humble part as an artist, I try to serve the public nobly – without anxiety about gain or loss – whether by pleasing, or by confronting, it. (Budapest, 10 February 1883)

---

17. Letter from Liszt to Olga of 15 January 1883

What was the point of Liszt's reference to Lamennais? The priest's honesty in his writings, such as *Paroles d'un croyant*, had been greatly admired by Liszt as a young man. However, by attacking the Roman Catholic Church's ties with the privileged classes, he had lost much of his Catholic following while acquiring support in socialist and secular settings. Liszt seemed to be claiming that he was attempting neither to 'please' nor 'confront' his public. In his letter in the *Gazette* he had done nothing to remove his association with the principal anti-Semitic passages in his book. It was Wagner, the day before his death, who saw the truth of the matter. Cosima's diary entry indicates that when her husband read this letter he told her: 'Your father goes to his ruin out of pure chivalry!' Walker notes[18] that the actual word Wagner used was '"Cavalerie" – a triple pun on chivalry, cavalry and Calvary'.

On 13 February Richard Wagner died in Venice following a heart attack. When he received the news, Liszt telegraphed Cosima offering to travel to Venice and accompany her and Wagner's body back to Bayreuth. His granddaughter Daniela answered for her, asking Liszt not to come. He appears not to have been disturbed by Cosima's refusal of his assistance, writing to Olga that 'between her and me there are bonds and dates far removed from ordinary relations' and to Carolyne that, as he disliked grand ceremonies, he would not attend Wagner's funeral but in some weeks' time 'unhurriedly and at my leisure, see Cosima again in Bayreuth'. However, Liszt seems to have misread his daughter. Later, he may well have come to realise that his decision not to attend Wagner's funeral in Bayreuth had been a serious mistake. Although his health was weakening, he was still capable of travelling and willing to travel long distances in response to invitations which he valued.

On his way to Weimar in April, Liszt stayed for some days in Vienna where he continued work with Marie on *St Stanislaus*. While he was there, Marie hosted a reading of the 'definitive' text in her own residence. Although his stay was short, Liszt wrote twice more to her suggesting further amendments and asking for her help in completing the text:

> The eternal conflict between Church and State is brought out strongly by Stanislaus and Bolesław. ... After the death of Stanislaus, Bolesław's penitential pilgrimage (orchestra alone) is to end at the Ossiach convent where the king sings the 'Out of the depths' and joins with the chorus in the 'Holy Poland'. (Vienna, 5 April 1883)

---

18. Ibid., p. 409, footnote 15.

> Please excuse my insistence, Your Highness, but I am preoccupied with the idea that the *St Stanislaus* Oratorio can only succeed under your aegis and with you presiding over the completion of the text. ... I have noted the modifications on it that seemed to me necessary: principally: the murder of the bishop, *at the cemetery*, after his brief apostrophe to the King: 'Behold here the arm of God, forever upraised to avenge the Truth!' (Vienna, 6 April 1883)

Having arrived back at his home in Weimar, Liszt attended another concert of his *St Elisabeth* in Marburg where he stayed with his cousin Franz von Liszt. From there he wrote an enthusiastic letter to Marie, thanking her for the text of *St Stanislaus* which he had received.

Liszt then journeyed on to Leipzig for the Allgemeine Deutsche Musikverein festival in early May where his symphonic poem *Prometheus* was being performed. From there, he had been expecting to travel on to Bayreuth to see Cosima. We know from Adelheid von Schorn's account of seeing Liszt in Leipzig that he had been greatly shocked to receive a letter there telling him again not to come: '... found him in a dreadfully excited state: he had received a letter from Wahnfried asking him to postpone his visit as Frau Wagner would see *no one*. That his daughter was shutting herself away from *everyone*, Liszt knew, but that *he* was to be no exception, hurt him bitterly.'[19] Whatever his private feelings may have been, Liszt continued to take an active part in the Wagner memorial concert for 22 May at the Weimar Theatre, coming to the podium at a certain moment to conduct the Good Friday Music from *Parsifal*.

There is unusually little correspondence from Liszt available to read for the following four months. Might this reflect Liszt's distress at his rejection by Cosima? We are thus only left with one letter to Carolyne and short notes to his granddaughter Daniela to provide further evidence on Liszt's state of mind in these months. His letter to Carolyne gives no hint of distress and attributes, rather sardonically, his delay in writing to his 'music writing' habits:

> Once again the reason, or rather the unreason, for the delay in my letters lies in my tiresome habit of writing music. To correct myself of it in my old days is no longer possible! Fontenelle used to say of his brother, the abbé: 'In the mornings he says mass; in the evenings he knows not what he says.' I resemble

---

19. Cited by Williams (ed.), *Franz Liszt: Selected Letters*, p. 899.

> the Abbé Fontenelle, with this variant that, in the evenings, worn out by the fatigues of the day – I no longer know what to say, and limit myself to corresponding mentally! (Weimar, 26 July 1883).

Perhaps more indicative of Liszt's feelings is his correspondence with his granddaughter:

> Very dear Daniela, your mother has genius of heart. Her reason is of the same level. I understand, admire and love her with all my soul.
> Your grandfather (Weimar, 7 May 1883)

> For today, very dear Daniela, I have not a word to say to you: Come on. On all matters, we will always understand each other very simply, even through silence. Your old papa (Weimar, 22 August 1883)

Liszt's mood is probably best reflected in some of the piano music he produced in the same period of time, including *R.W. – Venezia, Am Grabe Richard Wagners*[20] and, particularly, the disturbing *Schlaflos! Frage und Antwort*. Life had given him another jolt.

It has been suggested that Liszt in 1883 may have reached levels of depression similar to that of six years earlier.[21] However, this is unlikely to have been the case because in the intervening years Liszt seems to have developed more effective ways of dealing with negative thoughts. Nonetheless, one reason for suggesting similarities with his situation in 1877 is his repeated belittling of his musical composition. As before, he had been concentrating on writing music but was displeased with the results. Having heard Berlioz's opera, *Benvenuto Cellini*, in Leipzig both in August and September, he wrote to Carolyne in praise of the work and its 'youthful verve', which 'I don't weary of admiring', but, as a postscript, he commented negatively on his own current compositions: 'Despite the many interruptions, I continue to blacken music paper, and do nothing but cross out and erase. Most of the things I could write don't seem to me to be worth the trouble!' (Weimar, 29 September 1883).

---

20. Liszt wrote this piece on 22 May which would have been Wagner's seventieth birthday.
21. See, for example, Pesce, *Liszt's Final Decade*, p. 159.

It needs to be remembered that Liszt's plans to complete *St Stanislaus* had foundered yet again. His relatively few short letters to Olga do not reveal anything further about his state of mind, but simply express the devotion to her own well-being of her 'very aged' but 'constant' friend (Weimar, 1 October 1883). He refers hardly at all to Cosima in his letters to Olga but no doubt had many opportunities to speak to her directly about his daughter's behaviour towards him.

Promoting the Work of Others

Liszt's experiences in the following months gave him reasons to be hopeful about his musical legacy. Later in October, on the eve of Liszt's seventy-second birthday, the Weimar Court Theatre presented a stage performance of *St Elisabeth*, and in November he travelled to Leipzig to hear a concert of his works by his Russian pupil Alexander Siloti. In December he visited Meiningen on two occasions to hear its orchestra under Hans von Bülow. He was hugely impressed by Hans' performance, particularly his rendering of Beethoven's Great Fugue Op. 133 by more than 30 string players. For Liszt, these were rewarding events, about which he wrote enthusiastically to Carolyne. He also wrote to Otto Lessmann, the editor of *Allgemeine Deutsche Musikzeitung*, on 10 January to ask him to publish an article he had written on his impressions of the Meiningen orchestra.

He continued to promote the new Russian music, writing to César Cui, one of his friends among 'The Mighty Five',[22] to thank him for dedicating a new composition to him:

> Your musical style is raised far above ordinary phraseology; you do not cultivate the convenient and barren field of the commonplace. ... Doubtless *form* in Art *is* necessary to the expression of ideas and sentiments; it must be adequate, supple, free, now energetic, now graceful, delicate; sometimes even subtle and complex, but always to the exclusion of the ancient remains of decrepit *formalism*. (Weimar, 30 December 1883)

Liszt told Cui that he had met with the Tsar's cousin Grand Duke Konstantin, a patron of the arts, during his recent visit to Germany, and

---

22. An expression used to refer to five composers of the 'New Russian School' of music: Mily Balakirev, Alexander Borodin, Cui, Modest Mussorgsky and Nikolai Rimsky-Korsakov.

that he spoke to him about the importance of the recent developments in Russia. He also recommended Alexander Siloti to Cui's 'kindness' when his Russian pupil arrived in St Petersburg.

His manservant's declining health had prevented Liszt from undertaking his usual autumn journey to Rome. Achille Colonello had been his manservant for only three years but had already become greatly valued for the considerate care he had provided in Liszt's declining health. Liszt did not want to abandon him and for the first time in many years stayed in Weimar for Christmas. But having admitted him to the local hospital in the new year and realising he could do no more for him, Liszt left Weimar at the end of January, together with a young manservant who was loaned to him by Olga, to keep his appointments in Budapest. On the way he visited his biographer Lina Ramann in Nuremberg. It was she who delivered to him the news that Achille had died. She noted in her memoirs of Liszt: 'I gave him the telegram; he was very shaken, it trembled in his hand and a tear fell upon it.'[23] He paid tribute to his servant in a letter to Carolyne:

> In my last conversation with him, I urged him to exercise patience and to trust in Our Lord Jesus Christ – while assuring him that he would return to my service and join me again in Budapest. He answered me most affectingly: 'Per Vostra Eccellenza vengo a piedi.'[24] Achille was the best *cameriere* [valet] I have ever had – upright, quiet, home-loving, well-schooled, and not easily put out. His failings were certainly far fewer than those of his master, and his qualities very praiseworthy. (Nuremberg, 2 February 1884)

Despite the evident good humour shown in most of his correspondence, Liszt did acknowledge to some of his correspondents the very real problems he was encountering with his health. He explained to Henriette von Liszt, his cousin Eduard's widow, that his commitments had prevented him having a proper rest in Vienna on his journey from Weimar to Budapest: 'Such an extra is hardly my lot anywhere. My life is one continued fatigue. Someone once asked the celebrated Catholic champion Arnauld (the Jansenist) why he did not allow himself some rest. "We have an eternity for that", answered he.' (Budapest, 8 February 1884)

---

23. Cited in Williams (ed.), *Franz Liszt: Selected Letters*, p. 912, footnote 3.
24. 'For Your Excellency, I come by foot.'

Two months later Liszt expressed to Olga how his visual impairment was becoming worse:

> No news from here other than the disagreeable weakening of my sight. To write is becoming as difficult for me physically as mentally. Hence I am very far behind, not only in answering letters but in my promises to the publisher Kahnt, who is to bring out the *Stanislaus* fragment, announced in the programme of the next *Tonkünstler Versammlung*. (Budapest, 11 April 1884)

Yet, Liszt never complained about his untiring efforts to promote the work of other aspiring and neglected composers. He told Olga that he had asked Riedel to include in the forthcoming German music festival a piano concerto by Alfonso Rendano, like Liszt an infant prodigy, who had been born in obscurity but taken by his parents from Calabria to train in Naples. However, he feared both for him and for Giovanni Sgambati, another of his Italian protégés, that their works would be a victim of narrow-minded critics:

> It [Rendano's concerto] is a vigorous, original, and remarkable work which I greatly appreciate, while being of the opinion that the ears of pens of the leading critics will not receive it favourably.
>
> Hans Richter[25] recently praised Sgambati's symphony sincerely to me. The Vienna performance was fairly well received but in the *Presse* Hanslick was critical. Hence it is a failure. The public is easily discouraged by a newspaper article. With few exceptions, people believe what they read. (Gran, 3 February 1884)

He also took the trouble of writing to Felix Mottl, court opera conductor in Karlsruhe, to express his appreciation to him for presenting his former colleague Peter Cornelius' *Barber of Baghdad*, the reception of the first performance of which in Weimar in 1859 had sparked Liszt's resignation as court musician.

In his last letter to Olga before arriving back in Weimar, he took the opportunity to reassert his strong religious convictions. In his previous

---

25. A famous Austro-Hungarian conductor.

letters he had mentioned contact with the French author, 'free thinker' and editor of *La Nouvelle Revue*, Juliette Adam, who was visiting Hungary. Liszt's preference now was for a life of prayer rather than argument. He told Olga that in his recent visit to Cardinal Haynald in Kalocsa his focus had been on attending church services rather than other matters:

> These I attended regularly for at least four hours daily. This is not of much interest to you, but so long as there are human beings here below, their best course will be to say *Kyrie eleison, Christe eleison!* and *Pater noster!*
>
> There is a splendid remark by Napoleon I to Larevellière-Lépeaux, leader of the theophilanthropists: *Vous voulez du sublime, Monsieur; eh bien, dites votre Pater.*
>
> The illustrious Mme Adam is not of this opinion, and claims that Apollo suffices for everything. So be it for those, among whom I do not number myself, who are content with this. (Vienna, 22 April 1884)

On his way back from Budapest to Weimar Liszt stayed in Vienna for much longer than the previous occasion, spending time with Princess Marie and sharing with her his plans for *St Stanislaus*. Five short notes from Liszt to Marie survive from this period in which they agreed times to meet. A few weeks later he wrote a longer letter to her from Weimar, in which he referred to the life they had shared together with her mother:

Franz Liszt. Photograph by Louis Held, Weimar 1884.

> The pleasant memories you retain of Weimar, Your Highness, touch me keenly. Since the year of '47, I have become as if imbedded here. It is a heartache to me, that your mother does not condescend to return. I can only yield to certain fixed ideas. ...
>
> By Pentecost of '85, I hope to have finished the score of St Stanislaus. I write slowly – cross out three-quarters, and then do not know whether the fourth part can stand by itself. (Weimar, 30 May 1884)

In this letter to Marie, Liszt also referred positively to the German music festival which had just been held in Weimar and in which he conducted an orchestra for the last time. The pieces he chose were von Bülow's symphonic poem, *Nirvana*, and 'Salve Polonia' from *St Stanislaus*. Both pieces were performed from manuscript and the performances were far from perfect. Liszt had been received with great honour by the audience but his student Felix Weingartner, when he wrote his memoirs, recorded his sense of sadness: 'Over this unforgettable scene there lay a feeling of leave-taking. ... No one could fail to see that here was a tired old man whose clock was running down.'[26]

However, Liszt does not seem to have shared these feelings of sad decline. His correspondence with Carolyne suggests that his focus was now less on himself than on the overall success of the music festival. His previous note to her indicated his growing reluctance to dwell on his own compositions: 'Riedel is keen to give a second performance of my oratorio *Christus* in Leipzig, on 18 May. I have in vain tried to dissuade him – after they have been written, corrected and published, my poor works preoccupy me not in the least. I generally even advise against their performance.' (Weimar, 27 April 1884) After the concert he expressed himself satisfied with the performances, including of his own compositions, and of the warm response of his many friends:

> Mme Viardot, her daughter Mme Héritte, and above all my most excellent and illustrious friend Saint-Saëns, responded to it with emotion. I feel rather tired – just enough to begin to be sociable again at the performances of *Parsifal* at Bayreuth in July and August. The very valiant Arnauld used to say: 'Haven't we eternity to rest?' (Weimar, 29 May 1884)

His letters to Saint-Saëns show his overriding concern for the younger composer, who seems to have become his dearest friend in music among contemporary fellow composers. Three weeks later he had to admit his failure so far to make the progess he desired in promoting Saint-Saëns' works:

> I refused to suspect that there could be any ill-will against you in Budapest. Nevertheless I think it is strange and most unjust that your dramatic and symphonic poems have not yet taken the place which is due to them in Hungary. I have explained myself clearly about them several times, but the

---

26. Cited in Walker, *The Final Years*, p. 464, footnote 13.

theatre *ménage*, and even that of the Philharmonic Concerts, is formed outside of my influence. They are quite ready to accord me a general consideration, with the exception of arranging particular cases otherwise than I wished. For many people doubtful profits and manoeuvres contrary to their dignity exercise an irresistible attraction. (Weimar, 18 May 1884)

However, if Liszt was hoping for a warmer reception from Cosima when he attended the Wagner festival in Bayreuth in July 1884, he was to be gravely disappointed. It must have been particularly hard for him to accept that Cosima, having taken over responsibility herself for the direction of the festival, did not turn to him, despite his long experience of running musical events, for even one word of advice. Nor was he even allowed to stay in the family home but had to seek accommodation elsewhere. Yet Liszt had never wavered in his support for Wagner's music. In Bayreuth he attended every rehearsal as well as the final performances, but only had one fleeting encounter with Cosima herself, who tried to avoid any contact with the public. According to the report of his grandson Daniel Ollivier, who saw Liszt pass Cosima in the theatre corridor after a rehearsal, Liszt spoke to her but she walked past in silence.[27]

Liszt hid whatever pain he felt from his own correspondence. He wrote five times to Olga from Bayreuth and stressed his positive experiences there, beginning with his granddaughter Daniela coming to meet him at the station, and ending with his anticipation of Olga's own arrival in Bayreuth. To Carolyne, Liszt wrote with his usual huge enthusiasm for Wagner's genius and with only brief comment on Cosima:

Monday and yesterday, the first 2 performances of the revival of *Parsifal* in Bayreuth. Complete success with a large German and international audience, filled with enthusiasm for this wonderful masterpiece. It will continue in the same way for the whole fortnight. Wagner must be glorified – we had a presentiment of it in Weimar as early as '49. The following years confirmed our feelings – and today, the theatre is everywhere dominated by Wagner. His true glory is never

---

27. Cited by Williams (ed.), *Franz Liszt: Selected Letters*, p. 977.

to have deviated from his great calling – which he followed through many an obstacle. To him belongs the immortality of a great earthly renown! ...

My daughter remains engulfed in her mourning. I have not seen her again. Her children, whom I see every day, are prospering. (Bayreuth, 24 July 1884)

Nevertheless, once back in Weimar, he returned in a subsequent letter to his silent encounter with his daughter in Bayreuth: 'Cosima I caught a glimpse of for barely a minute, in the darkness at the end of one of the *Parsifal* rehearsals. Her mother in days gone by took as a motto: "In alta solitudine." Cosima's altitude is her widowhood!' (Weimar, 10 August 1884)

This suggests that the no doubt painful memory of this silent encounter in the dark with his estranged daughter had stayed with Liszt over the three weeks since it occurred. It seems significant that he connected this recent memory with a much older, but also sad, memory he held of her mother Marie d'Agoult.

A few weeks later Liszt travelled to Munich where he attended a performance of Wagner's *Rheingold*. From there he travelled to Schloss Itter in the Tyrol to be a guest at the home of Sophie Menter, whom he regarded as the most 'Lisztian' of all his female pupils and who was now at the peak of her career as a pianist and was about to sign a contract to become Professor of Piano at the St Petersburg Conservatory. His journey to the Tyrol reminded him of an earlier visit with Carolyne and her daughter in the summer of 1858 just before the fateful performance of Cornelius' *Barber of Baghdad*, Marie's marriage and the death of Liszt's son Daniel, both major losses to their respective parents. He wrote to Carolyne about the feelings it evoked:

At Schloss Itter I quietly thought back on our travels in the Tyrol with Magne, who was still rather unwell at that time. Even the *vetturino*,[28] the *zither*, and the Tyrolean songs, more vulgar than artless – seemed admirable, as you were there! Oh! that good and lovely time when the common run of people said we were unhappy! (Weimar, 11 September 1884)

---

28. Little carriage.

Liszt offered some spiritual reassurance. He had composed a motet on a psalm verse, his moving, *Qui seminant in lacrimis in exultatione metent*.[29]

In the same week he also wrote to one of his most combative supporters in his difficult earlier years in Weimar, the German music critic Richard Pohl. He thanked him and commented on Pohl's recently published book on Berlioz:

> In reading the first volume I was painfully affected by several passages out of Berlioz's letters, in which the discord and broken-heartedness of his early years are only too apparent. He could not grasp the just idea that a genius cannot hope to exist with impunity, and that a *new thing* cannot at once expect to please the *ancient order of things*. (Weimar, 12 September 1884)

Had Liszt understood this any earlier than Berlioz? The evidence from his own correspondence shows how he struggled with not being accepted as a valid composer for much of his life.

Liszt continued his life of constant activity, visiting Eisenach for the unveiling of a statue of J.S. Bach, followed by Leipzig for a concert of his own music given by his two Russian pupils Alexander Siloti and Arthur Friedheim. Fostering Russian music continued to be a major interest for him. He wrote to Mily Balakirev in St Petersburg in October to 'salute' the energy of the new Russian school and to accept the dedication of the composer's symphonic poem, *Tamara*. Liszt's final journeys of 1884 were to be particularly happy ones. He journeyed to Budapest via Nuremberg, where he discussed music theory, practice and aesthetics with his biographer Lina Ramann, and to Vienna, where, as usual, he stayed in his cousin's house and visited Princess Marie and various friends. In Hungary, he was the guest of Count Géza Zichy, who by now had become a very close friend, at his estate in Tetétlen on the great plain of Eastern Hungary. Zichy had built a small one-storey house next to his for Liszt's use, with room for friends as well. He wrote an account of his journeys to Olga and thanked her for translating from Russian an article about him. He agreed with the author's claim that Liszt's sympathy for Russian music had begun already in 1842 when he encountered Glinka's operas in St Petersburg.

---

29. Psalm 125/126:5, 'They that sow in tears, shall reap in joy'.

In further letters to Olga and Carolyne, respectively, Liszt described his experiences in Tetétlen. There was one experience he did not record but which Count Zichy did in his memoirs. On 10 November Liszt, with Zichy and his daughter, gave a concert for the local countryfolk:

> After the concert the great master excelled himself in kindness, waiting upon his unsophisticated guests, offering them food and filling their glasses with wine. ... After Liszt had captivated everyone, despite his inability to speak Hungarian fluently, a snow-white old man went up to him at the end of the meal and, glass in hand, said: 'What you are *called*, the Count has told us; what you can *do*, you have shown us; but what you *are*, we have seen for ourselves – and for that, may the great God of the Hungarians bless you!'[30]

Back in Budapest, Liszt helped Zichy with one of his own compositions. He described what he was doing in a letter to Olga:

> Your sagacity and perspicacity are rarely at fault. Thus they had rightly guessed that I'm going to undertake a friendly task on behalf of Géza Zichy. This is the orchestration and rearrangement of a long ballad: 'The Enchanted Lake' (*Zaubersee*), in which the composer has introduced three charming melodies which, however, do not combine happily. He is as ignorant of the difficult art of transitions as he is of that of orchestration. ... The instrumental ballad will run to about thirty printed pages. In order to complete them as I promised, I will stay here until Monday evening and only arrive in Rome Wednesday or Thursday. (Budapest, 4 December 1884)

His letters from Rome to Olga, Marie and others convey a picture of a man still very involved with life. Their content contrasts strongly with that of Adelheid von Schorn's memoirs which stress how shocked Carolyne was that Liszt looked so swollen and worn out. As Walker stresses[31] Liszt did not like complaining about his health. He tended only to do so when it hampered his everyday activities, and this was not the case at present. He was met at the station in Rome by his pupil Giovanni

---

30. Graf G. Zichy, *Aus meinem Leben*, 3 vols (Stuttgart, 1911-20), vol. 3, p. 61, cited in Williams (ed.), *Franz Liszt: Selected Letters*, p. 911.
31. Walker, *The Final Years*, p. 466.

Sgambati, and subsequently led a very active social life, attending musical soirées, at which Sgambati played, and dining well with his many friends in Rome, including Cardinal Hohenlohe. Overeating may not have been good for Liszt's health but he was not shunning contact as he had some years previously. On Christmas Day he was the guest of the Caetani family, who had been one of the first to welcome him to Rome more than twenty years before. He told Olga of the musical talent of his godson Roffredo Caetani. In the same letter[32] he let Olga know that he had told 'everyone' of her forthcoming arrival in Rome. What had previously not been advisable now was encouraged!

Liszt also wrote to Marie to tell her of his improved impressions of her mother and gave her news that would please her further about the placing of family images in Carolyne's apartment and the completion of her mother's *magnum opus*:

> The 25th volume of the 'Causes' – an immense work of a fierce fourteen-years' labour is being courageously completed. After the last page is printed, the author at (long) last intends to rest next summer, and even to take a trip around Italy in little daily stages – Assisi, Siena, Pisa, Florence, Bologna, Venice, etc., etc.: *mirabile visu*! (Rome, 17 December 1884)

He also continued his advocacy on behalf of others. A most striking example of this is a letter he wrote to Victor Hugo on behalf of a woman he admired greatly, Marie Espérance von Schwartz, a philanthropist who had done much for the people of Crete during their struggle for independence from the Ottoman Empire, founding hospitals and schools. She was also a supporter of Garibaldi and asked Liszt to write to Hugo to accept the dedication of her recent book on the Italian hero. It is noteworthy how Liszt could admire people who were of a different 'camp' to him. Hugo had been a fierce critic of Napoleon III, deciding to go into exile on the channel island of Guernsey during his reign. Liszt on the other hand had been a friend and admirer of Napoleon and was also certainly no supporter of Garibaldi in the conflicts over Italian unity in which he had sided with Pope Pius IX.

Liszt continued to send letters from Rome to his various friends. Virtually all of Liszt's letters have a named recipient but there is one letter he wrote from Rome in January 1885 to an unnamed person

---

32. Letter from Liszt to Olga of 28 December 1884.

which Adrian Williams deservedly includes in his collection. It shows Liszt encouraging a singer not to 'withdraw from the world':

> Without the shadow of a reproach, I am not of the opinion that you should withdraw from the world. To be sure, it hasn't only delights to offer: roses do not lack thorns and sometimes even thistles mingle with them. All the same, one must know how honourably to endure and adapt oneself. In your capacity as a singer of excellence, solitude doesn't suit you at all. Music is necessarily sociable, immediate, humanitarian. Come down, therefore, from your *Montagne Pistoiesi*, and, if it isn't inconvenient, come and see me again, not far away, at the Universe Hotel in Florence. I shall be spending two days there at the end of next week, and will telegraph you beforehand. (Rome, 16 January 1885)

While in Rome Liszt completed what was to be his last religious work, *Salve Regina*. In composing it, he returned to the harmonious style of his *Ave verum corpus*. It is a very beautiful piece, unusual for Liszt in that it was composed for unaccompanied voices, but unjustly neglected like so much of his religious work.

Journeying until the End

Liszt told Olga on his return to Budapest in February 1885 that he was only travelling now 'from a sense of duty, possibly illusory'. By comparison, writing music was still essential. In fact, his letters to Olga seem to convey a subtly changing view of himself, still dissatisfied with the products of his musical compositions but as firmly committed as ever to his continued efforts to compose:

> I am again guilty of being late, and for the same reason – or rather for the same fault as formerly. This fault is writing music, a task which tires me greatly and which I only carry out unhappily, finding my talent very inadequate for the lively expression of my thoughts. Everything seems to me listless and colourless. (Budapest, 26 February 1885)

> A very highly born young lady, having let herself be abducted by her lover, wrote to her mother: 'I am guilty, but not a

criminal.' Well, I confess to being both guilty and almost a criminal because of my delays in writing. Need I repeat that it is once again my silly music which has, this whole month, kept me from writing letters. (Budapest, 25 March 1885)

Pesce suggests[33] that Liszt was at last coming to terms with the doubts that had long plagued him about his music's worth. He no longer sought to be among the highest creators but simply accepted that he enjoyed composing. In spite of the depressive comment about his music ('listless and colourless'), he was enjoying his new achievements. He had indeed been working hard, writing during February 40 pages of music with a Hungarian character, including his Hungarian Rhapsodies No. 18 and No. 19 and a *Csárdás Obstinée*, the first piece intended for an exhibition of Hungarian culture at which his artist friend Mihály Munkácsy was also to be represented with a painting.

An important factor in Liszt's good humour may have been the result of the increasing role of a new woman in his life. He had been accompanied both in Rome and Budapest by a young pupil Lina Schmalhausen who had come to him with recommendations from the German court six years earlier. She now took it upon herself to care for Liszt in his old age. Liszt had supported Lina strongly in difficulties she had encountered in her career as a pianist so far, and also provided her with financial help.[34] Thus, he not only had a manservant, a Hungarian named Misha, but also a female carer who, besides taking lessons from him, helped him with letter writing as well as taking a more general interest in his welfare. Lina was not popular with Liszt's other students, nor with Olga. As a result, Lina no longer attended Liszt's classes in Weimar.

Based again in Weimar, Liszt showed his resolve not to put himself at the centre of attention. He made it clear to Alexander Siloti that he disapproved of the latter's intention to set up a 'Liszt Society' in Weimar: 'In Weimar it is wisest to keep oneself *negative* and *passive*. Therefore, dear Siloti, attempt *no* 'Liszt-Verein'. (Weimar, May 1885).

Siloti was by now one of the most outstanding pianists among Liszt's current performers. It was in this year that Liszt dedicated a spare but effective arrangement of a Russian folksong, *Abschied* ('Farewell'), to him. It makes poignant listening because it is one of the very last piano pieces Liszt composed. Perhaps the theme had been introduced to him by Siloti.

---

33. Pesce, *Liszt's Final Decade*, p. 163.
34. See Walker, *The Final Years*, pp. 413-14.

Through Triumph and Disaster (1881-86)   241

At the end of May, Liszt visited Karlsruhe for the Allgemeine Deutsche Musikverein festival of 1885. Despite his tiredness, he continued travelling to concerts in Mannheim, Strasbourg and Freiberg, followed by a visit to Antwerp to hear a performance of his Szekszárd Mass. From there, he wrote to Ferdinand Taborszky, his music publisher in Budapest, about his recently completed set of piano pieces dedicated to the memory of six Hungarian heroes and asked him to go with his housekeeper to his house in Budapest to fetch the copy of his *La Lugubre Gondola* and send it to him in Weimar. This late composition in its various arrangements had become special to him:

> I stupidly forgot there – in the bedroom, *not* in the *salon* – the beautiful and revised copy of a composition for piano and violin or violoncello, together with the transcription of the same for pianoforte alone. The title is *La Lugubre Gondola* (the funeral gondola). As though it were a presentiment, I wrote this *élégie* in Venice six weeks before Wagner's death. (Antwerp, 8 June 1885)

He then attended concerts in Halle and in Aachen before returning to Weimar. He expressed much appreciation of the performances in his correspondence to Carolyne and Olga.

The letters Liszt wrote in the spring and summer of 1885 show him in good spirits. In a letter to Carolyne in June he continued to express a humbler view of himself as a composer:

> I waste my time more or less voluntarily. Given the weakening of age, work becomes more difficult for me; nevertheless, I continue laboriously to fill music paper, and some people flatter me that my last compositions are not worse than the preceding ones. My estimation of both does not go beyond the most rigorous modesty. Without counting the great masters such as Palestrina, Lassus, Bach, Mozart, Beethoven, I consider myself very inferior to their successors Weber, Meyerbeer, Schubert, Chopin, etc., and bow profoundly before the immense genius of the *double eagle* Wagner, 'word and tone poet', as King Ludwig of Bavaria addressed him in his letters. (Weimar, 30 June 1885)

However, he was annoyed that his recent religious works, *Via Crucis*, *Septem Sacramenta* and *Rosario*, had been declined by the Catholic publishers, Pustet of Regensburg. Nevertheless, this would not stop him supporting their publication of the works of the German Society of St Cecilia whose composers were attempting to restore plainchant and renaissance polyphony to Catholic liturgy. His motto in this situation would remain: 'As you will do, I shall not do.'

In the middle of October 1885, Liszt left Weimar for Rome. Together with a group of his pupils he travelled via Munich where he attended a performance of *The Barber of Baghdad* conducted by Mottl, with the cuts suggested by Liszt. He then stayed with Sophie Menter again in the Austrian Tyrol before travelling on to Innsbruck where his birthday was celebrated in style by the local male voice choir. Back in Rome, he wrote a reassuring letter to Marie about Carolyne's health: 'As for her health, your mother is at *her* best – despite the prodigious activity and the extreme ardour of both the intellect and heart of the persevering patient, who only departs from her sublimity by her compliant amiability.' (Rome, 19 November 1885)

Liszt's letters to Marie, as well as to other correspondents, had become much shorter due to his failing eyesight and his reliance on others, usually his pupils, to write them. There was no longer any mention of completing *St Stanislaus*. In ending this same letter, he was more frank about his health problems but charming as always in the way he expressed his gratitude to Marie: 'My eyes are still getting weaker: my memory too, with the exception of that of my heart – described by a deaf-and-dumb person as 'gratitude'. This I place constantly before your feet.' Liszt's response to the sad news that Olga's third son Clément, who had been studying art in Rome, had died, was also much shorter than one might have expected:

> No man can know, let alone feel a mother's grief. It is not forbidden to condole with deep respect. ... Your son Pierre has written me some warm and noble lines. Be so good as to give him my enclosed reply, as I do not have his address.
>
> The religion of sorrows with the supreme hope of divine mercy is that of Christians. Let us keep it faithfully with all our soul. (Rome, 24 November 1885)

While in Rome, Liszt received invitations to attend concerts of his music in London, Paris and St Petersburg during the following year. It is amazing that in his weakened condition he was prepared to travel to all three. He felt obliged to come to London because of his friendship with Walter Bache who had been promoting Liszt's music for many years in England. However, he hesitated to accept the French and Russian invitations. He confided in Saint-Saëns that he did not want 'to expose myself to the discomfiture' that he had experienced in Paris in 1866. He wrote to Sophie Menter that he was incapable of conducting an orchestra or even playing the piano well and so could not justifiably claim a fee – but also he could not afford the expense of travelling and staying in Russia without financial help. Nevertheless, he told Olga that he probably would travel to St Petersburg because of the 'warm good will' shown him by Grand Duke Konstantin: 'Since one must live, one tries to do so as best one can short of mortifying oneself greatly.' (Rome, 23 December 1885)

Problems with his eyesight had now become a constant theme in Liszt's correspondence. Although he never liked being asked about his health, his growing blindness could not be ignored since it interfered with all aspects of his life, including composing. On his way back to Budapest he wrote Olga a letter containing his last substantial reflection on Christianity and ethics. It concerned Tolstoy's recently published *My Religion* which Liszt had already mentioned to Olga three months earlier. He now gave her his impression of it:

> On the way here, [Bernhard] Stavenhagen read me a good many pages from *Ma Religion* by Leo Tolstoy. This work may please people who enjoy fuzzy thinking. If, as on pages twenty-one and following, one advances the proposition *Ne résistez pas aux méchants*[35] as the <u>central</u> and supreme axiom of Christianity, this means continually straddling the false and the absurd. Indeed we must resist evil men by whatever means we can if we are not to suffer the worst fate here below. Without government, without judges, without military power, without resistance to evil, what kind of society can be organized? Are we to open our doors wide to thieves and bare our throats supinely to murderers? (Palazzo Malipiero, Venice, 27 January 1886)

His last days in Budapest were happy ones. He had told Olga that he had been spending a couple of hours each day with his students and several of them would soon achieve the rank of 'first-class' pianists. He enjoyed the fact that they brought new pieces to play for him, including a composition by one of his previous students in Weimar. A group of

---

35. 'Do not resist evil men.'

students accompanied him to the station as he took the night train to Vienna on 11 March. After visiting Marie in Vienna, he journeyed on to Liège to attend a Liszt concert. From nearby Argenteau he wrote to Carolyne about both the success of the concert and the family meal he shared with her daughter in Vienna. Marie, he told Carolyne, was 'physically, intellectually and morally getting along admirably!' He accepted the mammoth journeys facing him in his seventy-fifth year, comparing himself to 'a rolling stone which gathers no moss', 'rolling from Paris to London and then to St Petersburg'. He also kept in contact with Olga, and she was the first person he told that his trip to St Petersburg would have to be postponed until the autumn because the entire Russian court was moving to the Crimea for April.

Despite his initial worries, Liszt's return to Paris was a triumph. The performance of his Gran Mass went so well that it had to be repeated a week later. However, the pain of two of his friends' earlier disloyalty remained as we see from one of his letters from Paris to Carolyne: 'At midday, 2nd performance of the Gran Mass – rehabilitated henceforth, despite the contrary opinion of Berlioz in '66, and of his scribe d'Ortigue, a good Catholic and friend of my youth!' (Paris, 2 April 1886)

In letters the next day to Olga and to Marie, he also expressed his huge sense of satisfaction at his reception in Paris and, particularly, at the success of the Gran Mass. To Olga he wrote that his 'success in Paris exceeds all expectations'. To Marie he also the stressed the contrast with the reception the Mass had received in 1866 with the repeated performance in the same week being 'something almost without antecedents for a piece of Church music'. He continued to reflect on that change in attitude to his work in his subsequent letters even after his return to Weimar. In his letter of 22 May to Carolyne, in which he told her of further 'Parisian details', he described how 'a well-known preacher' had said to him that 'of all the musical works I know, it is the most theological' and added that 'this opinion is gaining credence, despite many hesitations'.

Liszt's visit to London in April was also a great success, as well as being filled with engagements. While he was there, he wrote a series of short notes to Carolyne, reporting the success of the two performances of his *Elisabeth* and of two other 'Liszt Concerts', held in St James's Hall in the centre of London and in the 'Crystal Palace', near to where he was staying as a guest of Henry Littleton, head of the Novello firm, in Sydenham. He also told her of his reception at the Royal Academy of Music and the establishment there of a 'Liszt Scholarship', as well as his meetings with Queen Victoria at Windsor Castle, the Prince of Wales, Cardinal Manning, the Roman Catholic primate of England, the actor Henry Irving and the distinguished religious scholar Max Müller, who invited him to visit Oxford in the following year. He played the piano himself both for Queen Victoria and for the students at the Royal Academy. He had been able to accept 'barely half' of the invitations he had received to dinner and lunch.

After a visit to Antwerp to stay with friends he returned to Paris where he was entertained in the house of Mihály Munkácsy and his wife Cécile. He also took the opportunity to see Agnes, who had also become acquainted with the Munkácsys. A further successful performance of the *Elisabeth* took place at the Trocadéro on 8 May. He described to Carolyne how his fellow composer Charles Gounod remarked, after the scene of the 'miracle of the roses', 'there are aureoles therein – it is haloed with a mystic dust' and, after the final chorus, 'the stones with which it is built are holy ones'. He promised that Émile Ollivier's wife would write to tell her more about it and his former secretary Gaëtano Belloni would send some newspapers to confirm the success. It was important to Liszt that Carolyne fully appreciated the extent of the acceptance Liszt had finally achieved in Paris.

On 18 May, the day after his return to Weimar, Liszt received an unexpected visitor, his daughter Cosima, who had been deliberately avoiding contact with her father for over three years. He gave no details of this meeting in the subsequent letter he wrote to Carolyne (nor in any of his other surviving letters), simply stating that, as a result of her visit, he had decided to travel to Bayreuth not only for the wedding of his granddaughter Daniela, but also for the summer's season of Wagner performances. One might have expected Liszt to have made some further comment on Cosima in this letter to Carolyne, but perhaps its limited character reflects the fact that Liszt was now generally dictating letters via his students and could not reveal much of a personal nature.

Liszt followed the itinerary he set out in this letter, but beforehand travelled to Halle for medical consultations both for the swellings in his legs and his increasing blindness. For the former, he was recommended water cures which he had always disliked. As he told Carolyne on 14 June, the operation to remove a cataract from his left eye which he had been promised was 'almost more attractive to me!' He wrote to Géza Zichy later in the month to thank him for the new piano sonata that he had sent. Since he could not read or write, he had asked his student August Göllerich to play it to him. He sent a kind letter back to his friend:

> It sounds good and when nicely played will make an effect. Without being a hunter of reminiscences – a very silly hunt – I was nevertheless struck by the similarity between the triplets in your first movement and the triplets in my *Tasso: Lamento e Trionfo*, and still more those in Rubinstein's *O! wenn es doch immer so bliebe*, a conservative song but no longer an unknown one. This kinship can't be helped, and you can therefore calmly admit to being a cousin. ... Your most affectionately devoted, F. Liszt (Jena, 25 June 1886)

One has to rely mainly on others' accounts of Liszt's actions and words over the last weeks of his life. He attended the annual festival in early June of the Allgemeine Deutsche Musikverein which in 1886 was held in Sondershausen. This was another most successful occasion for him as two Liszt concerts were held to mark his coming seventy-fifth birthday and many of his pupils and friends attended. Walker refers[36] to eye-witness accounts of how Liszt became animated in the rehearsal for his oratorio of *Christus*, encouraging the 'disciples' to become more agitated in the tempest scene and that 'Christ' should reproach them strongly 'as if to say, "What cowards you are!"' He was also in 'high spirits' as he travelled back to Weimar together with Walter Damrosch, Adelheid von Schorn and Paul von Zhukovsky, keeping them entertained by his comments on the festival and his reminiscences both in the train and back in Weimar where they dined with Zhukovsky. Damrosch recorded in his memoirs how they accompanied Liszt back to his house afterwards and how he was spellbound by Liszt pausing and asking them to listen to the sound of a nightingale, a sound Damrosch had never noticed before.

Liszt did write to Carolyne, Olga, Agnes and Sophie Menter from Bayreuth in early July, describing his granddaughter's civil and religious wedding ceremonies, and from Colpach in Luxembourg where he stayed with the Munkácsys in another of their houses. His letters show him still in good mood, praising Agnes yet again for the 'precision' and 'shrewdness' of her political mind, telling Olga of life with the Munkácsys, and promising to send soon a further report on life in Colpach to Carolyne. However, then, four days before his journey to Bayreuth, he

---

36. Walker, *The Final Years*, pp. 502-3.

wrote to Olga indicating that he had developed an unpleasant respiratory tract infection:

> To my physical condition, already so pleasant, has now been added these five days a most violent cough which plagues me day and night. To comfort me, the doctor says that this type of cough is very tenacious. So far, neither cough medicine nor infusions, nor mustard plasters, nor foot-baths have rid me of it. (Colpach, 17 July 1886)

This is the last surviving letter we have from Liszt. In a previous letter to Olga, he had indicated that he was dictating his German letters to his pupil Bernhard Stavenhagen and his French ones to Cécile Munkácsy. He seems not to have dictated any further substantial letters, not even the promised one to Carolyne. Nevertheless, despite his worsening condition, he attended a concert in his honour in Luxembourg on 19 July, during which he played the piano himself, and travelled by train with Stavenhagen and his manservant Miska (Mihály Kreiner) to Bayreuth two days later. While there, his health continued to worsen but he still managed to attend performances of *Parsifal* and *Tristan* on 23 and 25 July. He subsequently had to take to bed in his lodgings and died of pneumonia and heart failure just before midnight on 31 July 1886.

Although little information was provided at the time about Liszt's last illness, we now can read a translation by Alan Walker of a detailed eye-witness account of his last few days, written by his pupil and helper Lina Schmalhausen.[37] As Liszt's condition deteriorated, he specifically asked for her to come and join him in Bayreuth, which she did on 22 July, nine days before he died. Her story of Liszt's last days was first discovered by Walker in the Weimar archives in 1977. It appears that soon after his death Lina was asked to write this account by Liszt's first biographer Lina Ramann. However, her detailed and vivid account of what she witnessed each day, particularly, the poor medical care, neglect and insensitive support from Cosima and her children, was no doubt seen as so damaging to the received account of Liszt's death and to the reputation of several people involved, that Ramann decided not to include the material in her biography nor even to mention its existence.

---

37. A. Walker, *The Death of Franz Liszt Based on the Unpublished Diary of His Pupil Lina Schmalhausen* (Ithaca, NY: Cornell University Press, 2002).

The detail in Lina Schmalhausen's account of each day is so precise that it must be a reflection of her intense involvement in all that she observed taking place in Liszt's lodging. It also includes almost verbatim accounts of Liszt's conversations both with Lina and with others. Although her accounts of Cosima's and others' actions and motives may be biased, there are, as Walker argues, no good reasons to doubt the veracity of her factual reports. This I think applies also to her accounts of Liszt's own conversations. Lina was clearly devoted to him and treasured everything he said to her. From 22 to 27 July Lina had almost unhindered access to Liszt and spent large parts of the day with him. However, on 27 July Cosima forbade Lina to enter his sickroom after inadvertently witnessing Liszt's conversation with her and being shocked by the level of intimacy that was closer to that of a father or grandfather. Nevertheless, Lina persisted in attempting to maintain contact, through his manservant Miska and fellow pupils who were keeping guard over Liszt, and, when locked out, kept a watch from outside through the window of Liszt's ground floor room, taking care not to be observed.

What emerges from her account about Liszt's attitudes to his situation in the last days of his life? The following points are clear. Liszt appreciated the care and comfort Lina provided him. She read and played cards with him as his other pupils did, but she also stayed with him, holding his hand when he asked her. He prayed with her and asked her to read from his prayer book, which, although he knew it by heart, he said helped to calm him. Liszt was also concerned for Lina herself throughout these days, thinking especially of her financial situation and what others might think of her tending to his care. From the day she arrived he repeatedly expressed his concern that she should leave before the 'Baroness' (Olga von Meyendorff) arrived on 2 August. He gave his encouragement to her obtaining a musical position in Budapest and even advice on playing a composition of his, *Funérailles* from his *Harmonies poétiques et religieuses*, demonstrating with his fingers an exercise to loosen her fingers. Although irritated at times, he was generally kind and understanding to others. He excused his family's behaviour towards Lina – 'You must forgive them for not allowing you to see me, otherwise everyone would want to come.'[38] In conversations with others, he even had good words to say of Olga Janina, his pupil from 1869 onwards who had caused him so much difficulty – 'She was not bad, simply unbalanced. In my opinion she was decidedly talented.'[39]

---
38. Cited in ibid., p. 119.
39. Cited in ibid., p. 55.

Understandably, he was very unhappy with his situation but most of the time he put on a brave face. All this is consistent with the attitudes to life we have seen Liszt express in his writings.

What is disturbing to read is evidence of the negligent care that Liszt received from doctors and especially from his family. His situation was not taken seriously and, even when he was clearly dying, Cosima did not send for a Catholic priest to administer the last rites.[40] He received relatively little comfort after Lina's care was taken away from him. Nevertheless, Lina's account, although very critical of his daughter, records that at the very end Cosima did show some tenderness to her father and after his death 'took me in her arms, kissed me repeatedly, and brought me the Master's prayer book'.[41] Cosima also allowed Lina to cut a lock of Liszt's hair and to place forget-me-nots in his left hand, placing it over his heart.

Where was Liszt to be buried? We also know from Lina's account that Liszt did not want to die in Bayreuth. However, he had left instructions only to Carolyne as to where he should be buried. As the executrix of his will, she was opposed to Liszt being buried in Bayreuth, in the shade of Wagner, but this was precisely what Cosima wished. There was therefore yet another tussle between the two women over Liszt. Weimar, Budapest and Rome all had claims to his remains. Carl Alexander made determined efforts to bring his body to Weimar where he would have established a worthy mausoleum. Carolyne, in the end, supported the Hungarian claim and agreed that the most suitable place would have been in the Franciscan monastery in Pest. All this was to no avail against Cosima's strong will. In her reply to Carl Alexander, she argued that, if Liszt had wanted to be buried other than in Bayreuth, near his family, and where he died, he would have told her. Bayreuth was also appropriate, she hinted, as it was where now was 'blossoming' the 'seed' which her father had 'sown' in Weimar. This final defeat for Carolyne was too much for her frail condition. She survived the great love of her life by only a few months. She was buried by Cardinal Hohenlohe in the grounds of the German cemetery within the Vatican itself, a distinction given her at the end by the institution that had blocked her marriage to Liszt.

What about Liszt's other principal correspondents? Carolyne's daughter Marie[42] inherited all of Liszt's possessions, as these had been bequeathed in his will to Carolyne. She collaborated with Carl Alexander in preserving

---

40. The Roman Catholic sacrament then named 'Extreme Unction'.
41. Cited by Walker, *The Death of Franz Liszt*, p. 138.
42. Died in 1920, aged 82 years.

Liszt's memory in Weimar, creating a museum in the rooms of his lodging in the Hofgärtnerei. Carl Alexander[43] was well remembered for his support of the arts in Weimar and his attempts to restore it to the glory of its previous golden age. Émile Ollivier[44] spent his retirement writing the history of the reign of Napoleon III, including its disastrous ending in which he had been so closely involved. His records on the lives of Liszt and Marie d'Agoult were preserved by his son and their grandson Daniel. Olga[45] remained in Weimar until the onset of the First World War when she moved to Rome, living there until her death in apparent obscurity. Agnes,[46] fittingly for her enigmatic life, also disappears from the records completely, apart from the recording of her death in the surroundings of Paris. Cosima[47] lived the longest of all. The rest of her life was one of total service to the Wagner enterprise in Bayreuth that, unfortunately, became increasingly marked with overtones of Aryan racial purity.

It is possible to trace the careers of many of Liszt's pupils and his other great friends in music. Sophie Menter[48] left St Petersburg shortly after Liszt's death and followed in his footsteps as a travelling concert pianist. Fortunately, recordings of her playing survive which give us perhaps the closest copy we have to Liszt's style of playing. She acquired considerable fame and there is a remarkable portrait of her by Ilya Repin. Alexander Siloti[49] developed, as Liszt had done, great skills in piano transcription. After the Russian revolution he emigrated to the United States, as did his younger cousin, the composer Sergei Rachmaninoff, to whom he himself had taught piano. Lina Schmalhausen[50] obtained a position teaching music in Budapest soon after Liszt's death and five years later was invited back to Berlin to be court pianist. Her last years, however, were difficult and in the year before she died, at the age of 63, she had to have her right leg amputated and could not afford to pay for an artificial limb. However, her fellow Liszt pupils were told of her situation and provided the necessary funds. As Alan Walker aptly remarks, 'they helped Lina because Liszt would have helped her, as he had helped them all'.[51]

---

43. Died in 1901, aged 82 years.
44. Died in 1913, aged 88 years.
45. Died in 1926, aged 87 years.
46. Died in 1901, aged 81 years.
47. Died in 1930, aged 92 years.
48. Died in 1918, aged 71 years.
49. Died in 1945, aged 82 years.
50. Died in 1927, aged 63 years.
51. Walker, *The Death of Franz Liszt*, p. 2.

Through Triumph and Disaster (1881-86) 251

Liszt's young Hungarian friend of his last years, Count Géza Zichy[52] achieved great fame both as a composer and a pianist for the left hand, receiving praise even from one of Liszt's main opponents, the critic Eduard Hanslick. He published the last letter which he received from Liszt in his own memoirs. His tribute to Liszt echoes down the years:

> A few weeks later this great and noble man was dead. I received the sad news in a small, remote village in the Hungarian mountains, so late that I had no time to get to the funeral in Bayreuth. Franz Liszt is the most beautiful memory of my life. In loyal love and gratitude I remember my great friend, whose friendship constitutes the greatest pride and the greatest joy of my existence.[53]

---

52. Died in 1924, aged 74 years.
53. Cited by Williams, *Franz Liszt: Selected Letters*, p. 942, footnote.

3 avril, 86 Paris.

Contrairement au mauvais accueil et à la pitoyable exécution en 66, de la Messe de Gran, elle a fait bonne impression cette fois, — même à deux fois en huit jours — chose presque sans antécédents pour une œuvre d'église.

Les Préludes, Tasso, Orphée, ont été applaudis chaleureusement aux Concerts Colonne et Lamoureux. Plus le concerto brillamment exécuté par Planté, perpétuelle gratitude

F. Liszt

Liszt's last letter to Princess Marie de Hohenlohe of 3 April 1886. It contrasts the positive reception which his Gran Mass had recently received in Paris with its poor reception twenty years earlier.

9

Seeing Liszt Whole: Music, World and Spirit

Key Themes in Biographies of Liszt

This book has examined Franz Liszt's own written self-presentation in later life by means of a thorough consideration of his correspondence over the last 25 years of his life. Taking account of how people present themselves is a necessary starting point for understanding them. Many of Liszt's previous biographers have attempted to reach conclusions on Liszt's life and personality but there is little consensus among them. This seems to me to have been mainly the result of not seeing beyond the apparent contradiction between the spiritual and worldly qualities he displayed both in his personal life and in his career as a musician. The most thorough account of his life remains Alan Walker's three-volume biography in which the identifiable facts of Liszt's life have been assembled in narrative form from birth to death, alongside an analysis of his principal musical achievements. However, this has not prevented others from attempting more definitive statements about Liszt's character. For example, Oliver Hilmes' recent one-volume biography has been much praised for presenting a convincing story of Liszt's life. The actor and author Simon Callow, who has written a book on Richard Wagner, responded to Hilmes' book on Liszt with the comment, 'at last, we see him whole'.

However, Hilmes' conclusion that Liszt 'was a contradictory character'[1] seems to reflect Ernest Newman's description of Liszt, written the best

---

1. Hilmes, *Franz Liszt: Musician, Celebrity, Superstar*, p. 313.

part of a century earlier, of a 'soul divided against itself'.[2] There is too much evidence which is left unconsidered in both their accounts. Seeing a person 'whole' is difficult, perhaps ultimately impossible, but in seeking a more complete truth it is important not to overlook significant available material. In Liszt's case, we have a considerable number of written records, especially the very many surviving letters written by Liszt himself. On the basis of a study of his correspondence with Princess Carolyne zu Sayn-Wittgenstein and Baroness Olga von Meyendorff over the last ten years of his life, Dolores Pesce has argued, contrary to both Newman and Hilmes, that Liszt was not torn and, in fact, had achieved reconciliation between the worldly and spiritual sides to his character by the end of his life. I agree with this view. Nonetheless, there is also much more to learn from a more complete view of Liszt's correspondence and over a longer period of time than that which Pesce attempted. Certainly, in the last ten years of his life, Liszt encountered major personal crises, including problems with both his physical and mental health. However, for many years before that he had also been living a life with considerable stress and strain, achieving much but also facing disappointments both in the reception of his music and in his personal life.

Despite his personal popularity, Liszt's character and music were much maligned even in his own lifetime, most notably by previous friends such as Clara Schumann, and there remains a tendency to repeat some of this criticism today. Clearly, Liszt had his faults. There is no doubt that he made serious mistakes in his life but his reputation as a 'mere showman', and, as a result, 'insincere' and 'superficial' both in his words and actions, seems to me greatly mistaken. Now that we have so much more information on his attitudes, thoughts and feelings from his own correspondence, some of which has only emerged in recent years, we are able to make a more accurate assessment about how he faced up to difficulties in both his musical and personal life.

The present study of Liszt's correspondence has taken as its starting point his decision in his late forties to relinquish his position as musical director in Weimar. He had become by then so frustrated in achieving his musical aims in Germany that he was prepared to take a step into the unknown by moving to Rome, which at that time was far from the centres of European music that he knew well. His hope was to make a new musical career for himself together with Carolyne, his partner during the previous ten years whom he was intending to marry. She too had suffered greatly as a consequence of being ostracised from most of Weimar society

---

2. Newman, *The Man Liszt*.

because of her failure to obtain a divorce from her early marriage to a Russian prince and her intimate and continuing partnership with Liszt.

Before seeking some conclusions about how Liszt responded and adapted to the events of his later life, it is worth considering three topics which appear essential to any biography written about Liszt. The first and most significant of course is his life as a musician, both his early success as a pianist and his subsequent striving to compose new types of music of ever-increasing originality as well as to support the efforts of like-minded composers. Although his reputation as a brilliant pianist was never in doubt, he was often disappointed in the reception given to his own compositions by music critics and by the general public.

The second theme, which has preoccupied most of his biographers, is Liszt's relationships with women. Even a preliminary examination of his correspondence shows that women played a very large part in Liszt's life from youth through to old age but none of these relationships, although passionate and often long lasting, led to marriage. As a result, Liszt lived alone for large periods of his life and for nearly all of his later years. Although it is understandable that this question should be a focus for many popular depictions of Liszt's life, it is also one where there is the greatest danger of exaggeration and misrepresentation.

The third important theme in his life, which is of at least equal importance to the second, is his strong spiritual yearnings. However, while biographies have differed in the relative importance they have given to the first two themes, no complete biography written on his life, perhaps not even Alan Walker's, has given equal attention to Liszt's religious beliefs and the way he expressed them in his life and in his music. Indeed, some biographers have not taken his spiritual beliefs seriously enough. Yet, it is very clear from an examination of the correspondence of his later years, that questions of Christian faith, as well as responses to non-religious ways of giving meaning to life, which were coming into prominence in later nineteenth-century European society, were central to his sense of self. It is therefore this aspect of Liszt's life that I have sought to draw out in my examination of his correspondence.

Liszt the Musician

Much has been written and will continue to be written about Liszt the musician. He is remembered principally because of his achievements, as a performer, teacher and composer. His reputation as a pianist was established already at a very young age in Paris. It is much less well known that by mid-life music had also become a source of suffering for him. In fact, it appeared to him at least that his early established strong musical identity as a pianist stood in the way of his later attempts to gain recognition as a composer. Following the example of Paganini, he dazzled audiences throughout his life with his piano playing. He had no equal for both expressiveness and delicacy of touch but his ambition went further. From a young age he had also wanted to be a composer and, when, with the offer of employment as musical director in Weimar in his later thirties, the opportunity arose to concentrate more on composition, he was more than happy to give up his previous career as a concert pianist.

No one seems to have denied the exceptional quality of Liszt's piano playing. The Viennese music critic, Eduard Hanslick, one of the most consistent opponents of Liszt's musical compositions, praised Liszt's rare return to the concert platform in 1874 in fulsome terms:

> His playing was free, poetic, replete with imaginative shadings, and at the same time characterised by noble, artistic repose. And his technique, his virtuosity? I hesitate to speak of it. It suffices to observe that he has not lost it, but has rather added to it in clarity and moderation. What a remarkable man! After a life incomparably rich and active, full of excitement, passion and pleasure, he returns at the age of sixty-two, and plays the most difficult music with the ease and the freshness of youth.[3]

His last pupils also commented on his exceptional playing even in his final years. For example, Alexander Siloti in his memoirs described how he was enchanted by the memory of Liszt's interpretation of the opening of Beethoven's 'Moonlight' Sonata:

> Scarcely has he played the opening triplets when I felt I no longer existed in the same room; but when the G sharp entered in the right hand four bars later, I lost all sense of reason. He did not accent this G sharp, but it was a sound never heard before, a sound which even now, 27 years later, I can still hear clearly.[4]

Despite the beauty of his pianistic performances, however, the more conservative elements in European music continued to condemn the

---

3. Cited in Walker, *The Final Years*, p. 273.
4. Cited in E. Burger, *Franz Liszt: A Chronicle of His Life in Pictures and Documents* (Princeton, NJ: Princeton University Press, 1989), p. 302.

influence that Liszt was wielding on the future of music through his advocacy of new forms of composition. Their opposition could reach extreme forms. When Liszt was invited to conduct Beethoven's *Missa Solemnis* in Vienna at a festival in 1870 to mark the centennial celebrations of his birth, musicians such as Brahms, Joachim and Clara Schumann, all of whom had known Liszt well in earlier life, refused to attend. Other musicians recognised the unfairness in the way Liszt was treated by those whom he had formally helped, most notably the English pianist and conductor Walter Bache who had studied with Liszt in the 1860s. As he wrote to a mutual friend Jessie Laussot in 1877: 'Liszt is the most ill-used genius the world ever saw. All are ungrateful to him. No Wagner, Bülow, Joachim or Klindworth would be here but for Liszt. … I lose courage with my abominable fellow-creatures.'[5]

Fortunately, by the end of his life, thanks to the efforts of Bache and others, Liszt's orchestral, choral and piano music were being given more recognition. His influence was also being felt by future major composers. Walker has commented[6] on the affinities between Liszt's magnificent descriptions of water and the subsequent works produced by Claude Debussy. The two met in Rome in January 1886 and on this occasion Liszt played his *Au bord d'une source* from the first volume of *Années de pèlerinage* to the younger man. Debussy was later to defend Liszt's music from excessive criticism, as in his concert review of a performance of Liszt's 'Mazeppa' in 1903:

> This Symphonic Poem is full of serious faults; it is sometimes even cheap. Yet the tempestuous passion which it maintains to the end holds the listener enthralled with such force that one finds it magnificent without asking why. At the end of the concert you can feign disgust because it turns out so well. It is sheer hypocrisy, believe me.[7]

In a concert review of 1912, Maurice Ravel was prepared to go further and claim for Liszt a significant impact on subsequent orchestral composers:

> Are the failings in all Liszt's works really so important to us? Are there not sufficient strong points in the tumultuous,

---
5. Cited in Williams (ed.), *Franz Liszt: Selected Letters*, p. 952.
6. Walker, *The Final Years*, pp. 475-76.
7. Cited in Burger, *Franz Liszt*, p. 332.

seething, vast, and glorious chaos of musical material on which several generations of famous composers have drawn? Let us be honest: it is very much to these shortcomings that Wagner owes much of his disclamatory vehemence, that Strauss owes his overenthusiasm, Franck his prolix sublimity, the Russian school its occasional harsh and pittoresque style, and the French School the uncommon coquettishness of its harmonic charm. For all their dissimilarity, do not these writers owe the best of their qualities to the overflowing musical generosity of their great predecessor?[8]

Of all Liszt's musical contributions, the most neglected have been his religious works. This is despite the thorough account of his masses, oratorios and other choral works with religious themes published by Paul Merrick in 1987 and re-issued more recently.[9] Outside Liszt's native Hungary most of these works are rarely performed, even within the Roman Catholic Church for which Liszt wrote them. As is evident from his correspondence, the failure of the performance of his Gran Mass in Paris in 1866 was a source of long-lasting pain to Liszt, only alleviated by its success on his return to Paris a few months before his death 20 years later. The religious music of his last years was even refused publication. By then he had come to terms with disappointment and, as he himself admitted, he was by then writing for himself and for the future. His compositions may still have a major part to play since Liszt was acutely aware of the need for church music to be an enhancement, rather than a distraction, to the liturgical events being enacted. All of Liszt's religious music expresses the devout nature of his beliefs and some of it is of exquisite beauty. For example, his choral piece *Ave verum corpus* of 1871 can bear comparison with Mozart's much more famous setting of this medieval Eucharistic hymn.

A further aspect of Liszt's life as a musician that deserves stressing was his sense of responsibility and duty to fellow musicians. Not only was he a conscientious teacher, he was a very active advisor and advocate not only for his students but for many other musicians who asked his help. To the end of the life, he remained dedicated to the welfare of colleagues, present and future. This is well illustrated in his letter, written less than a year before he died, to Otto Lessmann, the Berlin music critic and editor of the *Allgemeine Deutsche Musikzeitung*, in which he argued that

---

8. Cited in ibid. p. 332.
9. Merrick, *Revolution and Religion in the Music of Liszt*.

Past pupils and friends of Liszt gathered together for the 100th anniversary of his birth in 1911. Count Géza Zichy is in the centre of the front row. Seated on his right side is Sophie Menter.

some of an artist's or musician's financial success should be employed to benefit subsequent artists or musicians. He was commenting on the early death of the successful pianist, teacher and composer, Theodor Kullak:

> With regret, and a firm conviction, I repeat to you in writing that Theodor Kullak's forgetfulness ought to be made good by his heir. Otherwise it would be severely denounced as unfaithfulness to his position as an artist. A fortune of several millions gained by music-teaching ought not to remain buried without any regard to music students. Unless the heirs prefer to found a *Kullak-Scholarship*, I consider that they are in duty bound to endow the four existing musical scholarships – those in the names of Mozart, Mendelssohn, Meyerbeer, Beethoven – with 30,000 marks each: total 120,000 marks. (Weimar, 5 September 1885)

Liszt and Women

Liszt had a great capacity for friendship with both men and women. Women, in particular, seemed to be held under his spell. Even the one female musician who came to express disapproval of both Liszt and his music, Clara Schumann, indicated her initial attraction to him. In the diary entry on 1 August 1886 after hearing of his death she wrote: 'As a young man he was deeply fascinating, but later on there was so much coquettishness about him, for all his intelligence and charm, that it often offended me.'[10]

As Alan Walker has stressed, Liszt was no 'Don Juan'. He respected women, was interested in their lives and treated them with care and respect. There seems to be no record of any woman ever being afraid of him. His positive attitude to women, together with his magnetic personality and exceptional pianistic ability, account in large part for his acquisition of so many female friends.

Nevertheless, Liszt's reputation as a 'ladies' man' was well founded and he himself acknowledged that he had problems in this area of his life. He found it hard to control his often-passionate response to women whom he found attractive. As he claimed his father had forecast, he also allowed women to play perhaps too prominent a part in his life. Liszt is sometimes represented as searching for his 'Beatrice', the ideal woman who would inspire and support him in his desire to be a successful composer. Each of his two important relationships can certainly be construed in this way. Both Marie d'Agoult and Carolyne zu Sayn-Wittgenstein saw themselves to some extent as his muse, although they were both mature, well educated women with ambitions of their own which Liszt encouraged.

Liszt's tendency to search for women did not disappear as he became older. He continued to acquire close women friends until his death and this sometimes caused conflict amongst them. Although Carolyne never seems to have realised the true nature of his intimate relationship with Agnes Street-Klindworth, even while all three were living in Weimar in the 1850s, she followed closely his relationships with other women when he returned to Weimar without her in the 1870s. In fact, she deployed Adelheid von Schorn, the daughter of her best friend in Weimar, as her 'spy'. Adelheid's reports back to her for the most part absolved Liszt from any evident misbehaviour, but Carolyne remained highly suspicious. She feared that Liszt could easily revert to his previous habits. Hilmes draws attention to the significance of Carolyne's long letter to his cousin Eduard Liszt after she became aware of the scandal around his relationship with his former pupil Olga Janina: 'For ten years in succession he led an abstemious lifestyle. Both in Weimar and in Rome. But he is weak, and if a woman wants to control him, he cannot resist her.'[11]

In this letter Carolyne named a number of 'guilty' women, including the singer Emilie Merian-Genast, Olga Janina and Olga von Meyendorff.

---

10. Cited in Burger, *Franz Liszt*, p. 330.
11. Cited in Hilmes, *Franz Liszt: Musician, Celebrity, Superstar*, p. 244.

In fact, as Walker emphasises, there is no evidence that Liszt had sexual relations with any of these three women or intensity of feeling comparable to his earlier romantic involvement with Agnes Street-Klindworth. However, there are suggestions from his correspondence with Olga von Meyendorff that he may have led her to expect more from him than he was prepared to give. She took over Carolyne's role as Liszt's principal organising host in Weimar and expressed dislike for some of the younger female pupils around him in his second period in Weimar, especially Olga Janina and Lina Schmalhausen, whom she thought took liberties with an older man.

Walker does acknowledge that Liszt's behaviour with his female pupils aroused comment: 'there was much stroking of the hair, kissing of the cheeks, and embracing of the entire person'.[12] Liszt's attraction to women was also evident to his male friends, including his patron Carl Alexander, but none seem to have reproached him for it. The Irish portrait painter Henry Jones Thaddeus, who came to know Liszt in Italy in his last years, was impressed by Liszt's long history of attracting women:

> Even in his old age women adored him, and followed him about as if he were a magnet attracting them. He told me that there is no exaggeration in the story of how in Russia after one of his concerts the ladies present, exuberantly enthusiastic, stormed the stage, battling to embrace him and obtain a memento of the occasion, and that he was in a fainting condition when, eventually he was rescued … from the midst of this surging, hysterical mob of women, minus much of his clothing, which had literally been cut off his back for souvenirs.[13]

We know that Liszt did express regret, at least to Carolyne, about his behaviour with women. Hilmes cites[14] a letter Liszt wrote to Carolyne in his sixtieth year in which he was open with her about his tendencies to lose control of himself in women's company and that he tried to master these passions:

> I have a long struggle ahead of me until I defeat my old and wild-eyed enemy, who is not the imp of polite conversation

---

12. Walker, *The Final Years*, p. 298.
13. From H.J. Thaddeus, *Recollections of a Court Painter* (1912), cited by Williams (ed.), *Franz Liszt: Selected Letters*, p. 933.
14. Hilmes, *Franz Liszt: Musician, Celebrity, Superstar*, p. 244.

but the demon of arousal and strong emotions. Knowing it, as I do, from the many times that it has laid me low, I now avoid all occasions when it could easily overwhelm me – and I hope to triumph over it completely thanks to the grace of God, which I pray for every day. (Budapest, 17 January 1871).

One wonders to what extent Liszt was helped in this struggle by his frequent practice of confession to a priest. What precisely would his confessors have advised him in addition to providing absolution for his sins? Carolyne had doubts about this matter too. In her letter to Eduard mentioned above, she urged him to appeal to his cousin's sense of honour: 'Tell him that the world would have forgiven all his secret infidelities but that it refuses to condone the public lack of respect for a woman he fully accepted and whose husband he should have been.'[15]

Liszt's last years would likely have taken a very different course if he had married. There are clear explanations for the final failure of his relationship with Marie d'Agoult and also for the cancellation of his marriage to Carolyne in 1861 after the failure of the annulment of her previous marriage. However, why did he not marry Carolyne after her husband died just over two years later and why did he give such an evasive answer to Carl Alexander when he raised the subject with him? Some biographers have concluded that Liszt lost the desire to be married to Carolyne when they met again in Rome after seventeen months of separation from one another. They have also taken note of Adelheid von Schorn's comment that Carolyne did not wish Liszt to marry her out of a sense of honour and Carl Alexander's comments in his diary, cited in Chapter 4.

I still think that the most convincing explanation is provided by the action Liszt took the following year in taking minor orders within the Roman Catholic Church. He would not have been able to do this if he had married Carolyne. The Church's rules of the time forbade that, as Merrick pointed out many years ago.[16] Nor would he subsequently have been allowed to enter into a marriage relationship and retain his clerical status. Carolyne would have realised this too. Liszt clearly thought that he owed it to Carolyne to become her husband after all the sacrifices she had made for him over so many years. However, the longer Liszt stayed in Rome this consideration became outweighed by his developing ambition to enter the service of the Church. We also know that Carolyne

---

15. Cited in ibid., p. 244.
16. Merrick, *Revolution and Religion in the Music of Liszt*, p. 67.

strongly supported Liszt in his vocation to Holy Orders. Although, when subsequently pressed on the subject of why he became an abbé, he once answered that it was in order to avoid getting married, this is likely to have been simply a response to an impertinent enquirer.

All his subsequent actions indicate that he continued to give Carolyne a special status in his life. He took great pains, together with her daughter, to support her in her health difficulties, defending her to both Cosima and to Olga von Meyendorff and, despite their quarrels, never detracting from her position as his most special friend and the executrix of his will. Only towards the end of his life did he admit to Cosima that he no longer saw eye to eye with Carolyne, and this was a very sad admission for him to make.

All Liszt's special women friends gave him something unique and as a result he often felt it necessary to keep them apart. Even at the very end of his life he was concerned to ensure that Olga von Meyendorff and Lina Schmalhausen should not meet each other, urging Lina to leave Bayreuth before Olga arrived. Earlier, he had prevented Olga and Carolyne from meeting in Rome. The sad irony of his situation in Bayreuth in 1886 is that, although he had taken care to have Lina with him when he knew he was becoming unwell, his daughter cruelly intervened to prevent Lina being beside him in his very last days. He realised that it was very unfortunate for him that he was dying in Bayreuth. In Weimar, Rome or Budapest it is likely that he would have died more peacefully and with proper care under the surveillance of Olga, Carolyne or Lina.

A proper analysis of Liszt's relationship with women would have to start from his early attachment to his mother. It is clear that he had a deep and trusting relationship with her. Anna Liszt appears to have understood her son well and stood by him throughout his life with only a few recorded occasions where she felt obliged to complain. After he distressed his mother by his sudden flight with Marie d'Agoult to Switzerland in spring 1835, Liszt wrote to his mother on her name day some weeks later to reassure her:

Liszt and his pupil Lina Schmalhausen. Photograph by Koller, Budapest 1885, with a dedication to Lina.

> Your letter made me very sad. You have known for a long time that I am muddle-headed, thoughtless. ... The life I have had to lead has perhaps made my innate shortcomings still

worse; but Heaven forbid that my heart ever knew of such intentions as you suspect to be in me. Trust me, trust me absolutely. My love for you is deep and immutable, and my memory of your goodness and self-sacrifice will never fade. I should like to be able to find words to convince you how very much I love you, how greatly my heart is filled with reverence and gratitude towards you. (Geneva, 26 July 1835)

In Liszt's last illness, Lina Schmalhausen, as she encouraged him to eat, reminded him of his mother's care: 'Master, what would your mother say if she were to see that her Franz was still the same? She would say, "As with eating, so with everything."'[17]

As Walker notes, Liszt must have told Lina that his mother had quoted this proverb to him when he was young. In fact, it can also be found in Liszt's letters to his mother reminding her of what she used to say to him as a child. Anna Liszt had cared for her son without reserve and with minimal criticism. She had been an encouragement and a tower of strength from his childhood onwards. It was a similar kind of relationship that he sought with subsequent women.

Liszt and Christianity

The intensity of Liszt's Christian faith has not received the quality of attention from his biographers that it deserves and this neglect, I believe, has largely contributed to the distorted presentation of his character in the many popular biographies written about him. Once he was settled in Rome in his early fifties his spiritual ambition to enter the service of the Church, which he had first experienced as a very young man, reasserted itself and took precedence over his feelings of obligation to marry Carolyne. Although a cynical view of Liszt's motives – avoiding having to live with Carolyne – might lead one to question this, it is important to look at the consistency of the evidence on Liszt's clerical vocation.

Even a hurried reading of Liszt's correspondence shows that Christian attitudes were central to him throughout his life. The Catholic priest and reformer, Félicité Robert de Lamennais (1782-1854), a fierce critic of the Church of his time and a forerunner of social Catholicism, was a major

---

17. Walker, *The Death of Franz Liszt*, p. 92.

spiritual influence on Liszt from his youth onwards.[18] His admiration of Lamennais' *Paroles d'un croyant*, published in 1834, which criticised the Church for its failure to stand fully with the poor rather than the rich, led Liszt to seek acquaintance with the man and to express his admiration in some of the early music he composed. Although Liszt did not follow Lamennais in his subsequent criticism of papal authority, he remained an important figure to Liszt for the rest of his life. For example, it was to his poetry that Liszt turned in his grief on the death of his son Daniel in 1859, which produced his composition *Les morts*. It is a pity, nevertheless, that we seem to have no further direct evidence of his relationship and attitude to Lamennais after Liszt's letters to him of 1845 regarding the well-being of his children.[19] Liszt's striving after social reformation diminished after the failure of the revolutions of 1848 in France, Austria and Hungary and he came to admire the figure of Louis Napoleon whose rise to imperial power as Napoleon III had been strongly deplored by Lamennais.

It is interesting that it was Carolyne rather than Liszt who became more critical of the Catholic Church as they grew older. She was warned even by Émile Ollivier that she was linking herself too closely to Lamennais.[20] By the time of the publication of the first part of *Des causes intérieures de la faiblesse extérieure de l'Église en 1870*, Liszt was very concerned about how it would be received by the Church authorities. By then Liszt had come to take a more nuanced stand in the religious conflicts within the Church of his time, supporting liberal reforms but not challenging papal authority, since he had come to believe that only a united Church could weather the storms of modernity.

For any student of Liszt's life, it is important to appreciate the extent of the drama and crisis within the Catholic Church in Rome in the period Liszt and Carolyne were living there in the 1860s. To the outside world it seemed as if the very existence of the Roman Church as the major form of Christianity was threatened, since it had seemed to stake so much importance on its hold of temporal power in central Italy (the papal states had been termed 'the robe of Jesus Christ' by Pope Pius IX himself[21]).

---

18. See also Merrick, *Revolution and Religion in the Music of Liszt*, especially pp. 7-38.
19. Lamennais died in Paris in 1854 without being reconciled to the Catholic Church and was buried in a 'common grave' without religious rites.
20. See Walker, *The Final Years*, p. 323.
21. Ibid., p. 328.

Even after complete unification of Italy was achieved in 1871, conflicts continued between liberal and conservative forces within the Church as to what precisely its new relationship should be with the secular world outside.

As he grew older, Liszt became more cautious in expressing opinions on Church as well as state politics where he had been gravely disappointed by the fall of the Second French Empire. Nevertheless, his close friendship with liberal clerics such as Cardinal Hohenlohe and Cardinal Haynald indicates his preferences. He came to see that the loss of the pope's temporal power had created a more advantageous situation for the Church's role in the world, rather than a hindrance, as he indicated in a letter to Olga: 'One need not be a disbeliever to feel that temporal power is more of a hindrance than an advantage to the Holy Apostolic See.' (Villa d'Este, 18 November 1880)

His failures in political prognostication had also made him more cautious. He had learned not to speak or write on issues in which he was not expert, especially with intellectual correspondents in philosophy such as Nietschze whose views he did not support and with whom he was wary of entering into correspondence. At the same time he never lost his determination to witness to the content and truth of the Christian faith.

His later correspondence shows that he consistently affirmed his Christian beliefs. Although on other matters he often varied his approach when writing to different correspondents, this was not the case with his faith. He expressed himself in similar terms to other strong believers, such as Carolyne, as to those of a more sceptical and questioning character, such as Olga von Meyendorff. Moreover, he rarely lost an opportunity to reinforce the faith of others, as in his regular letters to Carolyne's daughter Marie, and when writing to friends in difficult circumstances, such as to his friend Count Géza Zichy or in his final letters to his manservants, Fortunato and Achille.

In fact, Liszt could well be considered as a fine apologist for Christianity. He and Olga often exchanged reading material and debated religious and philosophical issues. The following passage illustrates Liszt defending St Paul in response to comments Olga had sent him from the French historian of religion, Ernest Renan:

> Thank you for the quotation from Renan. It is understandable that writers who persist in presenting Christianity as a historical fact, more or less complex but natural and devoid of any miracles, should find that St Paul is not free of the faults which are shocking in sectarians, and that 'his style is

ponderous'. His role was not to sit 'weary on the side of the road, or to waste his time in noting the vanity of established opinions'. His faith in Our Lord Jesus Christ was not an 'opinion'; he preached of Jesus crucified, resurrected, risen into Heaven; he fought the good fight and awaited 'the crown of justice which Our Lord will confer in the full light of day on those who love his coming'. Fine and great minds may understand nothing about all this; nevertheless, millions of souls are illumined and fired by the words of St Paul. (Schillingsfürst, 2 August 1873)

Despite threatening to do so many times, Liszt never relinquished his involvement with 'the outside world' and was fully aware of the questioning spirit of the age. Nor was his faith ever badly shaken by the contrary opinions he heard or read. At the same time his faith did not prevent him from appreciating the good qualities of his non-believing contemporaries: see, for example, the following letter to Carolyne recommending the German novelist Richard Voss to Cardinal Hohenlohe:

He told me he had had the honour of seeing you in Rome now and then. His opinions are those which predominate nowadays, even among princes and princesses of the blood – free-thought is very much the fashion in literature and the salons. It is the great temptation to which one must not succumb! As you know, Voss has a house in Berchtesgaden and stayed for several months in Frascati. His plan to write a volume on the Roman Campagna will soon be taking him back to those parts. The accommodation he would now prefer to any other is an apartment at the Villa d'Este – and he is of course fully prepared to pay for renting it. I am giving him a note of introduction to Cardinal Hohenlohe. Be so kind as to tell His Eminence that it would be more agreeable to me to recommend to him for the Villa d'Este a good Catholic, such as my friend Dimmler, than a free-thinker. Nevertheless, I hope Voss will find a good welcome and shelter there, for he has an agreeable and attractive personality. (Weimar, 11 September 1884)

Despite enjoying many of the pleasures of the artistic and aristocratic world in which he mixed, Liszt's regular religious practice, for example, attending early morning mass most days, took priority and helped keep

Liszt listening to a Mass by Palestrina in Rome. Pencil drawing by Gustave Durand, 1885.

his faith strong. It was also nurtured by constant religious reading. Of course, as a person in religious orders he was obliged to carry out regular reading and his close acquaintance with the New Testament and the Psalms is evident throughout his correspondence. Although his religious dress and manner in later life was seen by some as an affectation, those who knew him better recognised a person whose concentration in prayer showed a deep religious conviction. Nadine Helbig, one of his pupils from his first period in Rome, who also saw him in on subsequent occasions, was very clear on this point in the memoirs she wrote in later life:

> Liszt was devout through and through, devout to the point of ecstasy. I was often granted the privilege of seeing him pray, either in the old, venerable, and silent church of Saint Cosmas and Damian or in the Church of Our Lady of the Souls, either in the perfect stillness of a deserted sanctuary or during wonderful performances of Palestrina's Masses. He was no longer aware of earthly matters, but seemed transfigured.[22]

In his last illness he asked Lina Schmalhausen to read to him from his prayer book. Even though he knew the words by heart he told her that he also wanted to hear them spoken.

We know from his correspondence, especially with Carolyne and Olga von Meyendorff, that Liszt read widely on religious and philosophical subjects. As part of her investigation of Liszt's correspondence with Carolyne and Olga over his last ten years, Dolores Pesce has paid particular attention to the books of spiritual guidance that he referred to directly or seems to have read.[23] The early influence of his father's love of the Franciscans remained with him throughout life and he was admitted to its 'Third Order' in 1857. In Lina Ramann's interview with him in 1874, he recalled reading as a boy a *Life of Saint Francis*, as well as the New Testament and the spiritual classic from the later medieval period, *The Imitation of Christ*, written by Thomas à Kempis. We also know from his correspondence with his mother that the latter was a

---

22. Cited by Burger, *Franz Liszt*, p. 305.
23. Pesce, *Liszt's Final Decade*, pp. 111-29.

book he took special care to take with him when he left for Switzerland in 1835 with Marie d'Agoult, and at his death he possessed multiple copies, including one translated into French with commentaries by Lamennais. The theology of the *Imitation* is reflected strongly in Liszt's correspondence, in particular its teaching of accepting life's tribulations in imitation of the way Christ accepted his Cross.

Two other biblical figures feature often in his later correspondence, the 'good thief' who died beside Christ on the Cross, to whom the Christian churches have traditionally given the name of 'Dismas', and Job from the Old Testament book of that name, who endured undeserved suffering with acceptance. In letters to Carolyne Liszt often referred to Dismas. The portrait of the 'good thief' featured in Rubens' *Christ and the Four Repentant Sinners*, a copy of which Carolyne sent Liszt in 1866, and, after his serious disputes with her in his last years, he often signed himself 'Dismas', seeming thus to acknowledge his 'wrongdoing' while hoping for 'salvation'. He also mentioned the 'good thief' in one of his last letters to Olga von Meyendorff, while referring to Christ's promise of immortality.

It is interesting that by the end of his life Liszt was drawing differently on the Book of Job. He was no longer an image of suffering to be endured but of peaceful acceptance of God's will. Lamennais had also given Job as an example of calm resignation and hope for liberation. In a letter to Carolyne four years before his death, Liszt indicated that he was rereading Lamennais's earlier book, linking it with the Polish nation's current experience of suffering under Russian rule and *Books of the Polish Nation and the Polish Pilgrimage* (1832), the work of its national poet Adam Mickiewicz: 'The *Paroles d'un croyant* are drawn from the same source. I have read this volume with fervour, fright, terror, and compunction. It is Poland panting on the Cross! The prayer and litany which close the book of the *Pilgrims* made me sob.' (Weimar, 2 November 1882).

Liszt's correspondence over the latter part of his life shows that Liszt never diverted from giving allegiance to the Cross as an essential part of Christian belief and practice. The Cross is also strongly represented in Liszt's music by a motif taken from plainchant which Paul Merrick has demonstrated Liszt used throughout much of his most significant work such as his *Piano Sonata*, *Faust Symphony* and *Christus* oratorio.[24] The Cross has always been a hard teaching of Christ to accept but there is no doubt that Liszt's words reflect orthodox Christian teaching. It

---

24. Merrick, *Revolution and Religion in the Music of Liszt*, pp. 283-95.

can, of course, be understood also as Liszt's way of coping with the many insurmountable problems he faced as he grew older. However, more importantly, it reflected his long considered understanding of the meaning of life.

Liszt's Personality: Split or Integrated?

Liszt's reputation has suffered greatly from unfair negative presentations of his character. This occurred in his lifetime and even shortly after his death. When a proposal to bring Liszt's body back to Budapest was debated in the Hungarian parliament, the then prime minister opposed it, referring to Liszt as a 'common actor'.[25] Ernest Newman, whose damaging portrait of Liszt has served as a model for later presentations in books and in the cinema, described him in similar ways. He cast particular doubt on the genuiness of Liszt's religious faith which may have reflected Newman's own strongly held 'freethought agenda'.[26] Liszt's striking appearance and dazzling performances as a virtuoso pianist enthralled audiences but seem to have led some observers to cast doubt on the sincerity of his character. There were also other factors at work, including the way Liszt was depicted in the semi-autobiographical books written by Marie d'Agoult and Olga Janina. Late in his life there were also the unfortunate accusations of anti-Semitism following the publication of the revision of his book on Hungarian music which he had delegated to Carolyne. Liszt's image as a religiously inspired idealist, both tolerant and generous, was undermined.

Fortunately, because of his extensive surviving correspondence we know much more about Liszt's inner life. Some of it does show him in a negative light, particularly his unfaithfulness to Carolyne in Weimar with their mutual friend Agnes Street-Klindworth. Most people like to keep their negative sides hidden and Liszt certainly tried to do this, destroying letters he received and encouraging others to do the same to the letters he sent them. However, luckily for his biographers, most of his correspondents kept the letters he wrote to them, a sign of the importance which they attributed to their relationship with him. It is necessary to read all of these letters to get as complete a picture of the man as possible.

---

25. Cited by Burger, *Franz Liszt*, p. 328.
26. See P. Watt, 'Ernest Newman's *The Man Liszt* of 1934: Reading its Freethought Agenda', *Context: Journal of Music Research*. Vol. 31 (2007), pp. 193-205.

Critics of Liszt have drawn a contrast between the high standards of chaste behaviour associated with the Catholic faith that he professed and his own passionate involvement with married women at different points of his life. His seeking of love and attention does indeed appear at times to have the character of an addiction but it also needs to be born in mind that Liszt expressed shame about his behaviour in letters both to Carolyne and to Olga. He also admitted that he had a problem in this area of his life, and one may question why he did not receive more effective help from his spiritual confessors. One should also appreciate the fact that Carolyne forgave him and to the end of her life stressed her admiration for his many good qualities. Sexual morality is far too narrow a focus for evaluating Liszt's character. The Christian value he upheld most strongly in his writing was that of charity and this was strongly evident in his own actions throughout his life.

Liszt did not seek riches for himself and was generous to a fault. Both in his piano virtuoso years and at later opportunities he was more than happy to play for charitable causes without personal recompense. As a result, he never saved up large sums of money. Even in his last year, and despite his failing eyesight, he needed to produce piano transcriptions to fund his travelling and rather modest lifestyle. He lived up to his Christian ideals in many other ways, most notably in his conscientious attitude to those who appealed to him for help. His support to Wagner in the composer's early difficulties and throughout his musical career was outstanding. He took pleasure in the latter's success even when there was an open rift between the two of them. His admirable quality of responding generously to the achievements of others was evident even with composers who had criticised Liszt's own compositions, such as Brahms.

Liszt generally avoided judging others' behaviour, preferring to come to a deeper understanding first, as he wrote to Princess Marie: 'The time seems to be at hand when in most human relations, those who are wise will say increasingly: 'understand', and less and less: 'judge'. The Gospel commands us to do this.' (Weimar, 11 June 1880) He was an early opponent of the death penalty which, as he told Olga in a letter, he regarded as an 'abominable social crime'. He continued: 'It is obvious that we are all more or less guilty, deranged, or crazy, but it does not follow that we ought to be guillotined, hanged, or, as an act of mercy, shot.' (Florence, 29 January 1882) He also paid little attention to negative comments made about others, writing in June 1884 to Carl Gille, following an embarrassing accusation made about his friend, to tell him that 'gossip and tittle-tattle never count with me'.

Liszt rarely appears hypocritical in his correspondence during his later years. One example is the accusation he levelled against Cosima for her relationship with Wagner which her father condemned as an infatuation which would end badly. Perhaps the strength of his condemnation reflected the outcome of his own experience with an already married woman, Cosima's own mother. Marie d'Agoult had been central to his life through his twenties and thirties and it is likely that the lack of true healing of this broken relationship remained a major source of pain for him until he died. His harsh judgement of Marie in letters to Carolyne reflects badly on him. Why, one is entitled to ask, did he not show to Marie more of the human understanding he said was needed in human relationships? So important is this topic from a psychological and spiritual view of Liszt's later life that a separate section of this chapter will be devoted to his need for healing of painful aspects of his past.

Liszt's pupils for the most part remembered him with affection and not only because of his teaching. Emil von Sauer a pupil in his last two years, who became a distinguished pianist himself, paid tribute to his teacher later in his own life: 'Grand seigneur from head to toe, a fervent Catholic, stern towards himself, indulgent towards others, with integrity of character, a perfect model from all points of view, I found in him but one fault: an overabundance of goodness and clemency, of whose abuse he did not take cognizance.'[27]

Nevertheless, his English pupil and promoter, Walter Bache commented on how even his pupils could be unfair in their judgements on Liszt. Writing to Jessie Laussot he wrote:

> Is there *one* of us (even your dear self) who does not feel guilty of having sometimes judged the great Departed unjustly, even impertinently, according to our small views, and not in harmony with his much greater ones? I allude to many small matters which we put down to weakness, old age, etc., which now appear to me as parts of his enormous and unflinching plan of *self-abnegation*, in which he had reached a height that is almost in comprehensible to us.[28]

'Self-abnegation' is an interesting word. Bache was referring to Liszt's practice of self-criticism and self-denial which became stronger as he

---

27. *Emil Sauer: Disciple of Liszt* (New York: Musical Scope Publishers, 1975), cited in Williams (ed.), *Franz Liszt: Selected Letters*, p. 917.
28. Cited in ibid., p. 952.

grew older, including his taking of criticism intended for others on himself. Even Wagner was impressed by what he referred to as Liszt's 'chivalry' in shielding Carolyne from the criticisms of anti-Semitic passages which she inserted in writings published under his name. Such behaviour recalls his early spiritual influences, especially Thomas à Kempis' 'Imitation of Christ', and his growing involvement with the Franciscan Order throughout the latter part of his life. Unfortunately, such practices did not seem to bring Liszt peace of mind. He often referred to his 'secret sorrow' and his portraits in later life, of which there are many, often show an underlying sad expression. How is one to make sense of the complex mixture of emotions and motivations that Liszt presented as an older man?

For a proper understanding of Liszt's personality in late life one needs to consider his psychological development from his youth onwards. There is enough material to construct a plausible argument. The evidence we have on the young Liszt suggests that he would have scored above average on all the five primary personality traits: extraversion, agreeableness, openness to new experience, conscientiousness and affectivity. Individuals with such a set of characteristics would be likely to become high achievers if they could learn to manage effectively their high level of emotional reactivity. Traits, of course, provide only the bare structure on which personality develops. They encourage or put limitations on what is achievable, but the key motivations and interests that give structure to lives come from interaction with the outside world. Typically, at least in the modern western world, a person is given the opportunity during adolescence and young adulthood to learn about and to decide what goals are worth the effort of pursuing and what values to uphold. In Liszt's case circumstances contrived to give him an early choice between a vocation for the priesthood and the life of a musician. Adam Liszt was a major influence in persuading his son that he could combine and reconcile his spiritual and musical ambitions.

Contemporary forms of psychological analysis of personality development place a large stress on seeking to uncover a person's life goals and projects and the narrative understanding or story of his/her life which he/she constructs over time.[29] The latter approach assumes that most people seek to construct, or at least desire to construct, a coherent and relatively integrated account of themselves and their lives. The

---

29. B.R. Little, *Who Are You Really? The Surprising Puzzle of Personality* (London: Simon & Schuster, 2017); D.P. McAdams, *The Art and Science of Personality Development* (New York: Guilford Publications, 2015).

personal life story exists in the mind mostly in provisional shape but it builds up a firmer structure over time in a process of constant retelling, reworking and restructuring. Usually by later life certain elements will have become constant features of the story and remain relatively fixed thereafter. Dan McAdams' concept of a 'redemptive narrative'[30] appears highly applicable to Franz Liszt. It describes those who consider not only that they are born with special gifts but that these gifts can be used to benefit others and, therefore, they feel a strong call to make a difference to the world. Liszt's early encounters with the charismatic priest Felicité Robert de Lamennais seem to have convinced him that he could be such a person.

Of course, such a high ambition risks a greater probability of failure and, already by mid-life, Liszt was facing serious obstacles in the way of his ambitious goal of creating and promoting the desirable new types of music he believed in. The opposition from the music establishment had been far greater than he had expected. Moreover, he had made two difficult choices in finding a partner with whom to share his life, both resulting from a romantic passion for an unhappily married woman. Countess Marie d'Agoult had strongly supported his musical talent and been an important contributor to his early poetic compositions for piano. She had also borne him three children but subsequently resisted his ambitions for a more public life as a travelling pianist. A talented writer, she had ambitions of her own.

Princess Carolyne zu Sayn-Wittgenstein, by contrast, had fully provided the support Liszt needed, sacrificing herself in the interests of realising the opportunities provided of realising his musical project made possible by his appointment as court musician in Weimar. Their hoped-for marriage, however, was persistently obstructed by opposition from Carolyne's family to annulment of her marriage. As devout Catholics, she and Liszt had been unable to find a way around this obstacle and as the years had gone by Carolyne's less than ideal position in Weimar society had become increasingly unbearable. Liszt also came to realise that he needed a new way forward for realising his life's goals. The decision to make their new home in Rome must have appeared to Liszt, as well as to Carolyne, as an answer to all of their prayers. It would bring together his ambitions of making religious music for the Catholic Church and solemnising their marriage. Unfortunately, there proved to be obstacles in the way of both projects.

---

30. D.P. McAdams, *The Redemptive Self* (New York: Oxford University Press, 2005).

Such is the brief imagined summary of Liszt's developing life story up to his late forties. To go further with understanding the changing life purposes of a living person requires careful and sensitive interviewing over time. To do the equivalent for someone who can no longer speak or answer for themselves is impossible, of course. However, there are individuals, such as Liszt, of whom we have such extensive records of their expressed attitudes, thoughts, feelings and behaviour, in his case almost on a daily basis, to construct what their answers might have been. In fact, this material can be more valid than one-off interviews because the material has arisen more spontaneously, and across various situations, and has been expressed to different other persons. As a result, it becomes possible to analyse variation as well as uniformity in a person's self-presentation.

What Liszt made of the remaining years of his life has been the main focus of this book. However, it should be clear even from this simple account of Liszt's earlier life that his personality at fifty years of age was certainly not split. In spite of the setbacks he had received, he was still seeking an integration of his life around the development of music and contributing to the spiritual renewal of society in a period when religious life was wavering. These had been his principal aims from childhood onwards. At times they had clashed but he now saw a possibility of combining them together perfectly.

Liszt as an Older Man

Liszt lived a relatively long life by the standards of the nineteenth century and had to face physical and mental health problems as he aged. He lost some of his previous ease of mobility and experienced deteriorating eyesight from his seventieth year onwards. He also referred much to 'nervous' problems and clearly encountered some severe depressive episodes, especially in his later sixties, largely brought on by the conflicting stresses of his life. However, ageing also brought him some positive benefits, most clearly evident in his last years, as he developed a broader and less self-centred perspective on life. The physical, psychological and social changes associated with ageing often require a series of complex adaptations. These can lead to growth in personality and a final more complete integration of a person's aims and purposes.[31]

When Liszt arrived in Rome in 1861. He was then only in the early stages of ageing, relatively youthful in looks and with strong reserves

---

31. See Coleman and O'Hanlon, *Aging and Development*, especially pp. 133-159.

of energy. Nevertheless, he was by the life expectations of his day approaching the end of life and the will he wrote the year before indicates that he was well aware of this. The passivity in the attitudes he expresses to his situation in his correspondence during the preceding months suggests that the eventual prevention of the marriage did not come as a complete surprise to him. I agree, nonetheless, with Alan Walker that the evidence we have indicates that Liszt was certainly prepared to go ahead with marriage to Carolyne on his fiftieth birthday.

The last-minute prohibition of the marriage meant that Liszt had to develop new plans for the future. He presumably felt obliged to stay in Rome to support Carolyne in the huge disappointment she had suffered, but this also suited his new plans to focus on writing religious music. He had already discussed them with Archbishop Hohenlohe who subsequently became a close supporter of Liszt's activities in Rome and an intermediary between him and Pope Pius. In this context it is also easy to understand how Liszt came to take on minor religious orders in the Roman Catholic Church. Although it is difficult to judge to what extent he actually expected a musical appointment in the Vatican to result from this decision, the thought seems certainly to have been in Carolyne's mind and was probably in his as well. When it did not materialise, he began thinking not only of returning to his previous life in Weimar, to which had been invited back by Carl Alexander, but also to respond positively to the enthusiastic invitations he was receiving from Budapest to make a contribution to musical developments in his native land. By the late 1860s he felt that he was making insufficient musical progress in Rome and needed to return to the centre of European musical developments.

In making this decision, Liszt brought about a painful and lasting bone of contention with Carolyne. She had not expected Liszt to leave Rome and, especially, to return to Weimar. Should Liszt be considered selfish in his refusal to please Carolyne by continuing to establish his main residence near to her? Probably so, but they had already decided not to marry. Liszt's taking of religious orders precluded this. His musical ambitions had always taken a primary place in his life – they had led to his split with Marie d'Agoult – and Carolyne knew and seemed to have accepted this. With the exception of when there were difficulties, for example, after Rome's capture by the forces of the new Italian state in 1871, he dutifully returned to Rome every year to see her for the remainder of his life. He remained a close friend and supporter of Carolyne, sharing his ambitions, hopes and fears with her and also taking an interest in her own ambitious writing project to reform the organisation of the Catholic Church.

Nevertheless, it is also clear that, in developing an ever more complex and demanding lifestyle for himself, Liszt was making his later life more prone to stress and mistakes of judgement in balancing his many goals and interests one with another. The complexities of his life were further enhanced when his daughter left her husband, his former protégé Hans von Bülow, for Richard Wagner. Liszt was greatly displeased but eventually sought reconciliation with the new couple in 1872. To Carolyne, this was an even more unacceptable decision on the part of the man she had hoped to marry. She had expected him to persist in his condemnation of Wagner whom she regarded as an immoral and anti-Christian figure both as a person and in his music.

One of the most developed areas in the social psychological study of ageing is how older people learn to cope with the losses, change and stresses that the experience of ageing brings with it. In general, the research findings have been more positive than negative.[32] By and large, older people appear to have learned from experience to cope better with disappointments and unwanted change. Compared with younger people, they show improved control of their emotional reactions to stress, at least in the earlier stages of ageing. Liszt's successful adjustment to the limitations put on his mobility by his fall in Weimar in his seventieth year is a good example of this. Most important for him was to be able to maintain his ability to travel across Europe. However, was it wise of Liszt to continue such a high level of activity? Carolyne had advised him to restrict his movements. It is evident from his correspondence that Liszt did not like being asked about his physical health or describing it in any detail, let alone complain about it. Nevertheless, in his last years he did begin to admit to persistent problems, particularly complaints about his 'nerves' and it is clear that for many years his 'threefold' way, or 'fourfold' as he now called it, had become more onerous.

Although in the latter years of his life Liszt had the regular help of a manservant, travelling could be both long and uncomfortable. His letters show that he sometimes agreed to travel to a particular distant destination after initially having decided to refuse. He was even prepared to travel right across Europe from London to St Petersburg in his seventy-fifth year. Clearly, he was enjoying the belated success that came with the

---

32. R.S. Lazarus and B.N. Lazarus, *Coping with Aging* (New York: Oxford University Press, 2006).

greater recognition of his compositions. He also wanted to please those who were promoting his work. Moreover, he liked continuing to help and promote the work of other musicians. At the very end of his life, he travelled to Bayreuth to support Cosima even though he was unwell. He died there as a result of an infection he had caught on his travels which developed into pneumonia. This could perhaps have been prevented if Liszt had taken care to heal himself before embarking on what turned out to be his last journey but it was his sense of responsibility which drew him on.

Liszt's pursuit of multiple goals can be understood in contemporary psychological terms as a preference for pursuing 'assimilation' over 'accommodation', that is attempting to adapt the means of achieving one's goals rather than disengaging from any one goal. There is evidence from psychological studies that failure or inability to accommodate to declining powers with advanced age is associated with an increased probability of encountering depression.[33] Many older people find it difficult to diminish or cease involvement in tasks they see as important parts of their lives but which have become too demanding for their now more limited physical and mental resources.

Of course, continued engagement in meaningful activities remains vital as one grows older but these activities need to be chosen with care and consideration for what is still feasible. Liszt set himself a daunting task in maintaining friendships, roles and responsibilities across Europe, not to mention his continued desire to compose. He achieved this through continued extensive travel as well as correspondence. However, by his later sixties, he was struggling badly and this could be seen in the very evident symptoms of depression which he began to display in his later fifties and which reached a peak in the autumn of 1877 when he was 66 years old. His over-commitment led him to make mistakes, the most disastrous being his delegating the revision of his book on Hungarian music to Carolyne. Although understandable in terms of his wish to keep Carolyne part of his working life, this resulted in damage to his reputation in his native country.

Nevertheless, it is hard to identify which of the major responsibilities that Liszt took on in later life he could have rejected. His teaching in Weimar, his promotion of music in Hungary, his regular travel to attend

---

33. J. Brandtstädter, 'Adaptive Resources in Later Life: Tenacious Goal Pursuit and Flexible Goal Adjustment', in *A Life Worth Living: Contributions to Positive Psychology*, ed. M. Csikzentmihalyi and I.S. Csikzentmihalyi (New York: Oxford University Press, 2006), pp. 143-164.

musical events elsewhere in Europe, as well as his annual return to see Carolyne in Rome, had all become part of his identity. They comprised Liszt's 'life projects'.[34] He could not give any of these up. Perhaps the one area of his later life where it might seem he could and should have made changes was in his relationship with Cosima and Wagner. This was the source of his most bitter disagreements with Carolyne and eventually led to his death in circumstances he had wanted to avoid. Even Alan Walker, in his later volume of essays, *Reflections on Liszt*, is critical of Liszt on this point as he addresses him personally, beyond the grave, from his position of having studied his life over many years:

> Better by far never to have seen the precious pair again. But you proceeded to make one major blunder after another with regard to Wagner and Cosima. Beguiled by the man and his music, you became Wagner's leading ambassador and a major fund-raiser. You should have given Bayreuth a wide berth. Instead you became 'Bayreuth's poodle', to use your own self-disparaging phrase.[35]

In Liszt's defence one can point out the evident fact that Liszt never ceased admiring Wagner's music. As he wrote to Olga after his friend's death, his admiration for Wagner's achievements had not abated but, if anything, increased further:

> The press is full of obituary notices on the great poet-musician (*Wort- und Tondichter*,[36] as the King of Bavaria rightly called him), the supreme dramatist of an Ideal never realized before him in complete art: poetry, music, and the stage. Compared with this triple achievement the colossi, Beethoven and Goethe, are sublime fragments. From *Tannhäuser* and *Lohengrin* to the *Nibelungen* and *Parsifal*, complete art has been revealed. To see Wagner only as a celebrity or showpiece strikes me as a somewhat silly misconception. The branches of his genius rise from deeper roots. In him the superhuman dominates. (Budapest, 20 February 1883)

---

34. Little, *Who Are You Really?*, especially pp. 30-53.
35. A. Walker, *Reflections on Liszt* (Ithaca, NY: Cornell University Press, 2005), p. 252.
36. 'Word and tone poet'.

Liszt became willing at various points in his life to subjugate his own interests to those of a musician whose talent he clearly rated higher than his own, much to Carolyne's disapproval. This was even clearer in his last years, by which time he had become more modest about his own ability.

Thus, it was almost inevitable, given Liszt's interests, determination and his strong sense of duty that he would continue to pursue his many different goals right to the very end of his life, never reducing his commitments to any significant degree. Considering the various obstacles he faced, it must be said that he managed rather well. Although in his sixties he did succumb to serious episodes of depression, his last years at least seem to have been relatively free of low moods in spite of his declining health. One can only admire Liszt's courage and his resilience. The results of recent longitudinal case studies on people growing older illustrate that determined individuals can successfully pursue paths of continued engagement and independence, although not without significant personal cost, including the risk of major episodes of depression.[37] Although at times Liszt clearly wanted to be free of some of his commitments, his sense of obligation usually got the better of such thoughts. This was true of him even in the very last year of his life.

An important personal resource that Liszt could draw on in dealing with the problems he faced was his ability to make close and lasting friends. Reading his correspondence shows how carefully and warmly he cultivated friendships with so many people across Europe, many of whom could not be mentioned in the restricted space of this book. As he grew older, he naturally lost some important friends through their earlier death but was he able to replace them with other meaningful relationships. The death of Baron Augusz, his oldest Hungarian friend, was a major blow but probably as a consequence his friendship with Count Géza Zichy, his new younger Hungarian friend, came to mean so much to him in his final years.

Liszt had a huge capacity for friendship. He wanted to give as much as he received. His correspondence with Olga von Meyendorff illustrates how he was able to confide his own problems with her as well as to respond to her own difficulties. He had had a similar relationship with Carolyne but as she became a major source of his difficulties in later life

---

37. P.G. Coleman, C. Ivani-Chalian and M. Robinson, *Self and Meaning in the Lives of Older People: Case Studies over Twenty Years* (Cambridge: Cambridge University Press, 2015).

he needed another person with whom to share these problems. Despite the challenges it brought in his relationship with Carolyne, one could also regard Liszt's recovery of his previously close ties to Cosima and Richard Wagner as one of the great achievements of his last years, involving admission of error and humility on his part. As a result, Liszt became part of the extended Wagner family in their journeys across Europe and this itself was a source of new contacts and friendships for him.

Perhaps Liszt's greatest psychological weakness, surprising as it might seem to those who were acquainted only with the popular image of Liszt as the dazzling performer of his younger years, was his vulnerable self-esteem. He might have appeared confident in his public self-presentation throughout most of his life but, underneath the image he projected, he was acutely conscious that his lack of early education put him at a disadvantage in the aristocratic societies in which he mixed. He had read avidly from a young age but he did not consider that this compensated. Even in his last years, he returned to the subject and recommended the importance to young musicians of having a rounded education. His feeling of inferiority probably explains why he reacted so bitterly to Marie d'Agoult when she criticised him for his lack of breeding and depicted him as a failed artist in her autobiographical novel, *Nélida*. Fortunately, in his last years Liszt seems to have achieved a larger measure of positive self-regard, as a result of his many close friendships and the warm reception of the musical public. He was cheered on as the old warrior he had become not only in Weimar, Rome and Hungary, but also in Vienna, London and Paris.

By the time of his death Liszt had come to emphasise less the importance of his own musical compositions. He accepted simply that he enjoyed composing and that this in itself was sufficient reward for him. In fact, it is significant that he did not advertise some of the darker themed piano music he composed in his later years. These were clearly ahead of their time, have indeed influenced later composers and continue to fascinate by their prophetic character. Nevertheless, many of his compositions also seem to have come from a special place in Liszt's experience of old age, a place of anxiety and great sadness. Their music seems to express aspects of his inner feelings that are admittedly not as strongly evident in his writings, although he did from time to time refer to his underlying sense of sadness. From where did these feelings originate? One can look for a connection with the sadness he experienced as a young man in Paris and the doubts he expressed about how he should find the strength to continue to live. However, the sadness of his old age seems to me different from this. I think it may relate not so much to his anxieties about the present or future but to troubling thoughts about his past life.

Life Review and Reconciliation

'What makes old age hard to bear is not the failings of one's faculties, mental and physical, but the burden of one's memories.' This quotation from the author Somerset Maugham was cited by the American psychiatrist Robert Butler when introducing the concept of 'life review' in the 1960s as an important developmental task of ageing. The extent to which past memories weigh heavily on older people varies from person to person but is clearly a very significant factor for some.[38] It is only fairly recently that serious attention has been given to recognising the long-lasting effects of disturbing memories. Some, such as traumatic war memories, can be so distressing that they are best avoided. Less upsetting, but still painful, memories can be kept at bay by distraction but, in general, it is advisable to seek healing. Achieving a sense of peace and reconciliation with the past is central to good mental health in old age.

Liszt often referred to being troubled by past memories without being explicit on their origins, other than that they related to his own mistakes across his lifetime. Many of us have issues from our past that we are ashamed of and old age offers the opportunity to lessen their hold on us. In Liszt's case, this healing seems to have taken place to an insufficient degree. This may seem rather surprising since Liszt had access to the counsel of close friends and he also regularly received the sacrament of penance within the Catholic Church. Of course, we do not know what he confessed and what priests and other friends might have said to him in response. One may speculate though, as did Carolyne, that the confessional did not give him the opportunity to explore the origins and the repercussions of the failings he reported there. We can only look for further hints in his letters and the actions he took. For example, he often refers to 'misdeeds' in addressing both Carolyne and Olga and asks for their forgiveness. However, with both of them he could be frank and at the end of his life seems to have been at relative peace with both women. It is unlikely that either one was a principal source of his deeply felt sadness.

---

38. M. Johnson, 'Spirituality, Biographical Review and Biographical Pain at the End of Life', in *Spiritual Dimensions of Ageing*, ed. M. Johnson and J. Walker (Cambridge: Cambridge University Press, 2016), pp. 198-214.

One of the most obvious failings of Liszt's later years was his inability to achieve a true reconciliation with Countess Marie d'Agoult, the woman he eloped with at the age of 23 and lived with for five years during which time she became the mother of their three children. Their separation was long drawn out and painful and, although in later life there were attempts at reconciliation when Liszt visited Paris in 1861 and 1866, the end results were negative. Because of its likely importance to Liszt's sense of well-being, it is worth examining this subject in more detail.

Liszt's recent biographers agree that the original and principal source of Liszt's feelings of resentment towards Marie was her highly successful, autobiographical novel, *Nélida*, in which she appeared to belittle Liszt as a failed artist. She developed the idea for writing this book towards the end of their relationship and began writing it after their final stay together in Nonnenwerth in 1843. The novel attacked Liszt where he was most vulnerable in his central life project, his ambition to be a great composer. Although he denied that he recognised himself in the character of Guermann, he certainly recognised that Marie's writing was aimed at him. *Nélida* set Marie on the path to a successful career as an author and strengthened her reputation in the salons of Paris, but it was a decidedly cruel action on her part. To make matters worse, she decided to republish the novel twenty years later, in the very year of Liszt's much heralded return to Paris in 1866 where he was hoping for a positive response to his choral and orchestral compositions.

Although Liszt's pain and anger at Marie's actions are understandable, it is regrettable that in the remaining years left to him he seemed not able to forgive her. Whereas Marie appears to have remained nostalgic about their past love for one another, this was not the case for Liszt. There is, in fact, little evidence about his true feelings that can be gleaned from his correspondence. Some of his comments about Marie are enigmatic. For example, he apologised to Olga for not noticing in the French journal which she had sent him copies of the letters between the Italian revolutionary Giuseppe Mazzini and 'Daniel Stern' – 'perhaps', he added, 'as the fateful result of my old blunders with the author of *Nélida*' (Budapest, 12 December 1872). What did he mean by 'old blunders'? There were no further opportunities for Marie and Liszt to meet before Marie's death in 1876. Liszt's cold reaction to news of this in letters to Carolyne and Émile is surprising in a man who was later to express the belief that all could be forgiven if properly understood

More significant clues to Liszt's real feelings in regard to his relationship with Marie d'Agoult can be found in his music, both in his reception of the works that had been inspired during his time with Marie and in some of his later pieces. Alan Walker has commented that in Liszt's later years 'his own music seemed to be burdened with memories for him, some of them too painful to bear'.[39] For example, it was noticed that Liszt had long refused to hear his *Vallée d'Obermann*, from the first year of his *Années de pèlerinage*, when his pupils brought it with them to play for him. In the book that August Göllerich, one of his last pupils, wrote of his reminiscences of Liszt, he records that his teacher did once ask him to play the piece but eventually broke into tears, seemingly overwhelmed by the memories it produced in him.[40]

Also telling are the many versions of *Die Zelle in Nonnenwerth* ('The Cloister in Nonnenwerth') (at least twelve between 1841 and 1880, according to Leslie Howard's research).[41] Nonnenwerth was an island in the Rhine near to Bonn to which Liszt had been introduced by his friend Prince Felix von Lichnowsky in 1841. Romantic and sad legends were tied to the ruins on the island which moved Lichnowsky to compose a poem and Liszt to set it to music. In his enthusiasm for this place and perhaps with hopes for a romantic outcome, Liszt invited Marie to spend holidays with him there in the summers of 1841 and 1843, but without coming anywhere close to the peaceful reconciliation of their relationship that they both desired. That Liszt constantly returned to this melancholy, but hauntingly beautiful, melody suggests that he remained captivated with the associations Nonnenwerth had for him. These may not have been related only to the collapse of his relationship with Marie, but also to his memories of Lichnowsky, who had been murdered by a mob in Germany in the European uprisings of 1848. Liszt's last piano composition in 1880 on this subject can be considered one of the most beautiful of all musical representations of nostalgia and the loss of romantic dreams.

At the conscious level of correspondence Liszt seems to have kept at bay the deeper remembrances and feelings he may have had for Marie. In one of his last references to her, in a letter to Olga in 1882, he displays a deliberate distancing of himself from his real emotions. They had been exchanging comments on the published correspondence between Benjamin Constant, the French political thinker and activist, and Juliette Récamier (née Bernard). The latter had, like Marie, maintained a salon in Paris, although earlier in the nineteenth century, and become

---

39. Walker, *The Final Years*, p. 475.
40. Cited in ibid.
41. Leslie Howard, *Liszt. The Complete Music for Solo Piano – 25* (London: Hyperion Records, 1993), p. 5.

(in)famous for attracting men's attention and then rejecting them. Liszt criticised both correspondents and especially Mme Récamier for their pretensions in regard to one another and followed with a comment on Marie: 'Now, as I used to say to Daniel Stern, much to her annoyance, it is Dante who created and immortalized Beatrice, and not Beatrice Dante. Ladies with false ideals falsely imagine the opposite.' (Rome, 18 January 1882)

It is a pity that Liszt was not given more help in the important task of reconciliation. His very many love letters to Marie over the first part of his life dominate all others in compilations of his early correspondence. In themselves they are sufficient evidence of the need for a better ending to their story together. Who could have helped him to see her in a different light? Carolyne had from early on in her relationship with Liszt developed a negative opinion of Marie although she had never met her. She shared responsibility for advising Liszt in the later education of his children and seems to have fully supported Liszt in shutting their mother out of their lives. Thus, she was complicit with Liszt's condemnation of Marie as a person and as a mother. Émile Ollivier tried to promote harmony between the parents of his first wife and continued to remain close to both of them after Blandine's early death, but the task of promoting reconciliation seems to have been too difficult for him.

Cosima could have been the key intermediary but had perhaps an even more difficult relationship with her mother than with her father. There is little mention of Marie in their surviving correspondence and in what there is Liszt usually refers to Marie by her *nom de plume* 'Daniel Stern'. As with Olga, Liszt seems to have exchanged much information about literature with his daughter and, generally, to have been complimentary about the later writings of 'Daniel Stern', such as her history of the formation of the Dutch Republic. He also commented favourably to Cosima on her mother's correspondence with Mazzini. However, in the last two years of Marie's life, his comments to Cosima about her are consistently negative. After Marie's death he appears to have mentioned her hardly at all. Because of Cosima's closeness to her step-sister Claire, Liszt must have known about Marie's periods of mental disturbance. If so, he seems not to have shown any sympathy.

What other troubling memories would have beset Liszt in his last years? Certainly, he must have been very badly affected by Cosima's rejection of him after Wagner's death. This was something he did not and could not have expected. Liszt must also have reflected often on Carolyne and how much she had suffered by linking her life to his, losing her country and her property, being rejected in Weimar and finally failing to obtain her long desired marriage to him. Their relationship also became troubled but at least Liszt had an understanding ear in Carolyne's daughter Princess Marie, a much more important figure in Liszt's later life than has generally been recognised. She knew better than most the ties that bound the two together but also the differences that separated them. La Mara recorded Marie's own considered judgement on the history of their relationship after they left Weimar for Rome: 'these events marked the start of the tormented martyrdom of these two human beings, who had been everything to each other and who continued to search blindly for one another without ever finding what they were looking for'.[42] Marie perceived the tragic character in the frequent quarrelling and misunderstandings of their last years.

Seeing Liszt Whole: Music, World and Spirit

Liszt's reputation declined in the century that followed his death. His musical contributions were devalued and his personal life caricatured. Thanks to the efforts of more recent biographical researchers, particularly Alan Walker, we now have a much more rounded picture of Liszt's merits and failings. However, any serious analysis of Liszt's character needs to include a close examination of how he himself expressed his intentions and aims in life. These can be discerned in the large number of surviving letters he sent to others, which cover his entire lifespan with some small gaps. Although there is still no complete edition combining all his letters, compilations of those he wrote to his most important correspondents are readily available and most of them have been translated into English. Thus, anyone with a will to do it can read Liszt's own words and come to their own opinion on Liszt at the various different stages of his life. This book has given my own view on Liszt's later life and it is generally a positive one. From reading all the letters I could find for the last 25 years of his life, I have found that my original admiration for Liszt has increased rather than decreased. Despite experiencing many blows and setbacks both in his musical and personal life, he maintained his fundamentally hopeful, courageous and moral view on life.

Despite the disappointments he experienced, he never lost the strong spiritual call, which he had felt already as a youth, to contribute to creating a better world. He imagined that he could do this through the performance and composition of music and, in his efforts, he certainly succeeded in raising the status of musicians. His ambitions involved

---

42. Cited by Hilmes, *Franz Liszt: Musician, Celebrity, Superstar*, p. 185.

him further in a struggle to create new forms of music suitable for the modern age and the social, national, religious and other challenges it faced. His incompletely fulfilled ambition in this respect helps to explain a large part of the tension he felt in his later years, but it also, I feel, contributes to the continuing appeal of much of his music to many of his admirers. In his last years his music conveyed even more strongly, in its adventurous harmonies and experiments with atonality, his sense of the incompleteness of human existence. He had always been reaching for something beyond the normal and accepted ways of his time.

As to the quality of character he displayed in old age, the most striking evidence, I think, comes from the younger people who came to know him well in his last years. Count Géza Zichy was one such, the brave one-armed Hungarian pianist and composer who never forgot how his old friend had helped and encouraged him. In his autobiography he described his impressions of Liszt:

> If true nobleness of heart forms the substance and core of saintliness, Franz Liszt was a saint. A worldly, amiable saint. Capable of making a sacrifice, always willing to help, wholly lacking in vindictiveness, oblivious to the wrongs he suffered, one of the most noble and humane of human beings ever to set foot on earth. Strict and tolerant, and not one of those Catholics who can sometimes be so unchristian.[43]

At the same time, he was not blind to Liszt's faults. He could be too kind: 'His magnanimity and kindness of heart were even greater than his genius. He was incapable of turning down a request. He recommended everyone, which meant that his letters of recommendation lost much of their weight.'

Zichy also commented insightfully on the low moods which Liszt exhibited in his last years which seemed to be at odds with his basic character:

> Liszt was of a cheerful disposition and usually in good spirits, although he suffered sometimes from deep melancholia. The wretchedness suffered by those around him and human misery in general saddened him greatly. He must have been very fond of me to have repeatedly vented his grief in my

---

43. This and subsequent quotes from Zichy's autobiography are taken from Burger, *Franz Liszt*, p. 296.

presence. He could never speak of his son Daniel's premature death without tears in his eyes. 'That was the greatest affliction of my life', he told me.

He was concerned as well to counteract negative comments about Liszt, such as that he was a seducer, extravagant in his lifestyle or had become an alcoholic:

> Through living in the sultry atmosphere of the Eternal Feminine, his kindness of heart and incomparable courtesy brought him the reputation of a Don Juan, something he most certainly was not. He said to me, 'If women appear ingratiating and men remain steadfast, they are bound to be brutal or ridiculous. Both are difficult!' He liked splendour and magnificence, yet his own way of life was as simple and modest as possible. I dined with him for several months, and the menu always consisted of ragout, boiled vegetables, fruit, and cheese. He drank very little during the meal; his favourite drink was a light Hungarian wine and – unfortunately – cognac. He took sips of it throughout the day, but I swear that I never saw him in a condition unworthy of his person.

One of Liszt's last pupils, Alexander Siloti followed in Liszt's footsteps as an international pianist and conductor, as well as becoming an excellent transcriber. He often performed Liszt's orchestral and piano music both in St Petersburg and then in New York, after he left Russia following the 1917 revolution. He also stressed in his memoirs how sensitive Liszt was to individual needs rather than to his own importance. When, in 1884, he asked for a photograph of himself with his teacher to send back to Russia, Liszt agreed but insisted on what he regarded as the most appropriate way to do this:

> It is remarkable how Liszt found a special meaning in everything. For the photograph I wanted Liszt to sit on a chair with myself on the ground at his feet; but he refused to accept this, explaining that he was old, that he had said all there was to say, and that he could sit, but that I was still young and had my whole life ahead of me, which was why I had to stand in order to be ready to advance.[44]

---

44. Cited in ibid., p. 301.

Indeed, in this photo, as in other surviving ones taken with his pupils, Liszt deliberately looks away, whereas Siloti stands over him and gazes steadfastly at the camera.

Alan Walker in his reflections on Liszt's relation to Wagner's music both before and after the latter's death, has raised the important psychological question why 'self-abnegation prevailed to such a degree' in Liszt's later life.[45] The answer, it seems to me, depends on whose interests one puts first, whether one's own or those of someone else judged to be more important. Liszt put Wagner's music first because he genuinely believed it to be more valuable than his own. Whether he was mistaken in this judgement is a different question. Many of his admirers, of whom Carolyne was the foremost, thought that it was Liszt who provided the musical inspiration for Wagner and that his own musical achievements were just as significant, if not superior. However, the issue here is what Liszt thought himself. There was something about Wagner's production of 'total art', of music integrated with drama, that turned Liszt into a dedicated 'Wagnerian'. He genuinely believed that it was Wagner rather than he who was the gateway to the music of the future. When one takes this into consideration, it was perhaps not so inappropriate that on his deathbed Cosima had her father laid out between a bust of Wagner and a crucifix.

Liszt and his pupil Alexander Siloti. Photograph by Louis Held, Weimar 1884.

As he aged, religious and ethical principles became ever more dominant in Liszt's life, also in regard to acceptance of his own compositions. Of course, he was pleased when his music was appreciated and discomforted when it was rejected, but he tried to accept rejection as he thought a Christian should and, towards the end of his life, became more accepting, showing less interest in hearing his music played and even recommending other musicians not to perform it. Paradoxically, it was in his very last years that his compositions, even those for choir and orchestra that before had been unappreciated in Paris, were most warmly applauded precisely there. By then, however, Liszt had grown further in the pursuit of humility.

---

45. Walker, *Reflections on Liszt*, p. 252.

Liszt's increased practice of his Christian religious faith seems to me the key to understanding Liszt's development at the end of his life. Of course, Liszt as an 'abbé' was required to do daily religious reading and his close acquaintance with the Psalms and the Gospels are evident from his correspondence. Dolores Pesce's analysis of his letters to Carolyne and Olga from 1876 onwards provides numerous examples. For instance, in a letter to Carolyne of 29 November 1876, he explicitly distanced himself from the *Weltschmertz* of despairing and pessimistic writings to which he had devoted too much attention in his younger days.[46] Rather he had 'kept the trusting thirst for the sources which "spurt towards eternal life". They are revealed to us through Christ. He commands us to love the *next person*, not to judge and maltreat him, but to pardon him so that we will be pardoned.'

Also, Cosima came to acknowledge the developments her father showed as an older man in the account of him she wrote twenty five years after his death:

> He was poor and wanted to be so. Here we touch on a point which, above and beyond the irresistible charm of his being lent his present life its peculiar character, providing the key to his conduct towards others: love of his neighbour. This expression of Christianity animated his entire being and did so, moreover, to such a boundless extent that many who thought Christian love should be kept within certain bounds were unable to understand either him or his behaviour. That his help and advice were available to all, both worthy and unworthy; that he never asked on what ground his seed had fallen or whether his goodness had kindled even the tiniest spark of love: this was of course beyond the grasp of conventional souls. But anyone who saw him involuntarily removing his hat when giving alms to the beggar could say that he was in the presence of a Christian. At the same time, he once let slip the remark, 'I have no illusions about charity', a remark which, on the lips of a man who gave away everything, certainly means a great deal.[47]

---

46. Cited in Pesce, *Liszt's Final Decade*, p.124.
47. Cosima Wagner, *Franz Liszt: Ein Gedenkblatt von seiner Tochter* (1911), pp. 50-51, cited in Burger, *Franz Liszt*, p. 327.

Ultimately Liszt has to be judged by the standards he set for himself. These were Christian standards. He realised that he had not lived up to them and did not hide this fact from those he knew best. 'The only real tragedy in life is not to have been a saint.' This sentiment has been attributed to both of the French Catholic writers, Léon Bloy and Charles Péguy, in the years after Liszt's death. I think Liszt would have agreed.

Editions of Liszt's Correspondence Consulted

Hamburger, Klára, (ed.), *Franz Liszt: Lettres à Cosima et à Daniela* (Sprimont, Belgium: Mardaga, 1996)
Hugo, Howard E., (ed.), *The Letters of Franz Liszt to Marie zu Sayn-Wittgenstein* (Cambridge, MA: Harvard University Press, 1953)
La Mara [Lipsius, Ida Marie], (ed.), *Letters of Franz Liszt*, trans. Constance Bache; *Volume 1: From Paris to Rome: Years of Travel as a Virtuoso*; *Volume 2: From Rome to the End* (New York: Charles Scribner's Sons, 1894)
La Mara [Lipsius, Ida Marie], (ed.), *Lettres de Franz Liszt à la Princesse Carolyne Sayn-Wittgenstein* (Paris: Librairie Fischbacher, 1900)
Pocknell, Pauline, (ed.), *Franz Liszt and Agnes Street-Klindworth: A Correspondence, 1854-1886* (Hillsdale, NY: Pendragon Press, 2000)
Pocknell, Pauline, Malou Haine and Nicolas Dufetel (eds), *Lettres de Franz Liszt à la Princesse Marie de Hohenlohe-Schillingsfürst née de Sayn-Wittgenstein* (Paris: Vrin, 2010)
Tyler, William R., (ed.), *The Letters of Franz Liszt to Olga von Meyendorff, 1871-1886.* (Washington, DC: Dumbarton Oaks, 1979)
Williams, Adrian, (ed. and trans.), *Franz Liszt: Selected Letters* (Oxford: Clarendon Press, 1998)

Other References Cited

Brandstädter, Jochen, 'Adaptive Resources in Later Life: Tenacious Goal Pursuit and Flexible Goal Adjustment, in *A Life Worth Living: Contributions to Positive Psychology*, ed. Mihaly Csikszentmihalyi and Isabella S. Csikszentmihalyi (New York: Oxford University Press, 2006), pp. 143-64

Brussee, Albert, 'Franz Liszt at Lake Como', *The Liszt Society Journal*, Vol. 41 (2016), pp. 39-62

Burger, Ernst, *Franz Liszt: A Chronicle of His Life in Pictures and Documents* (Princeton, NJ: Princeton University Press, 1989)

Coleman, Peter G., Christine Ivani-Chalian and Maureen Robinson, *Self and Meaning in the Lives of Older People: Case Studies over Twenty Years* (Cambridge: Cambridge University Press, 2015)

Coleman, Peter G., and Ann O'Hanlon, *Aging and Development: Social and Emotional Perspectives* (London: Routledge, 2017)

Craft, Robert, 'The New Liszt', *The New York Review*, 5 February 1981

Dufutel, Nicolas, 'Liszt and Wagner', Foreword to *The Collected Writings of Franz Liszt: Dramaturgical Leaves, II (Richard Wagner)*, ed. Janita R. Hall-Swadley (Lanham, MD: Rowman and Littlefield, 2016), pp. xv-xxxviii

Hilmes, Oliver, *Franz Liszt: Musician, Celebrity, Superstar* (New Haven, CT: Yale University Press, 2006)

Howard, Leslie. *Liszt. The Complete Music for Solo Piano – 25* London: Hyperion Records, 1993.

Johnson, Malcolm, 'Spirituality, Biographical Review and Biographical Pain at the End of Life' in *Spiritual Dimensions of Ageing*, ed. Malcolm Johnson and Joanna Walker (Cambridge: Cambridge University Press, 2016), pp. 198-214

Lazarus, Richard S., and Bernice N. Lazarus, *Coping with Aging* (New York: Oxford University Press, 2006)

Little, Brian R., *Who Are You Really? The Surprising Puzzle of Personality* (London: Simon & Schuster, 2017)

McAdams, Dan P., *The Redemptive Self* (New York: Oxford University Press, 2005)

McAdams, Dan P., *The Art and Science of Personality Development* (New York: Guilford Publications, 2016)

Merrick, Paul, *Revolution and Religion in the Music of Liszt* (Cambridge: Cambridge University Press, 1987; reissued 2008)
Morrison, Bryce, *Franz Liszt* (London: Omnibus Press, 2014)
Newman, Ernest, *The Man Liszt: A Study of the Tragi-Comedy of a Soul Divided Against Itself* (London: Cassell & Co., 1934)
Nieveld, Gert, 'Caroline de Saint-Cricq: Siren with the Heart of Ice', *The Liszt Society Journal*, Bicentenary Edition, Vol. 31 (2011), pp. 28-70
Ollivier, D., (ed.), *Correspondance de Liszt et de sa fille Madame Émile Ollivier, 1842-1862* (Paris: Grasset,1936)
Pesce, Dolores, *Liszt's Final Decade* (Rochester, NY: University of Rochester Press, 2014)
Walker, Alan, *Franz Liszt: The Virtuoso Years, 1811-1847* (London: Faber & Faber, 1983)
Walker, Alan, *Franz Liszt: The Weimar Years, 1848-1861* (London: Faber & Faber, 1989)
Walker, Alan, *Franz Liszt: The Final Years, 1861-1886* (London: Faber & Faber, 1997)
Walker, Alan, *The Death of Franz Liszt Based on the Unpublished Diary of His Pupil Lina Schmalhausen* (Ithaca, NY: Cornell University Press, 2002)
Walker, Alan, *Reflections on Liszt* (Ithaca, NY: Cornell University Press, 2005)
Watt, Paul, 'Ernest Newman's The Man Liszt (1934: Reading Its Freethought Agenda', *Context: Journal of Music Research*, Vol. 31 (2007), pp. 193-205.

Index

Aachen 200, 241
Adam, Juliette 232
Agoult, Countess Marie d' (Daniel Stern) xiii, 15-25, 48, 50-55, 73, 98, 105, 117-18, 120, 130f, 158, 167, 170, 174-75, 185, 189, 235, 250, 260, 262-63, 269-70, 272, 274, 276, 281, 283-85
 Mémoires 52, 117
 Nélida 22-23, 52-55, 117, 167-70, 281, 283-84
Albano 202-03, 207
Allegri, Gregorio 75, 82, 89
 Miserere 82, 89
Amsterdam 118-19, 121
Andrássy, Gyula 140
Antonelli, Cardinal Giacomo 42, 62, 103
Antwerp 212, 241, 245
Apeldoorn 172
Arnauld, Antoine 230, 233
Assisi 90, 128, 167, 238
Augusz, Baron Antal 57-60, 71, 91, 114, 119-20, 133, 135-37, 148-49, 159, 166, 181, 184, 193-95, 280
Austro-Prussian War 1866 121

Bach, Johann Sebastian 88, 221, 236, 241
 Cantata 'Weinen, Klagen, Sorgen, Sagen' 88
Bache, Walter 88, 94, 242, 257, 272
Baden-Baden 212, 220
Balakirev, Mily 236
 Tamara 236
Baudelaire, Charles 149
 Fleurs du Mal 149

Bayreuth 144, 148, 152-56, 160, 165, 170, 172, 188, 194, 203, 214-15, 220-21, 226-27. 233-35, 246-47, 249, 251, 263, 278-79
Beaumarchais, Pierre-Augustin Caron de 157
 Le Mariage de Figaro 157
Beethoven, Ludwig van 11, 19, 58, 62, 65, 89, 159, 162, 171-72, 202, 221, 229, 241. 256-58, 279
 Grosse Fuge in B flat Opus 133 229
 Last Piano Sonatas 202
 Missa Solemnis 257
 'Moonlight' Sonata 256
 Piano Concerto no 5 171
Belgiojoso, Princess Cristina 192
Bellagio 18
Belloni, Gaëtano 245
Berchtesgaden 267
Berlin 31, 42, 50, 51, 70, 81, 98, 102-3, 119, 127,142, 188, 200, 212, 250
Berlioz, Hector 1, 3, 14, 27-28, 37, 65-66, 104, 117-18, 141, 186, 204, 220, 228, 236, 244
 Bevenuto Cellini 228
 Les Troyens 37, 66
 Symphonie Fantastique 65, 186
Biographies of Liszt (see under Liszt, Franz: Biographers)
Bismarck, Otto von 141, 174
Bizet, Georges 66
Bloy, Léon 291
Blüthner, Julius 172
Boisselot, Xavier 82

Bologna 238
Bonn 19, 135, 159, 284
Borodin, Alexander Porfiryevich 177, 195, 212
In the Steppes of Central Asia 212
Second Symphony 195
Bossuet, Bishop Jacques-Bénigne 180
Boulogne-sur-Mer 12, 168
Brahms, Johannes 28, 257, 271
Brendel, Franz 65, 74, 80-82, 85, 91, 93-95, 100, 115, 120, 158f
Brittany 15-16
Bruckner, Anton 150
Brussee, Albert 18
Brussels 109, 119, 121, 123, 212, 220
Budapest (Pest) 19, 26, 57, 109, 112-14, 124, 132-33, 141-43, 145-49, 151 153, 158-62, 164-65, 171-75, 178, 182-85, 192-94, 197, 199-202, 205, 211, 217, 219, 224-25, 230-31, 233, 236-37, 239-40, 241, 243, 248-50, 262, 270, 276, 279
Bülow, Blandine von 130, 210
Bülow, Cosima von (see Liszt, Cosima)
Bülow, Daniela von 50, 212, 215, 226-28, 234, 245-46
Bülow, Eva von 130
Bülow, Hans von 27, 31, 33, 50-51, 65-65, 100-2, 113-14, 119-20, 126, 130-32, 144, 149, 152, 179-80, 182, 194, 202, 212, 217, 220, 229, 233, 257, 277
Nirvana 233
Bülow, Isolde 114, 130
Butler, Robert 282
Byron, Lord George Gordon 17f, 85

Caetani, Michelangelo, Duke of Sermoneta 81-82, 238
Caetani, Roffredo 238
Callow, Simon 253
Carl Alexander of Saxe-Weimar-Eisenach, Crown Prince, later Grand Duke 25-27, 30, 40-41, 60-64, 69, 73-74, 80-81, 89, 91, 102-4, 107, 110, 126, 129, 132, 144, 146, 148, 165, 167, 169, 214, 222, 249-50, 261-62, 276
Cavour, Count Camillo Benso of 53-54
Charnacé, Claire de 130, 174, 285
Chateaubriand, François-René 14

Chopin, Frédéric xiii, 1, 45, 147, 173, 241
Nocturne 147
Cohen, Reverend Hermann 84-85, 142
Colonello, Achille 230, 266
Colpach 246-47
Como 18
Constant, Benjamin 284
Constantine, Roman Emperor 98
Constantine, Prince of Hohenzollern-Hechingen 42, 81-82, 102, 110
Constantinople 20
Cornelius, Peter 30, 44, 56, 186, 231, 235
The Barber of Baghdad 30, 56, 186, 231, 235, 242
Craft, Robert 153
Cui, César Antonovich 177, 229-30
Czerny, Carl 3, 10, 12, 86

Damrosch, Walter 246
Dante Alighieri 19, 81, 285
Divina Commedia 26f, 81
Debussy, Claude 257
De Leeuw, Reinbert 198
Dornburg 187
Dresden 21, 63, 84
Duino 169
Düsseldorf 179

Edward, Prince of Wales 245
Eisenach (Wartburg) 104, 126, 171, 236
Eisenstadt 10
Eliot, George (Mary Ann Evans) 28, 54
Esterházy, Prince 10, 86
Esztergom (see Gran)
Eugénie, Empress 33, 119
Euripides 173
Ezekiel, Moses 211

Flaubert, Gustave 209
Florence 190, 238-39, 271
Franck, César 258
Franco-Prussian War 1870 137-39, 141-42, 148, 174, 205
Frankfurt am Main 202
Franz Joseph I, Emperor 124
Frascati 267
Frederick II, 'The Great', King of Prussia 172
Freiburg, 212, 220, 241

Index

Friedheim, Arthur 236
Friedrich, Crown Prince of Germany 188
Fulda 39

Galileo 81
Garibaldi, Giuseppe 238
Geneva 17, 22, 84, 119, 158, 264
George IV, King of England 10
German Music Association (New German School of Music) 28-29, 54, 65, 74(f), 91
German Music Festival 100, 177, 195, 227, 231-33, 241, 246
German Unification 67-68, 100, 138, 205
Gille, Carl 96, 115, 172, 271
Glinka, Mikhail 236
Goethe, Johann Wolfgang von 17, 25, 54, 61-62, 132, 171, 279
Göllerich, August 246, 284
Gorchakov, Prince Michael 150
Gorchakov, Prince Alexander 151
Gottschalg, Alexander 91, 93
Gounod, Charles 66, 118, 245
Gran (Esztergom) 82, 91, 114-15
Grenoble 23
Grottammare 128-29

Halle 214, 241, 245
Hanover 171, 179-80, 186, 194, 202
Hanslick, Eduard 28, 202, 231, 251, 256
Haussmann, Georges-Eugène 125
Haydn, Joseph 10, 221
Haynald, Cardinal Lajos 219, 232, 266
Helbig, Nadine 268
Hébert, Ernest 134-35
Hohenlohe, Archbishop/Cardinal Gustav 38-39, 77, 95-96, 99-100, 105-7, 129, 144, 161, 172, 189-90, 198, 202-04, 238, 249, 266-67, 276
Hohenlohe-Schillingsfürst, Konstantin 31, 44, 78, 124, 147-48, 164-65, 173
Hohenlohe-Schillingsfürst, Princess Marie (see Sayn-Wittgenstein, Princess Marie von)
Horpács 163-64
Howard, Leslie 284
Hugo, Victor-Marie 194, 238
Hungarian Uprising 1848-49 28, 58, 71, 265

Innsbruck 242
Irving, Henry 245
Italian Unification 40, 67, 121, 138, 276

James, William 34
Janina, Olga 149, 153, 169, 184, 248, 260, 270
  Souvenirs d'une Cosaque 169, 184
  Souvenirs d'un pianist 169
Jena 15, 172, 220, 246
Joachim, Joseph 28, 257
Johannot, Tony 45

Kalocsa 219, 232
Karlsruhe, 100-101, 151, 212, 231
Kiev (Kyiv) 26
Klausenburg (present day Cluj-Napoca) 201
Klindworth, Georg 67, 97, 99, 121, 129, 141, 219
Klindworth, Karl 67, 257
Konstantin, Nikolayevich, Grand Duke of Russia 229, 243
Kraków 206
Kreiner, Mihály ("Miska") 240, 247-48
Krems 48
Kullak, Theodor 259

La Mara (Lipsius, Marie) 5, 34, 37, 67, 197, 286
La Révellière-Lépeaux 232
Lamennais, Abbé Felicité 14-18, 22, 27, 31, 84, 161, 225-26, 264-65, 269, 274
  Les Paroles d'un Croyant 14, 225-26, 265, 269
Lassus, Orlande de 241
Leipzig 75, 113, 123, 127, 172, 227-29, 233, 236
Lenbach, Franz von 210
Leo XIII, Pope 196, 199
Leopold I, King of Belgium 121
Lessmann, Otto 229, 258
Lichnowsky, Prince Felix von 284
Liège 244
Limerick 20-21
Lisbon 20
Liszt, Adam 9-10, 12-13, 48, 68, 85, 87, 141, 168, 273

Liszt, Anna 9, 13-14, 16, 20, 23-25, 33, 48-49, 74, 81, 88-88, 91, 93, 100, 104, 107-8, 115, 120, 141, 202-03, 208, 263-64, 269

Liszt, Blandine (Blandine Ollivier) 17, 24, 33, 48-51, 80-85, 87, 93, 100, 104-5, 120, 132, 285

Liszt, Cosima (Bülow, Cosima von; Wagner, Cosima) xiii, 6, 18, 24, 31, 48-51, 53, 68, 82, 85, 100-5, 113-14, 119, 126, 130-32, 141, 144, 152, 154-57, 160, 165, 170-72, 174-75, 182, 184, 188, 194, 207, 220, 222, 224, 226-29, 234, 245, 247-50, 263, 272, 278-79, 281, 285, 289-90

Liszt, Daniel 19, 20f, 31, 49, 55-56, 58-59, 88, 93, 103, 235, 265, 288

Liszt, Eduard 31-32, 39, 42, 47, 56-57, 79, 91-93, 113, 115, 126-27, 134, 147, 160, 170, 178, 184, 193, 200-02, 260, 262

Liszt, Franz – Biographers (including editors of correspondence)
  Hamburger, Klára 6f
  Hilmes, Oliver 4, 21, 108, 130, 170, 253-54, 260-61
  Hugo, Howard E. 6f, 44, 216
  Merrick, Paul 4, 258, 262, 269
  Morrison, Bryce 9
  Pesce, Dolores 4, 37-38, 228f, 240, 254, 268, 290
  Pocknell, Pauline 6f, 67, 109, 119
  Tyler, William R. 6f, 153
  Walker, Alan 3, 11-12, 15-16, 21-23, 34, 37, 46-47, 51, 55, 57-59, 63-64, 77-79, 87f, 88, 95, 104, 107-8, 114, 126-27, 130, 137, 161, 184, 187, 194, 197, 201, 211, 214, 217, 226, 237, 246-48, 250, 253, 255, 257, 260-61, 264, 276, 279, 284, 286, 289
  Williams, Adrian 6, 37-38, 48-49, 98, 239

Liszt, Franz – Compositions, Piano
  Abschied 240
  Am Grabe Richard Wagners 228
  Années de Pélerinage I 17, 257, 284
  Années de Pélerinage II 17
  Années de Pélerinage III 176, 189
  Au bord d'une source 257
  Aux Cyprès de la Villa d'Este 176, 189-91
  Ave Maris Stella 204
  Csárdás Obstiné 240

Die Zelle in Nonnenwerth 284
Évocation a la Chapelle Sixtine 89-90, 92
Funérailles 58, 248
Glanes de Woronince 147
Harmonies Poétiques et Religieuses 15, 248
Hungarian Heroes (Six pieces) 241
Hungarian Rhapsodies xiii, 28
Hungarian Rhapsodies Nos. 18, 19 240
Il Cantico del Sol di San Francisco d'Assisi 90, 92, 197, 213-14, 222
La Lugubre Gondola 224-25, 241
Le Lac de Wallenstadt 17
Legend, St Francis of Assisi: Preaching to the Birds 95, 103, 114
Legend, St Francis of Paola: Walking on the Waves 95, 103, 114
Les Jeux d'Eaux à la Villa d'Este 189
Marche Funèbre (for death of Maximilian I of Mexico) 124
Mephisto Waltz No. 2 214, 216
Nuages Gris 214
Ossa Arida 205
Piano Concerto in E Flat Major 29
Piano Sonata in B Minor 28-29, 269
Piano Transcriptions: Schubert Lieder 19
Piano Transcription: Wagner's 'Liebestod' from Tristan und Isolde 127
Piano Transcription: Wagner's 'Feierlicher Marsch zum Heiligen Gral' from Parsifal 224
Rákóczy March 58, 60, 114
Rosario 197, 241
R.W. – Venezia 228
Septem Sacramenta 196-97, 241
Sposalizio 18
Vallée d'Obermann 17
Variations on Bach's 'Weinen, Klagen, Sorgen, Sagen' 88, 171
Weihnachtsbaum (Christmas Tree) 197

Liszt, Franz – Compositions, Choral
  Ave Verum Corpus 239, 258
  Beatitudes (Christus) 102
  Beethoven Cantata 135-36
  Christus Oratorio 92-93, 103, 109, 114, 120, 122, 150, 160, 162, 171, 178, 195, 202, 233, 246, 269
  Hungarian Coronation Mass 124, 200
  Les Morts 31, 76, 265

Index

Missa Choralis 160
Missa Quatuor Vocum ad Aequales (Szekszárd Mass) 205, 241
Missa Solemnis (Gran Mass) 82, 91, 115-18, 160, 200-01, 204, 212, 244, 252, 258
Motet: Qui Seminant in Lacrimis in Exultatione Metent 236
Oratorio: Legend of St Elisabeth of Hungary 80, 82, 85, 88, 90-92, 109, 112-13, 115, 122, 124, 126-27, 151, 171, 227, 229, 244-45
Oratorio: St Stanislaus of Poland 133, 135, 139, 166, 172-73, 178, 206, 223, 225-28, 231-33, 242
Oratorio: St Stephen King of Hungary (projected) 133, 135
Psalm 12(13) 'How Long O Lord Wilt Thou Forget Me? For Ever?' 119
Psalm 18(19) 'The Heavens Tell Out the Glory of God' 38
Salve Regina 239
Schlaflos! Frage und Antwort 228
Stabat Mater Dolorosa 76
Stabat Mater Speciosa 76
Sursum Corda 191
Die Glocken des Strassburgen Münsters (The Bells of Strasbourg Cathedral) 205
Tu Es Petrus 115
Via Crucis 163, 174, 196-98, 241

Liszt, Franz – Compositions, Orchestral
Dante Symphony 28
Die Ideale 205
Faust Symphony 28, 33, 123, 217, 269
From the Cradle to the Grave 214-15, 222
Mazeppa 257
Prometheus 227
Symphonic Tone Poems 28, 46, 127, 212
Tasso: Lamento e Trionfo 246

Liszt, Franz – Compositions, Song
Ihe Glocken von Marling 201

Liszt, Franz – Life, General
Ageing 173, 192, 208, 211, 214, 225, 228-29, 240, 242, 272, 275, 277-78
Anti-semitism, accusation of 216-17, 220, 225, 270
As author 216-17
As composer 1, 12, 25-26, 33, 40, 46, 54, 61, 75-76, 80, 82, 91,93, 101, 113-15, 124, 163-64, 189-92, 196-98, 209, 212, 216-17, 222, 224-25, 232, 239-40, 243, 255-56, 271, 278, 281, 286-87
As conductor 28, 30, 113, 186, 227, 233
As pianist 1, 3, 10-11, 13, 20, 25, 212, 245, 247, 255-56, 270
As teacher 13, 81, 88, 117, 132, 217-25, 237, 243, 248
Appointment as court musician in Weimar 25, 33
Appointment to new music academy in Budapest 139-40, 144, 171, 173-74, 195
Birthday celebrations 129, 140, 148, 162, 170, 181, 204, 208, 229, 242, 246
Carolyne von Sayn-Wittgenstein, asserting independence of 193, 198, 221
Carolyne von Sayn-Wittgenstein, praise of 35-36, 40, 43, 62, 101, 125-26, 133, 136, 163, 165, 183, 187, 193, 199, 217
Carolyne von Sayn-Wittgenstein, prevention of marriage to 31, 39, 41, 77-78, 144
Carolyne von Sayn-Wittgenstein, growing strain in relationship with 129, 155-57, 161, 178-81, 186-87, 193, 198, 207, 209, 276, 280-81, 286
Carolyne von Sayn-Wittgenstein, support in her later life difficulties 161-69, 172, 182-83, 206-207, 276
Cosima von Bülow, concern about her marriage to von Bülow 102, 104, 130-32
Cosima Wagner, reconciliation with her and with Wagner 154-56, 277
Cosima Wagner, rejection of her father after Wagner's death 227-29, 234
Correspondence, character of 2, 5-6, 34, 68, 75, 91, 204, 234, 240, 245, 254-55, 270, 283, 285-86
Criticism of his compositions 1, 5, 8, 28, 58, 143, 150, 212, 214, 219, 254, 271, 274, 115-19, 122-23, 127-2, 150, 153, 205, 255-56
Death of his son Daniel 31
Death of his daughter Blandine 87-90, 92

Decision to leave his music directorship in Weimar 30, 61-62, 254
Diary 11, 85
Early life 8-11, 85-87, 141, 208
Education, views on importance of 109, 177, 281
Fall at his home in the Hofgärtnerei, Weimar 211-14, 277
Funeral arrangements 135, 160, 249
'Glanzzeit' 20, 143
Health problems in later life 222-23, 226, 230-31, 243, 245, 247, 254, 271-72, 275, 277-78, 280
Hungarian identity 23, 28, 59, 60, 81, 139-41
Influence on subsequent composers 257
Insensitivity to his children's needs 25, 49, 51
'La Vie Trifurquée' 143-46, 150, 277
Last Will of 1860 34-36, 38, 160, 165, 263, 276
Life in Rome 1861 onwards 77-85
Marie von Sayn-Wittgenstein, his good relationship with 43-47, 134, 136, 159, 164, 173, 193-94, 200-01, 206, 223, 242, 286
Marie d'Agoult, failure to reconcile with 21, 51-55, 117-18, 174-75, 272, 283-84
Neglect of his religious music 258
Ordination to clerical status as 'Abbé' 105-11, 143, 162, 165, 276
Praise of his compositions 113-14, 124, 277-78
Promotion and encouragement of others' music (see also Wagner, support of) 20, 26, 70, 177, 186, 195, 203, 229-31, 233-34, 236-37, 239-40, 246, 248, 258-59, 278, 286
Return to Weimar 132-33, 136
Reputation 5, 15, 67, 253-55, 270-71
Wagner, support of 28, 63-64, 101, 188, 203, 220, 227, 271, 279, 289

Liszt, Franz – Psychological attributes
Attitudes to music, its creation and its future 7, 13, 61-62, 65, 69-71, 92, 172, 182, 229, 231, 236
Attitudes to his own music 122-23, 174, 185, 188, 191-92, 194, 197, 204, 209, 216, 224, 228, 233, 239-41, 258, 281, 289
Complaints about letter writing 173-74, 177, 183, 185-86, 189, 204, 213, 225
Depressive episodes 14, 49-50, 72-73, 75, 88-89, 93,127-28, 130, 159-60, 164, 168-70, 174, 177, 179-80, 182-88, 191-92, 194-95, 207, 209, 228, 278, 280, 287
Depression, recovery from 199, 218, 228, 238, 241, 280
Identity, self-understanding and self-presentation 2, 5, 7, 19, 20, 34-36, 54-55, 57, 75, 110-11, 134-35, 139-40, 154, 162-4, 166-68, 174, 178, 186, 191-93, 195 199, 209, 213, 221-22, 225, 230, 239-40, 244, 255, 263-64, 270, 272-75, 279, 281
Life review/healing of memories 3, 85-87, 90-91, 92, 96, 195, 203-04, 207-09, 216, 219, 235, 244, 282-86
Personality/character 1, 7-9, 11-12, 16, 18, 21, 43, 73-75, 89-90, 93, 153-54, 163, 165, 168, 177, 212, 248-49, 253-54, 264, 270-81, 286-290
Psychological changes with age 5, 92, 192, 205, 208-09, 275
Psychological state in his fiftieth year 73-76
Relationships with women 1, 7, 21, 67-68, 73, 75, 158, 168, 170, 255, 259-64, 271, 274, 282-86, 288
Sadness in late life 281-82, 286
Self-abnegation, self-disparagement 272-73, 279, 289
Values, personal principles 58-59, 83, 142, 163-64, 168, 192, 207, 215-16, 218, 242-43, 270-71, 273, 278, 280, 286-87, 290
Ways of coping, personal resources 6, 151, 175, 218, 248, 270, 280-81

Liszt, Franz – Spiritual life
Christian faith, expression of 7, 65, 133, 138, 147, 150, 152-53, 162-63, 166, 170-71, 193, 197-98, 200, 216-18, 231-32, 243, 255, 264-71, 275, 289-90
Christian teaching on the Holy Cross 6, 34-35, 98-99, 142, 157, 157f, 158, 160, 194, 204-05, 218, 269-70

Index

'Dismas', reference to 204, 269
'Job', reference to 181, 215, 219-20, 269
Religious music 12, 14, 75-76, 91, 93, 152, 196, 200, 274, 276
Religious vocation 12, 14, 90-92, 95, 202-03, 208, 264, 273
Spiritual advice 146-47, 164, 170-71, 204-05, 230, 242, 266
Spiritual practice xiv, 2, 5-7, 9, 12, 14, 34, 58, 72, 82-83, 89-91, 96-99, 108, 116, 119-20, 159-60, 178, 183-85, 188-89, 203, 207, 248, 262, 268, 271, 282, 289-90
St Francis of Assisi, devotion to 6, 58, 213, 268, 273
Liszt, Franz von 227
Liszt, Henriette von 230
Liszt Society xiii, 14, 18f
Littleton, Henry 244
London 10, 21, 188, 242, 244-45, 277, 281
Longfellow, Henry Wadsworth 171f
Loreto 42, 128
Löwenberg 42, 62, 72, 81, 102-3
Ludwig, King of Bavaria 100-101, 119, 131, 142, 179, 241, 279
Lugano 19
Luxembourg 247
Lyon 15

Magdeburg 212
Maria Pavlovna, Grand Duchess (mother of Carl Alexander) 25, 29, 60, 63
Madonna del Rosario, Monte Mario 94-99, 103, 105-6, 108, 120-21, 129
Mannheim 241
Manning, Cardinal Henry Edward 245
Marburg 227
Marcus Aurelius, Roman Emperor 215
Marseille 101
Martellini, Marquise Maria 199
Massenet, Jules 118
Maugham, Somerset 282
Mazzini, Giuseppe 283, 285
McAdams, Dan 274
Meiningen 229
Mendelssohn Bartholdy, Felix 62, 70, 203, 221, 259
Menter, Sophie 235, 242-43, 246, 250, 259
Merian-Genast, Emilie 260

Metternich, Prince Clement 67
Meyendorff, Clément von 157, 242
Meyendorff, Felix von 150-51
Meyendorff, Olga von 4, 6, 150-54, 157-61, 164-75, 177, 179-80, 184-86, 188-92, 194-96, 199, 201, 203-05, 207-09, 213, 215, 217-20, 222-26, 229-31, 234, 236-44, 246-48, 250, 254, 260-61, 263, 266-69, 271, 279-80, 282-85
Meyendorff, Pierre/Peterle von 220, 242
Meyerbeer, Giacomo 241, 259
Michelangelo Buonarroti 89, 190-91
Last Judgement 89
Michiewicz, Adam 269
Books of the Polish Nation and the Polish Pilgrimage 269
Mignet, François-Auguste 192
Milan 18-19, 222
Montalembert, Charles de 14
Montez, Lola 21
Moscow 20
Mottl, Felix 231, 242
Mozart, Wolfgang Amadeus 10, 12, 58, 82, 89, 221, 241, 258-59
Ave Verum Corpus 82, 89, 258
Müller, Professor Max 245
Munich 70, 100, 109, 114, 119, 126-27, 130-31, 152, 171, 210, 235
Munkácsy, Mihály 24, 245-46
Munkácsy, Cécile 245, 247
Music wars of mid. 19th century 28-30, 63, 66, 116-17, 220, 256-57, 274

Napoleon I, Emperor 232
Napoleon III, Emperor 1, 33, 40, 53, 71, 97, 101, 119, 123-25, 134-35, 137-38, 141-43, 148, 160, 238, 250, 265
Newman, Ernest 154, 253-54, 270
New York 288
Nicholas 1, Tsar 25
Nietzsche, Friedrich 152, 170, 266
Die Geburt der Tragödie aus dem Geiste der Musik 152
Nieveld, Gert 14
Nonnenwerth 21, 283
Nuremberg 230, 236

Oberammergau 36
Okraszewski, Ladislaw 30-31, 39, 45

Olga, Queen of Würtemburg 188
d'Ortigue, Joseph 66, 244
Ollivier, Daniel 49, 85, 105, 141, 194, 234, 250
Ollivier, Émile 50-52, 55, 74, 76, 81, 87-88, 104-5, 107, 115, 117-18, 120, 124-25, 137-38, 141, 148, 170, 175, 194, 213, 245, 250, 265, 283, 285
Oven, Charlotte von 98
Oxford 245

Paganini, Nicolò 25, 256
Palestrina, Giovanni Pierluigi da 70, 80, 99, 219, 241, 268
Paris 8, 10-14, 16, 18, 20-21, 23-24, 28, 31, 33, 35, 48, 50-53, 59, 63-64, 66, 68, 73-74, 80-81, 83, 88, 91, 100, 104, 105, 115-22, 124-25, 127, 138, 141, 143, 160, 194, 199, 204, 212, 216, 242-45, 255, 258, 281, 283-84, 289
Pascal, Blaise 104, 139, 186
Péguy, Charles 291
Pest (see Budapest)
Petrarch, Francesco 19
Pisa 238
Pius IX, Pope 1, 31-33, 37, 39, 41, 71, 78, 85, 95-96, 99-100, 104, 106, 110, 134, 138, 151, 162, 168-69, 184, 193, 199, 238, 265, 276
Pohl, Richard 236
Potsdam 188
Pozsony/Pressburg (present day Bratislava) 26, 202
Prague 147
Proudhon, Pierre-Joseph 149
Pustet, Friedrich 197, 242

Rachmaninoff, Sergei Vasilyevich 250
Raiding 10, 86, 91
Ramann, Lina 12, 14, 195, 208, 225, 230, 236, 247, 268
Raphael, Sanzio da Urbino 18, 106
  Sposalizio 18
  Vatican Murals 106
Ravel, Maurice 257-58
Récamier, Juliette 284
Regensburg 132, 156-57, 242
Renan, Ernest 266
Rendano, Alfonso 231

Repin, Ilya 250
Richter, Hans 231
Riedel, Carl 158, 177, 195, 233
Rimsky-Korsakov, Nikolai Andreyevich 177, 203
Romanticism 8-9, 17, 36
Roman Catholic Church 26, 29, 35, 39, 65, 83-84, 115, 134, 152, 161-62, 167, 173, 184, 206, 208, 226, 258, 262, 264-66, 274, 276-77, 282
Rome 5, 19, 29, 31, 33-34, 38, 40-41, 45-46, 49, 68, 71, 75, 77-85, 87, 89-101, 104-5, 108, 110, 114-15, 120-23, 125, 127-29, 134, 136, 138, 140-51, 156-57, 161, 164-70, 172-73, 177, 179, 181, 183-88, 190, 192, 194-95, 198-99, 201, 203-07, 211, 215-17, 221-22, 237-340, 242-43, 249-50, 254, 257, 260, 262-65, 268, 274-76, 279, 281, 286
Rosmini, Rev. Antonio 161
Rossini, Giacomo 12, 66, 104, 118, 221
Royal Academy of Music, London 244-45
Rubens, Peter Paul 120-21, 269
  The Four Great Sinners 120-21, 269
Rubinstein, Anton 150, 246
  O! wenn es doch immer so bliebe 246

St Augustine 11
St Catherine of Siena 193
St Francis of Assisi (see also Liszt, Franz – Devotion to) 81, 90, 157, 160, 197
St Francis of Paola 45, 178
St Gregory 116
St John the Baptist 67
St John the Evangelist 189
St Mark 187
St Paul 11, 157, 266-67
St Stephen 113
St Teresa of Avila 193
Sagrado 133
Saint Petersburg 203, 230, 235-36, 242-44, 250, 277, 288
Saint-Cricq, Caroline de 13
Saint-Saëns, Camille 1, 118, 214, 216, 233, 242-43
Saint-Simonist movement 14, 65, 161
Saint-Tropez 87, 100, 105
Sainte-Beuve, Charles Augustin 225

Salvagni, Fortunato 79, 94, 102, 109, 146-47, 266
San Carlo al Corso 77, 79
Santa Francesco Romana 122-23, 148
Santa Maria degli Angeli 190
Sand, George (Aurore Dupin) 14, 65
Sauer, Emil von 272
Sayn-Wittgenstein, Princess Carolyne von, xiii, 4-5, 14, 16, 24-27, 29-31, 33-47, 49-50, 52, 55,57-58, 61-62, 64-68, 71-82, 85, 87-88, 93-97, 99-109, 113, 115-21, 124-26, 128-29, 133, 135-39, 141-44, 147-50, 152-74, 178-190, 193-96, 198-99, 201-09, 212-17. 220-21, 223-30, 233-38, 241-42, 244-47, 249, 254-55, 260-74, 276-83, 285-86, 289
Des Causes Intérieures de la Faiblesse Extérieure de l'Église 161-63, 179, 207, 238
Life of Chopin (with Liszt, Franz) 179, 216
The Bohemians and their Music in Hungary (with Liszt, Franz) 216-17
Sayn-Wittgenstein, Princess Marie von (Hohenlohe-Schillingsfürst, Princess Marie) 6, 26, 29-31, 37, 43-47, 61, 75, 78, 101, 124, 133-34, 136, 140, 147, 147f, 148-49, 158-59, 164-66, 168-69, 171-74, 178-79, 181-84, 193, 198, 200, 203-07, 214-16, 223-27, 232, 235-238, 242, 244, 246, 249-50, 252, 263, 266, 271, 286
Sayn-Wittgenstein, Prince Nicholas von 26, 29-31, 38-39, 41, 61, 77, 103-4
Schiller, Friedrich von 25
Schillingsfürst 267
Schlözer, Kurd von 108
Schmalhausen, Lina 240, 247-50, 261, 263-64, 268
Schopenhauer, Arthur 171, 218
Schorn, Adelheid von 169, 171, 227, 237, 246, 260, 262
Schorn, Henriette von 169f
Schubert, Franz 102, 241
Doppelgänger 102
Schumann, Clara 254, 257, 259-60
Schumann, Robert 1, 20, 45f, 203, 221
Schwartz, Marie Espérance von 238
Sgambati, Giovanni 81, 149, 224, 231, 238
Siena 67, 207, 238

Siloti, Alexander 229-30, 236, 240, 250, 256, 288-89
Sistine Chapel 80, 82, 89, 96, 99, 219
Society of Saint Cecilia 148, 242
Solfanelli, Rev. Antonio 28-29
Sondershausen 246
Sophie, Grand Duchess (wife of Carl Alexander) 41, 62, 132, 146, 148, 165
Strauss, Richard 258
Szeged 201
Stavenhagen, Bernhard 243, 247
Strasbourg 101, 205
Street-Klindworth, Agnes 6, 39, 66-74, 82, 96-101, 105, 108-9, 119, 120-25, 127, 130, 141, 152, 194, 196, 203, 219, 246, 250, 260-61, 270
Street-Klindworth, Georges 128, 194, 196, 219
Stradal, August 176
Strasbourg 241
Sydenham 244
Szekszárd 58, 83f, 114, 135-40, 181, 205

Taborszky, Ferdinand 241
Tausig, Carl 27, 123, 148, 152
Tchaikovsky, Pyotr Ilyich 177, 186
Second Symphony 186
Tétetlen 236-37
Thaddeus, Henry Jones 261
Theiner, Reverend Agostino 81, 94, 97, 149
Thomas à Kempis 12, 268-69, 273
Tiziano, Vecellio ('Titian') 187
Tolstoy, Lev Nikolayevich 243
My Religion 243
Triebschen 126
Turgenev, Ivan 132

Valenciennes 24
Vatican 31- 32, 78-81, 95, 106, 108, 114, 121, 138, 143, 161-62, 184, 249, 276
Vatican Council 134, 152
Venice 18-19, 114, 121, 215, 222-26, 238, 241
Verona 215
Viardot-Garcia, Pauline 132, 233
Victoria, Crown Princess of Germany 188
Victoria, Queen of England 188, 245
Vienna 10, 12, 19-20, 23, 28, 31, 39, 41-42, 44-45, 47-48, 55-57, 59, 70, 72, 75, 86, 91, 115, 119, 124, 127-32, 134-35, 147,

149, 156, 159-60, 162, 164, 171, 173, 178, 180-81, 200-02, 205-06, 212, 217, 219, 226-27, 230-32, 236, 244, 257, 281
Villa d'Este, Tivoli 99, 129, 134, 144, 164-70, 172-73, 176, 188-91, 195, 197-99, 204-09, 213-14, 266-67
Visgnola 18
Voltaire, François-Marie Arouet 139
Voss, Richard 267

Wagner, Cosima (see Liszt, Cosima)
Wagner, Richard 1, 27-28, 33, 44, 50, 54, 56, 61, 63-66, 68-71, 73, 81, 85, 100-02, 107, 114, 117, 119, 126, 130-32, 136, 141-42, 144, 148, 152-57, 160, 170-72, 179, 182, 186, 188, 194, 203, 207, 217-18, 220-24, 226, 234, 241, 245, 250, 253, 257-58, 272-73, 277, 279, 281, 285, 289
Der Ring des Nibelungen 64, 119, 144, 148, 171, 179, 188, 221, 279
Die Meistersinger von Nürnberg 85, 102, 126, 130
Kaisermarsch 141
Lohengrin 28, 63, 136, 279
Parsifal 157, 186, 188, 203, 207, 220-21, 223, 227, 233-35, 247, 279
Rheingold 64, 235
Rienzi 63
Siegfried 64
Tannhäuser 28, 63-65, 69, 126, 279
Tristan und Isolde 64, 69, 127, 221, 247
Walküre 64
Weber, Carl Maria von 241
Weimar 5, 8, 22, 25-29, 31, 33-34, 36, 39, 40-42, 45-46, 48, 54, 56-57, 59-63, 65-70, 72-76, 79-80, 96, 100, 102, 104, 125-26, 128-29, 132-33, 136-37, 141, 143-48, 151-52, 155-57, 160-62, 164-65, 167, 169, 171-72, 178-80, 182, 186-87, 193-94, 199-200, 202, 211, 217, 221-23, 226-36, 240-41, 243-45, 247, 249-50, 254, 256, 260, 263, 268, 270-71, 274, 276, 278, 281, 285-86
Weingartner, Felix 233
Wilhelm I, King of Prussia/Emperor of Germany 71
Wilhelmsthal 172
Willem III, King of the Netherlands 119, 138, 171, 179
Windsor Castle 245
Woronince 24, 126, 147, 181

Zaluski, Count Karol 190
Zhukovsky, Paul von 223-24, 246
Zichy, Count Géza 194, 201-02, 204-05, 213, 236-37, 245-46, 251, 259, 266, 280, 287-88
Der Zaubersee 237
Piano Sonata 245-46

You may also be interested in:

Blasted with Antiquity

Old Age and the Consolations of Literature

by David Ellis

Given the increasing number of old people, the proliferation of books about old age is hardly surprising. Most of these come from cultural historians or social scientists and, when those with a literary background have tackled the subject, they have largely done so through what are known as period studies. In *Blasted with Antiquity*, David Ellis provides an alternative. Skipping nimbly from Cicero to Shakespeare, and from Wordsworth to Dickens and beyond, he discusses various aspects of old age with the help of writers across European history who have usually been regarded as worth listening to.

Eschewing extended literary analyses, Ellis addresses retirement, physical decay, sex in old age, the importance of family, legacy, wills and nostalgia, as well of course as dying itself. While remaining alert to current trends, his approach is consciously that of the old way of teaching English rather than the new. Whether 'blasted with antiquity' like Falstaff in Henry IV Part Two, or with the 'shining morning face' of an unwilling student, his accessible and witty style will appeal to young and old alike.

> *'Ellis's book is a delight to read – a significant publication for scholars in literary age studies and an accessible volume for anyone interested in literary representations of growing older.'* – **Dr Jacob Jewusiak,** Newcastle University

David Ellis is Emeritus Professor of English Literature at the University of Kent and has published around twenty books on Shakespeare, leading figures of the Romantic era, and D.H. Lawrence. In 2012 he received the Harry T. Moore Award for distinguished services to D.H. Lawrence studies.

Published 2023

Paperback ISBN: 978 0 7188 9718 5
PDF ISBN: 978 0 7188 9717 8
ePub ISBN: 978 0 7188 9716 1

You may also be interested in:

A Time and a Place

George Crabbe, Aldeburgh and Suffolk

by Frances Gibb

> 'There anchoring, Peter chose from Man to hide,
> There hang his Head, and view the lazy Tide
> In its hot slimy Channel slowly glide …'

George Crabbe, eighteenth-century poet, clergyman and surgeon-apothecary, is best known for 'Peter Grimes', the tale of a sadistic fisherman that inspired Benjamin Britten's opera of the same name. The brutal crimes and 'tortur'd guilt' of Grimes play out within the bleak, improbably beautiful setting of Aldeburgh. While Crabbe has fallen in and out of fashion, the Suffolk town and its landscape have continued to captivate writers and artists, including Britten, Ronald Blythe, Susan Hill and Maggi Hambling – all drawn to the stark coastline, eerie mudflats and open skies.

In A Time and a Place, Frances Gibb engages afresh with Crabbe's writing – tracing, for the first time, the resonance of this place in his life and work. She delves into his creative struggles, religious faith, romantic loves and opium addiction. Above all, she explores the continual lure – for Crabbe and those who have followed – of the 'little venal borough', and the land and sea beyond.

> 'Gibb's book evokes both the literal and psychological landscapes of the poet's life and work…. a useful reminder that it was Crabbe who had first claim on Aldeburgh, and that his poems provide an unsettling and enduring portrait of a time and a place and its people.' – **Peter Parker, *The Spectator***

Frances Gibb is an award-winning journalist and former Legal Editor of The Times. She contributes to publications including The Times and Sunday Times, The Daily Telegraph and The Spectator, as well as to national radio. She read English at the University of East Anglia and has an honorary masters degree from the Open University. Her family has been connected with Aldeburgh and Suffolk for more than fifty years.

Published 2022

Paperback ISBN: 978 0 7188 9611 9
PDF ISBN: 978 0 7188 9612 6
ePub ISBN: 978 0 7188 9613 3

You may also be interested in:

Richard and Maria Cosway

A Biography
by Gerald Barnett

Richard Cosway was once a more famous artist than Gainsborough. His portraits of the fashionable were the rage in Regency London. From 1785 he became First Painter to the Prince of Wales – the only artist ever to have been accorded such a title. He and his wife Maria entertained everybody who was anybody. Herself a talented artist in her own right, she was also a composer, musician and authority on girls' education. Thomas Jefferson fell in love with her; Napoleon doted on her.

And yet, save for Richard Cosway's pre-eminence as a miniaturist, he and Maria have long been neglected by the public, their reputation tarnished by rumour and misrepresentation. Here, Gerald Barnett seeks to present them in a truer and clearer light, emphasising their achievements as artists and individuals and rehabilitating them as major figures in the artistic history of eighteenth-century England.

Richard Cosway was the subject of major exhibitions at the Scottish National Portrait Gallery (Edinburgh) and the National Portrait Gallery (London) from August 1995. Richard and Maria Cosway feature prominently as characters in the Merchant-Ivory film Jefferson in Paris.

A carefully researched biography of the Cosways, two fascinating but often neglected figures in 18th-century English art history, emphasises their achievements.

Gerald Barnett was born in Exeter and spent much of his life serving in the Royal Navy. Now retired, Commander Barnett has long been an enthusiastic collector of English portrait miniatures and drawings and has been a champion of the Cosways' reputation for much of the past 20 years.

Published 1996

Hardback ISBN: 978 0 7188 2944 5